Praise for *Reading the European Novel to 1900*

"Schwarz's study is chock full of judicious evaluation of characters, narrative devices, ethical commentary, and helpful information about historical and political contexts including the role of Napoleon, the rise of capitalism, trains, class divisions, transformation of rural life, and the struggle to define human values in a period characterized by debates between and among rationalism, spiritualism, and determinism. One experiences the pleasure of watching a master critic as he re-reads, savors, and passes on his hard-won wisdom about how we as humans read and why."

Daniel Morris, Professor of English, Purdue University

"Anyone reading or teaching these books at the college level for the first time will benefit from this book. . . Summing Up: Recommended. Lower- and upper-division undergraduates; faculty; general readers."

CHOICE

T0287833

READING THE NOVEL

General Editor: Daniel R. Schwarz

The aim of this series is to provide substantive critical introductions to reading novels in the British, Irish, American, and European traditions.

Published

Reading the European Novel to 1900

A Critical Study of Major Fiction from Cervantes' *Don Quixote* to Zola's *Germinal*

Daniel R. Schwarz

WILEY Blackwell

This paperback edition first published 2018
© 2014 John Wiley & Sons Ltd

Edition history: John Wiley & Sons Ltd (hardback, 2014)

Registered Office
John Wiley & Sons Ltd, The Atrium, Southern Gate, Chichester, West Sussex, PO19 8SQ, UK

Editorial Offices
350 Main Street, Malden, MA 02148-5020, USA
9600 Garsington Road, Oxford, OX4 2DQ, UK
The Atrium, Southern Gate, Chichester, West Sussex, PO19 8SQ, UK

For details of our global editorial offices, for customer services, and for information about how to apply for permission to reuse the copyright material in this book please see our website at www.wiley.com/wiley-blackwell.

The right of Daniel R. Schwarz to be identified as the author of this work has been asserted in accordance with the UK Copyright, Designs and Patents Act 1988.

Library of Congress Cataloging-in-Publication Data

Schwarz, Daniel R., author.
   Reading the European Novel to 1900 : a Critical Study of Major Fiction from Cervantes' Don Quixote to Zola's Germinal / Daniel R. Schwarz.
      pages cm. – (Reading the novel)
   Includes bibliographical references and index.
   ISBN 978-1-444-33047-2 (hardback) ISBN 978-1-119-51770-2 (paperback)
   1. Fiction–History and criticism.   I. Title.
   PN3491.S38 2015
   809.3–dc23
                                                                    2014007165
A catalogue record for this book is available from the British Library.

Cover image: Alfred Sisley, *View of the Canal Saint-Martin*, 1870. © Photos.com/Gettyimages

Set in 10/12.5pt Minion by Aptara Inc., New Delhi, India

1   2018

As you set out for Ithaka
hope your road is a long one
full of adventure, full of discovery,
Laistrygonians, Cyclops,
angry Poseidon – don't be afraid of them:
you'll never find things like that on your way
as long as you keep your thoughts raised high,
as long as a rare excitement
stirs your spirit and your body,
Laistrygonians, Cyclops,
wild Poseidon – you won't encounter them
unless you bring them along inside your soul,
unless your soul sets them up in front of you.

(Constantine P. Cavafy, "Ithaka," trans. Gail Holst-Warhaft)

For Marcia Jacobson – life partner, perceptive novel reader, splendid editor – with love and appreciation

Contents

Contents

Acknowledgments

I am grateful for the strong support of Emma Bennett, Publisher, Literature, Social Sciences, and Humanities Division, Wiley Blackwell, with whom I have had a productive professional relationship for many years. Brigitte Lee Messenger capably and thoughtfully managed the production process from copyediting through proofreading and indexing.

Teaching Cornell students at every level from freshmen to graduate students over the past 46 years has helped me refine my understanding of how novels work and what they say. Much of the credit for whatever I accomplish as a scholar-critic goes to the intellectual stimulation provided by my students as well as my colleagues.

My wife, Marcia Jacobson, to whom I owe my greatest debt, has read every word of the manuscript more than once and has given me countless suggestions.

My longtime Cornell friend and colleague Brett de Bary helped me understand translation theory and recommended the texts I should read on that subject. My Cornell colleague Gail Holst-Warhaft generously provided an original translation of Cavafy's "Ithaka." Professor Coleen Culleton (Buffalo University) gave me helpful advice on the *Don Quixote* chapter. A number of colleagues at Cornell and elsewhere, including Professor Caryl Emerson (Princeton), pointed me in the right direction when choosing translations.

It gives me great pleasure to thank two gifted students who have done independent study projects with me and who have contributed to the final manuscript. Natalia Fallas was a great help in editing, proofreading, and indexing. Joseph Mansky played an important role in early stages of the research.

Finally, I wish to acknowledge the continued support of the Cornell English Department and in particular Vicky Brevetti.

Daniel R. Schwarz
Ithaca, New York
May 6, 2014

Also by Daniel R. Schwarz

How to Succeed in College and Beyond: The Art of Learning (2016, Mandarin edition 2018)

Reading the Modern European Novel since 1900 (2018)

Endtimes: Crises and Turmoil at the New York Times (2012; new revised paperback edition 2014)

In Defense of Reading: Teaching Literature in the Twenty-First Century (2008)

Reading the Modern British and Irish Novel 1890–1930 (2005)

Broadway Boogie Woogie: Damon Runyon and the Making of New York City Culture (2003)

Rereading Conrad (2001)

Imagining the Holocaust (1999; revised edition 2000)

Reconfiguring Modernism: Explorations in the Relationship between Modern Art and Modern Literature (1997)

Narrative and Representation in the Poetry of Wallace Stevens: "A Tune Beyond Us, Yet Ourselves" (1993)

The Case for a Humanistic Poetics (1991)

The Transformation of the English Novel, 1890–1930: Studies in Hardy, Conrad, Joyce, Lawrence, Forster, and Woolf (1989; revised edition 1995)

Reading Joyce's "Ulysses" (1987; centenary edition 2004)

The Humanistic Heritage: Critical Theories of the English Novel from James to Hillis Miller (1986; revised edition 1989)

Conrad: The Later Fiction (1982)

Conrad: "Almayer's Folly" to "Under Western Eyes" (1980)

Disraeli's Fiction (1979)

As Editor

Damon Runyon: Guys and Dolls and Other Writings (2008)

The Early Novels of Benjamin Disraeli, 6 volumes (consulting editor, 2004)

Conrad's "The Secret Sharer" (Bedford Case Studies in Contemporary Criticism, 1997)

Joyce's "The Dead" (Bedford Case Studies in Contemporary Criticism, 1994)

Narrative and Culture (with Janice Carlisle, 1994)

Chapter 1

Introduction

The Odyssey of Reading Novels

She speaks of complexities of translation,
its postcolonial and diasporic nature,
how translated text
is torn from original
as if it were unwillingly
sundered from its parent.

As she triumphantly
concludes her perfectly
paced performance,
she crosses her arms,
returning to herself
as if to say
her ideas have been
translated into words
as best she could.

("Brett de Bary," Daniel R. Schwarz)

Beginnings

This book, the first of a two-volume study, includes major novels published before 1900 that are frequently taught in European novel courses. The high tide of the European novel was the nineteenth century but no discussion of the European novel can ignore *Don Quixote*. Thus there is well over a two hundred-year

Reading the European Novel to 1900: A Critical Study of Major Fiction from Cervantes' Don Quixote *to Zola's* Germinal, First Edition. Daniel R. Schwarz.
© 2014 John Wiley & Sons, Ltd. Published 2014 by John Wiley & Sons, Ltd.

jump from Miguel de Cervantes' *Don Quixote* (1615) to Stendhal's *The Red and the Black* (1830) and *The Charterhouse of Parma* (1839) and Honoré de Balzac's *Père Goriot* (1835). Much of this study deals with works by the great Russians: Fyodor Dostoevsky's *Notes from Underground* (1864), *Crime and Punishment* (1866), *The Brothers Karamazov* (1880), and Leo Tolstoy's *War and Peace* (1869) and *Anna Karenina* (1877).[1] Among the French nineteenth-century novelists, in addition to the aforementioned, I include Gustave Flaubert's *Madame Bovary* (1857) and *Sentimental Education* (1869) and Emile Zola's *Germinal* (1885).

I have been rereading most of these books for a lifetime, although important new translations of Dostoevsky, Tolstoy, and Cervantes have been published in recent decades. But do we really reread or is every reading a fresh reading? As Verlyn Klinkenborg rightly observes, "The real secret of re-reading is simply this: It is impossible. The characters remain the same, and the words never change, but the reader always does."[2] We are different readers each time we pick up a text, maybe a different reader each day, changed ever so slightly depending on our life experience, our psyche that day, and the texts we are reading. For reading is a transaction in which the text changes us even as we change the text. While Klinkenborg has written that, "Part of the fun of re-reading is that you are no longer bothered by the business of finding out what happens" (ibid.), I find that rereading makes me aware of nuances I missed, even while making me aware that my memory of what happens is not accurate. What we recall is not a novel but a selection and arrangement of the novel, and as time passes what we retain is a memory of a memory rather than the full text in all its plenitude.

I am addressing the novels under discussion not only diachronically but also synchronically. That is, I am aware of the evolution of the novel and how major novels strongly influence their successors. For example, we will see in *Don Quixote* how the first person narrator's familiarity with his readers, his combining realism with fantasy and tall tale, his efforts to distinguish story from history, provide a model for subsequent novels, including *The Brothers Karamazov*. As Harold Bloom would argue, each major novelist is a strong misreader of his predecessors and thus each is also an original. We read major texts, as T. S. Eliot rightly contended in "Tradition and the Individual Talent," not only in the context of their predecessors and the possible influence of those predecessors, but also in the context of their successors. Thus each major work changes our view of its predecessors.

I also want to think of the novels on which I focus as being in conversation with one another, as if they were all present simultaneously at the same discussion or colloquium and were making claims for how and why they exist. Put another way, if we substitute "words" for "object," our novelists are all following Jasper Johns's oft-repeated axiom for art: "Take an object. Do something to it. Do something else to it."[3] I want to think about what is unique to what the novelist in each *doing* has created, and how these *doings* are similar and different.

I have not written completely symmetrical chapters. But each of my chapters will: (1) first and foremost provide a close reading of the novel or novels under discussion; (2) speak to what defines the essence of the author's oeuvre; (3) place the focal novel or novels within the context of the author's canon and culture; and (4) define the author's aesthetic, cultural, political, and historical significance. On occasion, I may focus on two works within a chapter when one adumbrates or complements the other.

We read in part to learn the wisdom of experience that the novelist fused in his vision of life and his historical scope. Those who provide notable wisdom include Tolstoy, Dostoevsky, Flaubert, Stendhal, and Balzac. These writers at times show what Thomas Mann – who might have been writing about himself – called in an essay on Theodor Fontaine, "classic old men, ordained to show humanity the ideal qualities of that last stage of life: benignity, kindness, justice, humor, and shrewd wisdom – in short a recrudescence on a higher plane of childhood's ancient unrestraint."[4] Of course there is no particular age when one achieves such a temperament. As we shall see in my Volume 2, Mann, writing *Death in Venice* in his thirties, as well as Albert Camus, had this temperament at quite an early age, and it pervades every page of Giuseppe di Lampedusa's *The Leopard*.

Why are there no women novelists in my study of the European novel to 1900? While Jane Austen, the Brontës, and George Eliot played a pivotal role in defining the nineteenth-century English novel, women played a much less important role in the European novel. Few would argue that George Sand (the pseudonym of Amantine Lucile Aurore Dupin, 1804–1876) was the equal of the aforementioned French novelists.

We do have fully realized and psychologically complex women characters in the person of the title characters of *Anna Karenina* and *Madame Bovary* as well as the Marchesa in *The Charterhouse of Parma* and Natasha in *War and Peace*. But in too many of the included novels, the women are depicted as objects of desire and relatively passive figures, as Madonnas or Mary Magdalenes, innocents or whores. Some of the more passive figures, like Grushenka in *The Brothers Karamazov*, do have some aspects of complexity.

Usually in the European novel before 1900, women – even fully realized ones – are not as intellectually gifted or ambitious in terms of achievement as men, and seem to be the creations of men who do not think of women as equals. How these male writers think of women is culturally determined, but it is hard not to wish for something more. It is the English novel where female writers – Austen, Brontës, Woolf – and their characters make their mark.

Indeed, even the male writers such as Dickens and Thackeray create more vibrant, rounded women characters than we usually find in the European novel.

Since I am writing in English, I occasionally make comparisons to the English and American literary traditions. It is by similarities and differences – the entire context of major novel texts – that we best understand how novels work formally and thematically.

The Function of Literature: What Literature Is and Does

According to Lionel Trilling, "[L]iterature has a unique relevance ... because literature is the human activity that takes the fullest and most precise account of variousness, possibility, complexity, and difficulty."[5]

Literature is a report on human experience, but, we need to ask, does its aesthetic form make it a privileged report and, if so, privileged in what way? Is literature part of the history of ideas, or only in a special sense where the aesthetic inflects the ideas? As a cause, literature, I argue, affects its historical context – its *Zeitgeist* – but literature is also a result of its historical context. Imaginative literature and, in particular, novels are indexes of a culture as well as critiques, but they do not – nor do other arts – exist in some separate higher universe. As Michael Chabon asserts, "[T]he idea for a book, the beckoning fair prospect of it, is the dream; the writing of it is breakfast-table recitation, groping, approximation, and ultimately, always, a failure. *It was not like that at all....* The limits of language are not the stopping points, says [James Joyce's] the *Wake*; they are the point at which we must begin to tell the tale."[6]

In this study, I try to balance the *how* with the *what*, and to balance the way that novels give us insight into human experience at a particular time and place and have significance for contemporary readers with how that is accomplished in terms of aesthetic choices and strategies. What a story means is why most readers read, and it is naïve and iconoclastic to think otherwise. How and what – form and content – are inextricably related.

What we read becomes part of our lives and how we experience both our culture and prior cultures. As David Foster Wallace observed, "Human beings are narrative animals: every culture countenances itself as culture via story, whether mythopoeic or politico-economic; every whole person understands his lifetime as an organized, recountable series of events and changes with at least a beginning and a middle. We need narrative like we need space-time."[7]

Traditional novels present the illusion of a comprehensible and at least partially rational world, with recognizable cause and effect shaping character and – beginning with the High Modern period (1890–1950) – the psyche. But we need to remind ourselves that there are other strands of novel history that eschew realism and rely more on romance, folklore, fantasy, myth, play, magic – including linguistic pyrotechnics – and deliberate send-ups of realism. In this study, *Don Quixote* may be the purest example, but Stendhal's *The Red and the Black* and especially *The Charterhouse of Parma* partake of this alternate tradition, one in which the very idea that books represent life is called into question. In English we think of Sterne's *The Life and Opinions of Tristram Shandy, Gentleman* and Joyce's *Ulysses* and *Finnegans Wake*, as well as, more recently, the work of Toni Morrison and Salman Rushdie; in Spanish, we have the magic realism tradition of Jorge Luis Borges and Gabriel García Márquez, among many others. As we shall see in my second volume, such Kafka texts as *Metamorphosis* and *The Trial* take the reader into a surrealistic world where normative cause and effect are suspended.

In general, especially in longer novels in the realistic tradition, characters need to typify a way of living a particular time and place and be shown to respond to social issues and political questions. Are the constructed imagined worlds of longer novels in which we live as readers for days, perhaps even weeks, different from the imagined worlds of short novels? What does it mean to say a novel has amplitude? For longer novels to qualify as masterworks, usually they need to raise major philosophical questions about what gives human life meaning and purpose and/or major political questions about how a country should be organized legally and morally.

By contrast, the very pace of shorter novels can be an asset. Their focus is usually on the dilemmas facing one man or woman, as in such short novels as *Heart of Darkness, The Secret Sharer, Bartleby the Scrivener, Daisy Miller*, or *The Dead*. Great short novels have the taut unity of poetry and short stories, with every word relating to major themes, and an experienced reader observes that unity – indeed, teleology – at first reading.

Longer novels often take a rereading to see how the discrete parts relate and may contain digressive material – such as Tolstoy's iterative commentaries on history and warfare that at times seem tangential even to a rereader – or characters that stray far from the center of the reader's consciousness and drift on the edges of our memory of the novel. In shorter novels, every character – indeed, every sentence – matters, in part because in one reading or even two within a day or so, we retain whatever the book presents.

In our age of shortened attention spans defined by smart phones, Twitter, social media, and Google searches, some of the masterworks I am discussing seem endless, especially to younger readers. Now when I assign a middle-length novel of four or five hundred pages, students respond the way earlier generations of students responded to 1,000 pages.

Recurring Themes

For most of the novel's history, notwithstanding the exceptions to realism I mentioned above, novels depended on relevance to historical contexts and contemporary social issues. As Georg Lukács observes, "Realists such as Balzac or Tolstoy in their final posing of questions always take the most important, burning problems of their community for their starting-point; their pathos as writers is always stimulated by those sufferings of the people which are the most acute at the time."[8]

Of course, the realistic tradition is still important today, as Joseph O'Neill's *Netherland*, Philipp Meyer's *American Rust*, and the novels of Saul Bellow and Ian McEwan make clear. As we shall see, major novels often had something of a pedagogical function even if they were not outright polemical and didactic – and they could be that too. Novels were expected to be readable and tell a story, but also expected to make you think. Although there were many exceptions, major novelists were less likely than today's novelists to write an account of the author's personal feelings – often in the voice of the narrator – and more likely to speak of social and political contexts. This was even truer of the European novel in the nineteenth and first half of the twentieth century than it was of the British and American novel of the same period.

European novels tend to balance the study of individuals' idiosyncrasies and families with a panoramic view of how political, cultural, and economic factors shape the ways that an individual thinks and behaves. Social hierarchies in eighteenth- and nineteenth-century Europe were different from our purported democratic and egalitarian twenty-first-century values, although we are still very much a stratified society with racial, ethnic, class, and gender inequities. In Russia especially, hierarchy was inherent in the social system; the aristocracy didn't court social inferiors but were expected to protect them and further their interests. Of course, there were abuses not only in Russia but also in most countries. In France, the French Revolution tried to redress some of those social incongruities and abuses, but with the Restoration and subsequent regimes, these abuses and inequalities continued in some form.

Recurring themes in our novels are the transformation of agrarian life due to machinery and the concomitant effect on traditional rural communities, the rise of capitalism, the evolution of the modern city, the attraction and disappointment of urban life, and the creation of a class of underemployed workers. Often reflected within our novels is class division, sometimes perceived more acutely by us twenty-first-century readers than by the authors.

In writing of the cultural and socio-economic significance of railroads Tony Judt observes, "[After 1830] trains – or, rather, the tracks on which they ran – represented the conquest of space."[9] Railroads transformed the landscape of much of the world. They made movement possible that was once unthinkable. Invented in the 1760s, the steam engine was the quintessence of the Industrial Revolution but didn't motor trains until 1825. The steam engine depended on coal, the subject of Zola's *Germinal*, to make it run. We see trains playing an important role in *Anna Karenina* and in *Sentimental Education*. As Judt puts it, "[M]ost of the technical challenges of industrial modernity – long distance telegraphic communication, the harnessing of water, gas, and electricity for domestic and industrial use, urban and rural drainage, the construction of very large buildings, the gathering and moving of human beings in large numbers – were first met and overcome by railway companies."[10]

Napoleon Bonaparte is also a thread that runs through the European novel from Tolstoy and even Dostoevsky (in *The Brothers Karamazov* his words are invoked by the precocious Kolya, who refers to him as "that pseudo great man" [IV.x.6.555]) to Stendhal and Balzac. In a sense he plays the role as fantasy superhero – even if viewed with some irony as an arrogant over-reacher – that chivalric heroes played for Don Quixote. As a man who rose from minor Corsican nobility to become not only a military hero but also the most dominant figure in Europe, Napoleon had more to do with nineteenth-century political and social history than any other figure. He is naïvely and obsessively idealized by Julien Sorel in *The Red and the Black*. His gigantic presence bestrides European history like a colossus. His civil reforms affecting laws and education, instituting government appointments based on merit, and building roads and sewers had a lasting effect on France and were a model for much of Europe. By allowing freedom of religion, the Napoleonic Code shaped Jewish history in Europe and led the way in emancipating the Jews, making the Jews equal citizens with equal civil rights and abolishing ghettoes in countries Napoleon conquered.

As we shall see, many of our novels examine the conflict between individualism and community standards, whether they be religious, political, or class strictures. Thus our novels often explore the value of subjectivity, self-awareness, and individual feelings, including sex and love. I am thinking not only of *The Red and the Black*, *The Charterhouse of Parma*, and *Madame Bovary*, but also of Tolstoy's and Dostoevsky's novels, despite the somewhat reductive religious solutions of authors. In many of our novels, personal sincerity and integrity become important values; how one behaves depends on individual choice rather than on rigid stipulations imposed by political and religious authority. Many of the novels I discuss dramatize the disruptive effects on individual characters of cosmopolitanism (*Père Goriot*, *Sentimental Education*, *The Red and the Black*), industrialism, and the movement from rural to urban culture and, in the case of *War and Peace*, Tolstoy's resistance to these developments.

As a genre the novel itself is often an expression of pluralism, secularism, and/or indifference to religion. The novels I discuss demonstrate diversity in religious, social, and political cultures (*The Brothers Karamazov*, *War and Peace*). These novels also address capital formation and ensuing class struggle (*Père Goriot*, *Germinal*) as well as freedom of thought and intellectual inquiry struggling with a sometimes monolithic and a decadent Catholic Church and autocracy (*The Red and the Black* and *The Charterhouse of Parma*). Indeed, some of the novelists in my second volume, such as Giorgio Bassani and Giuseppe di Lampedusa, suggest that traditional religion may close the door to subjective self-examination and self-knowledge, while responding to the needs of the individual psyche may free mankind from archaic and rigid morality and hierarchies. But are not these later novelists taking their cue from Balzac, Flaubert, Stendhal, and Zola?

The European novel rarely fell prey to what Ralph Rader – whose focus was the English novel – called "Victorian Rule," which requires "the subordination of the individual to the social" and defines "the highest good as the sacrifice of one's self for the common good."[11] It is this Rule that validates the behavior of such characters as William Dobbin, Esther Summerson, and Dorothea Brooke.

Balzac, Flaubert, Stendhal, and Dostoevsky are more cynical about the need to attend to the common good than Zola and Tolstoy. Even before the twentieth century, European novelists tend to be more concerned about how the individual in all his idiosyncrasies can remain human and how he or she can be happy both in the moment and looking forward without regard to the community good. In *The Charterhouse of Parma*, it never occurs to Fabrizio or the Duchess to think about the common good; without any compunction, including the effect on res publica, the Duchess will poison the Prince.

The Reader's Odyssey

Memory

Memory shapes our perceptions and identities, even in this age of Google where we may not have to remember as much. Our reading – particularly of masterworks that we read and reread – informs our memory and influences how our memory responds to experience. Our memories make us who we are and are a major basis for our values and character. Joyce Wadler reminds us: "What we consider a memory is actually a memory of a memory, which we refine every time we replay it in our mind."[12] Yet, as unreliable and fragmentary as memory is, it is how we make sense of our national, cultural, familial, and personal past and form our narratives, including stories about ourselves and our plans for our own future.

As the poet-critic Charles Simic put it, memory can be at once a "gold mine," a "garbage dump," and an "archive."[13] It is our own written and spoken words which give our memories shape, but for serious readers our memories are also shaped by the texts we read, and that is especially true when we enter into the sustained imagined worlds of novels. We make sense of our own lives by ferreting out significant details and facts and integrating significant pieces of the present with memories of past experience, including memories of our reading experience.

Turning our experience into stories, we can bring them to life for others and ourselves. For some, those stories are oral; for others they are written. Just as for the novelists we are discussing, imagination plays a role in filling our gaps and transforming our memories into the shape of meaning. We read to share the experience of others, and those of us who write do so to share their experience with others.

Sense-Making

Always skeptical of neat interpretations, Jacques Derrida reminds us: "A text is not a text unless it hides from the first comer."[14] But is this so different from Plutarch's claim that "The speech of man is like embroidered tapestries, since like them this too has to be extended in order to display its patterns, but when it is rolled up it conceals and distorts them"?[15]

Reading novels is an odyssey that takes us through adventures in sense-making as we journey through complex texts. As Jeanette Winterson observes, "What we write about fiction is never an objective response to a text; it is always part of a bigger mythmaking – the story we are telling ourselves about ourselves."[16]

We may meet resistance to our understanding, be held in the bondage of temporary puzzlement – even confusion about why characters behave and speak as they do – but eventually we emerge with some awareness of what the novel has enacted and how it has been accomplished.

Reading literature – especially of diverse cultures – broadens our sense of what it means to be human. Imaginative literature provides for the reader a detailed representation of the inner experience of being alive in a given time and place. Imaginative literature deepens our understanding of ourselves and our place in the world.

According to the Irish novelist John Banville, "[W]e go to fiction for many reasons – to be entertained, instructed, diverted, enlightened, entranced – but what we are really in search of is not fiction, but life itself. Like the figures in our dreams, the characters we encounter in fiction are really us, and the story we are told is the story of ourselves. And therein rests the delightful paradox that the novelist's transcendent lies are eminently more truthful than all the facts in the world, that they are, in [James] Wood's formulation, 'true lies.'"[17] Wood not only argues that "fiction is both artifice and verisimilitude," but also that "[E]ven when one is believing fiction, one is 'not quite' believing, one is believing 'as if.'"[18]

Authors work alone, but as they approach final drafts and publication, they often do not think of themselves as soloists. They are aware that they are in a duet with their audience whose full – albeit silent – communication is necessary to complete the hermeneutical circle. In formal terms, within their texts authors create a narrator who speaks to an imagined audience; sometimes authors expect the reader to cast a skeptical eye on unreliable and imperceptive narrators.

Formal criticism rightly demands that readers respond to themes and values enacted within the text as opposed to what the author says beforehand; the latter is called the intentional or biographical fallacy. Yet what an author says about his text or his personal, social, and political values – even if we consign those writings to the pre-critical or post-critical task of reading carefully – is another often relevant and corroborative piece of data.

Interpretive History

Readers change as history and culture evolve. What is the role of interpretive history in understanding a literary work? Do readers judge behavior differently in the complex world of novels than they would judge similar events in their own life? Do twenty-first-century readers respond much differently than the original readers of eighteenth-, nineteenth-, and twentieth-century texts?

The reading and reception of novels and authors change as times change; different cultures view texts and their authors differently. Such relativism of course is a dynamic process, and the meaning and value of literary texts will continue to evolve as historical circumstances and ideologies of reading – New and traditional historicist, deconstruction, feminist, Marxist, Aristotelian, etc. – evolve. As a pluralist, I resist one-dimensional readings that see every text in the context of "progressive" history and label texts as colonialist or fascist because they do not adhere to current political values. Yet I do not ignore the need for resistant readings that point out the oppression of women or the poor or minorities when texts (and authors) are oblivious to them.

Interpretive history is the various responses to texts over time. Because of transformations in cultural values, we need different readings than the original author intended. Historical contexts help us understand a text differently than the original audience was expected to perceive. For example, Chinua Achebe changed the discussion of *Heart of Darkness* in his 1977 essay "An Image of Africa: Racism in Conrad's 'Heart of Darkness,'" and so did Adam Hochschild's revelations in his 1998 *King Leopold's Ghost: A Story of Greed, Terror, and Heroism in Colonial Africa* about how the exploitive imperialism and lawlessness of Belgium's King Leopold II in the Congo were even worse than that of most other colonial powers. Another example of interpretive history: no one (except someone writing in a very thinly distributed gay journal before gay studies had a foothold) had ever mentioned in print the male homosocial relationship in *The Secret Sharer*. But when I edited a volume on *The Secret Sharer*, accompanied by five critical essays, all five contributions (including my own) mentioned it independently and without any prompting from me.

But, we need to ask: Do literary texts enable us to think like people of another time even if they show us how those people lived? In part, "yes"; we often become readers without much resistance to an author's perspective. But as contemporary readers we also have our own optics and our way of thinking. This is another way of saying that novels enter a dialogue with both the audience for whom the author wrote and those reading the novels today. Of course, we should not think that our thinking is always completely different from earlier members of a similar culture. Yet, the more different the culture we are reading about is from our own – for example, village life in Nigeria in Chinua Achebe's *Things Fall Apart* (1958) – the harder it is to think like the author and his or her characters and the more our own thinking deviates from author, narrator, and characters.

Is form only intellectually perceived or can we readers feel it as we develop a relationship with the narrator, experience iteration, and enjoy linguistic play? We might think of what I call *felt form*. Form is not merely perceived but felt in our literary experience and how we feel it can be communicated. Criticism that speaks of affects need not and should not be restricted to resistant readers but rather can be very much a part of authorial readings. In our criticism and in the classroom, we can describe how we experience an evolving text aesthetically as we understand its patterns and how it continually modifies, undermines, and reconfigures themes and characterizations. We might say that stories have "pleasurable intelligibility" derived from our understanding their meaning within a formal arrangement.[19]

Cognitive Poetics

Let us turn to the burgeoning field of cognitive poetics. Literary studies are now relying on cognitive psychology to explain why and how we read, and in some cases to relate our desire for complex plots to our evolutionary development. Blakey Vermeule observes, "Cognitive poetics is deeply humanistic. Its goal seems to be to understand what makes the experience of art so rich and powerful – not to explain the experience away or somehow nail it to the wall, as some of its critics fear."[20]

According to Patricia Cohen, literary studies has begun to look to the technology of brain imaging and the principles of evolution to provide scientific evidence for how and why we read:

· ·

This layered process of figuring out what someone else is thinking – of mind reading – is both a common literary device and an essential survival skill. Why human beings are equipped with this capacity and what particular brain functions enable them to do it are questions that have occupied primarily cognitive psychologists.

Now English professors and graduate students are asking them too. They say they're convinced science not only offers unexpected insights into individual texts, but that it may help to answer fundamental questions about literature's very existence: Why do we read fiction? Why do we care so passionately about nonexistent characters? What underlying mental processes are activated when we read?[21]

· ·

The Function of Criticism and My Critical Approach

What is the function of literary interpretation and comparison? Criticism begins as an act of self-understanding and continues in the act of sharing – in writing or speech – that understanding with readers.

These activities keep literary works alive in our minds, particularly if we propose our understanding in the spirit of "This is true, isn't it?" What we critics need to do is emphasize matters that may not be obvious, shine the light on meanings that are latent but represent, and in some cases stress what seems obvious but may have been neglected or misconstrued. We may seek to show that what seems a systematic, continuous, coherent, and unified text may be more complicated and/or ambiguous than we thought.

Novels are by humans, about humans, and for humans, and we forget this at our peril. Their subject is inevitably the human experience, notably the psyche and values by which humankind lives in a specific historically defined culture. As Tom Stoppard observed, "The reason we love the books we love – it's the people. It's the human mud, the glue between us and them, the universal periodic table of the human condition. It transcends."[22]

As readers of my literary criticism know, I try to balance "Always the text" with "Always historicize." This is another way I strive to be, as Henry James wrote in "The Art of Fiction," one those readers on whom nothing – or as little as possible – is lost. I rely on using close scrutiny of evolving texts to make my arguments about what values a text enacts and how texts shape the reader's response so as to understand these values. I focus on such formal issues as structure, narrative technique, and choice of language and argue for the inextricable relationship between form and content, between aesthetics and themes. Thus I stress that literature represents imagined "as if" worlds rather than real ones.

Significant form controls content. Necessary and sufficient ingredients for great fiction include how parts relate to the whole, rich dialogue that is lively and reveals speakers' psyches and values, dramatic scenes that are purposeful in terms of larger plot intentions and thematic patterns, and a compelling narrative voice to which we cannot help but listen.

I shall be arguing that the narrative voice has a human face, and that is a large reason why we read novels, namely that humans are talking to humans about human experience. When writing is great, contemporary novelist David Mitchell observes, "[Y]our mind is nowhere else but in this world that started off in the mind of another human being. There are two miracles at work here. One that someone thought of that world and people in the first place. And the second, that there's this means of transmitting it. Just *little* ink marks on squashed wood fiber. Bloody amazing."[23]

One aspect of my approach is what might be called pattern recognition – including recurrences, modulations, deviations, and transformations of plot, characterization, and language, and this means full attention to the words on the page rather than reference to an external theory. Attending to what Stephen Dedalus in the "Proteus" episode of Joyce's *Ulysses* calls "ineluctable modality of the visible" and later defines in "Scylla and Charybdis" as "What you damn well have to see," I am more an Aristotelian than a Platonist who focuses on a priori forms. Thus I seek to know what is the world represented by an author and what personal and historical factors caused an author to give that world shape. I believe in reason, but understand the need for intuition in reading texts imaginatively. Thus my discussions combine a mosaic of quotations and insights in the context of a reading that addresses major issues in the texts.

I try to define what is special and unique about each author by asking, "What kind of fiction did each of these authors write?" The novel is a flexible form without absolute rules, although it has multiple conventions of narration and dialogue. As 2010 Booker Prize winner Howard Jacobson puts it, "Here's the wonder of the novel. The novel is the great fluid form in which all those possibilities flow in and flow out. Nothing is definite, nothing is finished, nothing is determined."[24] Indeed, the novel form is so flexible that novels propose, even as they attend to their subjects, new modes of telling and viewing characterization, often in response to new ways of understanding how the human psyche works. Thus one of the narratives implicit in the pages that follow is a history of experiments with the novel form. While this history is an essential part of this volume with its strong component the realistic novel, the history of experiments in form is even truer of the twentieth-century authors on whom I will focus in Volume 2.

Aesthetic features always signify. The amplitude and conventions of novels often allow for different perspectives on events and characters; most novels eschew dogma, preferring to test different perspectives. Novels can propose, test, dispose of, reconfigure, and reformulate ideas.

While not inattentive to historical contexts following my mantra, "Always the text; Always historicize," my book's focus is on the formal and aesthetic dimensions of literature. For too long, historicism – in the name of cultural studies – has deflected us from attention to the text by claiming that a positivistic cause and effect between literary texts and one or another historical phenomenon is the fundamental reason for reading. Thus in some classes and scholarly essays, Leopold Bloom's carrying a potato in his pocket has been contextualized by long discussions of the Irish potato famine, while the novel *Ulysses* awaits impatiently for the teacher and the critic to return to the text. Another example would be scholarly essays that discuss the history of Parma without attending to Stendhal's form.

I do not treat aesthetic matters in isolation from social, political, and historical issues. Rather I show how the aesthetic choices artists make shape the presentation of these issues, even while their understanding of these issues shapes their aesthetic choices. A novelist's awareness is historically determined, although certainly individual personality enters into the choice of how events and characters as well as form are presented. Often novels – and especially the European novels under consideration – are in a dialogue with history, or should we say interpretations of history? Thus Russian and French novels reflect the glory and torment – the triumphs and vulgarity – of Russian and French (or, in Stendhal's case, Italian) history.

I also am cognizant of the difference between what is sometimes called authorial reading, which responds to the author's intended structure of effects, and various resistant (often contemporary) readings, which might notice sexism, racism, class snobbery, and homophobia, of which the author was unaware or chose to ignore or minimize.

In showing how authors build a structure of effects with their readers in mind, I write for both readers and rereaders. I stress the respect authors have for readers and their desire to shape their readers' responses. In the discussions that follow, I will be attentive to the narrator – who is speaking about character and history, albeit always in written form – and his relationship to the reader. Novels are not written in a vacuum and we sometimes forget how important a figure the reader is to authors when writing. Our authors are much aware of the reader when creating their narrators, knowing that who narrates and how is crucial to communication. Usually the narratee – the audience addressed by the narrator within the text – is a surrogate for an imagined reader at the time the text was written, whereas a reader of a later generation may more likely be resistant to a kinship with the imagined narratee. But in each case the reader plays an active role in constructing the text.

I consider myself a pluralist, making use of diverse approaches, depending on the novel. At times, I take as my inspiration a line from Wallace Stevens: "It can never be satisfied, the mind, never" ("The Well Dressed Man with a Beard").

I have tried to avoid the shortcoming of my approach – which I have elsewhere called "humanistic formalism" – namely, that it oversimplifies aesthetic structure and significant form in its quest for unity and coherence. I have learned from deconstruction, but try to eschew its tendencies both to stress every possible nuance of thematic confusion or formal dissonance and to enter into abstract discussion that takes us away from the experience of reading about lived life.

An Aspect of Realism: The Author in the Text

According to Zadie Smith, "Realism is built [upon three credos]: the transcendent importance of form, the incantatory power of language to reveal truth, [and] the essential fullness and continuity of the self."[25]

Thinking of traditional realism, Smith asks some compelling questions: "Do selves always seek their good, in the end? Are they never perverse? Do they always want meaning? Do they sometimes want its opposite? And is this how memory works? … Is this how time feels? Do the things of the world really come to us like this, embroidered in the verbal fancy of times past? … Is this really Realism?"[26] Some of the novelists I discuss in this volume challenge these ideas of realism and are aware of these paradoxes. Dostoevsky, Flaubert, and Stendhal know that characters act contrary to their own interest and eschew the most obvious lessons that experience teaches. In my second volume, we shall see how Kafka, Camus, and Saramago stress illogical behavior. Smith reminds us that "most avant-garde challenges to realism concentrate on voice, one where this 'I' is coming from, this mysterious third person."[27]

A convincing and plausible voice is the essence of realism and such a voice is often rooted in personal experience. Writing about Colm Tóibín but also thinking of other writers Tim Parks observed, "We may even ask if the satisfaction of achieving an aestheticized expression of personal suffering does not preserve the pain by making it functional to the life of the sufferer turned artist."[28] Does not the narrative voice in Dostoevsky, Stendhal, Balzac, and Flaubert often describe the behavior of despised characters as if the author were denying and

15

disguising aspects of himself that he does not wish to reveal or may not even be fully aware of?

The author's presence in the text takes many forms. This is what Ralph Rader called "the fiction of the actual" or – a term I like less – the "similar" novel.[29] As James Phelan and David Richter put it, the form of some novels "moves away from the 'as if' quality of the novel to represent in fictional form real people and events."[30] Such novels are, they argue, radical versions of "the way authors make room for representations of themselves and their own personal conflicts within otherwise fictional literary creations."[31] We need to be aware of the oscillating distance between author and characters even in so-called novelists of the actual like Tolstoy, Flaubert, and Zola – and, in the twentieth century, Mann, di Lampedusa, Bassani, Proust as well as Woolf and Joyce – all of whom use their novels to define their aesthetic, personal, and social values. We need to be aware, too, that authors pretending to take a cosmological perspective – whether Tolstoy, Dostoevsky, or Kafka (or, in the Anglo-American tradition, Hardy, Conrad, Hawthorne, and Melville) – often reveal a great deal about themselves.

In such novels as *Don Quixote* and *The Charterhouse of Parma*, Cervantes and Stendhal propose a parodic form of the fiction of the actual – what we might call "the fiction of the actual manqué" – where the narrator calls attention to himself as if he were a surrogate for the author, but in fact he or she is not a surrogate.

Reading Translations

Translation is necessarily the recontextualization of cultural artifacts because translation is a kind of plagiarism, an appropriation of one book to make another, or a kind of, to use a current term, remixing.

Translation has been called "creative betrayal" because the original can never be fully rendered.[32] Translating a text means transforming it, but how does a translated text get closest to the original? Is it by seeking equivalence or is something more subtle and nuanced required? The best translators are artists in their own right. To an extent a translation always implies the culture of its new language. Should we translate into another language "He hit a home run," if it were used by a contemporary American author, to mean: "He has done very well"?

Let us think about the issues raised by working with translations. Octavio Paz has wisely noted: "No text can be completely original because language itself, in its very essence, is already a translation – first from the nonverbal world and then, because each sign and each phrase is a translation of another sign, another phrase."[33]

Commenting on Stanley Corngold's translation of Goethe's *The Sufferings of Young Werther* (1774), J. M. Coetzee has remarked:

. . . .

[Corngold] follows Goethe's German closely, even at the risk of sometimes sounding foreign. He takes pains not to use words that were not part of the English language by 1787.

The reason for the 1787 cutoff date is obvious: to avoid anachronism. But anachronism is not only a matter of word choice [but of prose style].... With works from the past, how should the language of the translation relate to the language of the original? Should a twenty-first-century translation into English of a novel from the 1770s read like a twenty-first-century English novel or like an English novel from the era of the original?[34]

. . . .

These are essential questions and the tendency recently is towards the latter position but, more importantly, towards keeping the spirit of the original prose to the extent it is possible.

To retain, say, Tolstoy's nuanced and playful use of repetition of a word becomes a challenge to a translator. Does he simply repeat or does he try to find equivalents to the subtle nuances? As Caryl Emerson asserts, "The Pevear and Volokhonsky translations [of Tolstoy] don't paraphrase, respecting the Tolstoyan period as one would a poem. They observe Tolstoy's repetitions (same word in Russian = same word in English, because Tolstoy is incantational). [They d]on't soften his dogmatic nonsense, and in [*War and Peace*, leaving in the French]; in [*Anna Karenina*] the LONG sentences, like waves in the sea. Mostly sustaining the sense that the fellow never gave up."[35]

The obvious problem in discussing novels in translation is that we are not dealing with the original primary texts. In terms of close verbal analyses, I shall be using well-known translations. While translations can't replicate the original and always produce different texts, they can give the original text new life, not only with different words but sometimes also with different nuances. For some expressions there is no translation because the original belongs to the culture. Sandra Bermann observes, "Translations are texts in which other languages can be heard – whether as distant echoes or as distinct dialogues.... [L]inguistic translation means cultural translation. Yet no matter how well-prepared and carefully wrought, no matter how deep the linguistic and cultural knowledge of the translator, translation does not and cannot reproduce its already complex source.... Translation allows a text to live on in another culture and time.... But translation also questions and disrupts a text from a new cultural standpoint, raising unanticipated questions in the cultures that now read it."[36]

Translating is a hermeneutic activity. As Lawrence Venuti puts it:

. . . .

[A] hermeneutic model treats translation as an interpretation of the source text whose form, meaning, and effect are seen as variable, subject to inevitable transformation during the translating process.... Translating never gives back the source text unaltered. It can only inscribe an interpretation, one among many possibilities, through lexical and syntactic choices that can alter source-textual features like meter and tone, point of view and characterization, narrative and genre, terminology and argument.

The translator inscribes an interpretation [that]...mediates between the source language and culture, on the one hand, and the receiving language and culture, on the other.[37]

. . . .

As James Campbell observes, "The question of translators' fidelity to the works they are charged with smuggling across the border has been much debated. Every thoughtful practitioner is aware that he is creating something new."[38] But, as Campbell also notes, "Translators take fewer liberties nowadays," with the result of what has been called "'internationalist' translatorese" that is responsible for the "standardization and flattening of foreign texts."[39] Thus, while I am writing about that "something new," I am also in some cases dealing with the aforementioned problem of standardizing and flattening of a foreign text.

Good translations can be close to replications or iterations. But because the original language is culturally determined, sometimes, to create a parallel reading experience, it is necessary to find *different* language rather than replication of the translated language. In a sense a good translation has two different goals. A good translation needs to be torn free from its original cultural context and given a fresh one in the new language even while paradoxically doing its best to retain as much of the cultural original as possible. In her introduction to *Nation, Language, and the Ethics of Translation*, Sandra Bermann observes:

. . . .

[E]ach language bears its own vast and endlessly transforming intertext of socially and historically grafted meanings, along with their graphic and acoustic imagery.... Yet even in its imperfect, or simply creative negotiations of difference, translation provides a necessary linguistic supplement that bridges cultural chasms and allows for intellectual passage and exchange.... If we must translate in order to emancipate and preserve cultural pasts and to build linguistic bridges for present understandings and future thought, we must do so while attempting to respond ethically to each language's contexts, intertexts, and intrinsic alterity.[40]

. . . .

In a sense a translation is an Afterword, a commentary in another language coming as it does after the original writing is finished. Languages have a cultural and national history and the best translations respect idioms and silences and speech patterns, but also know that some things – especially word play – resist translation. With his puns, neologisms, portmanteau words, and stream of consciousness that jumps from one thought and sensation to another, Joyce's writing is most difficult to translate, especially *Ulysses* and *Finnegans Wake*. But the authors I discuss here also require deft and subtle translation. In recent years, Edith Grossman's wonderful translation of *Don Quixote* and Richard Pevear and Larissa Volokhonsky's translations of Dostoevsky and Tolstoy have taught us that a great translation, reflecting the translators' understanding of the words and the context in which they were written, can bring us a richer and more authentic reading experience than prior translations. Grossman observes: "For me this is the essential challenge in translation: hearing, in the most profound way I can, the text in Spanish, and discovering the voice to say (I mean, to write) the text again in English. Compared to that, lexical difficulties shrink and wither away. I believe that my primary obligation as a literary translator is to recreate for the reader in English the experience of the reader in Spanish."[41]

What happens when translation goes off track is that the translation has strong resonances of the culture in which the translation takes place. Thus Constance Garnett's translation of *The Brothers Karamazov* has lower-class characters speak in Cockney English, which doesn't work for American readers, and more importantly does not address the history of serfs and servants in Russia.

Yet translation at its best is also collaboration between the original artist and the translator, a creative act in which a new voice is achieved. We are hesitant to call a translator an artist because we like to think of the artist as someone who wrenches art out of his soul, possibly out of a process of lonely suffering, perhaps combined with the difficulty of coming to terms with the major examples of his or her art while creating. But we might remember that in the latter case appropriation often takes place. Is not, for example, *Ulysses* an appropriation of Homer?

Translations are intellectual travels from one country to another, perhaps something like border crossings, but the borders are not always clear. Major texts that are translated into many languages are cosmopolitan and diasporic, but our focus in my book will be on these major texts immigrating into the English-speaking world. Yet the very act of translation is cosmopolitan by situating a text in two worlds. Although postcolonial theorists regard translation as an act of colonialism, I regard translation as a political, intellectual, and social act of globalization because it erases borders and creates cultural dialogue. In that sense it has a progressive social function because it gives us access to other worlds in other places.

Edith Grossman, who has produced the renowned translation of *Don Quixote* that I am using in this book, has remarked:

Translation not only plays its important traditional role as the means that allows us access to literature originally written in one of the countless languages we cannot read, but it also represents a concrete literary presence with the crucial capacity to ease and make more meaningful our relationships to those with whom we may not have had a connection before. Translation always helps us to know, to see from a different angle, to attribute new value to what once may have been unfamiliar. As nations and as individuals, we have a critical need for that kind of understanding and insight. The alternative is unthinkable.[42]

Familiarity not only with the original language but also with the culture and history of the nation and the particular region or city where the events described take place is essential to a good translator. Not all translators subscribe to the same assumptions of what constitutes a good translation. One approach is to stay close to the original, following every sentence, and retaining the order of ideas and metaphors, even reproducing inconsistencies in tense or punctuation. That is, the translator is meticulous about staying close to the original and does not try to improve on a masterful artist. Yet translations that hew too close to the original can create misunderstandings, in which case some imaginative recreation might be preferable.

Grossman observes, "Where literature exists, translation exists. Joined at the hip, they are absolutely inseparable, and, in the long run, what happens to one happens to the other. Despite all the difficulties the two have faced, sometimes separately, usually together, they need and nurture each other, and their long-term relationship, often problematic but always illuminating, will surely continue for as long as they both shall live."[43]

Richard Howard concludes his discussion of Grossman's *Why Translation Matters*: "In the end, Grossman warmly (after all) and gratefully rehearses the twofold answer to the question of her title: translation matters because it is an expression and an extension of our humanity, the secret metaphor of all literary communication; and because the creation of any literary translation is (or at least must be) an original writing, not a pathetic shadow or tracing of the inaccessible 'original' but the creation, indeed, of a second – and as we have seen, a third and a ninth – but always a new work, in another language."[44]

We might close this section with a cautionary note about our reading translations from a discussion within the text of *Don Quixote*. When presiding over which books to burn and choosing one because the author has been a translator, the priest remarks to his friend, the barber: "[H]e took away a good deal of its original value, which is what all who attempt to translate books of poetry into another language will do as well: no matter the care they use and the skill they show, they will never achieve the quality the verses had in their first birth" (1.VI.48; trans. Grossman). I take this as an admonition that I am writing on European novels in translation, even though I, consulting a wide range of colleagues, have tried to find the best translations.

Conclusion

In the following pages I shall discuss major European novels in translation. I shall bring to this project my lifetime of reading and writing about literature, including some expertise about the form of the novel and the unfolding experience presented by the words on the page. While I acknowledge previous scholarship on each writer, I do not claim to be a world-class authority on either the individual novels or novelists that I discuss.

With each chapter I have included study questions to guide teachers and readers towards what I feel are the most salient issues. I invite you to join me as I celebrate the experience of reading some of the masterworks of Western literature.

Notes

1. I considered for inclusion Ivan Turgenev's *Fathers and Sons* (1862) but ultimately did not consider Turgenev to be at the same level as Dostoevsky and Tolstoy.
2. Verlyn Klinkenborg, "Some Thoughts on the Pleasures of Being a Re-Reader," *New York Times*, May 29, 2009.
3. Quoted in Roberta Smith, "Sculpture in High Relief," *New York Times*, May 20, 2011.
4. Quoted in Philip Lopate, "The Best German Novelist of His Time," *NYR* 58:3 (Feb. 14, 2011), 35–38; see p. 35.
5. Quoted from *The Liberal Imagination* (1950), in Louis Menand, "Regrets Only," *New Yorker*, Sept. 29, 2008, 80–90.
6. Michael Chabon, "What to Make of *Finnegans Wake*?" *NYR* 59:12 (July 12, 2012), 45–48; see p. 48.
7. Quoted in Wyatt Mason, "Smarter than You Think," *NYR* 57:12 (July 15, 2010), 12.
8. Georg Lukács, *Studies in European Realism* (London: Hillway, 1950), 12.
9. Tony Judt, "The Glory of the Rails," *NYR* 57:20 (Dec. 23, 2010), 60–61; see p. 60.

10. Judt, "The Glory of the Rails," 60.
11. Quoted in James Phelan and David Richter, "The Literary Theoretical Contribution of Ralph Rader," *Narrative* 18:1 (Jan. 2010), 73–90; see p. 82.
12. Joyce Wadler, "Though Memory May Fail Us, What I Recall Was Truly Love," *New York Times*, Sept. 15, 2013.
13. Charles Simic, "Grass: The Gold and the Garbage," *NYR* 57:5 (March 24, 2011), 23–24; see p. 23.
14. Jacques Derrida, "Plato's Pharmacy," in *Dissemination*, trans. Barbara Johnson (Chicago: University of Chicago Press, 1981), 69.
15. Plutarch's "Life of Themistocles," quoted in Roderick Conway Morris, "Weaving a More Modern Narrative," *IHT* (June 14, 2011), 11.
16. Jeanette Winterson, "A Classic Passes 50," *New York Times*, Jan. 29, 2012.
17. John Banville, "The Prime of James Wood," *NYR* 55:18 (Nov. 20, 2008), 85–88; see p. 88.
18. Quoted in Banville, "The Prime of James Wood," ibid.
19. Quotation from Ralph Rader, "Fact, Theory, and Literary Explanation," in Frances Ferguson, "Ralph Rader on the Literary History of the Novel," *Narrative* 18:1 (Jan. 2010), 91–103; see p. 100.
20. Blakey Vermeule, "Room for Debate: Can 'Neuro Lit-Crit' Save the Humanities?" *New York Times*, April 5, 2010.
21. Patricia Cohen, "Next Big Thing in English: Knowing They Know That You Know," *New York Times*, March 31, 2010; http://www.nytimes.com/2010/04/01/books/01lit.html?src=me&ref=arts (accessed February 14, 2014).
22. Tom Stoppard, quoted in Wyatt Mason, "David Mitchell, the Experimentalist," *New York Times Magazine*, June 27, 2010; http://www.nytimes.com/2010/06/27/magazine/27mitchell-t.html?pagewanted=1&8dpc (accessed February 14, 2014).
23. Quoted in Mason, "David Mitchell, the Experimentalist," ibid.
24. Howard Jacobson, quoted in Sarah Lyall, "Booker Prize Winner's Jewish Question," *New York Times*, Oct. 18, 2010.
25. Zadie Smith, "Two Paths for the Novel," *NYR* 55:18 (Nov. 20, 2008), 89–94; see p. 89.
26. Smith, "Two Paths for the Novel," 91.
27. Smith, "Two Paths for the Novel," 92.
28. Tim Parks, "Life at the Core," *NYR* 58:6 (April 7, 2011), 58–59; see p. 58.
29. Ralph Rader, "Exodus and Return: Joyce's *Ulysses* and the Fiction of the Actual," *UTQ* 48 (Winter 1978/9), 149–171.
30. Phelan and Richter, "The Literary Theoretical Contribution of Ralph Rader," 82.
31. Phelan and Richter, "The Literary Theoretical Contribution of Ralph Rader," 84.
32. Verena Conley, "Living in Translation," *Profession 2010*, 18–24; see p. 18.

33. Octavio Paz, "Translation: Literature and Letters," in *Theories of Translation: An Anthology of Essays from Dryden to Derrida*, ed. Rainer Schulte and John Biguenet (Chicago: University of Chicago Press, 1992), 152–162; see p. 154.
34. J. M. Coetzee, "Storm Over Young Goethe," *NYR* 59:7 (April 26, 2012), 17–22; see p. 21.
35. Professor Caryl Emerson, Princeton University, March 31, 2008, email to Daniel R. Schwarz.
36. Sandra Bermann, "Teaching in – and about – Translation," *Profession 2010*, 82–90; see pp. 84–85.
37. Lawrence Venuti, "Translation, Empiricism, Ethics," *Profession 2010*, 72–81; see p. 74.
38. James Campbell, "Creative Misreading," *New York Times Book Review*, June 12, 2011, 35.
39. Campbell, "Creative Misreading," 35.
40. Sandra Bermann, "Introduction," in *Nation, Language, and the Ethics of Translation*, ed. Sandra Bermann and Michael Wood (Princeton, NJ: Princeton University Press, 2005), 5–7.
41. Edith Grossman, "Translator's Note to the Reader," in Miguel de Cervantes, *Don Quixote* (New York: HarperCollins, 2003), xix.
42. Edith Grossman, "Prologue," in *Why Translation Matters* (New Haven, CT: Yale University Press, 2010), x–xi.
43. Quoted in Richard Howard, "Duet for Two Pens," *New York Times*, April 8, 2010; http://www.nytimes.com/2010/04/11/books/review/Howard-t.html (accessed February 14, 2014).
44. Howard, "Duet for Two Pens."

Chapter 2

Miguel de Cervantes'
Don Quixote (1605, 1615)

Inventing the Novel

Introduction

We begin our discussion of individual works in the early years of seventeenth-century Spain with *Don Quixote* (1605, 1615), an experimental and innovative novel that became a paradigm for subsequent texts that I am discussing. For Cervantes addresses the question that Ken Johnson asks: "If objectivity is a myth and the truth always elusive, who is really pulling the strings on the puppet show we take for reality?"[1]

Cervantes (1547–1616) not only ponders how to differentiate factual history from imaginary history, but also strives to present the essence of life during the high tide of Imperial Spain by focusing on two individuals who are irrelevant to political life. Within his remarkable text, he uses fiction to represent different ways of thinking and ways of being as well as to capture the socio-economic world in which his characters live. Even while interesting us, his readers, in the idiosyncrasies of two odd characters, Don Quixote and Sancho Panza, Cervantes makes us realize that we have a great deal in common with them. Cervantes combines reasonable explanations for behavior – what we think of as a grammar of motives – with incomprehensible and uncanny behavior. Put another way, Cervantes would have approved of Lady Gaga's musing: "I believe magic is real. I believe fantasy is real. I live halfway between reality and fantasy all the time."[2]

Reading the European Novel to 1900: A Critical Study of Major Fiction from Cervantes' Don Quixote *to Zola's* Germinal, First Edition. Daniel R. Schwarz.
© 2014 John Wiley & Sons, Ltd. Published 2014 by John Wiley & Sons, Ltd.

Cervantes creates a knowing and often ironic narrator, an editor-translator who has privileged information, some of which he shares and some of which he hides with a knowing wink. Realizing that a knight must have a lady to serve, Don Quixote invents Dulcinea as surely as Cervantes invented Don Quixote. For the most part, Cervantes' editor-translator and his other major narrator, Cide Hamete, balance comedy with compassion, sympathy with judgment, and objectivity with empathy when presenting the all-too-human behavior of his principals and secondary characters.

We begin, too, with a text that stresses the power of reading and reminds us that we are what we read. It also reminds us to be wary of losing all distance between what we read and ourselves. Were we to take too seriously such passages from Shakespeare as "Life's but a walking shadow, a poor player, / that struts and frets his hour upon the stage, / and then is heard no more; it is a tale / told by an idiot, full of sound and fury, / signifying nothing" (*Macbeth* V.v.24–28), or "Men must endure/ their going hence, even as their coming hither: / Ripeness is all" (*King Lear* V.ii.9–11), we might ourselves despair.

Cervantes' Digressive Imagination

As Christopher Benfey observes, "Getting lost appears to be a major theme in European literature. From Odysseus' long detour home, to Dante's midlife crisis … to the abandoned children of the Brothers Grimm, it would seem the 'straight way' is rarely the best way to make an interesting story."[3] Not only Don Quixote in his adventures but also his creator, his narrators, and the reader experience long detours on the journey through the text.

I want to discuss *Don Quixote* from both a formalist and humanist perspective, thinking about what Cervantes contributes to the novel form, including his relationship with readers, and thinking of *Don Quixote* as a human drama. As a humanist I will be concerned with the values and psyches of Don Quixote and Sancho Panza, even while realizing that there is an element of the uncanny in Cervantes' characters and that their behavior challenges and defies rational description if we are looking for the consistent and intelligible behavior patterns of the nineteenth-century novel of Flaubert or Dickens. While the Don seems to have retired from sexuality, the interpolated stories often speak of love and passion as if to point up his asexuality and perhaps his incompleteness if not emptiness.

Nor can we find a consistent grammar of motives for many of Cervantes' other characters, especially the Bachelor Sansón but also the priest, the barber, and Altisidora. Cervantes challenges twenty-first-century readers to accept uncanny and weird behavior in some of the characters in the interpolated tales. For the interpolated stories also include other examples, in addition to the Don's, of extravagant behavior and fancy gone astray. I am thinking of Anselmo's testing his wife's fidelity by talking his best friend Lothario into seducing her; or Marcela's rejection of Grisóstomo and Grisóstomo's assertion that she neither loves nor despises anyone (1.XIV.100); or the beautiful Dorotea's rejection by the Duke's son Fernando in favor of Luscinda, who is herself married, after Dorotea foolishly agreed to consummate their relationship on his promise of marriage (1.XXVII.218). Ultimately, after Dorotea coincidentally meets Luscinda and Fernando at an inn, Fernando with some reluctance embraces Dorotea as his true love, but what lingers in the reader's mind is his harsh and inconstant behavior towards the lower-born Dorotea.

Cervantes is modern in his awareness that we do not have a consistent self; he is acutely aware that circumstances determine human behavior and that we behave differently, depending on the situation and how our past experience has shaped us prior to a particular situation.

As a formalist, my comments on *Don Quixote* will focus on the self-consciousness of the text, what is often called textuality. That self-conscious textuality is an important strand that recurs throughout my discussions in this volume on the European novel to 1900, and even more so in my next volume. Some of the fun of Part Two of *Don Quixote* in particular is the characters' awareness – and of course, the reader's – of the existence of the published version of Part One. Perhaps that playful awareness is one reason that I, as a formalist interested in the study of narrative and how it shapes readers' responses and fulfills our need for imposing order on events, found Part Two, contrary to most readers, to be just as satisfying as Part One, if not more so. Is Part Two more fun because there are fewer digressions from the main characters, although to an extent the adventures in Part Two – and perhaps this is inherent in most picaresque novels – are themselves digressions?

Many of the claims for the importance of *Don Quixote* are extra-literary. These range from crediting Cervantes for his contribution to a sense of Spanish nationhood to praising him for his response to previous literary forms as if this were a sufficient claim for a work's excellence. For example, Ramón Menéndez Pidal discusses the genealogy of chivalric romances, citing instances where *Don Quixote* draws on ballads and the *romancero*, popular Spanish heroic poetry of the time.[4] Pidal describes the beginning of *Don Quixote* as a response to "Entremés de los Romances," a short play written around 1591 about a peasant who goes crazy from reading too many ballads. But discussion of the original context of production is not why readers reread a text again and again. What redeems *Don Quixote* is that Cervantes has a deep sense of human nature and folly. Moreover, it is often hilarious.

Don Quixote is an elegy for a world that never was, but it alludes to a world where the conventions of knighthood and traditions of chivalry did have considerable standing. By the time Cervantes wrote, gunpowder and artillery as well as the modern nation-state had emerged to render the conventions and traditions of knighthood and feudalism obsolete. Machiavelli had written *The Prince* (1532) and Ariosto had written *Orlando Furioso* (complete version, 1532), and Cervantes was very much aware that the ideals of chivalry and the cult of virginity – what C. S. Lewis has called the religion of love – had given way to a much more complex view of human nature. He was aware of the foolishness of violence for its own sake, the pretensions of chivalry and class differences, and the notion that one man or way of seeing the world had a monopoly on truth.[5]

What Ingrid Rowland writes of Ariosto's *Orlando Furioso* is equally true of Cervantes' *Don Quixote*: "Seldom … have the contradictions of knighthood been laid so bare, from the useless violence of constant jousting to the confusing mores of aristocratic society: the cult of virginity is praised to the heavens, but that fact stops few of Ariosto's knights and ladies from sporting vigorously."[6] Cervantes, the seventeenth-century modernist, cannot accept the pretensions of the chivalric traditions. As Ken Johnson aptly notes, caricature depends on the audience members relating what they read or see to something within their own experiential world: "Because his job is to make the fantastic seem viscerally real, the caricaturist must be skilled in the art of naturalistic representation. For caricature to exist in the first place there has to be a tradition of mimetic realism in place. The Renaissance provided that for European artists."[7]

Don Quixote is written in the narrative form known as the picaresque, a genre in which a human ventures from his home to find himself through a variety of episodes. As Roberto González Echevarría puts it, "*Don Quixote*'s narrative structure owes a great deal to [the picaresque], not only in the episodic plot … but also in all the scenes in inns and roads, with their colorful gallery of rogues."[8] The *picaro* – or rogue – is usually a low-born figure, although Don Quixote de la Mancha is less a rogue than an innocent and is more middle class than poor.

The Don and Sancho Panza as Characters

Don Quixote, the dreamer and idealist, and Sancho Panza, who is more anchored in reality but has his own aspirations, are among the great characters in fiction. As Anthony Cascardi writes, "Don Quixote fashions an identity for himself, wins his self, achieves his individuality, without forsaking moral choice; conversely, he is able to act ethically without sacrificing his personal autonomy."[9] The same can be said of Sancho Panza, who grows in maturity and self-knowledge within the text, especially in Part Two. Sancho Panza does love his creature comforts, but he is less Don Quixote's opposite than – with his aspirations to governorship and marrying his daughter to a count – a kind of earthy peasant counterpart to Don Quixote. It is his unfailing optimism that allows him to take Don Quixote's condescension and at times even emotional abuse. From the moment in their early adventures when Sancho is tossed about in a blanket at the inn and physically abused, he participates in Don Quixote's nonsense.

The title character, whose real last name is Quexana, lives in the provinces in obscurity until his reading of knightly tales stirs his imagination to the point where he becomes transformed into an obsessive and humorless fool, albeit a well-meaning and courageous one. The texts he reads make him dissatisfied with who he is; he models himself on preposterous romances that speak of giants and wizards and impossible heroic deeds. Don Quixote is satirized as a well-meaning figure who has become so immersed in tales of knights and chivalry that his imagination verges on madness. Before deciding he will became a man of action in the form of a chivalric knight, he is single, middle-aged, and sedentary. His real quest is not for money but for fame and self-fulfillment, but what the quest brings him, finally, is self-knowledge.

Thinking of himself as a chosen one and a member of an elect group because he is a knight errant, he is at times also an arrogant elitist and a snob. Don Quixote makes clear to his sometimes more rational and practical companion Sancho Panza – who himself is diverted by promises that he will rule an island – that he regards his squire as a lesser being whose feelings and thoughts do not matter.

Cervantes' novel is about what happens when we humans forget who we are. On the one hand, Don Quixote is living in a world of dragons, giants, and spells; on the other he has real-life experiences and ensuing disappointments that baffle his understanding. Cervantes is very much aware of the place of eros and the foolishness of pretending that it doesn't motivate behavior. He stresses how silly it is to test virtue and to ignore human desires, passions, and physical needs.

Don Quixote takes himself very seriously, but most of the other characters within the novel either mock him or humor him while laughing behind his back. With his peculiar steadfastness and fundamental decency combined with an active imagination that more than half creates what he sees, Don Quixote gets himself into trouble battling perceived evils in the name of his fantasy lady, Dulcinea del Toboso.

Believing that a knight must serve a lady, the Don wants to idealize Dulcinea as the paradigm of beauty, chastity, elegance, and refinement, but he has no desire to have sex with her. He is a lifetime bachelor and seems uninterested in sex; one could even argue that he embraces the role of errant knight because it frees him from the complications that might ensue in relations with women. In the Prologue, Cervantes' author-surrogate speaks of the Don in the last paragraph as "the most chaste lover and the most valiant knight seen in those environs [the district of Campo de Montiel] for many years" ("Prologue," 8–9).[10]

Fixated on his Dulcinea, he subscribes to a religion of love in preference to traditional religious values. The Don claims to have loved her for twelve years, although he has seen her only four times. Dulcinea is really a local peasant woman named Aldonza Lorenzo who lives nearby and whom the Don knows can neither read nor write (1.XXV.199). She is known for her strength and loud voice and is something of a "trollop" if we can believe Sancho Panza (1.XXV.199–200).

After Sancho objects to the Don's transforming this peasant girl into Dulcinea of Toboso, Don Quixote, in one of his rare moments of clarity, acknowledges: "[I]t is enough for me to think and believe that my good Aldonza Lorenzo is beautiful and virtuous; as for her lineage, it matters little, for no one is going to investigate it in order to give her a robe of office, and I can think she is the highest princess in the world.... I imagine that everything I say is true, no more and no less, and I depict her in my imagination as I wish her to be in beauty and in distinction" (1.XXV.201). The Don knows that most women in literature are not "really ladies of flesh and blood" but rather "are imagined in order to provide a subject for [authors'] verses" (1.XXV.201).

When Sancho presents the peasant girl as Dulcinea and tells Don Quixote that the Don is enchanted if all he sees is a peasant girl, we see that Sancho has become more inventive and imaginative. Sancho's imaginative fantasy in which he will eventually be in the position to govern an island – *insula* is the Latin word for island – shows that he shares some of Don Quixote's capacity for self-delusion. Yet when he does get to govern, if not an island, a community, he is something of a pre-Enlightenment rationalist. Cervantes implies that we need a balance between imagination and reason. After all, Don Quixote – and then Sancho Panza – invents Dulcinea, just as Hamete, the "author" of the novel, invented Don Quixote and just as Cervantes invented both Hamete and the fictional Spanish translator. Given that *ingenioso* in Spanish means to be quick with inventiveness, the full title *The Ingenious Hidalgo Don Quixote of La Mancha* points not only to Don Quixote's overactive imagination, but also to Cervantes' creativity in writing his fiction.

Gradually Don Quixote becomes a multi-faceted character whose interest for the reader depends on how the Don responds to human situations in Catholic Imperial Spain. We learn how various classes live, from the idle rich who, like the Duke and Duchess, have nothing to do and are served by a large staff, to the peasants – like the stocky Sancho Panza – who eke out a living from the land. We meet innkeepers and shepherds, religious zealots and charlatans, book publishers and puppeteers, and gradually begin to understand the social and economic mosaic of late sixteenth- and early seventeenth-century Spain.

As Echevarría puts it: "Don Quijote and his creator both invent themselves in a quest for freedom that their advanced age makes urgent, breaking on the one hand with literary tradition and on the other with social expectations.... Cervantes' protagonist has had such lasting appeal because he embodies a … yearning to shape one's life according to one's desires, together with the confidence that such a thing is possible by an act of will undeterred by natural or man-made obstacles."[11]

In Chapter XLV of Part One, the Don has a touching moment of semi- clarity in which he acknowledges that the way he sees the world is a function of his belief in his social role: "Perhaps because you have not been dubbed knights, as I have, the enchantments of this place will not affect your graces, and your minds will be free and able to judge the things in this castle as they really and truly are, and not as they seem to me" (1.XLV.392). Here Don Quixote realizes that what he sees is a function of the role he has assumed but also acknowledges that he does not have a monopoly on reality and truth.

Cervantes and the Form of the Novel

Reading *Don Quixote* depends on understanding the ironic disjunction between the view of Cervantes' narrator – the Spanish editor-translator –and Don Quixote's very limited perspective. Cervantes stresses that we are also the stories we tell ourselves and others, and that is one point of the interpolated stories. Wasn't Cervantes a pioneer in introducing multiple perspectives in fiction? Didn't that relate to his skepticism of monolithic truth articulated by the King and Church and his awareness of the infinite variety of human life in the face of efforts to control it? Part of the novel's fun derives from the differences in perspectives among the narrator, Sancho Panza, and Don Quixote, to say nothing of the various figures in the interpolated stories.

The prologue is written not by Cervantes' invented Hamete but by Cervantes himself, or at least his narrative surrogate, who addresses us "idle reader[s]"; that surrogate is the fictional Spanish narrator – who is also the fictional editor. Thus the writer claims to be the "stepfather," not "the father" of the book. As the "stepfather of Don Quixote," he wants us to appreciate his linearity and balance and sometimes mocks Cide Hamete's punctiliousness in including every detail ("Prologue," 3). He leaves out details of Don Diego's house: "[T]he translator of this history decided to pass over these and other similar minutiae in silence, because they did not accord with the principal purpose of the history, whose strength lies more in its truth than in cold digressions" (2.XVIII.568). Here "translator" seems to mean not the person who originally translates Cide Hamete into Spanish (see 2.XXIV.614) but the narrator who presents the story to us. Grossman's translation does not always make this distinction clear, perhaps because she believes that Cervantes wants the ambiguity. But it is more likely that, notwithstanding Cervantes' brilliant experiments with various modes of telling, there is some inconsistency in how the Spanish narrator – who presents the Don's story to the reader – knows what he knows and who translated what. In other words, there is a continual problem of multiple, often unidentified, sources of information for both Cide Hamete and the narrator-translator.

Much criticism has been directed at the appearance of the "second author" at the end of 1.VIII. Is it Cide Hamete or another figure taking the place of the fictionalized narrator-translator whom we met in the Prologue? If the latter case, the narrating "I," beginning in 1.IX, is unidentified. But I think we may be mistaken to try to use the aesthetic standards of Henry James to resolve the narrative strategies and experiments of Cervantes. Indeed, as Colleen Culleton has observed, "The lack of reliable information about sources of information is fundamental to the work, because of what it does to the reader," namely, calling into question for the reader the invisible line that separates reality from fiction and the relative and provisional nature of truth.[12]

With its emphasis on multiple ways of seeing and its questioning of monolithic and authoritative explanations, *Don Quixote* is an example for the dialogic nature of future novelists. No one speaks for the King or the Catholic Church, or indeed for the dominant clerical or political presence in the world Don Quixote inhabits. Indeed, the double perspective by which the Don is idealist and narcissist as well as humane friend but also at times – by our twenty-first-century standards – a harmless, borderline psychotic is a further example of Cervantes' novel containing multiple perspectives. As readers we oscillate among various responses to the two major characters. We regard Don Quixote and Sancho Panza as well-meaning, decently motivated characters and at the same time as naïve fools. Especially in Part Two, when they are often buffeted by circumstances and less worthy characters, they earn our sympathy.

Don Quixote is so inclusive that it contains its own opposites, or in contemporary terms, deconstructs itself. Thus the Canon, who has read a bit of chivalric literature but has never finished a novel of chivalry, offers a critique of books that stray widely from the truthful: "[T]he more truthful the fiction, the better it is, and the more probable and possible, the more pleasing.... [V]erisimilitude and mimesis ... together constitute perfection in writing.... [The style of books of chivalry] is fatiguing, the action incredible[,] ... the language foolish.... [F]inally, since they are totally lacking in intelligent artifice, they deserve to be banished, like unproductive people, from Christian nations" (1.XLVII.412). Yet no sooner does he denounce chivalric literature than he acknowledges he has been writing in this genre and that when it is done "in a pleasing style and with ingenious invention, and is drawn as close as possible to the truth, it no doubt will weave a cloth composed of many different and beautiful threads, and when it is finished, it will display such perfection and beauty that it will achieve the greatest goal of any writing, which ... is to teach and delight at the same time" (1.XLVII.413–414). That *Don Quixote* is an example of both chivalric texts and their own critique is part of the novel's inclusiveness.

What does *Don Quixote* teach us about novel form? With so few precedents (particularly among major works) for striking a balance between history and imaginative fiction, Cervantes deserves to be considered the first novelist. *Don Quixote* is Cervantes' inquiry into the distinction between history (which purports to be true, even if one historian's truth is not necessarily another's) and fiction (which allows for invention); that inquiry provided a paradigm for successors. We might note that both history and fiction have a narrative that organizes events into a pattern.

Hardly a literary luminary at the time, Cervantes wrote the first volume in 1605 at the age of fifty-eight. Cervantes did not know what novels were and insists for the most part that he is writing history, although he allows for the selection and arrangement necessary to maintain the story's forward thrust. Bruce W. Wardropper observes, "We have to deal, then, with a story masquerading as history, with a work claiming to be historically true within its external framework of fiction."[13]

Digression is a major theme and structural concept in *Don Quixote*, and this is appropriate for characters whose purpose is to sally forth and engage in whatever adventure they find. These characters have no religious, political, or material goal and they go where fate takes them. Virtually every tale and speech could be edited and, indeed, has been in multiple abridged editions.

Novels are a lived life, but for those who read them – at least serious and complex novels – they are an enriching and enlightening digression. With relatively little precedent, Cervantes' first novel enacts that idea. As a fiction, Cervantes' *Don Quixote* is a digression first and foremost from factual and documentary history; Don Quixote's adventures as a knight errant are a digression from his own life as a fifty-year-old bachelor who is a member of the rural gentry with limited income who lives with a housekeeper, a niece approaching twenty, and a man who does chores for him. He eschews hard work and spends his very considerable leisure time reading about chivalry. His foolishness extends to selling arable land – another digression – and using the money to buy books about chivalry. Don Quixote is an idealist, motivated by his desire to do good, "for there were evils to undo, wrongs to right, injustices to correct, abuses to ameliorate, and offenses to rectify" (1.I.24). But the path he follows is folly, and he is both oblivious to the real world and dangerous to himself and others.

Reading about chivalry is a digression from work; indeed, Don Quixote "became so caught up in reading that he spent his nights reading from dusk till dawn and his days reading from sunrise to sunset, and so with too little sleep and too much reading his brains dried up, causing him to lose his mind" (1.I.21). If Cervantes' purpose is to discredit the chivalric form – really a version of romance that emphasizes make-believe – does not *Don Quixote* give credence to other kinds of fiction, particularly those that are more in touch with the real world?

Cervantes recognized that we humans need sustaining fictions – whether in books or our imagination – but we also need to distinguish, as Don Quixote can't, between fiction and reality. Therefore our fictions must, as Wallace Stevens also understood, negotiate between our impossible dreams, on one hand, and the actual and the possible, on the other. And stories will teach us more if they are aware of human behavior in all its complexity rather than attribute what happens to enchanters. As George Haley puts it, "In proposing to discredit the chivalric novel, Cervantes does not suggest that we not read chivalric novels, but only that we read them properly for what they are, outlandish and sometimes beautiful lies."[14]

In modern psychological terms, Don Quixote alternates between an obsessive-compulsive disorder – imagining himself as a knight errant serving a lady he has never seen – and an attention-deficit disorder. During his two adventures on the road, he often digresses from his purpose when he abandons one adventure to pursue another. In speech, too, he is digressive; he is extremely long-winded and digresses from his subject, something that is echoed in his squire's digressive propensity for a plethora of proverbs, many of which are far from the point of the events he addresses.

Historical and Philosophic Implications

Sometimes in fiction what is absent tells us as much as what is present. What is striking in *Don Quixote* is the absence of ethnic variety. Jews and Moors had to convert or leave Spain in 1502. Many Moors remained. In 1609 King

Philip III decreed the Expulsion of the Moriscos, that is, Moslems who had converted to Christianity in 1502 rather than leave Spain. Hundreds of thousands of Moriscos were expelled, some of them probably sincere Christians. Cervantes has some nostalgia for when Arabs and Catholics – and maybe Jews, too – lived together. He regrets Philip III's tyrannical Catholicism and what we now call ethnic cleansing, which sanitized Spain from Jews and Moors.

On the one hand, the entire narrative, including the interpolated stories, depends on simple distinctions and a belief that words like good, evil, beauty, courage, and virtue have absolute meanings that are culturally shared. But, on the other hand, to Cervantes, good and evil do not come to earth unblemished and untouched by each other. As Captain Ruy Pérez de Viedma, who, in one of the interpolated tales, rescues the Moorish princess Zoraida, observes: "[T]he good rarely, if ever, comes to us pure and simple, but is usually accompanied or followed by some disquieting, disturbing evil" (1.XLI.363). This blurring of absolute good and evil is inherent throughout much of Cervantes' entire novel.

An important aspect of Cervantes' modernism is his awareness of the relativity of truth and the danger of moralistic simplification. We see this not only in Don Quixote's treatises or Sancho's proverbs, but also in how we are asked to respond with a double optics of judgment and sympathy to Don Quixote's well-meaning but extraordinary actions and explanations, including the concept of enchantment that he invokes to explain his weird behavior. Arguing that the relativity of truth in Cervantes' novel is perhaps the result of the Counter-Reformation, Bruce W. Wardropper maintains: "One cannot apprehend the whole truth; one can only get glimpses of partial truth. This is the great lesson of historiography if not of history itself.… Who can say when Don Quixote's lucid intervals begin and end?"[15]

As we learn from Don Quixote's often pretentious and stilted language and Sancho's proverbs, reality is, paradoxically, a function not only of what one sees but also of the language that one chooses to talk about what one sees. In the case of Don Quixote's beloved Dulcinea, what one man sees as beautiful, another may see as ugly. How we think in turn shapes how we see and how we talk. Caught in the chivalric-romance linguistic system, Don Quixote is culturally determined to such an extent that he lives at an oblique angle to the rest of the world. Thus when the innkeeper's daughter and her maid, Maritornes, tie him up, he attributes events to enchanters. But these events are caused by simple human motives. His braggadocio is hilariously at odds with the reality we as readers see, as when – in stilted and archaic language he has learned from his reading of chivalric texts – the Don describes his hand to Maritornes, whom he believes is wooing him: "[T]hou mayest gaze upon the composition of its sinews, the consistency of its muscles, the width and capacity of its veins, and from this conjecture the might of the arm to which such a hand belongeth" (1.XLIII.380).

Cervantes' Narrators

In the wonderful prologue, Cervantes or his persona quotes advice from his friend, advice that he avers he has taken:

....

[Y]ou should strive, in plain speech, with words that are straightforward, honest, and well-placed, to make your sentences and phrases sonorous and entertaining, and have them portray, as much as you can and as far as it is possible, your intention, making your ideas clear without complicating and obscuring them.... [K]eep your eye on the goal of demolishing the ill-founded apparatus of these chivalric books, despised by many and praised by so many more, and if you accomplish this, you will have accomplished no small thing. ("Prologue," 8)

....

Cervantes' – or his surrogate's – difficulty in writing the prologue is solved by his shaping it around his bemused and relaxed friend's pragmatic advice: "[T]here is no reason for your book to preach to anyone, weaving the human with the divine.... It has only to make use of mimesis in the writing, and the more precise that is, the better the writing will be" ("Prologue," 8). Elias L. Rivers maintains, "[T]he supposedly discursive prologue is converted into a narrative: the present-tense monologue in which the writer (in the first person) addresses the reader (in the second person) has become a past-tense narrative about a third person, or non-person, and what he said."[16]

Cervantes uses the convention of the discovered manuscript, a convention he borrowed from chivalric manuscript, but, as Echevarría notes, his "most radical creation is the character of the Spanish narrator of *Don Quixote*, who styles himself a sort of editor of the story, presumably first written by Arabic historian Cide Hamete Benengeli and translated into Spanish by several translators."[17] When the aforementioned narrator-editor finds the rest of the incomplete manuscript, he needs to hire someone to translate it and both the narrator-editor's and this translator's comments are included in the final text.

What we need to understand is that Cervantes, who does not have the paradigm of the realistic novel and the omniscient third person narrator, is creating a narrative puzzle, and that the puzzle – perhaps cumbersome to a modern reader – is part of our reading experience. The "sources" of the fictional narrative become a kind of conundrum for the reader to solve and something of a running joke. In the early chapters the Spanish narrator-editor seems to be relying on a variety of sources: "Some authors say his first adventure" (1.II.25); "[T]here is a certain amount of disagreement among the authors who write about [the Don's real name]" (1.I.19). The effect of the narrator-editor's quest for sources is to throw into doubt the absolute nature of truth and facts and invite the reader into a world of relative judgments and values. Such an invitation would have been quite radical in seventeenth-century Spain, a country where the Inquisition was not abolished until 1834.

But at this point the narrator-editor hasn't mentioned Cide Hamete. Only after he has begun his story and presented it in eight chapters does he come across the notebooks and papers (1.IX.67) of Cide Hamete Benengeli – self-identified as "an Arab historian" – and he finds a Morisco Castilian who can read Arabic. At first the narrator takes a rather critical view of the Arab author, whom he later praises. He tells us that Arabs "are very prone to telling falsehoods" (1.IX.68), and he presents himself as more sympathetic than Hamete to Don Quixote: "[W]hen he could and should have wielded his pen to praise the virtues of so good a knight, it seems he intentionally passes over them in silence…. [I]f something of value is missing … in my opinion the fault lies with the dog who was its author rather than with any defect in its subject" (1.IX.68–69). Since no one in 1605 Spain could own a book written by an Arab, Cervantes may be taking an ironic view of the cultural repression in place in Spain.[18] Yet, as the Christian narrator tells the story, he becomes more and more sympathetic to and impressed with Hamete.

Who, we need to ask, is this fictional author Cide Hamete? We might note that Cide Hamete Benengeli means something like "Lord Hamete of the Eggplants." At times he is omniscient, and at other times he invokes documentary sources, but he is also concerned with artistic presentation. A kind of self-appointed ombudsman, he selects and arranges the evidence he presents. As George Haley writes:

. . . .

Cervantes was able to set before the reader a novel viewed in the round and depicted in the process of becoming: the dynamic interplay of a story, its dramatized tellers, and its dramatized readers…. The characters in this corollary tale are all involved in the mechanics of telling and transmitting Don Quijote's story. Their adventures … are the search for source materials in Manchegan archives, the creation of a continuous narrative from fragmentary and sometimes overlapping sources, the translation of the continuous narrative from Arabic to Castilian, the recasting of the translation and the publication of the revision, with intrusive commentary at every stage.[19]

. . . .

Cervantes or his fictional surrogate, the Spanish narrator-editor, has arranged for the translation of Cide Hamete's book; he seems to be the speaker at the end of Part One, and has purchased documents about Don Quixote's final days. Or, we wonder, could that be Hamete's voice?

Our Spanish narrator-editor tells us how Hamete sometimes needs editing to keep the story on track. We assume he knows this from Hamete's manuscript. In a sense, he becomes our surrogate reader of Hamete. He tells us what he includes and omits. Thus at times the Spanish narrator-editor makes a point of leaving out such subjects as how Don Quixote's horse relates to Sancho Panza's donkey in friendship, a subject to which Hamete devotes "particular chapters" (2.XII.528).

Part One: The 1605 Text

There is a once-upon-a-time simplicity to the early chapters. The narrator does not specify in which village in La Mancha is to be found the Don's home, but we know it is in the region of Campo de Montiel. At first the narrator patronizes Don Quixote as a ridiculous figure, if not a lunatic – the sun "would have melted his brains if he had any" (1.II.25) – and the reader joins him. It is as if at first the narrator is implying that because Don Quixote does not look like the traditional hero, he is not worthy of our full attention: "[H]is complexion was weathered, his flesh scrawny, his face gaunt" (1.I.19). His horse Rocinante is also skinny rather than a steed we would expect a heroic figure to ride.

Although *Don Quixote* is mostly comedy, it is often comedy noir – and the interpolated stories are often not comical at all. We pity Don Quixote because his punishments and suffering – resulting in physical injury – are often disproportionate to his behavior. We might understand the response Cervantes is evoking if we recall that during the Renaissance, what we think of as pity and fear were rendered as *compassione* and *horrore*. We might think of our response to Actaeon in Titian's *Diana and Actaeon* (1556–1559), where Actaeon's misfortune seems disproportionate to his behavior; because he sees Diana naked, he is turned into a stag and torn apart by dogs.[20] Don't we feel that the Don is suffering beyond all measure, and does that not evoke not only our pity but also our fear for a world in which this innocent fool is unjustly punished? The difference between the Don's suffering and real tragedy is that for the most part he has the physical resilience of a cartoon character.

The digressions structurally diminish the Don by pushing him away from the reader's attention. Digressing from the life of Don Quixote, the narrator interpolates other stories, especially in Part One, to the point where it is easy to forget that Don Quixote is the focus. Put another way, for extended periods, Don Quixote virtually disappears into the mist of interpolated stories. While some of these are simplistic and tedious, one can make a case for their being part of the branches of the novel's root themes such as chivalry, sexual temptation, and the quest for freedom from tyrants (recall that Cervantes was imprisoned). Yet the modern reader becomes used to and perhaps impatient with Don Quixote's story being increasingly superseded by digressive tales, which have a sameness in plots that contain a large fantasy element. Lacking more than a superficial relationship with the real and possible, these tales do not have a plausible grammar of character motives; nor do the rapid plot twists and turns enact complex values.

Do these long interpolated stories make the novel a tough read? Are they too digressive or do we need to consider that Cervantes' ideas about storytelling derive from different models – folk tale, fantasy, myth, romance, and various oral traditions – than the realistic novel? Probably these stories derive from an oral tradition in which stories are retold as entertainment, somewhat differently on each occasion, but with a core moral lesson. Yet, while one can always make a case for the relevance of each interpolated tale to themes and issues raised by the Don's adventures – often fidelity, constancy, and freedom to choose one's beloved on the part of man or woman – this does not make these sometimes prolix tales any easier to read.

In Part One, after hilarious early chapters featuring his tilting at windmills and fighting armies that turn out to be sheep, Don Quixote becomes more and more a supernumerary in the novel in which he is the title character. The narrative itself seems to adopt the innkeeper's perspective "[W]hen he told [travelers] that this was Don Quixote and there was no need to pay attention to him because he was out of his mind" (1.XLIV.384). But for Cervantes the quest for freedom includes the opportunity to pursue one's dreams and to digress from one's place in society and career path, even if the resultant behavior is flagrantly idiosyncratic – as is the case with Don Quixote's compulsive foolishness in his devotion to chivalry – as long as others are not harmed.

His squire and companion Sancho Panza is motivated as much as Don Quixote by the hope of transforming himself, in his case to a rich and powerful man. He, too, is digressing from his life path as a peasant laborer. Nor is he above lying and stealing. Sancho Panza tells a big lie when he says to the goatherd that he left untouched the saddlebags of The Ragged One of the Gloomy Face when in fact he rifled through them and took a good deal of money (1.XXIII.178–179).

But Sancho Panza is also tempted to return to the real world, especially in Part One. Thus when prospects for success are dim or he is overcome by fear, he wants to return to his wife and children (1.XXV.190). Sancho Panza finds that talking quells his fears, but we see the same verbosity in the Don when he repeats his chivalric mantra. Indeed, while Don Quixote finds Sancho Panza loquacious, the Don talks far more than he does.

Don Quixote's Character and Psyche in Part One:
Good Intentions, Bad Results

Don Quixote's behavior is what happens when a reader loses aesthetic distance and thinks he is a character in a story. His behavior is an example of strong misreading; put another way, he becomes a captive of allusions to other chivalric romances, allusions that he applies to his experience. Sancho Panza, who cannot read or write, reminds Don Quixote and us that taking books too seriously is "very dangerous to your health and very damaging to your conscience" (1.X.73). Living in a world of allusions and illusions created by books leads Don Quixote astray and ultimately is responsible for his demise. After Sancho and Don Quixote suffer a series of mishaps, Sancho characteristically relies on a concatenation of hoary clichés: "And the better and smarter thing, to the best of my poor understanding, would be for us to go back home now that it's harvest-time, and tend to our own affairs, and stop going from pillar to post and from bad to worse, as they say" (1.XVIII.125).

On one hand, Don Quixote cannot tell fantasy from reality: "Because at all times and at every moment his fantasy was filled with the battles, enchantments, feats, follies, loves, and challenges recounted in books of chivalry, and everything he said, thought, or did was directed toward such matters.... [I]n his imagination he saw what he did not see and what was not there" (1.XVIII.126–127). On the other hand, there is something attractive, indeed noble, in his idealism: "[T]o defend those who are defenseless, and to avenge those that are wronged, and to punish malfeasance" (1.XVII.121).

Good intentions, Cervantes implies, do not always result in doing good. Cervantes makes clear that Don Quixote is a self-immersed narcissist with delusions of grandeur whose foolishness harms not only himself but also his loyal follower Sancho Panza. Often, if not deranged, he is both a fool and a simpleton.

Notwithstanding his ideals, the Don is pathetically ineffective, in part because his judgment and reason are skewed. But he is also a victim. The barber and priest may mean well, but are they justified in putting the Don in a cage and encouraging him to think that he is the victim of enchanters? That the barber and priest do the Don wrong makes him a more sympathetic figure to us. Do they, we need to ask, get too much satisfaction from reducing Don Quixote to a pathetic lunatic? Are they too pleased with themselves?

Isn't Cervantes also – anticipating Dostoevsky, Kafka, and Mann – reminding us of human irrationality and inability to learn from experience, and showing us how humans make choices contrary to their own interests? Don Quixote is something of a masochist in allowing himself to continually be beaten without learning his lesson. Indeed, one of his shortcomings is that he learns nothing from his experience due to his obsession with chivalry. The Don's behavior has

Figure 1 Don Quijote Beset by Monsters, *Francisco de Goya. Brush drawing in gray-brown ink and wash, 207 × 144 mm, c. 1812–1820. © The Trustees of the British Museum*

a compulsive quality; even though he loses part of an ear, many of his teeth, and is constantly wounded, he throws himself into battle against various chimeras. He thinks the world is controlled by enchanters who are tricking him and takes no responsibility for his own behavior, claiming paranoically that he is reacting to various schemes beyond ordinary visual evidence or comprehension by lesser mortals.

When Don Quixote feigns madness, citing the example of Roland, he becomes self-parodic; without realizing it, he describes his own behavior: "The great achievement is to lose one's reason for no reason…. Mad I am and mad I shall remain until you return with the reply to a letter [to Dulcinea]" (1.XXV.194). Given his history, feigned madness and actual madness are not always easy to distinguish.

Cervantes reminds us that even well-meant actions could have unfortunate consequences, and that thinking that one's actions are justified by one code or another does not mean they are in fact right or just. Good intentions, when encoded in chivalry – or religion or politics – can have deleterious effects. Because Don Quixote thinks a knight errant does not have to pay, he cheats an innkeeper: "[They, the knights errant,] never paid for their lodging or anything else in any inn where they stayed, because whatever welcome they receive is owed to them as their right and privilege" (1.XVII.121). In sum, while courageous in the face of peril, real and imagined, and foolishly bold, Don Quixote is often an egomaniac and a braggart. His misjudgments hurt others, as when the bachelor Alonso López, who has taken his first vows towards becoming a priest, reminds him that in supposedly righting wrongs, Don Quixote has done him wrong by breaking his leg: "I don't know how you can speak of righting wrongs…. [For] you have certainly wronged me and broken my leg, which won't ever be right again…. [I]t was a great misadventure for me to run across a man who is seeking adventures" (1.XIX.138). Cervantes emphasizes that compulsive pursuit of one's dreams – even if they include supposed righting of wrongs and generous service – can in actual fact have a cost to others.

Part Two: The 1615 Book

I will use the term Part Two for Cervantes' second 1615 book focusing on the Don's further adventures. (Grossman uses the term "part" for each of the four sections of Part One rather than – as Raffel does in the Norton edition – simply dividing the text into the 1605 and 1615 books and calling them "volumes.") With more emphasis on Don Quixote and with far fewer interpolated tales, Part Two is more tightly structured than Part One and is less digressive. Because of the emphasis on the human feelings of Don Quixote and Sancho, it is also less farcical. We feel for Don Quixote, who is the victim of jokes at his expense.

If in Part One, as Henry W. Sullivan puts it, "Don Quixote's injuries arose from attacks he undertook at his own free will, however ill-advised, and punishment was meted out to him by rightly outraged persons," in Part Two he is the victim of those who use him for their own amusement – what Sullivan calls "jocose cruelty."[21]

Even Sancho, his usually loyal squire, convinces him that Dulcinea is transformed into a peasant girl by an enchantress. That Don Quixote's fantasy has transformed a peasant girl into his idealized Dulcinea gives Sancho Panza's ploy some ironic justice. After all, Don Quixote – always blaming enchanters for his setbacks – would be the primary enchanter in the novel were it not for our realization that such an accolade belongs to Cervantes himself. But we also feel that the Don is a victim of Sancho's disloyalty, and we empathize with his being duped by the person he trusts most.

Cervantes' narrator makes fun of Don Quixote and Sancho Panza, but he is gentler in Part Two. He also pokes fun at narrative conventions, as when Don Quixote remembers a slew of poems during the theatrical presentation that he heard once at Camacho's wedding party, which turned into Basilio's wedding party (2.XX.587–588).

Is Part Two more fun because of its references to and resonances of the published text of Part One? Does not Sansón as Knight of the Mirrors subtly call attention to the doubling and mirroring of Part One with Part Two?

In Part Two, Cervantes depends on the fiction or conceit that his literate characters are familiar with the published version of Part One because they have read it. By pretending that his imaginative fiction is reality that shapes the lives of others, Cervantes is glorifying the artist who can create a reality in which readers participate. In a sense, we have a fiction in Part Two that depends upon a fiction, namely the book that is Part One.

Some of the playfulness in Part Two comes when Cervantes is urging himself to keep writing by having his characters encourage another volume. For me, one of the funniest scenes is the discussion early in Part Two when Don Quixote and Sancho Panza ask the Bachelor Sansón Carrasco about the audience response to the book of their adventures. Rather comically, they are discussing looking for and publishing a manuscript about events that haven't yet taken place (2.IV.482). It is as if the major character were not Don Quixote but the author. According to Sansón, "[A]s soon as [the author] finds the [second part of Don Quixote's] history which he is searching for with extraordinary diligence, he will immediately have it printed" (2.IV.482). When Don Quixote objects to the inclusion of events that "belittle the hero" (2.III.476), Bachelor Sansón Carrasco defends the fictive Moorish author Cide Hamete Benengeli (who hired a translator in

Toledo) as an historian writing – in contrast to the poet – about things "not as they should have been, but as they were, without adding or subtracting anything from the truth" (2.III.476).

Rather comically, Part Two partly depends on Don Quixote's pride in being the subject of a book he hasn't read as well as his concern that the author has not done him justice. The Don is cranky when he hears that some of the bathetic episodes have been included and that his heroic stature may be diminished. He expresses his "fear that in the history of my deeds, which they say has been published, if the author by chance was some wise man who is my enemy, he will have put in certain things instead of others, mixing a thousand lies with one truth, digressing to recount actions other than those required in the coherent narration of a truthful history" (2.VIII.504). He attributes such putative lies to the author's envy.

Cervantes the formalist uses secondary characters to shape our response to the Don. To an extent, Sansón becomes a surrogate for us readers; he wants Don Quixote to have further adventures, even though we are told at the end of 2.VII that Sansón had consulted the barber and priest, who had taken Don Quixote home for his own good in Part One.

Concerned with the physical safety of the eccentric and often mentally unbalanced Don Quixote, Don Quixote's housekeeper is also a surrogate for a realistic reader; "The first time they brought him back to us lying across a donkey, beaten and battered. The second time he came home in an oxcart, locked in a cage and claiming he was enchanted, and the poor man was in such a state that his own mother wouldn't have recognized him: skinny, pale, his eyes sunk right into the top of his head" (2.VII.496–497). The Don's niece is another surrogate for the realistic reader, explaining to Don Quixote – while he is home in between the first and second series of adventures – "[Y]ou have been struck by such great blindness and such obvious foolishness that you try to make us believe that you are valiant when you are old, and strong when you are ailing, and that you right wrongs when you are stooped by age, and most of all, that you are a knight when you are not" (2.VI.493).

In Part Two, perhaps even more than in Part One, both the Don and Sancho Panza live in their own word worlds. Sancho lives in proverbs, some of which he gets wrong, but Don Quixote lives in his treatises on everything from marriage to poetry. Both are great talkers and both get immersed in their telling to the point where they become oblivious to others.

Sancho is more of a personality in Part Two; he is more proactive and articulate (and he does know an astonishing number of clichés and proverbs for a simple man). Part of the fun of the opening chapters of Part Two arises when Sancho Panza and his wife Teresa speak in proverbs, some of which they deliver in confused fashion. Teresa's "[W]here laws go kings follow" is an inversion of "Where kings go laws follow" (2.V.488). The narrator facetiously remarks: "[W]hen Sancho wanted to speak in an erudite and courtly way, his words would plummet from the peaks of his simplicity into the depths of his ignorance" (2.XII.528). But Sancho Panza often does speak without pretension and does make sense, and thus represents a reality principle that Don Quixote requires but ignores.

In one astonishing moment – one that takes place in this chapter raising questions about Don Quixote's probity – Sancho Panza tells Don Quixote, "Be quiet, Señor" (2.XXII.601). We cheer for Sancho's insisting on common humanity and refusing to bend to the Don's patronizing snobbery and will. Earlier Sancho had reminded Don Quixote of an agreement that he, Sancho, could "talk all I wanted as long as I didn't say anything against my neighbor or your grace's authority" (2.XX.584).

Part Two includes plot recapitulations, which remind the reader not only where Don Quixote has been but who he has been (2.X.516). The Spanish narrator-translator reminds us of the danger of digression, a central problem in both the telling in Part One and the knight errant's picaresque journeys. The narrator-translator tells us that while the "author" – Cide Hamete – does not say whether the peasant girls (whom Sancho Panza wants Don Quixote to believe include Dulcinea) are riding male or female donkeys, "since not much depends on this, there is no reason to spend more time verifying it" (2.X.516).

In Part Two, it becomes harder to patronize Don Quixote. Often he shows great wisdom, especially when he advises Sancho about governance (2.XLII, 2.XLIII). Indeed, the Don is far less a fool in Part Two. As the narrator-translator notes, "[H]e spoke nonsense only with regard to chivalry, and in other conversations he demonstrated a clear and confident understanding, so that his actions belied his judgment, and his judgment belied his actions" (2.XLIII.732). Indeed, on such occasions, the distance between Don Quixote and Cervantes narrows a great deal.

Not only does Don Quixote grow in stature, but also so does Cide Hamete. At the outset of Chapter XXIV in Part Two, the translator "found in the margin, written in [Cide Hamete Benengeli's] own hand, these precise words: 'I cannot believe, nor can I persuade myself, that everything written in the preceding chapter [about Don Quixote's adventures in the Cave of Montesinos] actually happened in its entirety ... [because] it goes so far beyond the limits of reason.... [I]f this adventure seems apocryphal, the fault is not mine, and so, without affirming either its falsity or its truth, I write it down'" (2.XXIV.614).

Two important things happen in this passage. First, by questioning this one episode pertaining to the Don's descent into the Caves of Montesinos, Cide Hamete actually gives ballast to the authenticity of the other episodes, for he reveals himself as a discriminating and reliable voice. The narrator-translator's title for 2.XXIII, derived from Cide Hamete's skepticism, encourages the reader to believe he is getting a balanced version of the Don's adventures: "Regarding the remarkable things that the great Don Quixote said he saw in the depths of the Caves of Montesinos, so impossible and extraordinary that this adventure has been considered apocryphal" (2.XXIII.604).

The second important aspect of the passage I cited above from 2.XXIV.614 is that both Cide Hamete and the original translator (our narrator's source, who is described "as the man who translated this great history from the original"), as well as the different figure who is our editor and translator all put themselves on the reader's side by suggesting that the reader is not gullible and has the perspicacity to separate fact from fiction. As Cide Hamete puts it, "You, reader, since you are a discerning person, must judge it according to your own lights, for I must not and cannot do more" (2.XXIV.614). Lest we doubt his authority, Cide Hamete adds a revelation that he knows the whole story that he is telling from beginning to end and that he is looking back after Don Quixote's death: "[I]t is considered true that at the time of Don Quixote's passing and death, he is said to have retracted it, saying he had invented [the Cave of Montesinos adventure] because he thought it was consonant and compatible with the adventures he had read in his histories" (2.XXIV.614). Of course this doesn't surprise us because we know that Don Quixote cannot always separate fact from fiction and is prone to bizarre fantasies.

Don Quixote's Sexuality in Part Two

Cervantes wants readers to understand that what the Don desires is not the presence and reality of a flesh-and-blood sexual partner, but the fantasy of an unattainable partner.

Much of the fun of Part Two depends on the comic fear of sexuality on the part of Don Quixote, especially when faced with the bold advances of Altisidora, one of the Duchess's maidens. The Don's reluctance to respond sexually to Altisidora is a male resonance of Marcela in 1.XIII and 1.XIV, who did not respond to male desires and preferred living among shepherdesses; she rejected the view that because a male loves her, she is "obliged to love" in return (1.XIV.99). She embraces "chastity [as] one of the virtues that most adorn and beautify both body and soul" (1.XIV.99). If Marcela rejects sex as presumptive male privilege, the Don, by rejecting the promiscuous female, shows that for males, too, sex is a matter of choice.

Altisidora, the young teenager who wants to sleep with Don Quixote, represents sexuality, an aspect of life with which Don Quixote has great difficulty. The Don is more comfortable in the company of men. As Henry W. Sullivan observes, "[T]he sexual attentions of Altisidora … attack the very heart of Don Quixote's difficulties with sexuality and conjure up the terrifying prospect of a sensual, desiring woman."[22] We realize the Don requires distance from his idealized fantasy lover, Dulcinea, because he is uncomfortable with sex.

The Role and Function of the Duke and Duchess in Part Two

Even while lavishly entertaining Don Quixote and Sancho Panza, the high-spirited but self-regarding Duke and Duchess arrange elaborate embarrassments for the Don and Sancho. The Duke and Duchess, who are familiar with the published version of the Don's adventures, seek their own amusement at the expense of their guests. The Duchess reminds Don Quixote that, according to the published history of his adventures, he has never seen Dulcinea: "[I]f … we are to believe the history of Señor Don Quixote that only recently has come into the world to the general applause of all people[,] … she does not exist in the world but is an imaginary lady, and that your grace engendered and gave birth to her in your mind, and depicted her with all the graces and perfections that you desired" (2.XXX.671–672).

Cervantes satirizes the conspicuous consumption of the self-indulgent Duke and Duchess. They demonstrate the narcissism, sloth, and arrogance of the wealthy who can afford to indulge their humor at the expense of Don Quixote and Sancho Panza by turning them into court jesters. Cervantes is very much aware of seventeenth-century class distinctions, with Don Quixote a small landowner, Sancho Panza a peasant, and the Duke and Duchess representing the aristocracy. Becoming increasingly impatient with the Duke and Duchess, the narrator-translator approvingly cites Cide Hamete, who quite bluntly puts them in their place, although readers have already judged their elaborate shenanigans at the expense of the Don and Sancho, shenanigans that make the Don and Sancho more sympathetic: "[D]eceivers are as mad as the deceived, and the duke and duchess came very close to seeming like fools since they went to such lengths to deceive two fools" (2.LXX.914).

The Duke and Duchess have little regard for the feelings of Don Quixote and Sancho Panza; in an elaborate performance arranged by the Duke and Duchess, Sancho Panza must suffer 3,300 self-inflicted lashes to free Dulcinea from enchantment. Is there anything funny, Cervantes is asking – and the question has implications for what has preceded in his two-part novel – about deliberately humiliating two well-meaning people?

Cervantes' narrator is much less tolerant of those taking advantage of the now aging Don. In Part Two Don Quixote is wiser and more articulate, except when he disappears into his own fantasy world of enchanters, Dulcinea, and his sense of responsibility as a knight errant. The more Don Quixote is made fun of, the more he engages the reader's sympathy, in part because we know Don Quixote does not mock others. Often we see that he is a victim of elaborate jokes like those performed by the Duke and Duchess and in Barcelona by Don Antonio Moreno, even though the latter "sought ways to make [Don Quixote's] madness public without harming him; for jests that cause pain are not jests, and entertainments are not worthwhile if they injure another" (2.LXII.864). We are put off by Don Antonio's wife inviting friends to "enjoy his incomparable madness" (2.LXII.865).

Growing in stature and independence throughout Part Two, Sancho is often Don Quixote's true friend. He often displays considerable wisdom in advising the Don. Nor does he take part in humiliating Don Quixote, like the Don's other supposed friends. We remember the barber and priest humiliating Don Quixote when at the conclusion of Part One he was returned in a cage under their auspices.

Sancho does not forget his self-interest. He believes in his own self-preservation and is a realist about his need for the food he likes, wine, and sufficient sleep; he takes very good care of his donkey. To be sure, Sancho does apply the lashes to the Don that are prescribed by Merlin to free Dulcinea from enchantment when and how he pleases. And Sancho does tell the Big Lie about the peasant girl's being Dulcinea transformed by an enchanter. Sancho Panza often garbles proverbs, but he has an amazing memory, especially in light of his inability to read.

Don Quixote's Final Renunciation

We feel sadness for Don Quixote when he is defeated by Sansón Carrasco as the Knight of the White Moon. While Bachelor Sansón is supposedly acting in Don Quixote's interests by bringing him home, Sansón also wants to revenge his own defeat as the Knight of the Mirrors, "a defeat and a fall that ruined and destroyed all his plans" (2.LXX.913). So, the reader muses, is the Bachelor really a friend? By now we know that Cervantes is aware of multiple motives in human behavior.

Are we not moved by Don Quixote's final renunciation of his identity as errant knight? "I was Don Quixote of La Mancha, and now I am, as I have said, Alonso Quixano the Good. May my repentance and sincerity return me to the esteem your graces once had for me" (2.LXXIV.937). Don Quixote has lost his spirit and returns to die rather than serve a one-year moratorium: "melancholy and low spirits were bringing his life to an end" (2.LXXIV.935); they were brought on by his defeat and "his unsatisfied longing to see

Dulcinea free and disenchanted" (2.LXXIV.934). Without his imaginative life, he cannot sustain himself. What Charles Simic wrote about Téa Obreht's *The Tiger's Wife* is applicable to my reading of *Don Quixote*: "[I]t is a book about story-telling and its power to enchant as it wards off death and postpones the inevitable."[23]

Paralleling Don Quixote's increased stature, Cervantes' narrator becomes increasingly a sympathetic and humane voice validating decency; thus he concludes in the last chapter: "[W]hether Don Quixote was simply Alonso Quixano the Good, or whether he was Don Quixote of La Mancha, he always had a gentle disposition and was kind in his treatment of others, and for this reason he was dearly loved not only by those in his household, but by everyone who knew him" (2.LXXIV.936). This reaching out on the part of the narrator to include and respect readers as sharing a common humanity, both with him and with the novel's characters, is often characteristic of the novel form. But at times the very oddity of the characters in Part One creates a distance that leaves the reader observing the more bizarre aspects of the story, and especially Don Quixote's behavior, from a patronizing and iconoclastic perspective.

Conclusion to Part Two

In Part Two Cervantes shows his displeasure with the author Avellaneda, who has created another Don Quixote. (We don't know the identity of Avellaneda, although it may be a pseudonym for Lope de Vega, with whom Cervantes had a difficult relationship.) The Norton editor Diana de Armas Wilson describes the Avellaneda text as a "wretched novel that chronicled the slapstick and mechanical adventures of two puppets impersonating Cervantes's main characters, Don Quixote and Sancho Panza."[24]

Cervantes has his Don Quixote meet a character in Avellaneda's book, Don Alvaro Tarfe, and disabuse him as to who the real Don Quixote is: "I am Don Quixote of La Mancha, the same one who is on the lips of Fame, and not that unfortunate man who has wanted to usurp my name, and bring honor to himself with my thoughts" (2.LXXII.926). We know that the description of Don Quixote taking part in jousts at Zaragoza, described by Avellaneda, is bogus. We have been told by our Spanish narrator-translator that there exists no authentic document for the so-called third journey that reputedly took place. Our Spanish narrator finds out about Don Quixote's end from information in a lead box possessed by an "ancient physician" discovered in the foundation of an old hermitage under renovation (1.LII.445). That the Spanish narrator, who calls himself "the trustworthy author of this new and unparalleled history" – rather than Hamete – is our source is stressed by the discovered material being in

Castilian, a dialect spoken in the historic area of Castile in northern and central Spain (1.LII.445).

Cide Hamete's conclusion is to claim the field as the author of the true history by sweeping aside the rival text by Avellaneda: "For me alone was Don Quixote born, and I for him; he knew how to act, and I to write; the two of us alone are one, despite and regardless of the false Tordesillan writer" (2.LXXIV.939). Previously, Cervantes has his Arab surrogate Hamete cite Don Quixote's denunciation of his rival's history, which he had encountered at a printing house in Barcelona: "[T]he truth is I thought it had already been burned and turned to ashes for its insolence; but its day of reckoning will come, as it does to every pig" (2.LXII.875). And the narrator-translator has been effusive in his praise for Hamete, who "depicts thoughts, reveals imaginations, responds to tacit questions, clarifies doubts, resolves arguments; in short he expresses the smallest points that curiosity might ever desire to know. O celebrated author! O fortunate Don Quixote! O famous Dulcinea! O comical Sancho Panza! Together and separately may you live an infinite number of years, bringing pleasure and widespread diversion to the living" (2.XL.713).

Don Quixote as a Long Read

Honesty compels us to acknowledge a place for an abridged version of Cervantes' masterwork in which the Don Quixote episodes are maintained, including his great comic wrong-headed battles with an assortment of wizards and giants and his comical faith in his own perceptions and judgment. That he can convince himself that x is y is often hilarious but also reminds us readers how we all are half-creating what we see. That Don Quixote has immersed himself in chivalric literature reminds us not only that we are what we read, but also that who we are is often in large part culturally created. The Don begins as a comic character, but there is much that is poignant in his well-meaning madness. His simple-minded embrace of the chivalric code has a strong idealistic inflexion which he carries through both parts and is a welcome counterpoint to the self-serving behavior of many of those he encounters; he believes that there are "evils to undo, wrongs to right, injustices to correct, abuses to ameliorate, and offenses to rectify" (1.II.24).

I am divided about whether *Don Quixote* is overly long and one of the canonical books that could be presented to undergraduates in an abbreviated form. It is the only text I discuss in my book about which I feel that this might be a good idea. One can open the book blindly and start reading and find great pleasures, but for me the lack of character development – even in the Don and Sancho Panza episodes – does at times make *Don Quixote* a long-winded digressive text. It may well be I would feel differently if I read Spanish, but my book is one that addresses major translations in English.

Even while knowing that Cervantes' presentation of the major character, Don Quixote, is part of the novel's inquiry into the nature of verisimilitude, the reader does at times become impatient with the digressions, interpolated stories, and repetitions as well as some inconsistencies in who translated what and where information comes from. But we need to remember verisimilitude, consistency, and organic unity are our standards, not necessarily those of Cervantes or his audience.

The basic story of Don Quixote is preposterous. Random events disguised as coincidences occur at least every few pages. Motives are implausible. The very unpredictability of events becomes a kind of sameness. The uncanny dominates to the point that it becomes expected. Thus chapters of great originality are undermined by our awareness of the limitations and excesses of Cervantes' imagination. At times, *Don Quixote* becomes tedious in its repetitiveness, and we become impatient with its allusive if not minimizing historical contexts. We may wish for an imagination that is less indifferent to historical contexts and discussed the banishment of Jews and Moors, the power of Philip III, the place of the Catholic Church and the role of the Inquisition in shaping seventeenth-century Spain.

Yet why do we enjoy reopening *Don Quixote* and turning to any number of our favorite scenes? Perhaps, taking Erich Auerbach's suggestion, we also need to think of *Don Quixote* as recreation, gaiety, and "brilliant and purposeless play."[25] We need to enjoy Cervantes' fertile imagination and his presentation of diverse scenes and settings as well as his high-spirited sense of the comic and ridiculous.

Afterword

Don Quixote belongs to a literary tradition where the reader is invited by the author to help him or her in judging narcissism and misplaced feelings as well as the social and personal cost of such failings. Cervantes' strong insistence in establishing the authenticity of his teller in *Don Quixote* became implicitly and explicitly part of the ensuing novel tradition. Because the novel makes claims on truth, actuality, and reality, the credentials of the narrator as truth teller who knows what he is talking about and knows his characters become important. This does not mean the author has to imply or claim omniscience for his or her created narrator, but it does mean he needs either to assure the reader that such a narrator knows what he is talking about, as is almost always the case in Cervantes' novel, or to create an alternative model where the reader understands the narrator's unreliability and/or lack of perspicacity. In some cases, an author may present a combination of both.

Study Questions for Cervantes' *Don Quixote*

1. How does Cervantes distinguish between history and fiction? What does *Don Quixote* teach us about novel form? In what ways can digression – including most of the serendipitous adventures of the Don and the interpolated stories – be considered as a formal principle in *Don Quixote*?

2. If Cervantes' purpose is to discredit the chivalric form, can we give credence to other kinds of fiction? Or is Cervantes' point that, while all fictions can deflect us from reality, we nevertheless not only require sustaining fictions – whether in books or our imagination – but also need to distinguish, as Don Quixote can't, between fiction and reality?

3. Do the interpolated stories – including Anselmo's test of his wife's fidelity when he talks his best friend Lothario into seducing her – make the novel a tough read? Are these stories too digressive?

4. Is *Don Quixote* repetitious? Do the major characters, Don Quixote and Sancho Panza, vary and evolve enough to engage our interest?

5. Does the humor of Don Quixote's misperception wear thin? Is Part Two – which some readers write off – better artistically because it is less digressive? Is Part Two more compelling in part because there are fewer digressions from the main characters?

6. How does Part Two relate to Part One structurally, thematically, and rhetorically? Is Part Two more satisfying in part because of its resonances and references to the published text of Part One? Or do you prefer Part Two and, if so, why?

7. How would you define the roles of the Moor Cide Hamete Benengeli, the Spanish translators, the voice of Cervantes' narrator-editor as well as that of Edith Grossman, the English translator and other translators of *Don Quixote* that you might have read? Is the Cervantes narrator consistent in explaining how he knows what he knows and who translated what?

8. What is admirable about Don Quixote? Is it hard to patronize Don Quixote, who often shows great wisdom, especially when he advises Sancho Panza about governance in 2.XLII, 2.XLIII? Although Sancho Panza often garbles proverbs and has his own fantasy about owning an island, does he have some basic sense?

9. Consider secondary characters: What are the roles of Don Quixote's niece and housekeeper? What are the roles of the barber and the priest? What is the role of the Bachelor Sansón in Part Two? What are the implications of his being the Knight of the Mirrors? Are we sympathetic to the Duke

and Duchess, who, for their own amusement, arrange elaborate embarrassments for Don Quixote and Sancho Panza?

10. Are James Joyce's words for his *Ulysses* – "this chaffering allincluding most farraginous chronicle" (*Ulysses* 14.1412) – apt for *Don Quixote*? How would you shorten the novel into a more forward-moving read? Or is this fulsomeness, digressiveness, chattiness, and inclusiveness integral to our reading experience?

Notes

1. Ken Johnson, "Unfiltered Images, Turning Perceptions Upside Down," *New York Times*, Aug. 26, 2011.
2. Lady Gaga, quoted in Jon Pareles, "The Queen Pop Needs Her to Be," *New York Times,* May 22, 2011.
3. Christopher Benfey, "Bend Sinister in Wales," *NYR* 60:13 (Aug. 15, 2013), 40–41.
4. Ramón Menéndez Pidal, "The Genesis of *Don Quixote*," in *Cervantes' Don Quixote: A Casebook*, ed. Roberto González Echevarría (Oxford: Oxford University Press, 2005), 63–94.
5. See Ingrid D. Rowland, "Having a Good Time with Ariosto," *NYR* 57:20 (Dec. 23, 2010), 86–91.
6. Rowland, "Having a Good Time with Ariosto," 90.
7. Ken Johnson, "Mockery, Alive and Well Through the Ages," *New York Times,* Sept. 16, 2011.
8. "Introduction," *Cervantes' Don Quixote: A Casebook*, 5.
9. Anthony Cascardi, "Personal Identity in *Don Quixote*," in *Don Quijote*, trans. Burton Raffel, ed. Diana de Armas Wilson (New York: Norton, 1999), 792.
10. All quotations from the text are taken from Miguel de Cervantes, *Don Quixote*, trans. Edith Grossman (New York: HarperCollins, 2003).
11. *Cervantes' Don Quixote: A Casebook*, 3–4.
12. Email to Daniel R. Schwarz, Oct. 14, 2013.
13. Bruce W. Wardropper, "*Don Quixote*: Story or History," in *Cervantes' Don Quixote: A Casebook*, 142.
14. George Haley, "The Narrator in *Don Quijote*: Maese Pedro's Puppet Show," in *Cervantes' Don Quixote: A Casebook*, 262.
15. Wardropper, "*Don Quixote*: Story or History," 154.
16. Elias L. Rivers, "Cervantes' Revolutionary Prologue," in *Don Quijote*, trans. Raffel, ed. Wilson, 798.
17. *Cervantes' Don Quixote: A Casebook*, 6.
18. See Georgina Dopico Black, "Canons Afire," in *Cervantes' Don Quixote: A Casebook*, 112–113.

19. Haley, "The Narrator in *Don Quijote*," 241–242.
20. See Andrew Butterfield, "Titian and the Rebirth of Tragedy," *NYR* 57:20 (Dec. 23, 2010), 16–21.
21. Henry W. Sullivan, "The Duke's Theatre of Sadism," in *Don Quijote*, trans. Raffel, ed. Wilson, 830–833; see p. 832.
22. Sullivan, "The Duke's Theatre of Sadism," 833.
23. Charles Simic, "The Weird Beauty of the Well-Told Tale," *NYR* 58:9 (May 26, 2011), 18–19; see p. 19.
24. *Don Quijote*, trans. Raffel, ed. Wilson, 765.
25. Erich Auerbach, "The Enchanted Dulcinea," in *Cervantes' Don Quixote: A Casebook*, 59.

Chapter 3

Reading Stendhal's *The Red and the Black* (1830) and *The Charterhouse of Parma* (1839)

Character and Caricature

Stendhal (Marie-Henri Beyle, 1783–1842) and Balzac wrote at a time when, as Sanford Schwartz puts it, "Images of families, solitary artists, or courting couples in modest living rooms or studies with a window open to the city or even leafy views outside perhaps say that private, apolitical persons are now poised to have more of a stake in what happens in the world beyond them."[1]

Following Lorenz Eitner's 1955 essay, Schwartz dates this phenomenon to the early nineteenth century when "age-old autocratic social orders were being questioned or dismantled."[2] As we begin our inquiry into the French nineteenth-century novel – works by Stendhal, Balzac, Flaubert, and Zola – we might observe that these writers create characters for whom, to cite Schwartz's phrase, the "unheroic and uneventful moments in middle-class lives" are not enough.[3] The turn towards politics and engagement in the material world may be more applicable to Balzac and Stendhal than to Flaubert, although, as we shall see, that turn has a place in *Madame Bovary* and *Sentimental Education*. This engagement is particularly marked in Stendhal where Julien in *The Red and the Black* (1830) and Fabrizio in *The Charterhouse of Parma* (1839) are caught up in the very political intrigues that they want to avoid and live apart from.

Côme Fabre has written about how in post-Napoleonic times the "deceptively clear distinction between enlightenment and obscurantism" was replaced by "a new, grey, frightening and uncertain world in which no sharp lines could be

Reading the European Novel to 1900: A Critical Study of Major Fiction from Cervantes' Don Quixote *to Zola's* Germinal, First Edition. Daniel R. Schwarz.
© 2014 John Wiley & Sons, Ltd. Published 2014 by John Wiley & Sons, Ltd.

drawn between good and evil."[4] And that frightening and uncertain world dominated by moral ambiguity and corrupt politics is the world of Stendhal's novels.

If we understand that Stendhal's themes are selfishness, narcissism, and solipsism as well as complete disregard for public interest in favor of private motives, then we can see the roles that both comedy of manners and social satire play in his fiction. In this decadent world the characters rarely discuss anything that doesn't pertain to their immediate self-interest. In Stendhal, the provinces corrupt, and Paris corrupts absolutely. In Book I of *The Red and the Black*, no sooner does Stendhal expose provincialism, cronyism, and materialism – all part of the Mayor de Rênal's world – as well as the hypocritical Church, than he shows us in Book II that Paris is even worse. In Paris, "love-in-the-head ... a single disposition [which] can never last more than two days" prevails, whereas in provincial Verrières, Julien shares a genuine felt and ongoing passion with Mme. de Rênal, who "loved him more than life itself" (II.xix.290; I.xvii.74).[5]

Paul Valéry has observed: "What is most striking in a page of Stendhal, what declares his immediate presence is ... his *tone*. He possesses, and what's more, he affects, the most individual tone in all literature.... [I]t makes the man himself so present.... [H]is inner pretensions lead him to attempt the accumulation in a work of all the most expressive tokens of *sincerity*."[6] Stendhal's individuality – his idiosyncrasies – may explain why we cannot fully explain his characters in terms of a realistic psychology of motives and responses. Stendhal's epigraph to *The Red and the Black*, "Truth, bitter truth" (which he attributes to Danton, although it has never been located in Danton's writing), refers more to the themes and truths revealed by his satire than to a realistic plot or characterizations.

Indeed, Stendhal has much in common with the caricaturist Honoré Daumier, whose satirical energy and keen eye for the crystallizing detail influenced him in depicting the hypocrisy, self-interest, narcissism, and corruption of the rich and powerful aristocracy that dominated politics. Few human follies and social pretensions escaped Daumier's insightful social vision. Daumier flourished in the wake of the satirical journals founded in the early 1830s, journals made possible by a new liberal press law in France of December 1830.[7]

1. "Perhaps": *The Red and the Black* as Psychological Novel and Political Anatomy

....

"Julien is a young man whose social style is nearly always clumsy.... He is above all a plebeian in revolt, driven far less by the thought of immediate advantage to be gained than by a sense of outraged dignity and pride. And, besides, he is absolutely deprived of any moral sense at all …"[8]

. . . .

Introduction

Like Cervantes, both Stendhal and Balzac consider the relationship between history and story and regard their stories as historically shaped. The subtitle of *The Red and the Black* is *A Chronicle of 1830*. Stendhal's realism, according to Erich Auerbach, "sprung from resistance to a present which he despised[; he] preserved many eighteenth-century instincts in his attitude.... [T]he heroes of his novels think and feel in opposition to their time, only with contempt do they descend to the intrigues and machinations of the post-Napoleonic present."[9]

Balzac and Stendhal present a fictional history of the decadent present; Balzac, in particular, regretted much that was lost in the French Revolution. In both writers, we see a note of melancholy nostalgia for a simpler world in which the brio of Napoleon – or the passion of Romeo or the larger-than-life desire of Don Juan – had a place. Yet, notwithstanding this nostalgia, one can hardly claim that either writer gives specificity or depth to a heroic past.

Unlike Balzac, Stendhal does not give us full descriptions of buildings and streets; what interests him in particular, as Giuseppe Tomasi di Lampedusa, author of *The Leopard* notes, are "the meanness of the provincial atmosphere, the perpetual feeling of mistrust at the seminary," and the frivolity and intrigue which inform the central circles of Parisian and provincial life.[10] Stendhal – and di Lampedusa, as we shall see in my next volume on the European novel in the twentieth century – are both interested in how human behavior is much defined by the culture and institutions in which one lives.

A major Stendhal theme is the transitory nature of history as well as individual life. In many ways, his novels question the Enlightenment and see it as just another provisional narrative in a long series of European narratives, including clerical history and intelligent design reflecting God's will, Greek and Roman history, medieval history, and the ebbs and flows of dynasties and revolution. We make patterns or narratives of events as ways of giving meaning to our lives and our culture. But ultimately if we take the long view, history, according to Stendhal, teaches us the irrelevance of power and empires.

Stendhal believed that history is finally ephemeral, and ideologies that stress progress or teleology moving towards human perfectibility are wrong. If he were alive today, Stendhal would have cast a skeptical eye on those drawing momentous conclusions about so-called progressive or, alternately, devolutionary patterns of human behavior. For Stendhal, the only lesson that history teaches us is that there is no one lesson that fits all.

In a sense Stendhal's focus is on the "perhaps," the possibility of what we might be, that is the intersecting of circumstances beyond our control with those in which we have a choice. "Perhaps" is the unwritten text of our lives before we begin to make the choices and run into events that comprise our life narrative. Indeed, the narrator empathizes with the poignancy of Julien's regret after he is convicted: "I alone know what I might have done ... For the others, I am at most nothing but a PERHAPS" (II.xlii.391).

The Red and the Black's Historical Context

Like Balzac's *Père Goriot*, Puccini's *La Bohème*, and Hugo's *Les Misérables*, Stendhal's novel revolves around the chaotic 1830s when revolutionary forces struggled for supremacy against others, notably the Orleanists, who wished to return to the Bourbon days, and when fierce political, economic, and social debates about the direction of France prevailed. Furthermore, at this time the Catholic Church was divided between Jesuit and Jansenist factions.

Erich Auerbach argues for the importance of understanding "the political situation, the social stratification, and the economic circumstances ... in which France found itself just before the July [1830] Revolution" in *The Red and the Black* and stresses the subtitle, *Chronique de 1830*:

. . . .

> Even the boredom which reigns in the dining room and salon ... is no ordinary boredom.... [L]ife is governed by the fear that the catastrophe of 1793 might be repeated. As these people are conscious that they no longer themselves believe in the thing they represent, and that they are bound to be defeated in any public argument, they choose to talk of nothing but the weather, music, and court gossip. In addition, they are obliged to accept as allies snobbish and corrupt people from among the newly-rich bourgeoisie.... [F]rom his earliest youth [Julien] has felt nothing but loathing and scorn for the piddling hypocrisy and the petty lying corruption of the classes in power since Napoleon's fall. He is too imaginative, too ambitious, and too fond of power, to be satisfied with a mediocre life within the bourgeoisie ...[11]

. . . .

Julien Sorel is the outsider challenging this decadent society, even while he is being created by it.

Stendhal believes the Restoration and the ensuing years culminating in the return of the Orleanists created an opportunity for mediocrity and triviality to flourish. He shares Julien's nostalgia for Napoleon as well as Mme. de La Mole's – her first name is Mathilde – for the sixteenth century because in both periods ambition, passion, and bravery had a place. He would endorse Mathilde's view that "Exposure to danger livens the spirits, and saves one from the bog of bore-dom" (II.xi.250). The aristocracy is paralyzed by fear of a second revolution, and the nouveau riche are, as Georg Lukács puts it, "a mob of self-seeking and ignorant upstarts indifferent to cultural values."[12]

By subtitling his novel *A Chronicle of 1830*, Stendhal chooses the year that Louis-Philippe's bourgeois monarchy replaced the Bourbon regime that ruled during the Restoration following Napoleon's defeat in 1815. Julien's most enthu-siastic passion is for Napoleon as a model of a bold heroic figure, who took chances and made his way in the world: "Oh, Napoleon! What a joy it was in your day to rise through the perils" (I.xxii.111). For Julien, Napoleon is an envied model of upward nobility and a self-made man; he not only has sublime energy that Julien hopes to emulate, but is also a paradigm of standing alone and observing the world with an iconoclastic attitude. At odd moments, the manipulative abbé whose only causes are his self-promotion and sex looks to Napoleon as a model of passion, courage, and fulfilled ambition.

It is almost as if a corrupt society undermines private relationships and ren-ders them vapid. Neither Mathilde de La Mole nor Julien are, after their con-summation, transported by passionate love. With a mixture of irony, disap-pointment, sadness, and pity, the narrator informs us: "To tell the truth, their transports were a bit *conscious*. Passionate love was still more a model for them to imitate than a reality" (II.xvi.277).

Historical context is essential to understanding *The Red and the Black*, includ-ing understanding the depth of Stendhal's harsh political critique. Indeed, Auer-bach believes that the behavior of characters is more historically determined – shaped by "contemporary historical conditions" and "contemporary political and social conditions" – than in any earlier novel. As Auerbach notes, "[T]he inadequately implemented attempt which the Bourbon regime made to restore conditions long since made obsolete by events, creates, among its adherents in the official and ruling classes, an atmosphere of pure convention, of limitation, of constraint and lack of freedom, against which the intelligence and good will of the persons involved are powerless."[13]

With satiric energy, Stendhal strongly emphasizes the hold that the Catholic Church – albeit venal, hypocritical, and corrupt – has on its followers. Thus the narrator ironically renders Mme. de Rênal's inner life as soon as her son Stanislas recovers from an illness which she takes as God's punishment for her adultery: "I am damned, damned without hope of pardon.… [W]ho wouldn't be terrified at the prospect of hell?… I would sin again, if my sin were still before me. Let God simply forbear to punish me in this world, and through my chil-dren, and I'll have more than I deserve" (I.xix.92). Doesn't this passage evoke from readers a grim cynical smile blended with compassion for Mme. de Rênal's naïveté and simplicity?

In an odd intrusion, recalling both *Don Quixote* and Sterne's *The Life and Opinions of Tristram Shandy, Gentleman* (1759–1767), the fictional author-narrator – from whom we have heard earlier (II.xix.289) – intervenes to speak as a character in his own novel. He has the task of dealing with a twenty-six-page trial transcript; he claims that it is his publisher who insists upon specific political references: "If your characters don't talk politics, says the publisher, then they are no longer Frenchmen of 1830, and your book is no longer a mirror, as you claim" (II.xxii.304).

Technically, in this passage Stendhal is using the rhetorical device of *occupatio*, where the author proceeds to do the very thing that he says he is reluctant to do. For the characters do talk about everything but the essential political issues of the day. It is fair to say that Stendhal's interest as an imaginative writer is to catch the quality of the civilization at the period in which he is writing and to place it in the larger historical context of French and even European history. Thus he evokes the morally and politically bankrupt environment of the Restoration.

Not only Julien but also Stendhal and his fictional narrator have a somewhat skewed and myopic reading of Napoleon, the historical figure. For them, Napoleon makes his way with élan, chutzpah, and boundless self-confidence in his abilities. In their minds, Napoleon hovers over the 1830s world as an *Übermensch*, a superhuman, someone whose reach for a time exceeded the dreams of mortals. Stendhal is of Napoleon's party without fully knowing it. Just as Julien sees Napoleon as a model of social mobility and temerity, his fictional narrator sees himself as an undervalued and socially unconnected writer who, like Napoleon, boldly needs to assert himself.

In *The Red and the Black*, Stendhal's historicism, especially in its evocation of the sixteenth century, has aspects of the uncanny that are not quite explained by the facts of the narrative. Is Stendhal serious or ironic in his praise of the sixteenth century as a time of passion? His history of the sixteenth century is relatively accurate – indeed, more so than his nineteenth-century history – if focused on the violent and weird (II.x.243). Mathilde de La Mole seems to admire the sixteenth-century Queen Marguerite of Navarre, who asked for and buried the head of her lover – Boniface de La Môle – after an unsuccessful insurrection.

Stendhal's Artistry

Stendhal has written an urbane and sophisticated, often angry, satirical novel of manners posing as a *Bildungsroman*. Hardly a Puritan where sex is concerned, Stendhal is not writing *The Scarlet Letter*. Indeed, manners are the function of a decadent age in which politics are defined by power struggles between Church and state, liberals and conservatives, reformers and predatory exploiters of economic opportunity.

In Book I Julien begins as a naïf but becomes somewhat worldly for a man of the provinces. Yet that worldliness hardly serves in Paris, where much more is required in the way of cynicism, hardness, duplicity, and disguised feelings. Imaginative, intellectually arrogant, and proud, Julien admires Napoleon, whom he believes was a self-made, larger-than-life character.

For Stendhal, Catholicism is a major antagonist and a prime target of his satirical energy. While not a believer, Julien casts his lot with the Church because he believes that a petty bourgeois can make a career in that powerful institution, although we never hear about his religious beliefs. Julien is totally lacking in spirituality or faith and indifferent to religious strictures about adultery.

Parallel incidents, recurring characters, and Julien's memory of provincial life stress the ongoing comparison between provincial life in Book I and the Parisian life of Book II. Mme. de Rênal and Julien share a more passionate and idealized love than the self-interested power plays that dominate Julien's Parisian affair.

Characters do not reveal themselves by what they say, but rather by what they think. As the narrator puts it, "one could talk freely about anything whatever," as long as it was a subject that didn't involve "the use of free speech," and politics was "never talked" about: "The smallest live idea seemed like a gross indiscretion" (II.iv.202). At dinner parties, "The young people who attended out of duty were afraid to talk of anything which might arouse suspicion that they had been thinking, or reveal that they had read some prohibited book" (II.iv.202). As Lampedusa notes, "Stendhal strives to avoid direct discourse; he prefers to report because that procedure offers to an author as expert as he is the opportunity to comment, *to qualify what has been said*."[14]

Paradoxically, what makes Stendhal a realist is that long dialogues do not reveal the characters' innermost thoughts. Stendhal realizes we often conceal in our words as much as we reveal – wearing masks and adopting postures to suit circumstances – and that it is in our thoughts, silences, and impulsive gestures that we are most ourselves. Julien is a master at standing aloof and deflecting direct approaches, even while showing off his cleverness and Latin learning. In response to Mathilde's glances, even as he is being captivated in spite of himself by the attentions of "a pretty woman of high fashion," he assumes a "gloomy, cold expression" (II.xii.257–258).

Self-Delusion: Is Julien Who He Thinks He Is?

For Stendhal, self-knowledge is a value but often self-delusion is disguised as self-knowledge. One of Stendhal's major targets is human folly, especially how people delude themselves into thinking they are different from whom they are. Isn't this true of all the major characters in *The Red and the Black*? Thus Stendhal shows that we never know who we are, and the word "perhaps" hovers over all self-defining formulations. What better illustrates this self-delusion than Julien's reductive concluding summary three days before he is to be guillotined, when his romantic self-pity recalls Goethe's *The Sorrows of Young Werther* (1774, 1787)? "[N]o human eye will ever see Julien weak, primarily because he isn't. But my heart is easily touched; the most ordinary word, if spoken with a genuine accent, can soften my voice and cause my tears to flow. How often the hard-hearted people have despised me for this failing! They thought I was begging pardon: that is what I will not endure" (II.xlii.391).

Anticipating Friedrich Nietzsche, Julien claims to be outside traditional morality and immune to the judgment of others less worthy than he. In fact, Julien alternates between seeing himself as superior to his fellows and having serious doubts about himself; put another way, he alternates between self-diminishment and self-aggrandizement, although as the novel progresses he does become surer of himself.

Yet for all that, the narrator is, especially at the outset, empathetic to Julien's class position and his need to make his way in the world on his own. Julien is a self-immersed narcissist and his ruling passion is ambition; he doesn't care if he makes his way in the world as a soldier or a priest. At times he is a despicable scoundrel. For all Julien's conniving, Stendhal's narrator manipulates the reader to find touching the passion between Mme. de Rênal and Julien, whom he calls "a man of feeling" as opposed to M. de Rênal, whom he ironically calls "a man of power and position" as well as "this little man" (I.xxiii.118). The hothouse sexuality in which Julien and Mme. de Rênal risk getting caught is a welcome counterpart to the cynicism of everyone else's behavior, including that of Julien. Mme. de Rênal's naïveté makes her appealing; she alternates between paroxysms of pleasure and guilt-ridden suffering for her sins.

Gradually the reader becomes resistant to Julien. On each rereading our optics change. Julien seems increasingly more of a rascal, notwithstanding that he is a victim of an abusive father and brother. Selfish, self-absorbed, opportunistic, responding to life as a sporting event with winners and losers, Julien is no better than the small local oligarchs whom he despises in the provinces and the larger ones whom he despises in Paris. Julien in Paris often reverts to thinking of the purity of his former love with Mme. de Rênal, ignoring of course its adulterous nature and the mixed motives that propelled him forward. But we recall that Julien's passion is motivated not so much by his attraction to the mayor's wife as by his ambition.

Narrative Strategy and the Function of the Narrator in
The Red and the Black

Throughout *The Red and the Black*, we hear the voice of a worldly, urbane, angry, cynical, anti-clerical, intolerant narrator. In his role as privileged reporter and author, he is a character on whom the reader depends. So much in the Verrières section depends on the ironic distance between the narrator's historical vision and his characters' focalization, especially Julien's, but also that of both M. and Mme. de Rênal. At times the narrator dislikes Mathilde and the world she lives in so much that the ironic distance dissolves and the narrator expresses repulsion and disgust: "With these bold, proud people, it is always just one step from self-hatred to fury against other people; when this step is taken, transports of rage give them keen pleasure" (II.xxx.296).

When the fictional author-narrator, a surrogate for Stendhal, emerges in his own person and justifies his depiction of nineteen-year-old Mathilde de La Mole in all her eccentricity, fickleness, and neuroses, he speaks of the novel as a kind of perambulatory mirror: "[A] novel is a mirror moving along a highway. One minute you see it reflect the azure skies, next minute the mud and puddles of the road" (II.xix.289). Defending himself against accusations that show the mud is his fault, the narrator continues: "And the man who carries the mirror in his pack will be accused by you of immorality! His mirror shows the mud and you accuse the mirror! Rather you should accuse the road in which the puddle lies, or, even better, the inspector of roads who lets the water collect and the puddle form" (II.xix.289).

Is the fictional author-narrator reliable? He knows the thoughts of the major characters and shares them with the readers as the characters evolve. Thus he shows Mathilde awakening from her boredom to realize that she is interested in Julien. When Julien feels impassioned sympathy for a poorhouse inmate singing on the other side of the dining room wall – whom M. Valenod silences – the narrator ironically remarks, "Fortunately nobody noticed [Julien's] moment of ungentlemanly emotion.... I confess that the weakness which Julien displays in this monologue gives me a poor opinion of him" (I.xxii.111).

As much as the narrator detests M. de Rênal's cupidity, arrogance, and pomposity, he detests M. Valenod, the poorhouse director, even more so. Described by the narrator as "ashamed of nothing[,] ... shaking off humiliations, and laying claim to no personal dignity," the latter writes anonymous letters to M. de Rênal about his wife's cuckolding him (I.xxii.116). It is hardly surprising that Julien finds the manners at M. Valenod's house disgusting after experiencing de Rênal's house, where, of course, he is doted on by Mme. de Rênal.

In *The Red and the Black* we are aware of the cost of everything, as if everything depended on how much money is available. Stendhal stresses the materialization of all feeling on the part of M. de Rênal, who will put up with anything so as not to lose Mme. de Rênal's inheritance. For M. de Rênal, his wife has the function of preserving the value of his social domain. M. Valenod talks about the price of every object in his house: "Everything in it was splendid and new, and [Julien] was told the price of each piece of furniture" (I.xxii.110).

The narrator regards Mme. de Rênal as provincial, naïve, and lacking in self-understanding. With some glee, Stendhal has his narrator reveal the latent sexuality of the mayor's wife, who has become caught in a web of boredom. Indeed, the narrator extenuates Mme. de Rênal, who lives in a claustrophobic world where the husband is "master" (I.xi.53) and the woman has little to do: "The boredom of married life is sure to destroy love, whatever love has preceded the marriage. Indeed, a philosopher would say, it even leads (where people are rich enough not to have to work) to a profound boredom with all tranquil satisfactions. Yet among women it is only the dried-up souls whom it does not predispose to love" (I.xxiii.124).

Is there any major novel that uses the word "boredom" more often? For Mme. de Rênal, Mathilde de La Mole, and Julien, boredom is a personal demon; boredom becomes almost materialized as a force that needs to be wrestled with. It takes the place of the temptation of desire, or, for the believer, of the devil offering an evil path. Isn't the narrator ironically excusing Mme. de Rênal's adultery? She lives with such slight satisfaction from her husband that it is understandable that she needs a way of overcoming almost debilitating boredom.

Julien overcomes boredom by means of spasmodic bouts of passion, ambition, and cynicism, while Mathilde relieves her boredom with intermittent sexual passion and feisty challenges to her wealthy and prominent father's social position and values.

Nor does the narrator allow the reader to be complacent or patronize Julien. Thus he warns us: "Let us not think too poorly of Julien's future; he was inventing, with perfect correctness, the language of a sly and prudent hypocrisy.... Later, circumstances permitted him to approach closer to fine gentlemen; no sooner had he done so than he was as skillful with gestures as with words" (I.viii.37). The narrator is not unsympathetic to Julien's self-invention and his learning how to make his way in the world, even if that way goes amiss. Indeed, Stendhal and his narrator are in some awe of the way that the monomaniacal Julien is master of the three "R's": resilience, resolve, and resourcefulness.

The extremely cynical narrator manipulates the reader to like Julien, who seems the worst person in the novel's world except for most of the others. In the early chapters leading up to the successful seduction of Mme. de Rênal, the narrator looks down on the behavior of Julien, "for whom hypocrisy and cold calculation were the ordinary means of refuge" (I.xii.59), and the reader is conscious of an enormous ironic distance between narrator and character. In a way reminiscent of Chekhov, the narrator mocks "our hero" (I.xv.69), but, given the context, he is rather tolerant of Julien's foibles, machinations, and even his manipulative hypocrisy.

What makes Julien ultimately attractive to the reader and the narrator is that he is a tsunami of independence and energy. Julien's passionate nature – his most attractive quality – awakens dormant feelings in Mme. de Rênal and, especially, Mathilde. He impulsively takes great risks when he climbs a ladder to visit Mme. de Rênal's bedroom before leaving for Paris, and he does the same thing to enter Mathilde de La Mole's bedroom.

When rendering Julien's thought processes, even when they seem complex, what the narrator often stresses is Julien's naïveté, immaturity, lack of experience and illogic. But in these qualities, Julien has found his counterpart in Mme. de Rênal. Flirting with her, "Julien thought it was his *duty* to make sure that the hand was not withdrawn when he touched it. The idea of an obligation to fulfill, and of ridicule, or at least a sense of inferiority, to be endured if one did not succeed, immediately drove the last trace of pleasure from his heart" (I.viii.42). Rereading Book I after our first reading of Book II, we may find Julien even more appealing; after he and Mme. de Rênal become lovers, the narrator points out how he has discovered love: "In the first days of this new life there were moments when he, who had never loved or been loved by anybody, found such delicious pleasures in sincerity that he was on the point of confessing to Mme. de Rênal the ambition that had been, up to this point, the secret essence of his existence" (I.xvi.73). Of course he doesn't make that confession, in part because she disapproves of his admiring Napoleon.

Julien is more appealing in Paris, because his Lilliputian Machiavellianism is out of its league in the machinations and self-immersion of the Parisians. The de La Mole world is composed of voyeurs whose values revolve around watching and gossiping about tiny social deviations. De La Mole himself is plotting for an occupation by foreign powers supported by reactionaries as a way of staving off a repeat of the Revolution.

At first in Paris, Julien is rendered comically as something of a naïf; the narrator is sympathetic to his plight in the de La Mole world: "[T]he poor fellow still had very little polish, so that when he rose to leave the drawing room, his clumsiness was complete and everyone noticed it" (II.xx.295). Julien cannot fathom how Mathilde's mind functions: "He understood not at all the character of the singular person whom chance had rendered absolute mistress of all his happiness" (II.xx.296).

Stendhal stresses the relationship within the French 1830 culture between, on the one hand, political hypocrisy and, on the other, the insincerity, narcissism, and emotional vacuity that mark personal and social behavior. Put another way, political decadence is fed by personal and social decadence.

Thus Mathilde's wealth (or her father's) and her position as beautiful heiress give her an exemption from consistent emotional behavior. Indeed, her inconsistency borders on the weird; Stendhal – probably deliberately – does not provide a rational grammar of motives. The proud and pretentious Mathilde de La Mole, who has experienced a short lifetime of hyperbolic praise, suffers powerfully from the boredom of courtship. No sooner does she declare her love than she seems to withdraw it. The narrator ironically mocks the moments when Julien expresses how he really feels because in this world one is expected to disguise one's feelings. When Julien says, "So you no longer love me, and I adore you," the narrator reveals to us readers: "Mathilde, confident of his love, despised him completely" (II.viii.285).

The Ending of *The Red and the Black*

Why does Julien shoot Mme. de Rênal? We need to recall that soon after he and Mathilde consummate their relationship, he contemplates killing Mathilde; she had spoken regretfully to him of giving herself "to the first comer" (II.xviii.281). When Julien seizes an old sword in the library, she thinks excitedly, "So I have been on the verge of being killed by my lover!" and, thinking longingly back to the turmoil of the sixteenth century, finds his violent passion quite exciting: "The idea carried her back to the finest years of the age of Charles IX and Henri III" (II.xvii.281).

What attracts Mathilde to Julien is that he lives unconstrained by court customs and rules and is an "inferior being" dependent on her for stature and at the same time an outsider, even an outlaw, according to the Restoration world in which she lives: "Far from living in continual dread of a revolution, like my cousins … I shall be sure of playing a role, and a great role, for the man I have chosen has character and boundless ambition" (II.xvii.286).

As the novel progresses, Julien increasingly lurches between self-reflection and bursts of spasmodic energy. Isn't his shooting Mme. de Rênal the final symptom of a passionate, erratic, maniacally energetic, ardent, at times self-destructive and obsessive egotist who, despite the appearance of control, is in fact lurching out of control? Henri Martineau emphasizes how Julien rushes pell-mell into shooting Mme. de Rênal without his usual self-interrogation: "[Stendhal] clearly understood that Julien had suddenly become incapable of registering anything at all: he scarcely notices the most commonplace impressions of the outside world, the ordinary mill of associated ideas no longer turns within him."[15]

Rather than flouting conventions and becoming a self-made man living by his own rules, Julien has been defeated by the social constructs he despises and, indeed, has lost his bearings and become emotionally unhinged. In a sense the novel does not fully provide an answer to why he shoots Mme. de Rênal because Stendhal wants us to see that no grammar of motives to which narrator or reader can have access fully explains Julien's derangement. Julien's behavior has left the world of rational and comprehensible explanations.

Stendhal's Originality

Before turning to the later *The Charterhouse of Parma*, in which we shall see further development of the qualities that are original to *The Red and the Black*, let us consider what Stendhal brings to the novel form in *The Red and the Black*.

1. More than many of his nineteenth-century contemporaries, he understands that human feelings are not fixed but in constant flux; without employing a modern psychological terminology to describe human behavior, Stendhal renders the ebb and flow of love, hatred, jealousy, pettiness, anger, and frustration. He understands that character and personality are inconstant and that we have multiple and conflicting selves.

2. Stendhal creates a complex narrator who is a character choosing what to present to his reader. The narrator assumes a reader who is not only sympathetic to his world view but also one who may be less perspicacious, less cynical, and more ingenuous than he about observing human behavior. While the often omniscient and always knowing narrator infrequently presents the actual words of the characters whom he is observing, he relentlessly reveals their failings.

   Stendhal reminds us that authorial intrusions did not begin with self-reflective postmodern fiction and that traditional novelists were very much aware of the act of telling and thought about it a great deal. The realistic illusion not only includes the presentation of the novel's events as if they were as real as events described in the daily newspaper or a biography, but also the creation of a social and intellectual relationship between teller and tale. The reader's emotional engagement depends on both forms of realism, even as one form may complement, undermine, and even puncture the other. In fact, discursive material in which the author confides to the reader the fictionality of the supposed realistic world he is describing plays a role in the fiction of, among others, Cervantes, Sterne, Fielding, and Melville.

3. *The Red and the Black* goes where Stendhal likes, very much like *Moby Dick*, and stops for satires, often in the form of vignettes revealing the quality of provincial life in Book I or Parisian life in Book II. Plot often is secondary to exposing the superficiality of Parisian aristocratic social life or the intrigues of provincial life. The France of the 1830s becomes the dominant character. Julien and Mathilde and her family and the de Rênal family are often far from foregrounded. Stendhal has digressive moments, but when focusing on the vertical ladder of class as a crystallizing theme, Stendhal has deft structural control of his plot and themes, wryly and cynically juxtaposing the rural focus of Book I with the Paris culture of Book II. That underlying formal control is even more prevalent in *The Charterhouse of Parma*.

4. With his sense of fun and play along with the overriding cynicism that extends to his own work, Stendhal is innovative in his self-referential parody of his own artistry and his awareness that even if art has a factual underpinning, it succeeds as an illuminating distortion. In a sense *The Red and the Black* parodies itself by embedded narratives that raise questions about the authenticity of narratives. We can cite several examples of this; Julien's narrative, which he sends to Fouque (his reader); Mathilde's drawing of him; and the historical narrative that M. de La Mole charged Julien to write – and then digest and memorize to present to an unnamed Duke – about the conspiratorial political meeting. As we shall see, that combination of self-parody, cynicism, and noir humor is very much part of *The Charterhouse of Parma*.

5. Anticipating modernism and postmodernism, *The Red and the Black* and *The Charterhouse of Parma* raise questions about whether one can describe originating events, how we organize our perceptions, whether we can depend on memory, and whether even multiple perspectives can provide a truth beyond "perhaps."

Study Questions for *The Red and the Black*

1. What is the necessary historical context for reading *The Red and the Black*?
2. Why is Napoleon important? How and why does Julien identify with him?
3. What motivates Julien?
4. In what ways is Stendhal a realist and in what ways is he not a realist?
5. How would you define the narrator's values? Are they the same as Stendhal's? In what ways are Stendhal and his narrator more sympathetic to Julien and Napoleon than they acknowledge?
6. Can the novel be both an anti-pastoral and a rejection of urban sophistication?
7. What is Stendhal's attitude to the Catholic Church?

8. What does *The Red and the Black* say about the power of social class? In what ways is Julien's behavior transgressive of class structure?
9. What is the significance of the ending?
10. How does Stendhal use his art to show us that "perhaps" – implying that there might be alternative stories to both Julien's life and the corrupting decadence in France – was possible?

2. *The Charterhouse of Parma*: Narrative as Energy, Reading as Play

Before we turn to *The Charterhouse of Parma*, we need to foreground two relevant biographical facts. Stendhal was a survivor of the 1812 French retreat after the failed effort to conquer Russia as well as a professional diplomat in northern Italy familiar with court intrigues. Stendhal wrote – or rather dictated – this, his last completed novel, from November 4, 1838 to December 26, 1838 and there are some rough spots despite Balzac's lavish praise in 1840, praise which did much to establish its original reputation. Among the rough spots: the eccentric poet and assassin Ferrante Palla should have been introduced earlier and the ending is rushed. And we need to ask, why the title, since the Charterhouse is not mentioned until the final sentences? Compared to *The Red and the Black*, the pace and momentum of *The Charterhouse of Parma* are less deliberate and restrained and deflect the reader from taking a more careful look at what is happening. Yet a young Henry James, whom we think of as the early apostle of organic unity, considered it in an 1874 article for the *Nation* "among the dozen finest novels we possess."[16]

In his deft and subtle use of interior monologue and narrative summary, Stendhal in *The Red and the Black* is more interested in character psychology than in *The Charterhouse of Parma*. He probes less deeply into Fabrizio's feelings and motives than he did into Julien's. The result is that, compared to Julien, we have a less intense and continuing sense of Fabrizio as a troubled figure whose emotional education does not always keep up with events. The ironic narrative distance and high-spirited irony that we see in *The Charterhouse of Parma* are often missing in *The Red and the Black*, notwithstanding similar operatic scenes and dialogue.

Politics and History

Does, Stendhal asks, political community in the 1830s have any moral value when it depends simply on individuals maneuvering for power to fulfill sexual and materialistic needs as well as to placate envy and desire for revenge? Is the European nation-state system based on various shams? Has the nation-state system developed beyond feudalism? Is it organized for its citizenry or for the privileged life of the few whose pleasures are protected while the common good is disregarded? For example, does the narcissistic Prince of Parma stand for anything or care about anybody? Is Mosca or the Duchess any better? Aren't the minor characters like Marietta and Fausta and Giletti merely parodies of the major ones?

Major themes of *The Charterhouse of Parma* are the exposure of the folly of absolute monarchy and, as in *The Red and the Black*, the superficiality of court life. Stendhal was himself a follower of Napoleon but, as Mendelsohn puts it, disgusted with "the bourgeois complacency" of the French.[17] In post-Restoration France, Stendhal dismisses what he sees as French pretensions, hypocrisy, and claims for reason, and favors the impulsiveness, depth, and passion of Italian emotions, although he also sees the turbulence of these emotions leading to all kinds of hypocrisy, as when Clelia will only see Fabrizio at night because of her oath to the Madonna. Stendhal is fascinated by the larger-than-life, imaginative, emotional, cynical, and selfish Italians, who are driven by private passions to manipulate both public policy and the private lives of others. Thus, to further her own purposes and those of her lover, Count Mosca, the Duchess convinces Prince Ernesto, who is in love with her, to speak to his neglected wife (vi.121ff.).

What Kind of Fiction is *The Charterhouse of Parma*?

Stendhal's two major novels dramatize a profound uncertainty about the forms of society in a world where nothing is fixed or stable. Neither the form of the novel nor the world it dramatizes seems to have traditional moral restraints; in a sense, Jane Austen's novels of manners and morals are its polar opposite in terms of the narrator's including standards by which to measure characters' behavior.

Even more than *The Red and the Black*, the very pace of the plot in *The Charterhouse of Parma* puts everything in doubt and leaves the reader in a whirl. Reflecting on the effect of the novel's being written in seven weeks, Mendelsohn has commented: "The swiftness of its composition is reflected in the narrative briskness for which it is so well known – the 'gusto, brio, élan, verve, panache' of which [Richard] Howard is rightly conscious in his translation – and, as even die-hard partisans of the novel would have to admit, in passages where compositional speed clearly took a toll in narrative coherence."[18]

With a chatty narrator, jittery pace, extraneous characters that deflect the reader's attention and simply disappear, a shaggy dog plot, repetitious and prolix rendering major characters' thoughts as well as the narrator's analyses of the same characters, and final pages that rush through three years and many crucial events before the demise of the major characters (Fabrizio, Clelia, and the Duchess Gina), Stendhal violates every tenet of the paradigmatic formal novel in the James–Flaubert tradition. Rather than an organic plot with a cause-and-effect relationship for events and a grammar of motives for characters, Stendhal's episodic plot lurches this way and that.

Indeed, one could argue that, if what defines the realistic novel is its warp and woof that emphasizes particularity in the service of representative figures of a larger cultural and historical pattern – what we will be seeing in Balzac and Flaubert as well as in Tolstoy – then *The Charterhouse of Parma* is more a parodic anti-novel than a novel. "From a practical point of view," as Adam Begley notes, "'The Charterhouse of Parma' makes a lousy guidebook. An ardent fan of all things Italian, and a brilliant, impressionistic travel writer, Stendhal could have bequeathed to the ages an unforgettable prose portrait of Parma, the small, sleepy, provincial northern Italian city where most of the action of his great novel takes place. But instead he made it up; his Parma is imaginary."[19] The absurdity and illogic of the novel's events and the characters' motivation have more in common with a postmodern writer such as T. Coraghessan Boyle than the aforementioned realists.

In *The Charterhouse of Parma*, even more than in *The Red and the Black*, Stendhal's goal is to give pleasure; much of the novel is stylish escapism. Some of the episodes are light confections containing unbelievable circumstances. For long stretches we do not take the characters too seriously, even though their lives are at stake. Yet the novel has elements of genius. Stendhal makes the illogical seem reasonable and distracts us from thinking about the mad world of his plots. What makes the novel work is that Stendhal's characters believe in their lives. They don't think they are funny even if Stendhal does. Indeed, he urges us to see that their taking themselves seriously is part of the fun. To let his readers know that we should not always take his characters as seriously as they take themselves, he winks on occasion at the reader in part through his epithet "our reader," and in part because he expects us to smile at his often reductive and implausible distinctions between the French and Italians.

Put another way, *The Charterhouse of Parma* is a page turner. Its major themes include the waste and folly of war, the magnetism of sexual attraction, and how the political labyrinth created by kings and generals ensnares and shapes the lives of individuals and nations. Equally important focal points are the dominance of human foibles, limitations, and such vices as greed, jealousy, stinginess, and lust. Stendhal's major characters – most notably the Contessa, Marchesa, and Fabrizio – enact these themes. Plot details fade from the reader's memory as the novel moves at a rapid pace from one impossible and unpredictable event to another, often within a few pages. Indeed, Stendhal relies on the reader to fill in the blanks about character motivation and decision as well as the cause and effect which might make an implausible plot more plausible. As Begley rightly observes, Stendhal "prefers contour to detail, favoring a kind of figurative indistinctness that invites the reader's imagination to fill in the blanks, to join in the creative endeavor."[20]

Stendhal owes a good deal to the example of *Don Quixote* (1605, 1615). Indeed, he is something of a Don Quixote, or at least his narrator is. The narrator simply forges ahead without any regard to what might be expected or what has preceded. Like Don Quixote, he does not learn from his own mistakes. He is not deflected from rushing pell-mell through telling one adventure and then moving on to the next.

In picaresque style, Stendhal's inventive novel with its naïve hero recalls Cervantes' masterwork. Fabrizio does his share of tilting at windmills. Like Don Quixote, novels and poems play a role in shaping his sense of reality; as Mendelsohn writes, "[Fabrizio] keeps checking up on himself, as if trying to conform to some hidden master plan for being, or for loving.... No wonder he so often expresses himself in the interrogative."[21]

Stendhal as an artist subscribes to one of the two major traits he attributes to the character of the Duchess Gina, namely: "[S]he never gave further thought to a decision once she had made it. In this regard, she used to quote a remark of her first husband's, the charming General Pietranera: 'What insolence to myself! ... Why should I suppose I have more sense today than when I made up my mind?'" (xxi.365).[22] Indeed, the narrator also has much in common with the other major trait of her character: "[W]hat she wanted once she wanted forever" (xxi.364–365).

As Mendelsohn notes, the Duchess Gina "is one of the great creations of the nineteenth-century novelistic imagination: brilliant, flirtatious, cunning, vulnerable, passionate, extraordinarily self-aware, and yet helplessly the prey of a forbidden passion for her beautiful nephew."[23] But, despite her plotting, is she really self-aware or does she live by the illusion of control? She lives by her emotions; she poisoned her father in revenge for his treatment of Fabrizio. After sleeping with the repellent Prince once and accomplishing her purpose – the freeing of Fabrizio from prison – she discards him.

French novelists, as Georg Lukács and others have stressed, tend to be more aware than other European novelists of the way that economic contexts and social milieu shape characters and more concerned about how, despite this, the individual with all his or her idiosyncrasies can remain human and be happy in the moment without regard to the community well-being. As Georges Poulet observes, "[In Stendhal, t]he impulsive being is therefore not a free being, he is on the contrary a being tyrannized by the emotion to which he is subject."[24] Prey to impulse and deflection from espoused goals, Julien and Fabrizio, one might say, both have trouble with telling themselves a consistent narrative that might structure their behavior for some length of time. Put another way, both characters fail to look to the consequences of impulsive moments, and often these consequences take place in the context of political ructions.

Paradoxically, what matters in Stendhal's fiction is the quality of private life that can be found in a world of often unpredictable political crises and turmoil. Public position is often an accident by which we make our way and organize our economic and personal arrangements, but it is private needs and desires that direct human action.

Notwithstanding his role in Parma's political leadership, Count Mosca's obsession for Gina the Duchess and hers for Fabrizio play a large role in driving political machinations in Parma. Fabrizio is the ultimate realist, serving and despising the despotic Prince and later his son. Yet Fabrizio was once a follower of Napoleon and longs to be a Napoleon, whom he sees as a paradigm for someone who shapes his own destiny. Fabrizio settles for being an Archbishop, although he is something of a rake until he meets and becomes obsessed with Clelia. The latter's spasmodic and iterative oscillations between guilt and passion make her decidedly less dynamic than Gina, whose plots – directed by her extravagant emotions – move the novel forward.

Plot and Structure

The Charterhouse of Parma is not the art novel of Flaubert, whom we will be discussing in a later chapter, or of Henry James. The incredible pace and momentum of telling may reflect the novel's having been dictated by Stendhal. The telling takes precedence over the showing, and at the end Stendhal simply kills off Fabrizio, Clelia, and their son.

Balzac praises Stendhal's structural pace, what he calls "the streamlined concentrated structure," albeit he is thinking of *The Charterhouse of Parma*.[25] I take issue with that, finding in the plot, if not the satirical energy of his critique of Church and state, a somewhat digressive tendency.

As we read and are often surprised by what happens and by sudden shifts in focus, we understand that Stendhal's exuberant, uncanny plot is a metaphor for the impulsive and reckless behavior of the characters that the plot describes. What Balzac says about Stendhal's characters is as true of Stendhal the author: "*To feel* is the rival of *to understand* as *to act* is the opposite of *to think*."[26] Novels teach us how to read them, and Stendhal's fast-paced plot and high-spirited characters keep us off balance and, if we are not careful, make for a less than scrupulous first reading that may miss crucial details. The Duchess, the supposed father's younger sister, is not really Fabrizio's relative since it is Lieutenant Robert, a French lieutenant under Napoleon, who is Fabrizio's real father, something careful readers notice.

Stendhal's narrator assumes that the reader is aware that he is being guided through an imagined world and that the reader enjoys listening to the tale, even as he is aware of the fictional voice playfully creating diverse kinds of representation and reminding the reader that he is doing so. The narrator often mocks the characters whose behavior he describes. What could be sillier than Fabrizio making a career in the clergy while his raging desire drives his behavior? The reader responds by an awareness that his reading is an imaginative game and that he knows that the narrator, to use Thackeray's apt metaphor, is a puppeteer who can put the puppets back in the box and save them for a sequel; alternatively, he can end the story or strands of the story whenever he wishes and kill off most of the cast, as in fact he does in a few final pages.

Stendhal conflates time. Di Lampedusa has noted that "the duration of the actions *actually narrated* is less than the reading time" and speaks of the novel's fast pace or "gallop."[27] But the narrator's pell-mell telling is often undermined by a kind of free-spirited, even airy, chatty nonchalance in which there is time for the narrator to observe (at times obsessively) the distinction between French and Italian character, or tell side stories or intersecting stories about characters that interest him or drop those for whom he has little use, such as the Marchese del Dongo, or his real son, who plots against Fabrizio, or Lieutenant Robert.

When thinking of the high-spirited plot that becomes almost a parody of realism, we should look to the influence of Laurence Sterne. Stendhal knew Sterne's *Tristram Shandy*, which was well known on the continent, and he mentions *Shandy* in his autobiography, *The Life of Henry Brulard*. *The Charterhouse of Parma* has its digressive moments that recall Sterne's insouciant artistry in *Tristram Shandy* or Fielding's Man of the Hill. Most notable in this regard is Ferrante Palla, the misguided poet, follower of Napoleon, and anti-monarchist poisoner of the Prince who suddenly appears in the woods on the property of the Duchess's Sacca villa.

Stendhal's often necessary narrative interruptions remind us that when we tell stories we occasionally need to introduce missing strands of information. Thus, with a wink and a smile, he adds important information about political machinations involving Chief Justice Rassi, information that made it incumbent that Fabrizio escape immediately from prison: "Here a necessary detail, one which partly accounts for the Duchess's courage in advising Fabrizio to attempt such a dangerous course, compels us to interrupt, momentarily, the story of this bold enterprise" (xx.350).

The apparent randomness of the plot enacts Stendhal's view that luck is the determining factor in life. Often Fabrizio makes what seems a wrong decision – crossing into Austria – only to be saved. Thus when he is arrested, he is brought before a border official who is a friend of a man he killed – Giletti – and whose passport he is now carrying; the official lets him go because he thinks he is helping his friend.

To read *The Charterhouse of Parma* is to watch Stendhal at play. Charterhouse is an archaic term for a Carthusian monastery and the title monastery only appears in the second to last paragraph as the place to which Fabrizio retreats for his last year. Note that the French title is *La Chartreuse de Parme*. Indeed, postponing the title location is itself a kind of spoof of traditional titles and plots, since a more apt title would be *Fabrizio's Adventures*, or *Love and Intrigue in Parma*. With plot taking over entirely from character and with little logical cause and effect in either personal behavior or fictional history, do not Chapters xxvi and xxvii become a parody of realistic fiction?

Certainly the novel has its share of farce, particularly when we think about how the plot turns back on itself. When Clelia become a Marchesa, she has the same title Fabrizio's mother held when she committed the adultery that resulted in his birth. Fabrizio, like another follower of Napoleon, Lieutenant Robert, impregnates Clelia with an out-of-wedlock child, Sandrino, as he had himself been conceived.

In a sense Fabrizio's various sexual conquests are iterations of his first. Given that one conquest can hardly be distinguished from another, it is as if Stendhal created a plot with repetition compulsion. With Fabrizio's death and that of Clelia, his son, and the Duchess, the plot erases the manic energy that gave it life. It is as if the pervasive talk of poison touches the plot in the form of death, and death becomes a metonym for the reader's experience of taking leave from the novel. We might say that the final pages are a kind of erasure of what precedes, or at the very least, for the reader a goodbye to the energy, passion, and vitality that gave the novel urgency and pace. The last words, "To the Happy Few" – the same words with which Stendhal concludes *The Red and the Black* – form an ironic epigraph to those who survive: the Count, whose beloved Gina is dead, and the corrupt and inept Prince, who in his way also loved Gina. Not only are we reminded that both are *not* happy but also that *The Charterhouse of Parma* dramatizes the idea that sustained happiness eludes all mortals on earth. Stendhal emphasizes that the art of living is always elusive and that not only circumstances beyond our control but also, finally, mortality will always trump our aspirations.

Because Stendhal dramatizes extravagant and hyperbolic scenes, which simultaneously invite human sympathy and ironic distance, our reading, our experience, is quite different from our experience in reading such realists as Balzac, Flaubert, or Zola. To be sure, mixing genres is not unique to Stendhal, but continually inviting discordant responses to virtually every major turn of plot and revelation of character behavior, as Stendhal does most notably in *The Charterhouse of Parma*, is. Nor is the dialogue realistic; rather, it is often stilted and parodies how real people speak; an example is the dialogue between Fabrizio and the Duchess (vi.117) when she is urging him to build his future by entering the priesthood.

Farce and comedy are often interspersed with and qualify serious if not operatic moments. When Clelia rushes into the prison to save him, Fabrizio first claims, contrary to fact so as to win her further sympathy and not loosen her embrace, that he has eaten the poisoned meal. No sooner does she exclaim, "O my only friend! … I shall die with you," than her clothes begin to fall off, arousing Fabrizio's sexual passion: "She was so lovely just then, her gown slipping off her shoulders and in such a state of extreme passion, that Fabrizio could not resist an almost involuntary movement. Which met with no resistance…" (xxv.433). Fabrizio's confession that he had not eaten the poisoned meal, we smilingly realize, is as much motivated by desire as by moral rectitude: "In the enthusiasm of passion and of generosity which followed extreme rapture, he murmured to her quite foolishly: 'No unworthy falsehood must cast a shadow over the first moments of our happiness'" (xxv.433). Quite possibly they have sex, but as is often the case, the reader must fill in the contours of the scene, and that is especially true of sexual scenes. (While sexual scenes in French nineteenth-century novels are quite different from contemporary fiction, Flaubert, Balzac, and even Stendhal in *The Red and the Black* linger long enough to be more explicit.) The narrator often gallops forward without stopping to give us quite enough information. Thus often the scenes and the narrator's explanations are under-determined, leaving the reader to guess at, as in some postmodern fiction, what is going on.

Indeed, *The Charterhouse of Parma* is a fictional crucible in which Stendhal makes words and charters (rules) for his fiction and the Chartreuse is his artistic monastery. Stendhal knew that fiction was an open form for which each novelist makes his own rules and creates his own space and time. He knew that a lifespan or a short discussion could take the same number of pages. The Battle of Waterloo can take less time than an interview between the Duchess Gina and the Prince. Like Waterloo – and life – Stendhal's fiction seems to be more about disorder than order, chance rather than system. He sometimes seems to be implicitly saying to his reader, "Now what am I to do with these characters that I have created out of thin air and that seem to be so quirky and idiosyncratic? Should we take them or me seriously?"

Fabrizio

Fabrizio, all of five feet five – short but not very short for this period – is a blank slate onto which others project their feelings and needs. He is handsome, with his "Correggio countenance" – Correggio was Stendhal's favorite painter – but we don't really know what he looks like. Beginning with his comic and pathetic participation in Waterloo at the behest of Napoleon, things for the most part happen to him; rarely is he the originating agent of important action. His mother, the Duchess Gina, and Count Mosca direct his development as if he were their puppet.

Along with aspects of farce, noir, and tragedy, *The Charterhouse of Parma* has aspects of drawing room comedy where characters continually misunderstand one another. Half knowing, half strategic, Fabrizio gradually emerges from adolescence and responds to the machinations of Gina – the Marchesa and later the Duchess – especially after he kills a man. Romantic at the core, Fabrizio and the Duchess assert their freedom in response to cultural norms and expectations. Whether it be religion or politics or sexual love, they assert their right to be themselves and to define their values. Notwithstanding his lack of interest in Catholicism or any religion and his utter disdain for celibacy, Fabrizio follows Mosca's insidious plan to make him an Archbishop.

It never occurs to Fabrizio or to the Duchess to think about the common good; because the Prince doesn't keep his word about releasing Fabrizio after Gina sleeps with him, she will poison the Prince without compunction or worrying about the effect on res publica. Poulet observes: "Thus, as there is the slave of the momentary, fugitive sensation, there is the slave of perverted passion. Is it not the spectacle of this sort of slavery that we witness when … we see the duchess, until then so exquisitely spontaneous, change disposition, become absorbed in the sense of injuries endured, and finally undertake the murder [of the Prince] who had wronged her?"[28]

Fabrizio and the Duchess are, like Julien in *The Red and the Black*, post-Enlightenment figures for whom reliance on reason alone is a travesty and for whom emotional life – whether it is in their interest or not – is the essence of life. Their heritage is the freedom of Romanticism with a strong Byronic and Goethean inflection; indeed, we recall that a number of chapter epigraphs in *The Red and the Black* are from Byron's *Don Juan*. In significant ways the darker side of Stendhal's selfish and self-deluding characters – including Julien Sorel, the Machiavellian couple the Duchess and Count Mosca – anticipate such Dostoevsky characters as the Underground Man, Raskolnikov, and Dmitri Karamazov, all of whom defiantly act against reason and sometimes their own self-interest.

Stendhal asks what it is to be human if our impulses overtake our reason and if political and personal morality is merely a convenient mask for fulfilling our obvious and dimly acknowledged psychic needs? Is life about reimagining oneself and redirecting nervous energy, which seem to be the activities at which the hyperactive Fabrizio excels? Given his restlessness, interrupted by various moments when he seems to surrender to nature's sublimity, his sexual athleticism, and his proclivity for violence, chases, and escapes, does Fabrizio, the contemporary reader might ask with a smile, have an attention-deficit disorder?

Incest hovers over the novel. Not knowing who his father is, Fabrizio thinks "[the Duchess] would be as horrified by any word that was too specific as she would be by incest itself" (vii.141). Seemingly believing that her brother is Fabrizio's father, the Duchess is apparently unaware that the man she loves is in fact not a blood "nephew" (xi.176) but the child of her sister-in-law and Lieutenant Robert. However, the reader is not given enough information to know for sure whether the Duchess knows who Fabrizio's real father is. Stendhal rarely gives us entrance into his characters' interior lives so that we can understand the complexities of their psyches.

Even if she is constrained by the incest taboo, the Duchess Gina never stops loving Fabrizio and her passion is mostly sexual. After Fabrizio has returned to Parma following his studying for the priesthood and right before Mosca's entrance to announce that Fabrizio will be named the Archbishop's Vicar-General at twenty-four, Fabrizio and his aunt fall into a deep embrace: "In a natural transport of feeling and despite all his reasoning, he took this charming woman in his arms and covered her with kisses" (xi.176). She had just noticed that her formerly "ever-obedient nephew" had become "a serious man by whom it would be delicious to be loved" (xi.176). Mosca is jealous when he sees how sexually captivated Fabrizio and the Duchess are with one another. Mosca hires spies and even thinks of killing Fabrizio. An important turn of the plot is when the jealous Machiavellian Mosca omits from an official letter the key phrase "*this unjust procedure will have no future consequences,*" the inclusion of which would have exonerated Fabrizio (xiv.242).

The Duchess balances a strong sexual drive – she loves Fabrizio – with practicality in the person of Count Mosca, her lover and later husband. The narrator is overwhelmed by the task of describing the impetuous and emotionally extravagant Duchess: "How to describe the despairing moment which followed this account of the situation, in a woman so little swayed by reason, so much the slave of the present sensation, and, without confessing it to herself, so wildly in love with [Fabrizio] the young prisoner?" (xvi.269).

Before meeting Clelia, Fabrizio thinks he cannot feel love: "I would still have nothing to offer [my aunt the Duchess] but the liveliest friendship, though without love; nature has deprived me of such sublime follies.... She will suppose I

78

feel no love for her, whereas I feel no love for anyone; she will never be willing to understand that" (vii.142). Soon after the narrator intrudes in the first person: "Fabrizio had an Italian heart; I seek no pardon for him: this defect, which will make him less loveable, consisted chiefly in this: his vanity came only in sudden bursts" (viii.150).

Clearly Fabrizio has an outsized libido and little restraint, although he has taken vows as a priest and is to be the Archbishop's Vicar-General. While pursuing Marietta, Fabrizio is distracted by the singer Fausta, who responds to his interest, and in the midst of that sexual segue he becomes distracted by Bettina, Fausta's maid, with whom he becomes "infatuated" as soon as he discovers her following him to give him Fausta's message (xiii.225). As the narrator puts it, "The little chambermaid was quite pretty, which did away with Fabrizio's moral reveries" (xiii.224). Rather than tell us Fabrizio slept with the girl described as "charming" (xiii.225) and "pretty" (xiii.225), the narrator slyly and knowingly reports: "It was only at dawn that he parted from the little chambermaid, herself quite satisfied with the manners of the young Prince" (xiii.225). In an explanatory letter to the Duchess, Fabrizio castigates himself: "I cannot raise myself higher than vulgar pleasures" (xiii.227).

Stendhal's ironic narrator often holds characters at a distance but does empathize with Clelia's and Fabrizio's love, frustration, and loneliness. For Clelia, although not without her own quirks and even subtle evasions and justifications – adultery, she rationalizes, is permissible in the dark! – is comparatively ingenuous. Without guile, Clelia is the novel's one innocent; when she thinks of Fabrizio imprisoned, the narrator writes: "She was a very pious, very timid girl, and her heart, usually so tranquil, was beating with unaccustomed violence" (xv.267).

When Fabrizio falls in love with Clelia, he becomes something more than a Byronic rake and superficial twit, and begins to take on the role of romantic hero: "Fabrizio had no experience of the kind of emotion produced by a woman one loves; it was a sensation he had never felt, even in its faintest nuance" (xix.322). For once he falls in love with Clelia, he has a complete change of values. He chooses to stay in prison just to be near her: "[I]ntensely he felt that life, without Clelia's love, could be nothing for him but an endless round of bitter disappointments or unbearable tedium. It seemed to him that it was no longer worth living to rediscover those same delights which had seemed so interesting before he had known love" (xx.334).

That Stendhal seems puzzled about how to zero in on the two lovers in isolation is a result of his open form. Fabrizio is physically imprisoned; Clelia, who has rebuffed all prior men and knows of Fabrizio's fickleness, is imprisoned by her own fear and doubts. Fabrizio's imprisonment opens the door to a puzzling structural iteration where the plot becomes static, major characters don't move off dead center, and the now enervated narrator seems in the clutches of inertia in a novel where rapid pace and movement – both the plot's and the characters' impulsive, impetuous, and improvised behavior – had been part of the fun. That the novel seems stuck is an instance of the fallacy of imitative form because Stendhal has trouble getting off dead center – as do the lovers – and the reader becomes impatient.

With Chapter xxi, when the Duchess meets Ferrante, the pace resumes, but let us look in detail at Chapters xviii through xx. After Fabrizio is imprisoned and begins to communicate with Clelia – the daughter of the Governor of the Fortress whose name, Fabio Conti, has a deliberate resonance of Fabrizio's – the pace of the novel slows down and for the first time feels repetitive. Fabrizio becomes something of a bird in Clelia's aviary, but so does the reader. Her fastidiousness about whether to love him becomes rather tedious and her progress seems snail-like after the tsunamis of most other characters' behavior, especially that of the Duchess: "[T]here is something sinful in our relationship, I cannot doubt that some sort of misfortune awaits us" (xx.349). Fabrizio doesn't want to escape, and is imprisoned by love, something he hasn't felt before, for nine months. As Mendelsohn insightfully notes: "One ironic measure of [Fabrizio's] inability to master the art of living as a free man is that he finds true happiness only in the womblike security of his prison cell in the Farnese Tower ... from which he is loath to escape after he falls in love with Clelia."[29]

Clelia loves Fabrizio despite herself. She thinks he and the Duchess are lovers, and fears that she is merely "a distraction for his tedium" (xx.342). That she is governed by a hermeneutics of suspicion is shown by Stendhal's rendering of her thoughts: "This prisoner having made a name for himself in the world by his courage, he supposes he can prove that his love is something more than a passing fancy by exposing himself to such great dangers in order to continue seeing the person he imagines he loves" (xx.342). In Clelia we see how a rational, idealistic but wary innocent, uncorrupted by court manners, loves in contrast to the intrigues and lust that dominated court and street life. Trusting the protean narrator, at least to a point, the reader wants to believe in Fabrizio's transformation.

Sex and Love; Love and Sex

In Stendhal's politically corrupt world of Parma, where characters live on the edge, sex is the drug of choice, very much as it was – as Milan Kundera shows in *The Unbearable Lightness of Being* – for intellectuals, artists, and other political outsiders in Communist countries behind the Iron Curtain. Aware that the reader knows of Clelia's adulterous relationship with Fabrizio that will result in a son, the narrator ironically observes: "Many people at the court of Parma were astonished that no intrigue should be known in connection with a woman so remarkable for her loveliness and for the loftiness of her soul" (xxviii.491). Are not the narrator and reader sharing an awareness that "loftiness of soul" has become equated not with fidelity but with sexual desire and that the normative values have become passionate sexual pleasures rather than sustained monogamous love? With equal irony, the narrator calls Fabrizio's passionate, devoted, single-minded love an "unfortunate caprice of affection" (xxviii.491).

In Stendhal's novels, as in the novels of Mailer, Updike, Roth, and Bellow, "[s]ex," as Katie Roiphe writes, citing Updike's Rabbit specifically, "offers an escape, an alternate life – a reprieve, even, in its finest moments, from mortality…. These passages [about sex] are after several things at once – sadness, titillation, beauty, fear, comedy, disappointment, and aspiration. The writers were interested in showing not just the triumphs of sexual conquest, but also its loneliness, its failures of connection."[30] For Stendhal's heroes, notably Julien and Fabrizio – and, indeed, for many of his women from the Duchess and the Marchesa to Marietta and Fausta – sex is what Updike called an "imaginative quest."[31]

Stendhal's novels show how sex can be implied without pornography; mistresses abound. In the subplot, Theodolina, described as a "half-naked and quite pretty woman" (xi.189) who presides over a *trattoria*, has no compunction about entertaining her lover, Ludovic, without any thought of her husband. In this most libertine novel, their relationship is a comic parody of the Mosca–Duchess–Fabrizio triangle. Of course we also think of the Lieutenant Robert–Marchesa–Marchese triangle, which resulted in the birth of Fabrizio. We recall the inherited sexual lust that the mythological Pasiphae passed on to her daughter Ariadne, a model Stendhal may have had in mind when we think of the Marchesa's son, Fabrizio, who was conceived during a short affair.

The narrator has no use for social forms which interfere with love and which, along with religious constraints, generate a series of events that lead to disasters culminating in both Clelia's and Fabrizio's deaths. But in Stendhal's imagined world, sex and love are two distinct emotions, although often they intermingle. Despite hypocrisy and duplicity, when sex is combined with love it is something special that gives meaning to characters' lives. The Duchess, who marries for convenience a husband with whom she has no relations, has a lover, Count Mosca, who when she is widowed becomes her husband and who is a central figure in the political business of Parma. She also has a forbidden passion for a man she thinks is her nephew.

Napoleon as Metaphor

In fiction of the late eighteenth and nineteenth centuries, Napoleon is often the alpha and omega of history; he is the dominant historical figure in *The Charterhouse of Parma* and the figure in virtually every character's consciousness, and thus in the minds of Stendhal's readers.

As if to stress how Napoleon has become the centerpiece of European history, Stendhal's narrator focuses on how, in a series of accidents, Fabrizio comically follows Napoleon to Waterloo. Stendhal renders the Battle of Waterloo as one in which participants have no idea of the big picture. He knows that within the chaos and confusion of war, the participants are most worried about their own lives. Resulting in lost limbs and lives, war is ultimately the real theater of the absurd without rules. At one point, Fabrizio is not even sure if he has been in battle.

War, as we shall see later in Tolstoy's *War and Peace*, is a comedy of errors where individual soldiers are in the dark and their fate is determined by a series of accidents. Fabrizio's fate is shaped by the serendipitous encounters with the canteen woman and the wife of his jailer. Indeed, Tolstoy's presentation of the September 7, 1812 Battle of Borodino – the largest and bloodiest single day in Napoleon's French invasion of Russia – was influenced by Stendhal's coverage of the Battle of Waterloo.

Napoleon's army brings verve and gaiety to Milan. The narrator compares Napoleon to Don Quixote: "It was such follies of the imagination that induced Napoleon to surrender to a prudent John Bull [England] rather than trying to escape to America.... In every age, a base Sancho Panza triumphs over a sublime Don Quixote" (x.172). With its remarkable victories and ignominious defeats, doesn't Napoleon's life – particularly for a French reader in the years immediately after *The Charterhouse of Parma* appeared – become an apt reference point for the rise and fall of Fabrizio? Isn't it ironic that Fabrizio makes his way in the world by giving people "napoleons," coins that remind us of his fealty to Napoleon as an adolescent?

In seeing Napoleon as the pivotal figure in early nineteenth-century European history, Stendhal was far from alone. Napoleon is the cause of war, the paradigm of heroism and hubris, the romantic figure who came from nowhere and who is, as for Julien in *The Red and the Black*, the exemplar of the possibility of transformation. He is a small man who becomes expert in military strategy. He is almost ubiquitous, seemingly turning up all over Europe: Russia, Italy, France, Spain, and Austria.

As he did in *The Red and the Black*, Napoleon looms large in the *Charterhouse of Parma*. Napoleon represents self-creation due to bold and imaginative and courageous behavior. Implicitly and explicitly, every male character is measured against Napoleon's amazing accomplishments and failures, most notably his transformation into the most important figure in Europe. For Stendhal, he is the quintessence of possibility and hubris. He represents energy and sexuality, courage and bravura, arrogance and insolence.

In contrast to Napoleon's seemingly larger-than-life behavior, most of the characters are petty, small-minded, and engaged in intrigues. After the Duchess agrees to sleep with the ruling young Prince, he "fancied himself a little Napoleon" as if he had triumphed (xxv.442). Yet ironically, the Duchess whom he has bedded has participated in the assassination of the former Prince and the current Prince's father.

The Narrator

The best way to think of the narrator is as a surrogate created by Stendhal to tell the story, but a surrogate who defines himself as a separate figure by the story he tells. Thus Stendhal's narrator begins with an historical sweep, including a satire of Milan's nobility, especially the Marchese. Speaking in the first person in Chapter i, the narrator recalls: "[I]t would be impossible for me to give any notion of ... [t]his period of unforeseen happiness and intoxication" in the two years after Milan fell to Napoleon in May 1786 (i.7–8). His scathingly ironic narrator observes human behavior with a particular focus on folly and vainglory. Overcoming the boredom of a hundred years, the Italians embrace the invaders, especially the Marchesa, who has an affair with the French lieutenant, Robert. Her stiff, overbearing, cowardly, self-regarding, and parsimonious husband had "valiantly" taken refuge in his castle on Lake Como, "abandoning his sister and his lovely young wife to the chances of war" (i.7).

The narrator is a character in the novel and we learn a good deal about his hyperbolic imagination and cynicism from his generalizations. He has a hatred of the superficiality of court life, especially in a despotic regime where merit often takes a back seat to greed, lust, and power. The narrator disdains despotism, but he also mistrusts the political impulses of the bourgeoisie.

The narrator reductively and ironically defines liberalism as "the happiness of the greatest number," a principle diametrically opposed to the views of the Machiavellian Count Mosca, who "considered himself obliged to seek above all the happiness of Count Mosca della Rovere" (xv.277). Providing a model for the younger Fabrizio, who becomes a priest to advance his career, Mosca is cynically motivated by pure self-interest.

The narrator is even more scathing in his satire of religion and the Church. That the Church is completely corrupt is indicated by Fabrizio's career and the sexual ecstasies his preaching creates in women. The narrator knows enough about human nature to understand that Clelia's vow to the Madonna that she will never see Fabrizio is at odds with her passionate needs. Finally, Clelia withdraws from all meaningful communication except for the various codes and wiles she uses to speak to Fabrizio.

In the world Stendhal is satirizing, money is almost always in the foreground and never far from power struggles and the complicated business of love and sex. The Duchess marries for money. The Marchesa is deprived of money. Later in the novel, Clelia's life is further complicated by the desire of her selfish father to marry her to the wealthy Marchese Crescenzi, a marriage of convenience that echoes the marriage of Fabrizio's mother.

The narrator establishes a somewhat intimate and chatty relationship with the reader even as he has an oscillating but generally distanced relationship with his characters. He also continually stresses to his French audience the difference between Italy and France as if he were explaining to us readers the customs of a distant tribe: "The reader doubtless finds overlong the narrative of all these undertakings made necessary by the absence of a passport: such preoccupations no longer exist in France; but in Italy, and especially in the region of the Po, everyone talks passports" (xii.197). The narrator playfully points out Fabrizio's failure, notwithstanding his Jesuitical training, to realize that Count Mosca's intervention in his career is a form of *simony*, that is, paying for holy offices: "A Frenchman, brought up among features of personal interest and of Parisian irony, might in good faith have accused Fabrizio of hypocrisy at the very moment when our hero was opening his heart to God with the deepest sincerity and the profoundest emotional transport" (xii.200).

We need to remember Fabrizio is himself half French and half Italian. Part of the novel's humor is the double optics – that of Italian and French perspectives – and the frisson between the exaggerated presentations of cultural differences. The narrator takes the position of a Frenchman learning in wonderment about Italian behavior. Thus in Parma and other "despotic courts, the first adroit intriguer controls the *truth*, as fashion controls it in Paris.... [I]n countries where the great names are never subject to punishment, intrigue can accomplish everything, even against [the great names]" (xii.203–204, Stendhal's italics). The French–Italian dichotomy becomes almost an obsession of the narrator: "I am inclined to think that the immoral delight Italians experience in taking revenge is a consequence of their power of imagination; people of other countries do not, strictly speaking, forgive; they forget" (xxi.365).

Often the narrator's comments are high-spirited and unnecessary if not digressive, as if the narrator were as much a vaudevillian Master of Ceremonies as a storyteller. Remarking on the Duchess's failure to realize the irony that she, who used poison to get rid of the last prince, will now be the victim of poison if her beloved Fabrizio is poisoned, the narrator's comment is rather beside the point, if not perhaps deliberately fey: "In Italy, such reflections, in moments of passion, are taken as the sign of a vulgar sensibility, much as a pun would be regarded in Paris in similar circumstances" (xxv.435). In this case as in many others, the reader enjoys the delicious irony of plot iteration.

Reflecting Stendhal's cynicism, frustration, and anger in matters of court politics, the narrator is more energetic and pointed when he turns to satirizing the morally and politically bankrupt leadership of Parma. Thus he tells us that the Princess, Prince Ernesto V's mother, "regarded with marked repugnance any display of energy, which she found vulgar" (xxv.435). Or the Marchese Crescenzi, soon to be Clelia's husband, is overtaken by sloth and ineptitude when the Duchess wants him to intervene in Fabrizio's imminent poisoning; looking for excuses not to act, we are told: "[H]e hit upon an excellent notion: the oath he had taken as *Cavaliere d'Onore* forbade him to take part in any actions against the government" (xxv.436).

But at times the narrator becomes part of the hypocritical world he pretends to detest and employs a double standard. Indeed, not only does the narrator enjoy describing the satisfaction that his characters take in intrigues, but intrigue is also a modus operandi for the narrator himself. By this I mean he coyly uses insinuation and innuendo to undermine the stature of some characters, if not stab them in the back. The narrator casts a critical eye on those who live on the fault lines between passion and obsession, and at times he includes the Duchess in this category. But he generally suspends his harshly cynical satirical vision towards those he likes, most notably Fabrizio and even the Duchess, and excuses behavior that he condemns in others. His inconsistency extends to excusing Machiavellian behavior when it is in the service of the goals of the Duchess and Fabrizio.

Often wearing a mask of cool, wry detachment, although he himself is often deeply engaged and even impassioned in his judgments, the narrator describes the overheated emotions of the characters. As much as his characters, he can engage in role playing, alternately laughing and sympathizing, judging and empathizing with characters whose behavior breaks the norms of conventions. Sometimes he mocks his characters' over-the-top, even anarchic behavior that poses as reasonable, including that of the man who poisons the Prince.

Stendhal's narrator is something of a ventriloquist who adopts multiple perspectives. In a sense he is constantly in flux in much the same ways as the characters he describes. Thus he is not always consistent or trustworthy. The narrator is ironic at times in his treatment of all the characters. Usually less rigorous in criticizing Fabrizio, he separates himself from Fabrizio's inability to sustain feeling for others except Clelia. And he pokes fun at Fabrizio's convincing himself that he is having sublime moments with nature, as when he sits on a boulder on a promontory above Lake Como. Is Stendhal also parodying romanticism and perhaps Goethe's *Werther*? "[T]he mere aspect of such sublime beauty plunged [Fabrizio] into tenderness and dulled the sharp ache of his sufferings" (viii.150).

Does Stendhal not also parody realism by making the novel's most important building, which serves as a prison for the enemies of the autocratic Prince and his minions, 180 feet high? This is the building from which Fabrizio escapes with incredible daring and luck bordering on the implausible. Stendhal understands that in fiction we are not really in Parma but in a modified fictive universe – what Wallace Stevens would call the creation of the capable imagination – which allows for the flexibility to expand and contract at the author's behest.

Speaking in the third person about himself (and parodying the narrator), Ferrante Palla argues that "[H]is job is to rouse hearts and to awaken them from that false and altogether material happiness afforded by Monarchies" (xxi.358). Ferrante himself is a comic figure who keeps track of those he has robbed so as to someday make restitution. That he refuses to keep more than a hundred francs in his purse is a kind of satiric thrust directed at the ultra-liberals.

Conclusion

It happened that when J. D. Salinger died at the end of January 2010, I was thinking about what makes *The Charterhouse of Parma* so brilliantly original. At the time, David Lodge wrote that Salinger challenges "conventional notions of fiction and conventional ways of reading as radically as the kind of novels that would later be called post-modernist."[32] Doesn't Stendhal, more than any other major nineteenth-century novelist, do exactly that, and do it far more so in *The Charterhouse of Parma* than in *The Red and the Black*?

In many ways a unique performance, Stendhal's *The Charterhouse of Parma* flouts realistic conventions of plot and character and achieves a sui generis brilliance. Stendhal is indifferent to plot consistency and conventional narrative structure, including time, and relies on interpolated anecdotes and incredible events such as Fabrizio's escape, his communication with Clelia, and the Duchess's arranging the poisoning of the Prince of Parma by someone who conveniently appears. No matter how chaotic the political and military situation, letters crucial to the plot are delivered without problems as if there were modern post offices.

With his colloquial informality in the form of asides and his playful attitude to his reader expressed in comments about reading and about telling, his reductive yet hyperbolic winking generalizations about the difference between the Italians and the French, his blurring of lines between the fictional narrator and the real author, his radically oscillating tonal shifts between, on one hand, sympathy and empathy for his characters and, on the other, cynical irony about their behavior, Stendhal looks forward to modernism and even postmodernism.

Study Questions for *The Charterhouse of Parma*

1. Is *The Charterhouse of Parma* a realistic novel? What are the realistic and anti-realistic components?
2. What is the function of the narrator? Is the narrator French or Italian?
3. Is pace an aesthetic category? Is it a plus or minus in this novel?
4. What motivates Fabrizio? The Duchess? How does Stendhal present his characters' psyches?
5. What role do history and politics play in the novel?
6. Is the Clelia–Fabrizio relationship an effort to rescue the novel from cynicism by commingling passion, sex, and romantic love?
7. What motivates Mosca?
8. How does the ending modify what precedes it?
9. What are the differences and similarities between Julien in *The Red and the Black* and Fabrizio?
10. How does Stendhal satirize the Catholic Church? How does he satirize monarchy and autocracy?

Notes

1. Sanford Schwartz, "Looking into the Beyond," review of the Metropolitan Museum of Art's *Rooms with a View: The Open Window in the 19th Century* exhibition, *NYR* 58:10 (June 9, 2011), 26–27; see p. 26.
2. Schwartz, "Looking into the Beyond," 26.
3. Schwartz, "Looking into the Beyond," 26.
4. Quoted in Julian Bell, "The Angel of the Bizarre," *NYR* 60:10 (June 6, 2013), 24–26; see p. 26.
5. All quotations from the text are taken from Stendhal, *Red and Black,* trans. and ed. Robert Adams (New York: W. W. Norton, 1969). References to the Norton edition are hereafter cited as *Red and Black*, Norton.
6. *Red and Black*, Norton, 560–561.
7. Willibald Sauerlander, "The Genius of the Other Daumier," trans. David Dollenmayer, *NYR* 60:3 (Feb. 21, 2013), 17–18.
8. Henri Martineau, "The Ending of *The Red and the Black*," in *Red and Black*, Norton, 448.
9. Erich Auerbach, in Honoré de Balzac, *Père Goriot*, trans. Burton Raffel, ed. Peter Brooks (New York: Norton, 1980), 289.
10. *Red and Black*, Norton, 553.

11. Erich Auerbach, "In the Hôtel de la Mole," in *Red and Black*, Norton, 436–437.
12. Georg Lukács, *Studies in European Realism* (London: Hillway, 1950), 78.
13. Auerbach, "In the Hôtel de la Mole," 437.
14. *Red and Black*, Norton, 554, italics di Lampedusa's.
15. Martineau, "The Ending of *The Red and the Black*," 451.
16. Quoted in Daniel Mendelsohn, "After Waterloo," review of *The Charterhouse of Parma*, trans. Richard Howard (New York: Modern Library, 2000), *New York Times Book Review*, Aug. 29, 1999, 15–17; http://www.nytimes.com/1999/08/29/books/after-waterloo.html (accessed February 14, 2014).
17. Mendelsohn, "After Waterloo."
18. Mendelsohn, "After Waterloo."
19. Adam Begley, "Stendhal in Parma, Italy," *New York Times*, Dec. 23, 2009.
20. Begley, "Stendhal in Parma, Italy."
21. Mendelsohn, "After Waterloo."
22. All quotations from the text are from Howard's translation (New York: Modern Library, 2000).
23. Mendelsohn, "After Waterloo."
24. *Red and Black*, Norton, 476.
25. See Lukács, *Studies in European Realism*, 68.
26. *Charterhouse of Parma*, trans. Howard, 514.
27. *Red and Black*, Norton, 550, italics di Lampedusa's.
28. *Red and Black*, Norton, 479.
29. Mendelsohn, "After Waterloo."
30. Katie Roiphe, "The Naked and the Conflicted," *New York Times Book Review,* Jan. 3, 2010, 8.
31. Roiphe, "The Naked and the Conflicted," 8.
32. David Lodge, "The Pre-Postmodernist," *New York Times,* Jan. 29, 2010; http://www.nytimes.com/2010/01/30/opinion/30lodge.html (accessed February 14, 2014).

Chapter 4

Predatory Behavior in Balzac's
Père Goriot (1835)

Paris as a Trope for Moral Cannibalism

Introducing Balzac: Realist and Modernist

Honoré de Balzac's *Père Goriot* (1835) takes place in 1819 after the Bourbon Restoration (1814–1830), which was interrupted by the Hundred Days of Napoleon's return. While the restored monarchy was a constitutional monarchy, it was conservative and often indifferent to the lower classes, many of whom lived in poverty. Louis XVIII was king and did much to reverse the French Revolution and to give returning émigrés back their land. The Restoration also allowed the Church to once again become a major power. Balzac (1799–1850) shows us that in the post–French Revolution world of the Bourbon Restoration the aristocracy stands on the shoulders of the common people; as Peter Brooks puts it, "[T]he sordid realities of labor and economic exploitation become visible through the veneer of manners."[1]

According to Georg Lukács, "No one experienced more deeply than Balzac the torments which the transition to the capitalist system of production inflicted on every section of the people, the profound moral and spiritual degradation which necessarily accompanied this transformation on every level of society."[2] Notwithstanding his "legitimist royalism" and belief in a system based "on a Catholic legitimism and tricked out with Utopian conceptions of English Toryism," as Lukács puts it, Balzac's vision mirrored "the social realities" of the day[3] and he "exposed the vices and weakness of royalist feudal France and described its death agony with magnificent poetic vigour."[4]

Reading the European Novel to 1900: A Critical Study of Major Fiction from Cervantes' Don Quixote *to Zola's* Germinal, First Edition. Daniel R. Schwarz.
© 2014 John Wiley & Sons, Ltd. Published 2014 by John Wiley & Sons, Ltd.

Both Balzac and Stendhal cynically observe a culture bereft of values and principles. As in Stendhal, who also is writing about post–Napoleonic France in *The Red and the Black*, feelings and emotions in *Père Goriot* are for sale and become materialized into monetary value and/or social and political rank. While Stendhal's plots depend on unexpected reversals and are less realistic and more dependent on the uncanny than meets the eye, Balzac's plots tend to realism. Yet Lukács is right that Stendhal's world view owes much to the Enlightenment, whereas Balzac has troubles getting beyond "mystic Catholicism" and "political monarchism."[5]

Yet Balzac was a nascent capitalist. Always in debt, Balzac himself wrote for money; because he was paid according to length, revision meant expansion. *Père Goriot* began as a short story about how two selfish daughters brought their father to ruin. Expanded, it accommodates Vautrin's story and the ambitious Eugène de Rastignac's social rise. As the first novel in which *La Comédie humaine* begins to take shape and featuring characters – notably Rastignac, who appears in twenty-two novels, but also Madame de Beauséant and Madame de Langeais who will reappear – it plays a crucial role in the Balzac canon.

Balzac, as Henry James understood in "The Lesson of Balzac," was magnificent in defining the "*conditions* of the creatures with whom he is concerned,"[6] by which James meant the defining social and economic conditions: "what people are with what they do, of what they do with what they are, of the action with the agents, of the medium with the action, of all the parts of the drama with each other."[7] In *Père Goriot*, James believes, Balzac fuses "all the elements of the picture" into a "supreme case of composition, a model of that high virtue that we know as economy of effect, economy of line and touch."[8]

For Lukács, important distinguishing qualities of the great realists' conscious world view are conflicts within the "world seen in their vision," as in the case of Balzac. What emerges is "the real depth of their *Weltanschauung*, their deep ties with the great issues of their time, their sympathy with the sufferings of the people [which] can find adequate expression only in the being and fate of their characters."[9]

Notwithstanding Balzac's reputation for realism, Peter Brooks has rightly stressed his melodramatic representation: "The narrative voice … overtly adopts the breathlessness of melodrama from the opening page."[10] Brooks reminds us that the novel revolves around "a few thunderous and decisive scenes."[11] It is these crucial scenes that dominate the reader's memory, especially those involving Rastignac. Do we ever think about *Père Goriot* without recalling Rastignac's view – through the keyhole – of Goriot melting silver bowls and transforming them into an ingot? Brooks calls *Père Goriot* not a comedy of manners but a "melodrama of manners."[12] To put it another way, Balzac's focus

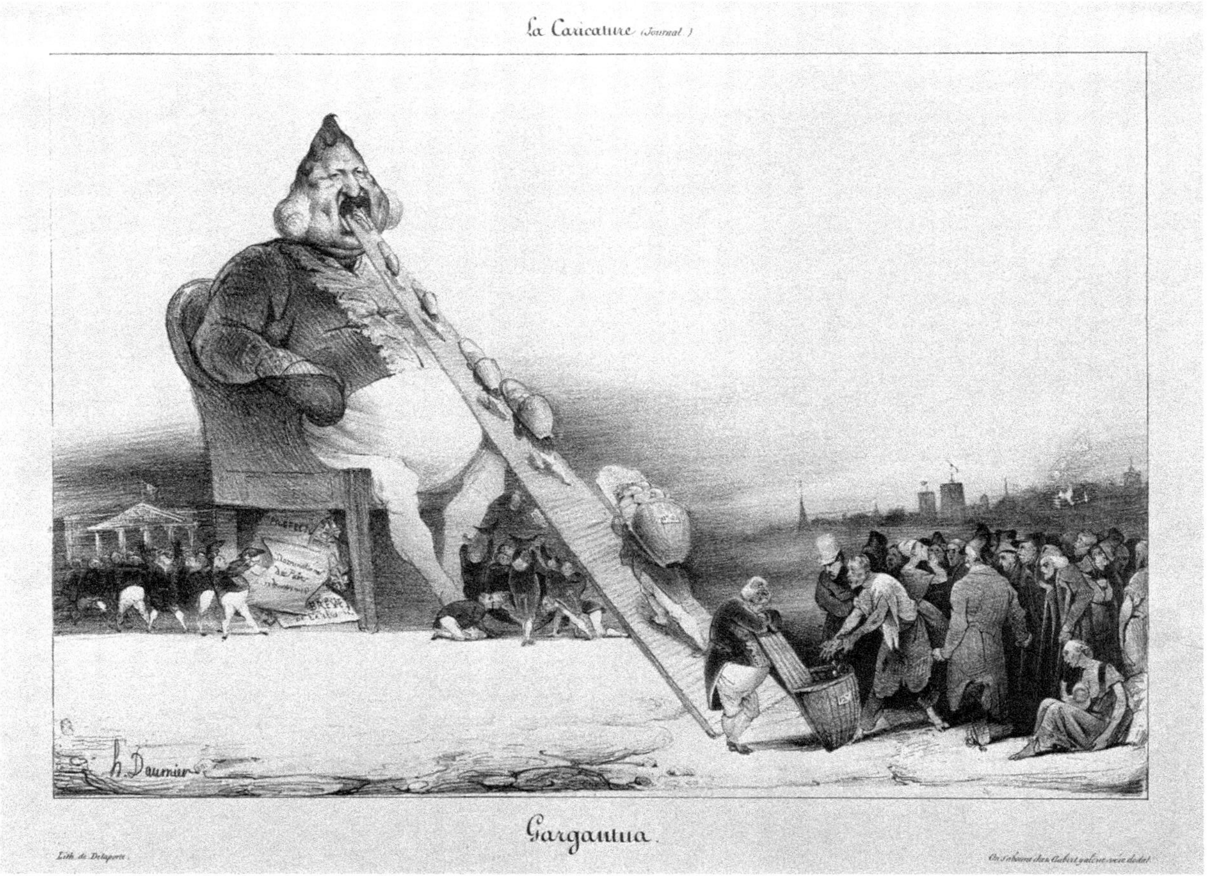

Figure 2 *Daumier's* Gargantua, *lithograph for the newspaper* La Caricature, *1831.*
Source: akg-images

on illuminating distortions of certain details deflects his realism into comic hyperbole with a noir inflection.

Balzac has a strong visual imagination. Like the most innovative painters of his day, he was depicting not religious or even historical subjects but what he saw in contemporary life. Anka Muhlstein observes, "Novelists of the time so clearly recognized their affinity with artists that they would often draw inspiration from a painting or even, in certain cases, from an artistic technique. In Balzac's case, for instance, Baudelaire noted that 'his prodigious taste for detail … forced him however to lay greater emphasis on the most important outlines, in order to preserve the overall perspective.' … Certain of Balzac's caricatural descriptions owe a great debt, by his own admission, to the coded visual language that illustrators and caricaturists frequently employed, incorporating plants and animals in drawing human figures."[13]

Baudelaire no doubt was thinking of Honoré Daumier.[14] Daumier provided Balzac with a model for satirizing Parisians by means of caricature, and his emphasis was on the foibles of the bourgeoisie and the incompetence of an abusive legal system and of self-interested politicians.

Balzac is a polemicist who uses the structure of *Père Goriot* to enact his themes. While he can be ironical, his characteristic style is loud, brash, excessive, and hyperbolic. More often than not, his focal unit is the chapter rather than the elegant and nuanced sentence, but he can provide a striking, crystallizing image. His images are direct – indeed, often in-your- face – and almost the stuff of graphic novels, like the gradual and striking deterioration in Goriot's appearance, his living quarters, and, finally, his health. Take the narrator's focalization of Rastignac's first view of Goriot's room: "The old man lay on a ramshackle bed.… The floor was damp, too, and covered with dust.… The canopy over the bed, attached to the ceiling by a rag, consisted of a faded piece of some cheap red and white checked material.… The chilling comfortlessness of the room wrung the heart; it might have been the most dismal cell in a prison" (III.ii.130–131).[15] The narrator hilariously describes Madame Vauquer dressing up to seduce Père Goriot into marriage: "Fully accoutered and ready for the fray, Madame Vauquer bore an undeniable resemblance to a well-known advertisement for boiled beef" (I.ii.26–27). (Probably Balzac's original audience would have had a more specific reference point, but we think of the usually parsimonious landlady serving herself up as a tasty meal.) Indeed, one can imagine the graphic novelist Art Spiegelman doing illustrations for an edition of *Père Goriot*.

Balzac is a realist, but he is also a precursor of modernist multiple perspective. Indeed, Balzac is more a precursor to Cubism – in which several perspectives coexist – than has been noticed. Coexisting in *Père Goriot* with realism are set melodramatic scenes where husbands and wives trick one another into doing their bidding. Passion rather than reason rules behavior, although passion often takes the form less of love than of a competitive zeal to gain one's ends, as when Rastignac uses Delphine – and even the modest means of his sisters and mother – to achieve his economic goals.

Cutting up and rearranging the ingredients of the plot enabled Balzac not only to postpone revealing secrets, but also to keep each character – and the reader – from quite seeing the whole as it unfolds. Instead we have diverse and limited perspectives at any one moment. Each character's perspective takes place in a limited time and space and almost completely excludes the time and space of others. The narrator only resolves the various perspectives in a partially unified vision at the end.

The reader is a voyeur and an eavesdropper. "The busy reader" becomes complicit by his or her interest in this world and by seeing parallels to his or her own foibles and aspirations. Just as Vautrin and Rastignac spy on Goriot, just as every character is watching the others, so we as readers are peeping through the keyhole with the narrator (I.i.12).

While there is an ironic distance between the narrator's point of view and that of Rastignac, Goriot, and even Vautrin, we also see the world to some degree through each of their limited points of view. We might say that Rastignac looking through a keyhole at Goriot is a crystallizing image of how we see only very partial and limited truths.

Balzac is a detective novelist who withholds information from his readers. He based Vautrin on Eugène François Vidocq, a confidence man turned criminologist and detective whose memoirs included his criminal exploits. But Balzac is also a sentimental novelist who can wrench every ounce of pathos out of a scene; a good example is when Goriot is dying and feels his cherished locket – containing the hair of his wife and the names of his daughters, Anastasie and Delphine – upon his chest (VI.268).

In terms of genre, *Père Goriot* is also a novel of manners manqué in that Balzac's text plays against the conventions of that genre. For what remains of manners in the higher social spheres is a hypocritical and superficial social plane where money is the driving force.

Balzac dramatizes how, in Brooks's words, "the upper social sector is dependent on exploitation of the lower, the surface dependent on the sinister and sordid thing behind."[16] That sinister and sordid thing is Madame Vauquer's boarding house and the secrets that live there in the persons of Goriot, Vautrin, and Victorine Taillefer. What ties these figures together is their frightening aloneness; no matter how desperately they seek connections, they are dependent on themselves. Victorine Taillefer's rejection by her father parallels the rejection of Goriot by his daughters. Together, these dysfunctional families undermine the traditional family paradigm as a source of order.

In *Père Goriot* characters do not evolve psychologically but, rather, are relatively consistent. Features of characters are brought out by social and economic conditions. More than in English novels, vice and virtue – in the rare times we see virtue – are functions of social and economic circumstances.

Paris

Paris is perhaps the major character, a living organism, where people of diverse social classes coexist, sometimes in the same neighborhoods due to their economic circumstances. In 1819, the population of Paris was about half a million and the railroad network, which later would bring a major population shift, did not yet exist. In one sense its various thoroughfares – from narrow twisting streets in the medieval center to extravagant entrances to palaces – and diverse neighborhoods are the story.

Balzac's noir vision of Paris and of the shortcomings of human behavior dominate *Père Goriot*. Even Goriot, who made his money by exorbitant pricing, is not a paradigm. Under the sway of Paris mores, Rastignac unlearns moral character and increasingly puts guilt on the back burner. His ambition to rise by manipulating the social hierarchy takes the place of hard work. Notwithstanding occasional protestations of love and occasional solicitous interest in others on the part of a few characters in the world of *Père Goriot*, greed trumps sentiment and social pretensions and vanity trump decency.

Like Dostoevsky, Balzac understood that the seemingly indifferent and anonymous city was a self-generating text with a plethora of individual stories. For Balzac, one can almost say that Paris was a novel waiting to be written, and his *La Comédie humaine* or *Human Comedy* was his reading of it. With his sharp eye for the crystallizing details of Paris life, he only needed to look and listen to what was happening, season his observations with his imagination, and select and arrange them into narrative units. What he then needed to do was piece together these individual tales into a whole, much as Paris itself had unity composed of its vast array of characters.

While offering promises of prosperity and upward mobility – and for some fulfillment of those promises – for the most part cities in the early nineteenth century were often impersonal, dark, dank, dirty, demonic, and dangerous places. For most of its denizens, the city was an impersonal juggernaut and a socially dysfunctional space breeding physical disease and emotional dissonance. Trouble in the form of violent criminals and petty swindlers lurks in every corner. In Balzac's Paris, as in Dostoevsky's St. Petersburg, one finds loneliness, heartbreak, marginalization, poverty, breakdown of family ties, indifference, and cynicism, as well as opportunity, especially for the unscrupulous.

Loyalty, human affection, and even, as in Goriot's case, family ties take a back seat to self-interest.

We recall Rastignac's famous dare to the city: "A nous deux maintenant!" ("Between us two now!"). Somewhat ironically, his first act of defiance, rather than a bold, imaginative, and transformative action of the kind associated with Napoleon, is a limited act of social climbing, namely, dining at the home of Madame de Nucingen.[17]

Bringing diverse groups together in a limited space, the city has the potential for vast conflict and social disharmony, even as it requires social cooperation to make it work. As Lewis Mumford argues in *The Culture of Cities*:

. . . .

The city in its complete sense, then, is a geographic plexus, an economic organization, an institutional process, a theater of social action, and an esthetic symbol of collective unity. On one hand it is a physical frame for the commonplace domestic and economic activities; on the other, it is a consciously dramatic setting for the more significant actions and the more sublimated urges of a human culture. The city fosters art and *is* art; the city creates the theater and *is* the theater. It is in the city, the city as theater, that man's more purposive activities are formulated and worked out, through conflicting and cooperating personalities, events, groups, into more significant culminations.[18]

. . . .

For Balzac, as for Dostoevsky and later Joyce, the city is theater and spectacle and his narrator is the observer. We may think of the early nineteenth-century city as a site of pollution, overpopulation, and urban chaos, but we must not forget the metropolis was also regarded in the nineteenth century as a source of promise and wonder. Walter Benjamin has written, "The City is reflected in a thousand eyes, a thousand lenses ... Mirrors are the immaterial element of the city, her emblem."[19] Balzac's narrator has those eyes, those mirrors, but he materializes often into a voyeur, an observer, casting a judgmental gaze on the city.

Balzac understood the competitive social and economic scrum that underlies the modern city. To signify that Paris is a moral maelstrom wrapped in secret arrangements, Balzac envelops Paris in fog. Indeed, the opening of Chapter iv anticipates the opening of Dickens's *Bleak House*. After Rastignac returns from his first ball, "The next morning Paris was cloaked in one of the thick fogs that envelop and darken it so completely" (I.iv.42).

At breakfast that very morning at Madame Vauquer's, Vautrin – using Goriot's elder daughter Madame de Restaud's social ascendance and financial parasitism as his point of departure – observes: "Last night at the top of the wheel, at a duchess's.... This morning at the bottom of the ladder, at a moneylender's. That's the women of Paris for you. If their husbands can't keep them in insane luxury, they sell themselves.... There's nothing they won't do. I know them" (I.iv.49). This comment by Vautrin informs the entire novel. Those with a strong acquisitive spirit are the most likely to flourish. Sharpsters like Vautrin – a Runyonesque character living on his wits – prey upon one another. Others like Rastignac substitute social climbing for hard work as the key to upward mobility.

Yet the city is also about the possibility of transformation and exhilaration. To succeed one must learn its rules. As Rastignac writes his mother: "I can't manage without the tools they use to work the vines in these parts" (II.ii.88); the tools are money. Like Goriot's daughters – for whom Goriot pimps – one can reinvent oneself chameleon-like no matter what one's family background.

Balzac's Narrator

Balzac's omniscient narrator does not give away his story completely, although he gives us hints, as when Goriot's daughters visit. Incredibly cynical, the narrator knows and reveals the worst about everyone. He has a generally dark view of human nature that sometimes takes the form of black humor:

. . . .

> Madame Vauquer ... was like many people who distrust their own family and yet will confide in the first stranger they meet.... There are also some individuals, born ungenerous, who cannot be kind to their friends or relatives because they would be fulfilling a duty thereby; whereas if they are kind to a stranger, they feel an increase of self-respect. The nearer people are to them, the less they like them; the farther away they are, the more willing they are to help them. In Madame Vauquer both of these essentially shabby, false, and despicable natures were combined. (I.ii.27–28)

. . . .

Balzac saw himself as a social conservative who disdained his grasping, materialistic characters. But when Vautrin demeans Lafayette because Lafayette proposed the first version of *The Declaration of the Rights of Man and Citizen* that undermined the old order, we wonder where Balzac's sympathies lay (III.i.113–114). And the answer is complex. For we realize that Balzac enjoys watching Rastignac climb the social ladder and sometimes even revels in the machinations of such scoundrels as Vautrin, a kind of flâneur who "knew the ways of a lot of ... things," including "prisons" (I.i.19).

Does not the narrator – Balzac's surrogate – imply that he knows both the lower- and upper-class worlds and has earned this hard-edged wisdom from a lifetime of disillusionment? As readers, we often find that we are torn between nodding – and at times almost in spite of ourselves smiling – in complete agreement, and trying to demur from some of his mean-spirited observations. The narrator warns us that "the reader's mind must be prepared by dark colors and solemn thoughts: he must be made to feel like the traveler going down into the catacombs ... [of] withered hearts [and] empty skulls" (I.i.9). The catacombs are an appropriate image for Madame Vauquer's boarding house – a metonymy for the outré social echelons of Paris – in which people and their past are buried, and the narrator accompanies our "travels" through the catacombs. Put another way, Balzac's Paris is a version of Dante's Inferno and the narrator is our guide.

Balzac's narrative surrogate is angry and indicts his readers for indifference as if they were responsible for the moral cannibalism he describes. In the second person, he describes the reader as sharing indifference to outrages within their midst: "No! Realize this: This drama is not an invention; it is not a novel. 'All is true.' It is so true that you can see hints of it in your own homes, in your own hearts perhaps" (I.i.8). In French Balzac uses the formal "vous" rather than the intimate "tu." Two characters confirm the narrator's cynical view of the world: Vautrin, who is cynical from the outset, and Eugène de Rastignac, who gradually in this ironic *Bildungsroman* grows into the perspective the narrator holds from the outset. Rastignac oscillates between two very different father figures. He embraces Goriot as father and cares for him, but it is the rascal Vautrin whom Rastignac follows as a father figure, even though early on he had told Vautrin, "This Paris of yours ... is nothing but a cesspool" (I.iv.51). As much as Rastignac is at first repelled by Vautrin, Vautrin becomes his teacher and surrogate father, teaching him that money is what matters and that the rich pay little attention to either law or morality. That the criminal and even Mephistophelian Vautrin is right about human motives is one of the most disturbing aspects of *Père Goriot*. We want him to be wrong and we want to be repelled but we are not. As Pierre Barbaris puts it, "What makes no sense to others is perfectly clear to him."[20]

We should be aware of the narrator's switch not only to the present tense but even to the future tense as he predicts behavior that he regards as all but inevitable to render Eugène de Rastignac's participation in the superficial mores of Parisian social life, a period when "he will be filled with enthusiasm for frivolities that seem momentous.... These successive initiation ceremonies bring him out of his shell; his horizons widen, and he begins to distinguish the strata that compose human society" (I.iii.35). Of course, looking to the future depends on the narrator's knowledge of the completed story that he is unfolding in a series of episodes for the reader.

Indeed, Rastignac's education makes the novel a *Bildungsroman*, although it is an ironic version in which the protagonist's morality declines as his experience increases. Losing "his boyhood illusions, ... his provincial outlook" means entering a world in which he is attentive to social distinctions and social classes (I.iii.35). He abandons the ideal of "mak[ing] his way by his own unaided efforts…. He had observed how strong the influence of women was in social life…. Surely they would be forthcoming for a young man whose native wit and enthusiasm were reinforced by a smart appearance and just the degree of virile handsomeness that women so easily find attractive?" (I.iii.36). His ambition now takes the form of "great social conquest," which basically means sexual conquest (I.iii.37). He does resist taking advantage of Vautrin's having Victorine's brother killed, but that may be more because of his obsession with Goriot's daughter, Delphine, than from any moral scruples.

The Opening

Openings are a novel's Genesis, a beginning in which we see, ex nihilo, the creation of a world that is new to us.

The first chapters of *Père Goriot* open into an imagined world in which almost every sentence is informed by the social class and economic situation of a character. In Balzac's imagined world, social class and economic situation may be, as in the case of the title character, who is almost destitute but comes from a good family, quite different. Balzac's narrator cynically demonstrates that what matters is not the morality of how one behaves but where a character is located on the economic and social ladder.

The first chapter introduces Madame Vauquer's seedy boarding house – a "respectable establishment … no adverse comment has ever been made about its morals" (I.i.7) – although we learn that the house, in a rundown area of Paris between the Latin Quarter and the Faubourg Saint-Marceau, has more than its share of scoundrels and selfish boarders as well as Madame Vauquer herself.

Madame Vauquer's boarding house is located "between the hill of Montmartre and the heights of Montrouge … [in] that valley where suffering is always real and joy very often false, and the everyday turmoil so grim that it is difficult to imagine any catastrophe producing more than a momentary sensation there" (I.i.7). The house is in the grimmest possible area: "In the whole of Paris there is no district more hideous" (I.i.9). It hides secrets that polite society doesn't want to acknowledge, and gives identity to those who wish to remain anonymous as they unscrupulously prey upon others. Put another way, Madame Vauquer's house contains a microcosm of a world that polite society doesn't want to know.

Beginning with the narrator's description of Madame Vauquer, who treats her lodgers according to how much they pay, Balzac makes money almost a character: "[T]he care and attention she allotted to each of them were regulated with an astronomer's precision according to the amount they paid" (I.i.15). Balzac's characters and narrator are obsessed with francs: the luxuries that francs purchase, how much each person makes, and the financial arrangements of every potential business deal. For the narrator, everything is measured in francs; this perspective is shared from the outset by Vautrin and Madame Vauquer (note the similarity in their names as well as their close relationship) and one to which Rastignac is gradually educated.

Père Goriot's first chapter, with its undisclosed secrets and its metaphor of the house as a prison, anticipates what is to follow. Goriot is saved for last by the narrator. Selling flour at exorbitant prices during the French Revolution, Goriot has made his money in less than an admirable way. But because Goriot is an afterthought for his children and regarded by his fellow lodgers with a mixture of "malevolent scorn" mingled with "persecution and pity," we are sympathetic to him.

To an extent, do we not become ambivalent about leering into the grotesque world that Balzac satirizes with dramatic ferocity, whether it be the upper classes or the outsider world of Madame Vauquer's boarding house? In the opening pages, Balzac's characters are exotic, invidious, and demonic, but they are also metaphors for a downtrodden part of the population of Paris. Given that the residents of the boarding house are presented as inhabitants of a human zoo, we may even bridle at the narrator's arch iconoclasm. The narrator looks at the world he describes in this chapter – the ugliness of the furnishings, the meagerness of the lodging, the grim location of the house itself – from a disapproving and even patronizing vantage point. Yet we do share the narrator's righteous indignation at the plight of Goriot, whom he saves for last among Madame Vauquer's boarders.

Not far behind in Balzac's targets of satire is class-consciousness. Snobbery permeates virtually every social interaction. Ever cynical, the narrator revels in human comedy – selfishness, self-delusion, greed, psychosis, fixations, compulsions, and dimly acknowledged needs and motives – without using contemporary psychological language.

In Maison Vauquer, the inhabitants are all socially marginalized but they rent different kinds of space, some relatively more comfortable than others. The rooms that characters inhabit – and even how they enter and leave rooms – become telling indications of their character as well as their stature. Goriot's stature – always morally compromised by the way he made his fortune as Chairman of his District during the Revolution, selling flour at ten times what he paid for it (II.i.80) – declines as he moves into smaller quarters and his circumstances become strapped. By 1819, he is sixty-eight years old. Because Goriot showed no romantic interest in Madame Vauquer and because his economic circumstances continued to decline, he became an object of ridicule, in large part due to her: "Outraged at finding that he could not be attacked directly, she fell back on disparaging him to his fellow boarders, persuading them to share her dislike for him; and for their amusement they served her lust for revenge" (I.ii.29).

Here and elsewhere Balzac is a master at exposing human meanness and nastiness. His narrator's anger can rise to a fever pitch unalleviated by playfulness. Speaking of Madame Vauquer, whom he detests especially for her treatment of Goriot, with whom for the most part he is sympathetic, he remarks: "It is one of the meanest habits of pygmy minds to attribute their own meanness to other people" (I.ii.29). The narrator becomes judgmental when showing Goriot's naïveté in letting himself become a self-abnegating economic slave to his daughters.

Inhabiting the same boarding house, Rastignac and Goriot begin in a world defined by demeaning poverty but one in which the basics are provided. However, the rereader knows there is a level far below this one. Rastignac's rise is juxtaposed with Goriot's decline. One of Balzac's major themes is mutability. Mostly in response to who has money, the wheel of fortune keeps turning, moving some up and others down.

Indeed, Goriot has been deprived of his very name. The residents of Maison Vauquer speak of "m'lord Goriette" and a particularly dense Paris fog as a "Goriorama … [Y]ou couldn't see through it" (I.iv.55). Madame de Langeais, far up the social ladder, cannot remember his name and in one brief conversation confuses "Goriot" with Foriot, Loriot, Moriot, and Doriot as if to indicate that he no longer exists as a human being but has become a series of variable and inconsequential sounds. As she put it, "Old Doriot would have been nothing more than a grease spot in his daughters' drawing rooms" (II.i.81; also see II.i.80).

Beginning with the detailed description of Madame Vauquer's house, objects have a life of their own in determining meaning; often they become extensions of their owner. An example is the silver ingots that Goriot melts from his possessions; to his children he becomes interchangeable with portable wealth and his functionality as a source of money is what matters.

Rereading, one appreciates the novel's taut structure and how much of the entire novel is embedded in the brilliant first chapter, including how the narrator's anger, irony, and cynicism shape the telling. The novel itself – and Paris – is an extension of the issues presented in the first chapter. Madame Vauquer presides over her house: "To put it briefly, unpoetic poverty reigns here; pinched, concentrated, threadbare poverty" (I.i.12). Of Madame Vauquer's boarding house the narrator says, "The prison cannot be run without a jailer" and speaks distastefully of her "unwholesome corpulence" (I.i.13).

Erich Auerbach has stressed how Madame Vauquer is an image of and is imaged by her social milieu.[21] She and her dining room become metonymies for one another. Her face and body "are all of a piece with the reeking misery of the room, where all hope and eagerness have been extinguished and whose stifling, fetid air she alone can breathe without being sickened…. [H]er whole person … explains the house, as the house implies her person. The prison cannot be run without a jailer" (I.i.12–13). The prison metaphor recurs in the text, and often, we realize, refers to self-imprisonment by selfish, self-deluding, venal characters, whether they live in poverty or luxury.

Madame Vauquer's home is a metonymy not only for her social milieu but also for impersonal and cold Paris, which is depicted as a prison of cynicism, selfishness, snobbery, opportunism, and materialism. Rereading, we see that the novel, too, becomes a prison in which the dark human comedy takes place, presided over by the narrator as a kind of warden.

As a new resident of the boarding house, a tutor observes after Goriot dies, one can live without anyone knowing or caring, unless someone makes an effort to find out: "One privilege we have in the good city of Paris is that we can be born, live, and die here, without anyone ever noticing. We must make the most of the advantages of civilization" (VI.271). That those "advantages of civilization" are the tutor's evening meal at Madame Vauquer's table demonstrates how the cycle of pettiness and selfishness is perpetuating itself.

Rereading brings into focus the dense metaphorical structure that reinforces the plot. We have mentioned the pervasive fogs that "envelop and darken" Paris and represent virulent ethical obfuscation. But we might consider the narrator's image of Rastignac as a circus performer walking a tightrope, which hints, too, at how he is performing for an audience of a higher social class that doesn't care about who he really is: "To walk the tightrope and feel so certain of your acrobatic skill that you can give the rope a superb kick, with such a charming woman as your balancing pole" (I.iii.39).

Each of the characters, not just young Rastignac, is an acrobat walking the tightrope of life, always in danger of falling off, whether it be materially or sexually, as is the case with Madame de Restaud's husband, who puts up with her lover Maxime. Economically supported by his nearly destitute parents, Rastignac is something of a cynical social capitalist from the outset, trading on what little he has in terms of means and the bit more he has in terms of relationships to the class to which he aspires to belong. Rastignac learns there are many currencies, including beauty and sexuality.

Amorality in *Père Goriot*

Vautrin – whose real name is Jacques Collin, alias Trompe-la-Mort – is a pre-Dostoevskian character who proudly embraces amorality. Very much like the Underground Man and Raskolnikov, he prides himself on flouting moral convention, although Vautrin does not clothe his cynicism in idealism. The

Machiavellian and homosexual Vautrin most often invokes God but is actually depicted as a Satanic tempter.

Within Balzac's novel, is there a moral compass, a character who succeeds by virtue? We might answer, "The narrator." But by giving much of the novel's energy to Vautrin's Machiavellian plotting and mischief-making, the narrator becomes, whether Balzac intended it or not, a surrogate for the unscrupulous and cynical Vautrin. Like the narrator, Vautrin "knew, or had guessed, the secrets of everyone in the place; his own thoughts and activities no one could fathom" (I.i.20).

Knowledge is power and knowing "secrets," a frequently repeated word – about who sleeps with whom, who has money and who owes money, about wills – is power. Everyone has his or her secret, beginning with the inhabitants of the Vauquer boarding house, but no less so in the aristocracy.

Vautrin knows secrets that he can exploit for his profit. Rastignac, learning from Vautrin how to manipulate his opportunities, discovers Goriot's secret: "To be perfectly sure of the terrain before attempting his advance on the house of Nucingen, Rastignac needed to know all about Goriot's earlier life. Such reliable information as he managed to collect may be briefly summarized" (II.ii.91). And then the narrator gives us Goriot's history.

Rastignac is caught between, on the one hand, Vautrin, a pure criminal who becomes a surrogate father figure, and, on the other hand, hypocritical women who betray their husbands and for whom luxury, idleness, and sexual play are the components of life. Vautrin cynically asserts: "[S]tick to your opinions as little as you stick to your words.... Principles don't exist, only events. Laws don't exist, only circumstances. The intelligent man weds himself to them in order to control them" (III.i.113). Where is the alternative within Balzac's imagined world to Vautrin's predatory survival of the fittest morality? Surely not in Goriot's psychosis in which he trades everything – including, finally, his life – in the hopes of being loved by his daughter in whose life he pathetically tries to participate. He gives all for love and gets nothing in return. Does Balzac show us an alternative to Vautrin's view of Paris as a place where "Corruption flourishes, talent is rare.... In Paris, an honest man is one who keeps his mouth shut, and takes and doesn't share" (III.i.109–110)?

When Vautrin is revealed as a criminal, the narrator somewhat turns on him: "Collin ... was the epitome of a whole degenerate race, at once savage and calculating, brutal and docile" (IV.iii.196). But before this point Vautrin's reductive morality had been something of a valid position within the novel. After all, his cynical observations about courtship and marriage are validated by the novel's action: "Better to war with men than grapple with a wife" (III.i.108); he also remarks that one way to succeed professionally in Paris is "a wife's dowry" (III.i.108).

Unwilling to take the high road of work and dedication and led astray by the trappings of wealth, Rastignac has tied his kite to social climbing. At first he has no idea how to proceed in this other world, comically choosing the wrong halls in Madame de Restaud's home and ending up in the bathroom instead of the salon. Balzac seems to accept rather than judge Rastignac's decisions as if Rastignac had no real choice if he wanted to succeed economically. Rastignac, who becomes a master of duplicity almost equal to Vautrin as the novel progresses and whose moral stature deteriorates gradually, asks (not without some compunction) his mother and sisters for money without telling the mother he has written the sisters or the sisters that he has written his mother.

Eugène de Rastignac, Goriot, and the Family Manqué

Much of the thematic structure of *Père Goriot* revolves around how children treat parents and how parents treat children, with Goriot being the centerpiece. Taillefer's rejection of Victorine – whose "habitual sadness" and "general misery" (I.i.7) echo Goriot's – because her mother didn't have a dowry contrasts with the boundless and unconditional, and, yes, obsessive, love Goriot has for his daughters. Many family ties have an economic nexus, that is, what parents can provide for children and, implicitly in Goriot's case, vice versa. Rastignac is dependent at the outset on his family eking out 1,200 francs by means of "The constant privation that everyone nobly tried to conceal from him" (I.iii.36).

The novel's rhythm is of continuing rise and fall, economic, social, political, and biological. If the focus of Chapter ii is age – personified by Goriot's increasingly reduced circumstances at age sixty-six – Chapter iii is about youth, hope, and aspiration, personified by Rastignac. Goriot has an "air of stupefaction" and is "stuck at freezing-point" (I.iii.34).

Balzac's subject is greed, pettiness, spitefulness, and nastiness imaged by Paris fog and by the unpleasant setting of Madame Vauquer's boarding house. But what also makes the novel topical is the subject of old age. It is assumed, the narrator notes with bitter irony, that Goriot in his late sixties must be debauched, senile, or incompetent, or all three. He "now looked like a pale, feeble-minded dodderer.... Young medical students, noticing the droop of his lower lip and the significant sharpness of his facial angle ... declared that he was sinking into a state of cretinism" (I.iii.33). That he is in economic decline and lives in "arid poverty" makes these views all the more convincing (I.iii.34).

As the title character, we expect Goriot to be the central figure, but in fact he is more a subtle thread that ties together diverse stories which often foreground Rastignac, Vautrin, and, perhaps, more than any single character, Paris. Thus when Rastignac visits Madame de Restaud, whom does he see but Goriot, her father?

In a parasitic relationship with their father, Goriot's children thrive at his expense. So desperate is he to be loved that he becomes Rastignac's pimp in setting up an adulterous liaison with his younger daughter, Delphine de Nucingen. Indeed, given that he considers Rastignac a surrogate son, his pimping has an incestuous nuance, just as his excessive love for his daughters takes a grotesquely submissive and masochistic shape.

Ungrateful daughters recall Shakespeare's *King Lear*. Goriot had given his daughters material wealth, thinking he would be welcome in their homes, but their husbands turned him out. Lear's words are apt for Goriot's plight: "How sharper than a serpent's tooth it is to have a thankless child" (*King Lear* I.iv.279–280). Goriot has no Cordelia who cares about him, only Regan and Goneril. Lear loses his retainers and wanders about the countryside beset by stormy weather; Goriot moves to smaller and smaller quarters in Madame Vauquer's boarding house. Goriot, like Lear, dies a grim, impoverished death, abandoned by children whose every economic wish he tried to fulfill. He rants, sometimes deliriously, for several pages, oscillating between self-pity and anger. Finally he is buried as a pauper.

Balzac is bemused but also disgusted by human behavior and the depths to which a man may sink. In *Père Goriot*, material considerations disrupt human relationships, undermine family ties, and determine social and political status. Indeed, Balzac not only attributes his epigraph, "All is true," to Shakespeare, but surely expected some of his readers to know that "All is True" was the alternative title of Shakespeare's *Henry VIII*.

As Sandy Petrey writes, "Under the Bourbon Restoration, the nonaristocratic source of their wealth became an intolerable embarrassment to Goriot's daughters. In an effort to conceal their newly unacceptable origins, they first forced their father to give up his life in trade, then tried to hide his existence altogether by refusing to let him be seen with them. Elevated by the Revolution, Goriot was abased by its aftermath."[22] His descent into nonexistence is, as we have seen, underlined by Madame de Langeais's inability to pronounce his name despite Rastignac's insistence.[23]

Is the nature of Balzac's realism to show only the dark side of human nature and to show a world dominated by self-interest, cynicism, and greed? Isn't this a harsh realism that omits human potential for good? Everyone is taking economic advantage of everyone else, and husbands and wives make economic arrangements no different from those of pawnbrokers and money-lenders. Clearly, in *Père Goriot* unregulated capitalism is itself a villain. There is no safety net for poverty and illness.

The reader participates in the repellent process of Rastignac's education to see the world from Vautrin's perspective. At first, Rastignac wants to eschew Vautrin's way of being: "Like all men of character, he wanted to make his way by his own unaided efforts" (I.iii.36). Rereading we see that, with each succeeding chapter of the first six chapters, the narrator is distancing himself from Rastignac, whom he at first gives a partial pass due to his naïveté. In the company of Delphine, "The squandering of his time he disregarded; he was busy absorbing the seductive lessons of luxury.... In almost no time he had adopted the expensive habits of the fashionable young man-about-town" (IV.i.153).

To be sure, his rural relatives represent an alternative, but they are rarely present and seem ingenuous rubes whom he can take advantage of when he needs to raise a little money. To Rastignac's credit, he does pay them back with some gambling winnings and does care for Goriot in his final hours and shows gratitude for Goriot's generosity.

The Ending of *Père Goriot*

Balzac's ending is hardly the conversion to humanistic ethics that we might expect in the *Bildungsroman* genre or in a comedy of manners. In the novel of manners, either the major characters' values are often, as in Jane Austen, brought in line with those of the narrator – that is, they discover their shortcomings (Emma Woodhouse, Elizabeth Bennet) and become more insightful – or they are condemned as unsuitable for the best social and moral universe. Rather than moral education after presiding over Goriot's death and burial, Rastignac seems to learn only hardness and cynicism. In the final sentence the narrator, with considerable irony, observes that Rastignac "went back to dine with Madame de Nucingen," who, we know, has provided him with an apartment (VI.275).

Study Questions for *Père Goriot*

1. How does the first paragraph both engage and distance the reader?
2. How is Paris the main character?
3. Is Balzac more a storyteller whose plot matters than a formalist where every word counts and every episode and character are integrally related? Can a case be made that the first chapter – introducing Madame Vauquer and her boarders – is a masterpiece of significant form crystallizing the entire novel?
4. In spite of Balzac's reputation as a realist, do you think Balzac has a tendency towards hyperbole and exaggeration and a bent towards the melodramatic?
5. How is *Père Goriot* a *Bildungsroman*, if an ironic one? How does the narrator present Rastignac?
6. What is the role and function of money in *Père Goriot*?
7. How does Balzac use comic hyperbole to give Paris a noir aspect?

8. What is Vautrin's role? Are he and Rastignac (both self-inventing, plotting, and staging scenes) surrogates for the author and his narrator?
9. How is the narrator a character? Do we feel his angry judgments and engagement? Is he a secret sharer of Rastignac's amoral behavior?
10. What does the novel say about politics? About economic discrepancies among the rich and poor? About idealism?

Notes

1. Peter Brooks, "Balzac: Representation and Signification," in Honoré de Balzac, *Père Goriot*, trans. Burton Raffel, ed. Peter Brooks (New York: Norton, 1980), 314–328; see p. 318. References to the Norton edition are hereafter cited as *Père Goriot*, Norton.
2. Georg Lukács, *Studies in European Realism* (London: Hillway, 1950), 12.
3. Lukács, *Studies in European Realism*, 10, 12–13.
4. Lukács, *Studies in European Realism*, 10.
5. Lukács, *Studies in European Realism*, 77.
6. *Père Goriot*, Norton, 254.
7. *Père Goriot*, Norton, 255.
8. *Père Goriot*, Norton, 255.
9. Lukács, *Studies in European Realism*, 12–13.
10. Brooks, "Balzac: Representation and Signification," 314.
11. Brooks, "Balzac: Representation and Signification," 315.
12. Brooks, "Balzac: Representation and Signification," 317.
13. Anka Muhlstein, "Paris: The Thrill of the Modern," trans. Anthony Shugaar, *NYR* 60:8 (May 9, 2013), 14–15; see p. 14.
14. See Muhlstein, "Paris: The Thrill of the Modern."
15. All quotations from the text are from Honoré de Balzac, *Père Goriot*, trans. Henry Reed (New York: New American Library, 1962), Signet edition.
16. Brooks, "Balzac: Representation and Signification," 319.
17. See Luc Sante, "In Search of Lost Paris," *NYR* 57:20 (Dec. 23, 2010), 54–57.
18. Lewis Mumford, *The Culture of Cities* (New York: Harcourt Brace and Company, 1938), 480.
19. Walter Benjamin, quoted in *Manet 1832-1883* (New York: Metropolitan Museum of Art, 1983), 481.
20. Pierre Barbaris, "The Discovery of Solitude," *Père Goriot*, Norton, 305.
21. *Père Goriot*, Norton, 282.
22. Sandy Petrey, "The Father Loses a Name: Constative Identity in *Le Père Goriot*," *Père Goriot*, Norton, 329.
23. Petrey, "The Father Loses a Name," 329.

Chapter 5

Flaubert's *Madame Bovary* (1857) and *Sentimental Education* (1869)

The Aesthetic Novel

1. *Madame Bovary*: Literary Form Examining Provincial Manners and Desire

Introduction

Gustave Flaubert (1821–1880) brought to literary realism scrupulous aesthetic control and polish exceeding that of his predecessors. That every sentence – even every word – of *Madame Bovary* (1857) throws a slightly new light on what he is describing and resonates with other sentences and words makes it a paradigm of organic unity. Flaubert's eye for detail and his quest for the exact and precise word enable the reader to know the central characters intimately and to understand how and why they interact with others in the small worlds in which they live. Clearly such a nuanced style is a challenge for the translator.

James Wood insightfully observes: "Flaubert is able to achieve his two contradictory ambitions, to write on the one hand fiction that is densely detailed, densely involved with matter, and on the other hand fiction without matter.... His prose will not register emotionally what it depicts visually.... [By contrast, in Balzac] the emphasis is always on the abundance rather than intense selectivity of detail."[1]

Reading the European Novel to 1900: A Critical Study of Major Fiction from Cervantes' Don Quixote *to Zola's* Germinal, First Edition. Daniel R. Schwarz.
© 2014 John Wiley & Sons, Ltd. Published 2014 by John Wiley & Sons, Ltd.

Much like his contemporary Edouard Manet (1832–1883), who was often more interested in the act of painting – composition, colors, degree of paint thickness – than what he painted, Flaubert at times seems more interested in the act of writing – word choice, structure, pace, narrative distance, and irony – than his subjects.

Flaubert and Manet have much in common. Both are keen observers of how humans behave. Manet's oeuvre displays his exuberant response to the variety of French contemporary life: its range of classes, its stories of seeming insignificance, its energy, and its complexity. Like Flaubert, Manet sees the spontaneity and compulsiveness of human behavior – including its ugliness and foolishness – and he understands the human impulse for self-survival in an indifferent cosmos. Like Flaubert, Manet delights in the physical presence and quirks of his human figures and deftly balances sympathy with objectivity and irony. Like Flaubert, Manet depicts outsiders, the disadvantaged, and lower classes with gusto, and he does so without moralizing or pontificating. Like Flaubert, he explores various possibilities that thwart, offend, and undermine bourgeois family values. Probably Flaubert is the more cynical of the two.

In *Le Déjeuner sur l'herbe*, the naked woman is unselfconsciously looking away from her companions, perhaps to catch the attention of other men or women who are not within the scene, including us observers. Manet freed the female – here hardly a classical nude – from any pretense of idealism, placed her clearly in the realm of sexuality, and did so without sentimentalizing her. Cannot one say the same of Flaubert?

For Manet and Flaubert, technique is often pre-eminent. Especially in *Salammbô* (1862) and *Sentimental Education* (1869), Flaubert has an ironic detached interest in human behavior to the extent that we can say, again like Manet, that there is no subject that Flaubert does not aestheticize and turn into a technical tour de force, even if empathy and sympathy are sacrificed. For that reason there is something hard in his response to human foibles in *Madame Bovary* and even more so in *Sentimental Education*.[2]

More than any other writer discussed in this volume, Flaubert conceived the novel as an artistic creation and paved the way for James, Proust, Joyce, and Woolf. He once remarked: "What seems beautiful to me, what I should like to write, is a book about nothing, a book dependent on nothing external, which would hold up on its own by the internal strength of its style, just as the earth, with no support, holds up in the air."[3]

Flaubert's self-consciousness about the novel anticipates James's seminal essay "The Art of Fiction" and his Prefaces to the New York Edition. His letters tell us how burdensome a labor the writing of *Madame Bovary* was and

Figure 3 Edouard Manet, Le Déjeuner sur l'herbe, 1863, oil on canvas. Musée d'Orsay, Paris.
Source: akg-images/Erich Lessing

how each sentence demanded excruciating effort. According to Stephen Heath, for Flaubert art is "proposed as sole possible fulfilment, sole possible truth to which one therefore owes exclusive commitment.… Hence the story of the novel is also the story of its writing in a quite unprecedented way.… [H]e is living in and through and for words, the right words, suffering in solitude a whole martyrdom of creation. In his correspondence during the years of composition, he details in page after page, letter after letter, his torments as a writer."[4] Flaubert thought the future of art lay in "a book which would have almost no subject, or at least in which the subject would be almost invisible."[5] As Heath puts it, for Flaubert, "Art has priority over life, style is the term of this, the transformation of the real, but also an object in itself.… If Flaubert can refer to *Madame Bovary* as an 'exercise,' it is inasmuch as it represents what he understands as a deliberate movement from the personal to the impersonal, from lyric flow to the hard muscle of making sentences, achieving style."[6]

Flaubert's Satire of Provincial Behavior

The subtitle of *Madame Bovary* is *Provincial Manners* (*Moeurs du province*), which to Flaubert signified uncouth behavior, narrow-mindedness, and lack of imagination, as well as an outlook hopelessly grounded in day-to-day reality, materialism, and self-advancement. In this regard he was influenced by Balzac. Money and financial transaction are important in the novel's imagined world; as Heath put it the "economy of money" "in this ordinary, middle-class, mediocre *petit-bourgeois* world" where money is the promise of opportunity and money wields power.[7] Emma Bovary flouts the economic values that dominate life in her world and suffers for it; she is a reckless spendthrift and denies herself little. She and Charles marry for love, whereas Charles in his first marriage, like his father, married in part for money.

Flaubert's father was a Rouen doctor and Flaubert himself was brought up in the residential wing of the hospital. Today we forget that, before penicillin and other antibiotics, hospitals were more often places to die than places from which patients returned home, healed and ready to resume their lives. Flaubert suffered from nervous disorders, probably undiagnosed epilepsy, and was considered something of an invalid. He never married but did have an eight-year affair with Louise Colet (the subject of Francine Du Plessix Gray's *Rage and Fire: A Life of Louise Colet, Pioneer Feminist, Literary Star, Flaubert's Muse*) while she was married – one of her several affairs – and she was in part the inspiration for Emma Bovary.

What Does Emma Want and Need?

Emma's story is in the vanitas tradition so prominent in seventeenth-century Dutch painting. She lurches from feeling to feeling in an increasingly erratic pattern of expansion and contraction. As she becomes disappointed with her lover Léon, who is after all only a clerk, her imagination – like her sexuality and her material needs – becomes more and more inflamed and less anchored in her day-to-day reality: "But suppose there existed somewhere some one strong and beautiful, a man of valor, passionate yet refined, the heart of a poet in the form of an angel, a bronze stringed lyre, playing elegiac epithalamia to the heavens, why might she not someday happen on him?" (III.vi.206).[8]

The more her insatiable need for sensation is seemingly satisfied, the more she craves. Even as her fantasy reaches towards ecstasy, she deflates it as if she were moving from sexual arousal to post-coital deflation without fulfillment. Finally her curse is cynicism derived from boredom, for in the sentence that follows the one I just quoted, she thinks: "Besides, nothing was worth the trouble of seeking it; everything was a lie" (III.vi.206).

Madame Bovary has a thematic structure stressing that sex separate from love and affection whets the appetite it is meant to sate. Emma becomes increasingly obsessed with her lover Léon and thinks of having him followed (III.vi.205). Everything seems a failed fancy to her: "Every smile concealed a yawn of boredom, every joy a curse, every pleasure its own disgust, and the sweetest kisses left upon your lips only the unattainable desire for a greater delight" (III.vi.206). The "your" in this passage firmly places these thoughts within Emma's interior monologue but also looks beyond so as to implicate the voyeuristic reader in her disappointment.

Rereaders are often surprised at how quickly Emma is dissatisfied with her marriage and how Flaubert's narrator presents many early indications of her restlessness, boredom, and disappointment with married life. After Chapter I.iv in which she gets married and Chapter I.v when she discovers that she was mistaken to think she had been in love with Charles, the narrator takes us back in time to when Emma was an adolescent in the convent school and reveled in the mystic sensuousness of her religiosity before becoming disillusioned and bored. No sooner is she married than she begins to feel "undefinable uneasiness" (I.vii.29) and to realize what a plain and unsophisticated man she has married.

In the Norton edition translation by Paul de Man from which my quotations come, Emma's disappointed view of Charles is rendered by the narrator in terms appropriate to her reductive, dismissive thoughts: "Charles's conversation was commonplace as a street pavement, and every one's ideas trooped through it in their everyday garb, without exciting emotion, laughter, or thought" (I.vii.29). Ironically Charles, a narcissist in his own right, doesn't have a clue about his wife's feelings, and rises "in his own esteem for possessing such a wife" (I.vii.30).

Charles is humorless and bland, dresses very much like he talks, and has little flash. Emma's perceptions of him only confirm what we readers know from the narrator, who begins the novel as a boy describing Charles's entry into the narrator's classroom: "We were in class when the headmaster came in, followed by a new boy.... [H]e was very ill at ease" (I.i.1). It is worth noting that by defining himself as an acquaintance of Charles, the narrator puts himself not only within the bourgeois world of the characters, but also within the physical environs where the novel takes place.

Emma is a sensualist who feels life has dealt her an unfair hand. In current terms, she is depressed. But in terms of nineteenth-century concepts of character, what she lacks as a wife are loyalty and fidelity. She shows only intermittent interest in her child, whom sometimes she regards as an encumbrance. She detests her husband, whom she calls "this creature" and whom she believes "understood nothing, … felt nothing!" (II.xi.133). The more he dotes on her, the less she loves him. Soon after marriage, the narrator poignantly understates: "But as the intimacy of their life became deeper, the greater became the gulf that kept them apart" (I.vii.29). Here "intimacy" has a sexual connotation; the more sex they have, the less they love or understand each other.

Georges Poulet pointed out more than fifty years ago the way that Emma's consciousness tends to contract.[9] What needs to be stressed is how this contraction reflects her fundamental narcissism. She can never be satisfied by what she has, and in every quest for something new, she fails because she takes her dissatisfied craving self with her. Beginning with her dissatisfaction with the wedding plans – she "would … have preferred to have a midnight wedding with torches" (I.iii.18) – she exhibits a restless temperament that cannot find repose or equilibrium.

While a resistant reader might with some sympathy for Emma observe that provincial society has no place for this woman, no way for her to fulfill herself in a profession or to find her calling artistically or intellectually, Flaubert makes clear that she has significant failings. To be sure, we are aware that her father disposed of her to a limited, unimaginative boor, but Flaubert ask us readers to wonder if her sexuality and wanderlust could be contained within any marriage.

For Flaubert, personality as well as character is fate. Emma is unable to deal with day-to-day reality; her imagination continually betrays her, substituting what-might-have-been and what-might-be for reality. She is often seized by envy, restlessness, and disappointment with her circumstances and marriage.

Flaubert's narrator understands that something is missing in Emma, and she is an empty vessel with no chance of filling her emptiness. Flaubert sees evil as the absence of good; something is lacking in her which prevents her "find[ing] out what one meant exactly in life by the words *bliss, passion, ecstasy*, that had seemed to her so beautiful in books" (I.v.24, Flaubert's italics).

Rodolphe, her first lover, recalls Alec d'Urberville and Emma recalls Anna Karenina. He is a one-dimensional rake who, the narrator lets us know from his first appearance, is up to no good. His "brutality of temperament" is illustrated by his thoughts of discarding his present mistress when he meets Emma Bovary, whom he – "having had much experience with women and being something of a connoisseur" – thinks of as "one [who] had seemed pretty to him" (II.vii.93), as if he were picking out a farm animal or a whore. He is incapable of love, but isn't she also? Isn't her propensity for boredom a counterpart to his shallowness and gamesmanship?

Rendering diverse perspectives in terms of how characters think is Flaubert's genius. Rodolphe understands Emma because she, like him, constantly needs new sensations. A snob, Rodolphe despises Charles and patronizes Emma. Note the reductive crudeness of his perceptions: "I think [Charles] is very stupid. She must be tired of him, no doubt. He has dirty nails, and hasn't shaven for three days.... How bored she gets! How she'd want to be in the city and go dancing every night! Poor little woman! She is gaping after love like a carp on the kitchen table after water.... She'd be tender, charming. Yes; but how to get rid of her afterwards?" (II.vii.93). She is to him a chattel, a plaything; the word "gaping" glaringly suggests his interest in penetrating her. For him love and sex are interchangeable; love is the act of having sex.

What is striking in Flaubert's artistry is his narrator's understated and playfully ironic control of his telling and the way the novel shifts perspective. One thing that binds Emma and Léon, only twenty when he meets her, is their literary interest. He and Emma like the Romance genre with its hyperbole – as he puts it, "noble characters, pure affections, and pictures of happiness" (II.ii.59). She, like Léon with whom she will have an affair after her affair with Rodolphe, rejects the very kind of fiction Flaubert is writing: "I detest commonplace heroes and moderate feelings, as one finds them in nature" (II.ii.59).

Flaubert suggests the sensual parallel between religious and sexual fantasies in that they both depend on a kind of absolutism that he doubts. The voluptuary Emma is prone to embracing both. After having sex with Rodolphe, she returns home: "So at last she was to know those joys of love.... She was entering upon a marvelous world where all would be passion, ecstasy, delirium. She felt herself surrounded by an endless rapture" (II.ix.117). Emma had thought that she and Rodolphe would leave Yonville and live together. But Rodolphe runs off, and she turns her sensual imagination once more to God's embrace. Abandoned by Rodolphe and ill, "it seemed to her that her being, mounting toward God, would be annihilated in that love like a burning incense that melts into vapour" (I.xiv.154). She imagines "God the Father, resplendent with majesty, who ordered to earth angels with wings of fire to carry her away in their arms" (I.xiv.154). Whether it be the seduction of man or God, Emma is a prey to her hyperbolic imagination that deflects her from the tedium of her day-to-day provincial life.

Looking forward to the twentieth and twenty-first centuries, Flaubert is ironic – and indeed, self-ironic – about both the power and limitations of words and their propensity to distort. While knowing that his own novel has illustrated Rodolphe's concern – dramatized by Rodolphe's own behavior – that "exaggerated declarations … serve to cloak a tepid love," his narrator bemusedly remarks, "as though the abundance of one's soul did not sometimes overflow with empty metaphors, since no one ever has been able to give the exact measure of his needs, his concepts, or his sorrows. The human tongue is like a cracked cauldron on which we beat out tunes to set a bear dancing when we would make the stars weep with our melodies" (II.xii.138). The effectuality of our words often falls far short of our aspirations for them, and we are often little more than street performers who can get a bear to dance with a few notes.

When Léon returns to her life, he has become something of a manipulative rake himself. As she is compulsively drawn to Rodolphe, so Léon is to her. Given Rodolphe's calculated seduction, the shy and naïve Léon might be, to the reader, the more attractive of the two. In a perverse way the younger and rather aimless Léon becomes her child rather than Berthe. At first we may think of the Rolling Stones' "You can't always get what you want / But if you try sometime, you just might find / You get what you need," but we soon realize that nothing will satisfy Emma's restless soul.[10]

Note how Emma nourishes Léon's sensuousness as well as his idleness: "It often seemed to him that his soul, fleeing toward her, broke like a wave against the contours of her head, and was drawn irresistibly down into the whiteness of her breast … She called him child. 'Do you love me, child?'" (III.v.192).

Speech, Flaubert knew, both creates reality and reflects reality. As Léon and Emma, upon renewing their friendship, reconfigure their pasts, "each setting up an ideal to which they were now trying to adapt their past life," his narrator remarks: "[S]peech is like a rolling machine that always stretches the sentiment it expresses" (III.i.169).

Charles Bovary

Charles Bovary is a well-meaning mediocrity. From the outset, he is passive, not very intelligent, and ostentatiously inarticulate. That he cannot pronounce his own name – it comes out "Charbovari" (I.i.3) – is a metaphor for his not knowing who he is. After failing his exams the first time, Charles passes the exam to become a second-class doctor with the degree of "Officier de Santé."

The first Madame Bovary is his mother, who finds him his first wife, the second Madame Bovary, an ugly woman with an income. Emma is, then, the third.

When invited by Emma's father to declare his intentions, Charles can only stammer his future father-in-law's name: "Monsieur Rouault – Monsieur Rouault" (I.iii.18). Imperceptive, he is manipulated into a marriage proposal by father and daughter, without any awareness of the character of either of them. In a key early passage, the narrator describes how Emma, when nominally speaking to Charles, is really speaking to herself: "[A]ccording to what she was saying, her voice was clear, sharp, or suddenly all languor, lingering out in modulations that ended almost in murmurs *as she spoke to herself*, now joyous, opening big naïve eyes, then with her eyelids half closed, her look full of boredom, her thoughts wandering" (I.iii.16, my italics).

The narrator sees and understands far more than Charles, who doesn't realize what a coquette Emma is and how she is seducing him. After she offers to have a drink with him on one of his visits to the farm, ostensibly to see how her father's broken leg was mending, she takes only a drop in her glass: "As it was almost empty she bent back to drink, her head thrown back, her lips pouting, her neck straining … the tip of her tongue passing between her small teeth she licked drop by drop the bottom of her glass" (I.iii.16). Coyly, she is conveying the promise of sexuality. The narrator emphasizes how immersed Emma is in her own body. She is telegraphing her sexual needs not only to Charles but also to the reader, who is made to understand by the narrator that this woman cannot be contained by man or convention.

Later, when we see through Emma's eyes how Charles botches an operation to correct a clubfoot, we lose some of our sympathy for him and may even be slightly forgiving when Emma congratulates herself on her adultery with Rodolphe: "For [Charles] sat there as if nothing had happened, not even suspecting that the ridicule of his name would henceforth sully hers as well as his.… She revelled in all the evil ironies of triumphant adultery" (II.xi.133).

Léon and Rodolphe have in common with Emma that they are self-absorbed narcissists who seem to eschew work. Rodolphe appears to have an inheritance, but not much in the way of assets. Of course, Charles, too, is a narcissist, so self-absorbed that he has no clue what is going on. But he does work and he does love Emma far more than her lovers will. He is one of the most imperceptive figures in Western literature, unable to read his wife's feelings or recognize his wife's machinations. Indeed, there is something unbelievable about his stupidity.

Charles's secret is that he has no secret. He will do anything to preserve the façade of respectability and marital love that he craves until he finally discovers Emma's secret life with Léon. After that, he has a corrupting secret that undermines his façade.

Structure

The novel's taut organization is a major source of aesthetic pleasure. Consider the entire deft three-part structure. In the short Part One the young Emma and the widowed doctor Charles marry, and she begins to yearn "for masked balls, for shameless pleasures that were bound, she thought, to initiate her to ecstasies that she had not yet experienced" (I.ix.48). In Part Two in Yonville, after failing to consummate her relationship with Léon, Emma has an affair with Rodolphe, who stands her up when she expects to leave with him; she then becomes critically ill before meeting Léon at Rouen. In Part Three Emma's weekly rendezvous with Léon in Rouen – inflected with increasing boredom with him which echoes her boredom with Charles – and her financial ruin conclude with her suicide and, in Flaubert's noir denouement, Charles's insistence that Emma be buried in her wedding gown. Percolating through each part is Emma's materialism and her concomitant financial corruption, both of which lead her to rationalize cheating on her husband.

Interestingly Emma's suicide is the result of what we might call a nervous breakdown, although Flaubert, like his nineteenth-century contemporaries, lacks our modern vocabulary for psychological phenomena: "Madness was coming upon her; she grew afraid, and managed to recover herself, in a confused way, it is true, for she did not remember the cause of her dreadful confusion, namely the money. She suffered only in her love, and felt her soul escaping from her in this memory, as wounded men, dying, feel their life ebb from their bleeding wounds" (III.vi.228). While we might note the aptness of the metaphor of dying, what we should also realize is that she no longer substitutes money for love as she had for most of her married life. In the past, money and the things it can buy were sexual tributes that she craved.

Endings are apocalypses, the way novelists bring order to the world they observe, and this one could not be bleaker. Recall the rapidly devolving denouement: Emma's boredom, her desperate quest for new sensations, her economic collapse due to her own foolishness, her loss of pride as her world comes apart, her going to a masked ball from which she awakens not knowing what she has been doing, and, finally, her grim and awful death.

Her death is followed by a kind of epilogue. On the last pages the narrator opens up his lens to focus on Charles's deterioration (a "long-bearded, shabbily clothed, wild figure of a man" rumored to drink [III.xi.254]) and his demise; the self-serving and malicious Homais getting the Legion of Honor; the priest becoming more fanatic; and Berthe, the neglected, uneducated daughter, in the care of a poor aunt and working in a cotton mill.

Structurally, *Madame Bovary* is a masterpiece. To a rereader every incident ties together. Let us look at an early proleptic incident when Emma is drawn to money and decadent sensuality. After her marriage has become stale, but while she and Charles are still living in their first home at Tostes, a Marquis whom Charles has successfully treated invites the then young couple – after noticing Emma – to a party, and it is at this party that Emma bites into the apple of material envy: "In [her heart's] contact with wealth, something had rubbed off on it that could not be removed" (I.viii.36, 40).

The male attendees at the party also wear the mantle of decadence to which she is attracted: "Their indifferent eyes had the appeased expression of daily-satiated passions, and through all their gentleness of manner pierced that peculiar brutality that stems from a steady command over half-tame things, for the exercise of one's strength and the amusement of one's vanity – the handling of thoroughbred horses and the society of loose women" (I.viii.36). This early passage anticipates how Rodolphe will play with her, and how she and Léon play with each other, with Emma taking the lead the first time and he the second. But the rereader understands that, like Mann's Aschenbach, Emma is continually meeting versions of herself. Or, as Joyce put it in *Ulysses*, she "found in the world without as actual what was in [her] world within as possible."

Homais's private room, which "[n]o one in the world was allowed to set foot [in]," is an emblem for the secret agenda that motivates almost everyone's behavior (III.ii.179). The room containing pharmaceutical ingredients holds the arsenic which Emma locates for her suicide. After she has learned where the key to the room is, she tricks Justin, Homais's bullied assistant. Captivated by her sexuality, Justin cannot refuse her request to help her get the arsenic, which supposedly is to kill the rats that are disturbing her sleep (III.viii.229).

One of the great structural moments is in Chapter viii of Part Two when the narrator presents Rodolphe's seduction of Emma as an almost clichéd event. The seduction scene at the farm show takes place in the context of the cultural mediocrity epitomized by Monsieur Lieuvain's political nonsense. The chapter concludes with pharmacist Homais's verbose and vapid article about the farm show (II.viii).

Part of our pleasure in reading complex literary works are subtle resonances and repetitions within a unified structure. For example, the recurring image of the desperately poor, blind but aggressive beggar with a misshapen face is an image not only of mortality but also of human corruption. This troubling figure foreshadows Emma's spiritual deterioration as well as the internal disintegration of her body after she takes arsenic.

Emma cannot escape her superstitious feeling that the beggar's misery is related to her or that his condition is a judgment on her human frailty. Described as a "wretched creature" with an "idiotic laugh," the blind beggar sings a song apropos to Emma's own life – "Often the warmth of a summer day / Makes a young girl dream her heart away" (III.v.193). At the moment she lays dying in her room she hears his voice as he sings the very same lines on the pavement outside, as if he had mysteriously turned up in Yonville to pass final judgment (III.viii.239). As black stuff comes from her mouth, the narrator implicitly compares Emma with the disgusting blind man whose singing she hears as she is dying.

The narrator stresses how this beggar becomes Emma's double and how he arouses her anxiety. His voice "filled Emma with dread. It went to the very depths of her soul, like a whirlwind in an abyss, and carried her away to a boundless realm of melancholy" (III.v.193). Hivert, the coach driver, "would lash out savagely at the blind man with his whip" (III.v.193). Later, when Emma is leaving Rouen for the last time, Homais – the know-it-all pharmacist and a parody of Enlightenment rationalism with his belief that all problems can be solved – shouts out to the beggar his quack remedies for his deformity. Disturbed and frightened, Emma gives the beggar her last five francs in response to his "uttering a sort of low howl like a famished dog" (III.vii.219).

The Function of the Narrator

The narrator is a character in the text who reveals a good deal about himself in the very telling. He is repelled by both the insularity of provincialism and the pretensions of urbanity. At times he seems as misanthropic as Swift in his impatience with human foibles such as pride, greed, and snobbery. Among other things, *Madame Bovary* is a scathing satire of human behavior.

We need to note the assumed worldliness of the narrator, who despises his characters, especially Léon and Rodolphe, but also Emma, Charles, and Homais. Yet we also need to remember he was once in the same provincial classroom as Charles.

The narrator detests the grasping and Machiavellian shopkeeper and moneylender Lheureux, who manipulates the Bovarys into financial ruin; the patronizing and pompous councilor Lieuvain; the narrow-minded, petty, and envious innkeeper Madame Lefrançois, whom the narrator refers to as "the fat widow" (II.viii.95); and the predatory tax collector Binet. When Emma asks him for money, Binet ineptly tries to ask her to trade sex with him for it and brushes his knee against her boot (III.vii.221). (Flaubert wants us to notice the structural resonance; Rodolphe had begun seducing her by brushing his leg against hers [II.ix.114].)

The narrator does not spare any characters. He withholds malice but not irony from his poignant depiction of Catherine Leroux, a peasant who has worked on the same farm for fifty-four years and is awarded twenty-five francs: "Something of monastic rigidity dignified her. No trace of sadness or tenderness weakened her pale face. Having lived so long among animals, she had taken on their silent and tranquil ways" (II.viii.108). That this provincial woman has lost the distinguishing qualities of feeling that make her human gives the reader pause in condemning Emma's need for more than Charles.

Ever so subtly, the narrator does make a case against Emma's lust, materialism, and need for new sensations. Writing about Emma's appeal to Rodolphe for money after all else fails – an appeal that is a disguised desperate effort to sell herself sexually and an appeal that the narrator calls "prostitution" (III.vii.225) – the narrator observes with considerable irony: "If he had had [the three thousand francs that she has requested], he would probably have given the money, although it is generally unpleasant to do such fine things: a demand for money being, of all the winds that blow upon love, the coldest and most destructive" (III.viii.227). Another example of his increasingly judgmental tone is when he remarks, after Emma has consummated her adultery in the carriage with Léon in Rouen: "[I]n her heart she felt already that cowardly docility that is for some women at once the chastisement and atonement of adultery" (III.ii.178).

Flaubert balances an external view of the characters with their individual perspectives. Thus Flaubert's narrator shows the characters seeing and being seen by other characters and himself. In her bold sexuality and exaggerated passions, Emma becomes "sinister" if not demonic to Léon: "She undressed brutally, ripping off the thin laces of her corset so violently that they would whistle round her hips like a gliding snake…. [S]he would throw herself against his breast with a long shudder" (III.vi.205). Her sexuality becomes increasingly desperate and violent: "[F]inding how experienced she was, he told himself that she must have passed through all the extremes of both pleasure and pain" (III.vi.205). It is as if sex is her drug of choice and she has become an addict.

It is the narrator's function to correct Emma's misperceptions, especially in regard to her lovers, and to give the readers accurate judgments. Thus the narrator regards Rodolphe as a lazy, self-serving rake whose attire "had the inconsistency of things at once commonplace and refined which enchants or exasperates the ordinary man because he suspects that it reveals an unconventional existence, a dubious morality, the affectations of the artist, and, above all, a certain contempt for established conventions" (I.viii.99).

Flaubert's Values

What are Flaubert's values? He despises the Church, materialism, foppery, pretensions, and the provinces, but he also dislikes Paris. Speaking as surrogate, his narrator condemns Emma's behavior. When the priest dips his right thumb in the oil to give supreme unction, the narrator summarizes Emma's behavior in a telling indictment: "First, upon the eyes, that had so coveted all worldly goods; then upon the nostrils, that had been so greedy of the warm breeze and the scents of love; then upon the mouth, that had spoken lies, moaned in pride and cried out in lust; then upon the hands that had taken delight in the texture of sensuality; and finally upon the soles of the feet, so swift when she had hastened to her desires, and that would now walk no more" (III.viii.237).

But is Flaubert more sympathetic to Emma than he realizes? Isn't the writing most energetic when he is writing about Emma's sensuality and lascivious behavior, even her reveling in dreams of orgies and decadence, as when she goes to a ball at Mid-Lent in a trashy costume after which she finds herself in a room with women of the "lowest class" (III.vi.212)? Describing Emma's response to this milieu, the narrator remarks: "[E]cstasies of imaginary ... love would exhaust her more than the wildest orgies" (III.vi.212).

The narrator is both judgmental and voyeuristic when presenting the episode where Emma and Léon spend hours driving around Rouen in a carriage while copulating in the back: "with all blinds drawn [the carriage] reappeared incessantly, more tightly sealed than a tomb and tossed around like a ship on the waves" (III.ii.177). We note the judgmental foreshadowing of Emma's accelerated rush to death with the word "tomb." We also note the voyeuristic implication that the bumpiness of the carriage ("tossed around") is owing in part to the continuous sex from noon to six. The only visible interruption – if indeed it is an interruption – is Emma's bare hand throwing out the letter of refusal to Léon that she never delivered.

Jonathan Culler points to the continually changing point of view in the scene where Léon picks up Emma in the cathedral followed by the six-hour coach ride in which they are having sex: "Léon and Emma vanish and are no longer even referred to by name."[11] They become no more than their sexual desire; Sartre remarks, "If [Flaubert] were to show the interior of the coach and the two lovers making love, Emma and Léon would have remained human in the same way as the coachman."[12] These central figures are reduced to anonymity because Flaubert artfully shows us what the townspeople observe and takes us into the mind of the puzzled coachman. Like the townspeople, we readers can only speculate on exactly what is going on in the coach.

More and more the narrator describes Emma's sexual needs as a compulsion, yet he does so with a puzzling and fascinated curiosity that wanders into the world of voyeurism. The narrator uses terms like "fierce lust" to describe her behavior (III.v.194). He underlines the relationship between her dishonesty to Charles and her financial chicanery as if one fed on the other, as in fact they do; she spends his money on frills to please herself and her lover. She pretends to go to Rouen to take piano lessons, and even plants a receipt to support that prevarication: "From that moment on, her existence was one long tissue of lies" (III.v.196).

Flaubert focuses much of the novel on Emma's point of view and creates a style appropriate to rendering her consciousness. At the same time he draws a circumference of independent judgment around her perspective. By means of a relatively small amount of dialogue and by entering other characters' consciousness and feelings briefly, he creates a kind of interior opera of diverse voices with Emma playing the lead.

Flaubert as Artist

Flaubert writes much of *Madame Bovary* from a woman's perspective, but the point of view varies, often several times within a sentence or even a paragraph. Culler speaks of "the predilection for continually shifting points of view which makes us uncertain who is speaking."[13] How many readers remember that the first word of the novel is "we" and that a classmate describes Charles as "a country lad of about fifteen" (I.i.1) who is "ill at ease" when he enters the room and something of a country bumpkin? Indeed, Charles's cap, "whose dumb ugliness has depths of expression, like an imbecile's face," is a kind of metonymy for how others – including, later, Emma – regard Charles, who, eventually, like his father becomes something of a misanthrope, "shut[ting] himself up … sick of men, he said, and determined to live in peace" (I.i.4). Note how the point of view has moved from the classmate to a voice with a historical view of the marriage of Charles's parent.

Madame Bovary is elegantly crafted; every word counts and the resonances of prior passages are part of the pleasure of a first reading, just as the foreshadowing of subsequent passages is part of the pleasure of rereading. Culler has written insightfully about the "puzzling inconclusiveness [of themes in Flaubert's work] as soon as we try to take them seriously as thematic statements."[14] In specifying and defining themes, my differences with Culler are more of degree than kind, I emphasize the richness and complexity of the themes of *Madame Bovary* as well as the need to ponder their implications.

For example, while a resistant reading can point to the lack of opportunities for women in the nineteenth century, Flaubert's point is that, no matter what the limits of French provincial culture are in producing his characters, something is lacking in Emma herself. Yes, we are left with what Culler calls "uncertainty," but there are degrees of uncertainty. Of course, with each reading every major work feels different, but I do not agree with Culler "that the flaw of the book lies precisely in the aspect of its theme which is firmest and most unambiguous, while its greatness derives from those areas of maximum indeterminacy, if not irrelevance."[15]

Put another way, if a major shortcoming of humanistic formalism is that it oversimplifies aesthetic structure and significant form in its quest for unity and coherence, a corresponding shortcoming of deconstruction is its tendency to stress – and often indeed to exaggerate – any and all nuances of thematic confusion or formal dissonance. We can and should find challenges to neat and monolithic explanations, but those challenges should not leave us with the sense that the quest for unity or meaning is without merit or that disunity and aporia are superior values.

Emma's life exemplifies the pathos of a repetition compulsion. From the outset her (and at first our) expectations are aroused by the promise of something better, only to be undermined again and again by boredom or betrayal based on her false and illusionary hopes. Her escape from farm to village to town by marriage is repeated over and over again in various forms (Charles, Léon, Rodolphe, Léon) – and indeed is anticipated by her escape from farm to convent and convent to farm – until we realize she is returning to the same place in her imagination after each disappointment and, in a sense, revisiting the same place over and over again, albeit with a different lover. Culler notes: "The successive episodes of the book record Emma's failure to find a life which accords with her expectations and show how the form of each failure leads to hopes which animate and direct her next attempt at self-fulfillment."[16]

Culler sees as an instance of Flaubert's uncertainty that we do not learn what is unique about Emma and why she has failed. Yet Culler sees this uncertainty as a virtue; what we learn in his reading is that "Purified desire is an empty form whose value is threatened by any realization, whether that realization be the meanings we attempt to read in our experience or the experience we postulate to fix the meanings."[17] Even if Flaubert demurs at fixed meanings, I would stress that he is aware in his ironic presentation of Emma that we cannot understand fully her psyche.

Perhaps the form of *Madame Bovary* has its own certainty. What is unique in *Madame Bovary* is that Flaubert has created an iterative structure that underlines Emma's repetition compulsion and implies the inevitable nature of her demise. The activity of reading this particular novel – responding to its structure of effects controlled by Flaubert's irony and shifting point of view to inflect that irony – creates the certainty of her demise, especially to a rereader.

Flaubert's self-conscious, sophisticated but artificial aesthetic that eschews naturalism, while employing inflected, even unstable points of view, has something in common with Italian Mannerism. Thus Flaubert, with his commitment to the rigorous but multi-faceted aesthetic that he demonstrates within *Madame Bovary*, is aware of what Culler describes as Flaubert's "ordering and interpreting fiction" that is "an indubitable case of desire" for meaning and wholeness that life may lack.[18] Put another way, Flaubert's desire for significant form is as strong as Emma's for sex.

If Flaubert's aesthetic has a Mannerist component and his scenes recall Manet's and Courbet's realism, in his desire to paint characters as we might see them with all their flaws – indeed, to highlight their conflicted expressions at crucial moments – Flaubert has a good deal in common with Caravaggio. Perhaps we should say he bestrides the borderline between Mannerism and Baroque. Mannerism, we recall, emphasizes intellectual sophistication and artificiality of style in contrast to more subdued, rational, and realistic modes of presentation. The Italian *maniera* roughly means "style." But we see Baroque in the exaggerated and heightened scenes such as the aforementioned carriage ride, where the stress is on highlighting and foregrounding some images at the expense of others; the idea is to achieve greater physical and psychological realism by creating illuminating distortions of what we see.

Madame Bovary: Final Thoughts

Madame Bovary emphasizes aesthetics and eschews polemics. With its focus on style, it has much in common with aestheticism – proposed by the Romantic movement – which argues that art has no other purpose than beauty; with its emphasis on Emma's uncontrollable sexuality, it anticipates the Decadent movement of Charles Baudelaire, Joris-Karl Huysmans, Théophile Gautier, and Oscar Wilde.

Why am I drawn to this wonderful novel and why do I reread it so slowly, savoring every word of de Man's translation? For one thing, I loved the descriptions of the provinces in France in the 1830s and 1840s; 1840 is the year Madame Bovary moves to Yonville and 1843 is the year she commits adultery. For another, I appreciate the pacing. No sooner are Emma and Léon drawn to one another in Part Two before he leaves than Flaubert dramatizes Emma's race to adultery with Rodolphe and then her even faster pace to adultery and subsequent ruin after she and Léon meet again.

Finally, Flaubert is a master psychologist in showing how loneliness, boredom, and desire feed one another, but he also knows how temperamental idiosyncrasies shape behavior. This is another way of saying that Flaubert's char-acters are less the product of their environment than Balzac's. Even living in a convent, Emma is a sensualist and hedonist, "softly lulled by the mystic languor exhaled in the perfumes of the altar.… The comparisons of betrothed, husband, celestial lover, and eternal marriage, that recur in sermons, stirred within her soul depths of unexpected sweetness" (I.vi.25). Flaubert takes an ironic perspec-tive towards Christianity, and specifically the Catholic Church, which, by plac-ing faith in an ideal God, offers to believers a substitute for the sensual worldly pleasures that often go hand in hand with idealizing people in ways unsupported by the evidence presented by their behavior.

2. Briefly Discussing the Puzzles of *Sentimental Education*

Introduction

To put the virtues of *Madame Bovary* in perspective and context, I want to segue briefly to Flaubert's last novel, *Sentimental Education* (1869). The novel takes place in the context of both the 1848 Revolution when King Louis-Philippe abdicated and the founding of the Second French Empire under Louis Napoleon that took place three years later. But *Sentimental Education* does not have the dialogue between the personal and political that we find in Tolstoy or even Zola. Frédéric Moreau, the protagonist, is swept along by events, but he possesses neither political vision nor commitment. Given *Madame Bovary*, we are hardly surprised by Flaubert's indifference to politics in *Sentimental Education*.

By contrast to *Madame Bovary*, I found *Sentimental Education* a bit too self-consciously mannered, even rococo in part, because to me it seemed labored, slow moving, less tightly structured, and at times over-determined in its elabo-rate and fulsome descriptions. Indeed, at times I thought it a second-rate work with tiresome characters who lack passion, brains, or motivation. Its sexual scenes seem more salacious than intimate. Although there may be great villains in the novels I am discussing, is there a more unpleasant protagonist in major nineteenth-century French fiction than Frédéric Moreau?

Sentimental Education is very much part of the Decadent movement in lit-erature, a fin-de-siècle novel before the fin de siècle. With its frequent talk of "amorous adventures," "assignation," and "Oriental orgy," the novel takes the reader into the sexual underground and demi-monde of Toulouse Lautrec (I.v.93; I.v.87).[19]

Even if *Sentimental Education* is, as Flaubert claimed, "the moral history, or rather the sentimental history, of the men of my generation," it reflects experiences of his own life – including his passion for an older woman.[20] *Sentimental Education* is dominated by often bored, materialistic characters that the narrator disdains and patronizes. Notable among these are Moreau, the sometime Flaubert surrogate, and Monsieur Arnoux, the husband of the woman on whom Moreau is fixated. The novel's focus is on a spasmodic and often inactive passion that not only includes Moreau's weird worship of his married beloved, Madame Arnoux, but also his narcissism, which takes the form of emotional masochism.

If I may recall – from my first chapter – Tim Parks's observation: "We may even ask if the satisfaction of achieving an aestheticized expression of personal suffering does not preserve the pain by making it functional to the life of the sufferer turned artist."[21] Are not these words applicable to Flaubert? The enervated narrative voice often cynically describes the narcissistic behavior of his characters as if – to again cite Parks – "The reader is invited to wonder, then, if [the story] isn't itself a reformulation of circumstances and emotions its author may not wish to disclose."[22]

Boredom and sloth are important failures of Emma Bovary, but she is also somewhat sympathetic as a victim of circumstances. Lacking ambition or self-knowledge, Frédéric Moreau, the focal character of *Sentimental Education*, is a spoiled adult waiting for a legacy and doing little good with it after he gets one. He is an emotional masochist putting himself in situations where he knows he will be hurt. Passively, he awaits events rather than managing or controlling them. The women connive at the expense of the men, but the men are no better, seeking to euchre one another out of funds and taking political stances out of self-interest or anger and envy resulting from their economic circumstances and career frustrations.

Flaubert rivals Balzac and Zola in giving a full sense of the geography and texture of individual neighborhoods in mid-nineteenth-century Paris and the specific details of décor in homes. Flaubert combines realism with the defamiliarization of the known or the uncanny when it comes to emotions and feelings.

Frédéric Moreau

And who is the chameleonic protagonist Frédéric Moreau? Whatever identity he assumes is shadowed by slippage, whether it be personal failure to connect with his beloved, his friends, and his family, or his fruitless quest to find a career. Moreau often is a twit when he is not completely repulsive. He is both a pathetic and often a comic character. He is compulsively and self-destructively obsessed with Madame Arnoux: "Something stronger than an iron chain bound him to Paris: an inner voice cried out to him to stay" (I.v.72).

Often in the throes of "idleness" and "boredom" (I.v.74), Moreau is a dandy, a snob, and a dreamer; "Frédéric furnished a Moorish palace for himself, and spent his life reclining on cashmere divans, beside a murmuring fountain, attended by negro pages" (I.v.64). He walks through the streets of Paris despising "the vulgarity" of "a vast torrent of humanity" and the "stupidity of their talk," and is convinced that "he was worth more than these men" (I.v.75).

A womanizing husband and an art dealer, Arnoux is an unscrupulous trickster. When Moreau visits looking for Madame Arnoux, her husband's "peculiar smile" tells us, but not Moreau, that he knows what is going on (I.v.74). He arranges for Moreau and his wife to be together and then chides Moreau for his lack of aggressiveness.

Fréderic is repressed and lacking self-knowledge, and his responses are at an oblique angle from the stimuli that produce them. He does not know what he wants and seeks loose women, like Rosanette and Madame Dambreuse (whom he doesn't even find attractive) because they provide temporary refuge from his loneliness and confusion.

Moreau often assumes a stoic melancholy and seems numbed by what is going on, and this certainly dominates many scenes between his occasional joyous interludes. Moreau is used by wealthy whores like Rosanette, who sleeps with others, including Madame Arnoux's husband, and is duped by petty swindlers, poseurs, and grubs who are like parasites feeding on him as an economic host. Notwithstanding his professions of love, does he really feel?

But, for the most part, Moreau's obsession for Madame Arnoux lacks passion. A voyeur and a sensualist, he savors small sensations like observing a costume party quadrille (II.i.123–124). A decadent who anticipates Huysmans's more explicitly gay figure Jean des Esseintes (in *A Rebours*, 1884), he is drawn to the demi-monde, the self-deluded, and the non-productive. He is confused about his own sexuality.

Perhaps Moreau is the adult Flaubert feared becoming, that is, a lonely man without a partner who has missed his opportunities for intimacy. Years later when Madame Arnoux visits Moreau, they part without having the sex that he thinks is being offered. Moreau's liaisons with Rosanette and Madame Dambreuse have come to nothing. Deslauriers (who is a double dealer more than a friend) has taken Louise from Moreau; she, seemingly uncharacteristic of anything Flaubert has shown us of her, runs off with a singer. Loved by four women in their way, Moreau is left without anything. He is as bankrupt in love as Arnoux is in business. Note how Deslauriers woos Louise: "[L]ittle by little Deslauriers informed [the Rocque family] that [Moreau] was in love with somebody, that he had a child, and that he kept a mistress" (III.iv.394). And prior to that he had spoken badly to Madame Arnoux about Moreau.

Moreau is an heir to Don Quixote, living in his fantasies and barely seeing reality. Madame Arnoux is his Dulcinea; while the former does appear, she is mostly a figment of Moreau's imagination, as we see from his obsessive behavior and declarations to her: "What is there for me to do in the world? Others strain after wealth, fame, power. I have no profession; you are my exclusive occupation, my entire fortune, the aim and centre of my life and thoughts" (II.vi.269). Of course, Moreau makes feints in the direction of wealth, power, and fame, but due to his attention-deficit disorder – to use a modern term – even his ardor for Madame Arnoux occasionally cools in the face of her continued loyalty to her husband, which is based not only on sexual morality but also on her sense that for her and her children to survive she needs to support his business foolishness. At one point Moreau actually thinks of taking advantage of an opportunity to kill Arnoux – also a rival for Rosanette, a courtesan who was sold by her mother – but demurs not only because of his ethics but also because he simply lacks the will to act: "Suddenly he felt that it was going to be put into action, that he was going to play his part in it, that he wanted to; and then panic seized him" (III.i.314).

When Moreau becomes temporarily engaged in the political ructions of 1848 and is "infected by the general madness," Flaubert's narrator describes Moreau as "the weakest of men" (III.i.298). That appellation could apply to both his behavior with money and his personal relationships, male and female. Isn't the narrator mocking his political engagement: "[Moreau] greedily breathed in the stormy air, full of the smell of gunpowder; and at the same time he trembled with the consciousness of a vast love, a sublime, all-embracing tenderness, as if the heart of all mankind were beating in his breast" (III.i.292)? This from an idle, bored man of some wealth who has just been having sex with Rosanette, a whore supported by the wealthy as well as perhaps the mistress of the husband of the woman with whom he is obsessed.

It is almost as if Rosanette and Moreau's dead baby becomes a metaphor not only for Moreau's unfulfilled emotional life – and that of the other characters, too – but also for the punctured dreams of the Republic. Moreau "felt that this death was only a beginning, that some worse misfortune was going to follow close behind it" (III.iv.395).

Moreau's obsessiveness crosses the border into serious pathology. When Madame Arnoux doesn't appear for a rendezvous, "He looked for omens in the number of coins grasped at random in his hand, in the expressions of passersby, in the colour of horses; and, when the augury was unfavourable, he refused to believe it" (II.vi.278). Yet when she turns up in March 1867 at his apartment, he restrains his desire and feels a "repugnance akin to a dread of committing incest" as well as "the fear of being disgusted later" (III.vi.415) because he has noted that her hair is now white; that knowledge "was like a blow full in the chest" (III.vi.414). Such an oblique yet hyperbolic response is what I mean by my claim that Moreau is at times emotionally uncanny. He transforms familiar feelings that we all share into something peculiar, if not weird.

Homosexuality and Decadence in *Sentimental Education*

Does the concept of "Sentimental Education" – that is, the education of Moreau's sentiments – include homosexuality? Current scholarship indicates that Flaubert at the very least experimented with homosexuality and that he believed, like the later Decadents, that a wide variety of life experiences – even some not sanctioned by traditional morality – was necessary to be a novelist.

There is a strong undertone of homosexuality in the male bonding in Moreau's circle; in code, the narrator often describes men who are not comfortable with women: "Senecal … asserted dogmatically that since prostitution was heartless and marriage was immoral it was better to abstain. Deslauriers [the man to whom Frédéric is most attached and vice versa] regarded women as a distraction and nothing more. Monsieur de Cisy was frankly scared of them" (I.v.68). He and Deslauriers, who sees the "feminine" in Frédéric Moreau – "Frédéric's physical appearance … had always exerted an almost feminine charm on him" (II.v.245) – are drawn to one another, sometimes to the exclusion of other male friends. Although Deslauriers will go off with a prostitute, he "inveighed against [women's] affectation, their stupidity; in short, they did not appeal to him" (I.v.85). We realize that the novel's discomfort with women extends to Moreau's obsession with Madame Arnoux. His obsession is a fantasy that takes the place of a relationship with a living woman.

With Deslauriers, Moreau finds comfort and intimacy that he does not have with women: "There would be endless confidences, unaccountable bursts of merriment, and occasional arguments about a smoking lamp or a mislaid book, brief quarrels which were quenched by laughter" (I.v.64). Why is he attached to Deslauriers, who is a kind of double attracted to the same women, finally marrying Louise after wooing Madame Arnoux (II.v.246) and hanging around Rosanette? Why does he put up with Deslauriers, who also abandoned Moreau's election campaign and is often a scoundrel in the mode of Dostoevsky's Svidrigailov? In 1867, after Deslauriers's wife leaves him, Frédéric and Deslauriers are "reconciled once again by that irresistible element in their nature which always reunited them in friendship" (III.vii.416).

In Moreau's quest for new sensations and his taste for opulence – he borrows money to give Madame Arnoux an expensive parasol – Moreau is a kind of

Dorian Gray and Arnoux is Lord Wotton. Moreau, who has a morbid streak resonant of Decadence, even thinks of suicide: "[H]e asked himself why he should not put an end to it all.... The weight of his head pulled him forward, and he imagined his corpse floating on the water" (I.v.86).

Style as Decadence

Writing this novel about solipsism, boredom, and sloth – qualities that he despised in *Madame Bovary* – Flaubert sometimes commits the fallacy of imitative form and replicates those emotions. I found the narrator's describing and dramatizing ennui not deserving of my *oui*. The inflexible cynicism of Flaubert's narrator replicates the unpleasant detachment and hard-edged views that he ascribes to generic "men": "For there are situations in which the kindest of men is so detached from his fellows that he would watch the whole human race perish without batting an eyelid" (II.vi 283); or "There are some men whose only function in life is to act as intermediaries; one crosses them as if they were bridges, and leaves them behind" (II.iv.242); or "[S]ome men enjoy making their friends do things which they find disagreeable" (II.vi.266).

Some of the descriptive passages are needlessly prolix and weighted down with the excesses of purple prose. At times the novel's voyeuristic description of lavish houses and sumptuous meals recalls the Silver Fork novels of England in the 1820s, including Disraeli's *Vivian Grey*. The breathless descriptions of the luxurious and profligate life of the aristocracy, and even at times the upper middle class, recall the response of Emma Bovary to such phenomena.

The narrator's cynicism is as much a part of his observations of political intrigues as it is of personal relationships. Isn't the novel's pervasive cynicism a kind of Decadence? Thus the unprincipled self-seeking Martinon, who spends his energy toadying to the banker Dambreuse, remarks: "When the lower classes make up their minds to rid themselves of their vices, they will free themselves from their wants. Let the common people be more moral and they will be less poor!" (II.iv.238). The novel emphasizes that the popular uprising that deposed the king is mostly the work of unprincipled leaders whose behavior is motivated by self-interest. Even the conniving capitalist Monsieur Dambreuse claims to be one of the people: "For after all, we are all workers, more or less" (III.i.296); his lackey Martinon concurs and talks of his peasant forebears. Terms like "mob," "rabble," "frenzy," and "hooligans" (III.289–290) describe the February uprising. One of the leaders, Hussonet, declares, "I find the common people revolting" (III.i.290).

Conclusion

Despite my reservations and my view that *Sentimental Education* is not one of the great European novels, it has much to recommend it. Paris is as much a character as any individual. Slowing down the novel's pace, Flaubert revels in describing the streets and shops of Paris as well as the interiors of rooms, clothing and jewelry, and the ample food at a festive meal. Flaubert uses these descriptions as metonymies for class and manners. Even while sustaining his own iconoclastic views, Flaubert's narrator mocks Moreau's snobbery. Indeed, one might ask what the narrator does like and value, since he is something of a dark, grumbling Thersites figure bordering at times on unpleasantness.

In both *Madame Bovary* and *Sentimental Education*, Flaubert's world is one in which his central characters – Emma Bovary and Frédéric Moreau – are immersed in libidinal dreams and materialistic fantasies punctuated by hard cash and the things it buys. For both, time is not money; money is money. Moreau's vice is sloth, and isn't that an aspect of Emma's issues when sloth takes the form of boredom? When Moreau finds out his mother has little and that he will have only 2,300 francs a year, he falls into the slough of despond. An inheritance of 27,000 francs from an uncle who didn't make a will rejuvenates his fantasy and temporarily alleviates his spasmodic depression. He returns to Paris with his goal of fulfilling his unrealized passion for Madame Arnoux. Frédéric Moreau needs to be educated away from materialism to sentiments (feelings) for others, but this transformation never happens. As in the case of Emma Bovary, who is also deficient in self-awareness and prone to narcissism and self-immersion, his own idiosyncratic if not weird pursuit of pleasure prevents personal growth.

Study Questions for *Madame Bovary* and *Sentimental Education*

1. How does the omniscient narrator function to reveal the diverse cast of characters and their passions and motives?
2. Why does Emma turn away from Charles?
3. Does the novel fulfill Flaubert's criteria for "a book which would have no subject, or at least in which the subject would be almost invisible"?
4. Why is Flaubert's prose more energetic when he is writing about Emma's sensuality and lascivious behavior?
5. How does Emma's life exemplify a pathetic repetition compulsion?
6. From the outset, why are Emma's (and at first our) expectations aroused by the promise of something better, only to be again and again undermined by boredom or betrayal based on false hopes? Why does Flaubert present Emma's story this way?

7. Why does Flaubert use a three-part structure in *Madame Bovary*?
8. Why does Emma commit suicide? Does Flaubert adequately describe her emotional condition? How would a later author do it?
9. Does Flaubert's ironic detachment undermine the narrator's creating a structure of affects that includes full commitment to empathy and sympathy? How does that affect our response to the behavior of Emma?
10. Does *Madame Bovary* fulfill Georg Lukács's definition of realism?

. . . .

The central category and criterion of realist literature is the type, a peculiar synthesis that organically binds together the general and the particular both in characters and situations. What makes a type a type is not its average quality, not its mere individual being, however profoundly conceived; what makes it a type is that in it all the humanly and socially essential determinants are present on their highest level of development, in the ultimate unfolding of the possibilities latent in them, in extreme presentation of their extremes, rendering concrete the peaks and limits of men and epochs.[23]

. . . .

11. If you have read *Sentimental Education*, how would you compare its themes to those of *Madame Bovary*?
12. What does Moreau have in common with Emma Bovary?
13. How is *Sentimental Education* a part of the Decadent movement in European literature?
14. Is Moreau's real passion for men? Is he bisexual?

Notes

1. James Wood, *The Broken Estate: Essays on Literature and Belief*, quoted in John Banville, "The Prime of James Wood," *NYR* 55:18 (Nov. 20, 2008), 85–88; see pp. 85–86.
2. See Julian Bell, "Manet: 'Sudden Sensuous Dazzle,'" *NYR* 58:12 (July 14, 2011), 16–19.
3. Letter to his mistress Louise Colet, Jan. 16, 1852, quoted in Stephen Heath, *Flaubert: Madame Bovary* (New York: Cambridge University Press, 1992), 7.
4. Heath, *Flaubert: Madame Bovary*, 2–3.
5. Letter to Louise Colet, Jan. 16, 1852, quoted in Heath, *Flaubert: Madame Bovary*, 7.
6. Heath, *Flaubert: Madame Bovary*, 7–8.
7. Heath, *Flaubert: Madame Bovary*, 58.

8. Quotations from the text are from Gustave Flaubert, *Madame Bovary*, trans. Paul de Man (New York: Norton), 1965. Hereafter cited as *Madame Bovary*, Norton.

9. Reprinted in *Madame Bovary*, Norton, 392–407.

10. "You Can't Always Get What You Want," Mick Jagger and Keith Richards, the Rolling Stones.

11. Jonathan Culler, *Flaubert: The Uses of Uncertainty* (Ithaca, NY: Cornell University Press, 1974), 121.

12. Quoted in Culler, *Flaubert: The Uses of Uncertainty*, 122.

13. Culler, *Flaubert: The Uses of Uncertainty*, 120.

14. Culler, *Flaubert: The Uses of Uncertainty*, 136.

15. Culler, *Flaubert: The Uses of Uncertainty*, 139.

16. Culler, *Flaubert: The Uses of Uncertainty*, 139.

17. Culler, *Flaubert: The Uses of Uncertainty*, 142.

18. Culler, *Flaubert: The Uses of Uncertainty*, 142.

19. Quotations from the text are from Gustave Flaubert, *Sentimental Education*, intro. and trans. Robert Baldick (New York and London: Penguin, 1964). Hereafter cited as *Sentimental Education*, Penguin.

20. Letter to Mademoiselle Leroyer de Chantepie, October 1864, in *Sentimental Education*, Penguin, 7.

21. Tim Parks, "Life at the Core," *NYR* 58:6 (April 7, 2011), 58–59; see p. 58.

22. Parks, "Life at the Core," 58.

23. Georg Lukács, *Studies in European Realism* (London: Hillway, 1950), 6.

Chapter 6

Reading Dostoevsky's *Notes from Underground* (1864) and *Crime and Punishment* (1866)

1. *Notes from Underground*: The Piano Plays Back

Essentials for Understanding Dostoevsky: Christianity and the Enlightenment

Dostoevsky is skeptical of abstract reasoning and logic that he believed dominated Western Europe and in particular the Enlightenment. He believed that the only way to contain man's darker impulses – self-love, passions, desires, narcissistic and destructive behavior – is to believe in God. He was skeptical that the clarifying light of reason could effectively organize human behavior and he was skeptical of philosophical ideologies such as utilitarianism and political systems such as socialism or democracy that made such claims. Nor does he believe, as did some of his Russian contemporaries who bought into Social Darwinism, that humans were upwardly evolving and fulfilling a teleological pattern to perfection, or at least a much-improved humanity.

Dostoevsky is something of a mystic who believes in the Russian soul as an individual and collective entity; he believes that Russia must find its own way derived from its own past and cultural traditions. He has great doubt that the scientific revolution would lead humankind to a better life or that humans can step by step accumulate universal truths by evaluating hypotheses according to evidentiary tests. Nor does he believe we can predict behavior from observation

Reading the European Novel to 1900: A Critical Study of Major Fiction from Cervantes' Don Quixote to Zola's Germinal, First Edition. Daniel R. Schwarz.
© 2014 John Wiley & Sons, Ltd. Published 2014 by John Wiley & Sons, Ltd.

as if a human being were an experiment within – to use a figure from *Notes from Underground* – a laboratory retort.

It is not enough to say that Dostoevsky is a conservative and a Christian as if he were an intellectual cousin of T. S. Eliot. To systematize his thought is to miss the interplay of voices, the concrete dialogue of personalities, the drama of interpersonal relationships that are at the center of his novels. One needs to imagine his characters sitting around a large circular table, each articulating his or her particular point of view, often in the form of self-justification. Perhaps the spiritual Alyosha, the hero of *The Brothers Karamazov* and both a believer in God and empathetic to humans, earns a special place at the head of the table, but only after we have heard the various perspectives.

Notes from Underground: Challenging Enlightenment Assumptions

Notes from Underground was originally published in two parts in the January and April 1864 issues of *Epoch*, a magazine edited by Dostoevsky's brother Mikhail. According to Richard Pevear:

> . . . .
>
> The two time periods of the novel represent two stages in the evolution of the Russian intelligentsia: the sentimental, literary 1840s and the rational and utilitarian 1860s; the time of the liberals and the time of the nihilists.... The "gentlemen" [whom Dostoevsky's speaker] addresses throughout his notes, when they are not a more indeterminate "you," are typical intellectuals of the 1860s. More specifically, they are presumed to be followers of the writer Nikolai Gavrilovich Chernyshevsky, the chief spokesman and ideologist of the young radicals [who] ... propounded ... "rational egotism," an adaptation of the "enlightened self-interest" of the English utilitarians.[1]
>
> . . . .

Dostoevsky's oscillating distance from his self-dramatizing narrator makes *Notes* a complex text. At times Dostoevsky is sympathetic to his narrator's rebellion against logic and reason and various Western social formulae, from British utilitarianism (as defined by John Stuart Mill and Jeremy Bentham) and its concomitant Hedonic Calculus to – according to Dostoevsky's reading – the Romanticism of Rousseau with its idealization of human behavior. Rousseau and his followers believed humans were born with an inherent propensity towards the good and beautiful; that propensity could be maintained in a state of nature were humans not corrupted by society.

Dostoevsky cast his lot with the Slavophils who were skeptical of Western ideas and thought Russia needed to maintain its differences, including spirituality, mysticism, and respect for the specialness of each individual. According to Robert G. Durgy:

. . . .

The Slavophils sought to dissociate Russia from the Western influence and to discover her peculiarity in the old peasant commune which was believed to reveal her socialistic soul. Whereas the Westerners' doctrines were either frankly atheistic or at least areligious, the Slavophils believed in the primacy of the moral and religious laws of the Russian Orthodox Church and favored a holistic, spontaneous reason over the lower logical and analytic reason they associated with western positivism.[2]

. . . .

Dostoevsky understands that we humans do not always act logically or in our self-interest. He knows we are driven by obsessions, compulsions, shame, and guilt. We may at times savor our enmities. We may make bad choices, but those choices are expressions of our idiosyncrasies.

While Dostoevsky identified with the Slavophils in discriminating between reason and spirituality, one could argue that in fact his focus on the individual soul in direct relation to God was a Western import. By contrast, the Russian Orthodox Church's emphasis on mysticism is underlined by the Iconostasis – or wall of icons and religious paintings – that paradoxically separates us from God while theologically bringing us closer to God. The Iconostasis is a representation of Christ as the interconnecting door between heaven and earth – between the nave (the holiest part of man's world) and the sanctuary (the place of God). We find the explanation in *Hebrews* 10:19–20: "Therefore, brethren, since we have confidence to enter the sanctuary by the blood of Jesus, by the new and living way which He opened for us through the curtain, that is through His flesh." Thus icons are not merely art objects but interactive entities – almost like spiritual guardians – which humans approached asking personal favors; these favors may take the form of earthly gifts and/or physical protection from illness, natural disaster, or political ructions.

What is missing in *Notes from Underground* but is present in the last pages of *Crime and Punishment* is a kind of literary Iconostasis. Rereading *Notes* after *Crime and Punishment*, we see what is missing in the inchoate, chaotic bundle of contradictory ideas and impulses that we find in the speaker's dramatic monologue, which is part confession and testimony. Perhaps Dostoevsky is implying that without an ordering faith in God, we are all, without realizing it, somewhat in the position of the Underground Man who is seeking to discover by reason, writing, and speaking the ineffable spiritual truth that eludes him.

Figure 4   *Russian icon painting, c. 1850. Private collection, Frankfurt. Source: akg-images*

Prelude to Modernism

Notes from Underground has two beginnings; the story begins with Part II, the discourse with Part I. Part I is informed by the consequences on the speaker's psyche of the events he narrates in Part II. According to Joseph Frank, Part II "satirizes the sentimental Social Romanticism of the 1840s just as the first part satirized the metaphysics and ethics of the 1860s."[3]

The Underground Man is an example of internal focalization because Dostoevsky limits what the Underground Man knows to his own experience. Such a narrator cannot accurately report the thoughts of other characters, although he may imagine the thoughts of others and even imagine the response of the putative audience. In this case, the narrator does both.

Because Part I is simultaneous narration – the narrator speaks as the story occurs as if he were speaking in real time – we have the illusion of listening to a desperately disturbed man for whom the stakes of telling are high. He needs to engage us; yet his nastiness and disdain distance us. Part II is a retrospective example of the same kind of psychotic telling that we saw in Part I. The events in Part II take place several years before the telling in Part I and are a justification for the rant and harangue of Part I. These events are also an explanation for why the speaker is what Herman Melville calls an isolato, separated from his hyperconscious, self-interested fellows.

The narrator is something of a conjuror in both parts, taking us in as he takes Liza in. Had we first read his more plot-driven monologue in Part II, and learned the full extent of his abusive behavior to Liza, we would have been less forgiving and more mistrustful when listening to Part I.

At times the rather circumlocutious, self-dramatizing narrator satirizes those holding illusions about human behavior and Western ideas about the perfectibility of human behavior and human communities: "[H]uman beings are still human beings, and not piano keys.... [E]ven if it should indeed turn out that he was a piano key [played on by the laws of nature], if it were even proved to him mathematically and by natural science, he would still not come to reason, he would do something contrary on purpose, solely out of ingratitude alone, essentially to have his own way" (I.viii.30–31). But at the same time, he inadvertently shows us that he is trapped in the very logic he despises, that his rebellion is pathetic and poignant, and that he is a narcissistic, self-hating, dysfunctional figure. Once we read Part II and see how he bullies, abuses, and manipulates Liza, how he holds out hope only to dash it, we realize that his philosophy in Part I is a function of long ago failures and that, in the guise of what we now call existential rebellion against conventions, he is seriously disturbed.

We need to remember that the man consumed with self-hatred in Part I has had the experiences in Part II, which can only be described, when pertaining to his behavior to Liza, as moral depravity. When Liza offers love, he cannot respond: "[F]or me love meant to tyrannize and preponderize morally.… I've reached the point now [presumably the time of the events of Part I] of sometimes thinking that love consists precisely in the right, voluntarily granted by the beloved object, to be tyrannized over" (II.x.125). Until the end of the epilogue of *Crime and Punishment*, we should note, such a definition of love informs most of the relationships in that novel, excepting Sonya's love for Raskolnikov, and maybe Razumikhin's for Dunya, Raskolnikov's sister.

What differentiates Dostoevsky from traditional users of a first person narrator is the lack of a consistent ironic distance between himself and the self-dramatizing narrator. Bakhtin has used the term heteroglossia to describe Dostoevsky's technique of speaking with many different voices. In part this is because the chameleonic speaker is addressing an imagined audience of "gentlemen" whom he is trying to convince of the rightness of his point of view; at the same time, he is distancing them by defining himself as a self-described nasty mouse indifferent to anyone's opinion. And yet he is often anticipating objections, as if some of his audience might jump in and object to his inconsistency or his misanthropy or his small-mindedness or his bullying. This is what Bakhtin calls the "highly characteristic anticipation of someone else's reaction."[4]

That Dostoevsky has his narrator tiptoe to the very precipice of outrageous interruptions, contradictions, and hyperbolic statements – and the reader learns to expect them – is what makes the text so dangerous and thrilling, yet so frightening. Dostoevsky has created a character whose presentation in Part I is intellectual skydiving without a parachute, and we root for him sometimes in spite of ourselves. Sometimes this character is Dostoevsky's surrogate, sometimes a despised darker self who becomes the other self.

For both first readers and rereaders, the problem is locating Dostoevsky's ever-shifting attitude to the Underground Man. Joseph Frank argues that Dostoevsky is always in complete control: "The first section shows the underground man in the ideological grip of the Nihilism of the Sixties; the second, as a perfect product of the social Romanticism of the Forties.… [I]t is a brilliantly ironic Swiftian parody remarkable for its self-conscious mastery, satirical control and Machiavellian finesse."[5]

In my judgment, Frank sees (and seeks) a clarity and consistency that are not there, but it may well be that the text of *Notes from Underground* is richer for their absence. I think Dostoevsky frequently shifts ground, empathizing with the speaker's rebellion against logic and reason but also showing us that (a) he is trapped in the very system against which he rebels; and (b) often his rebellion is pathetic and pathological. Without Christian belief, Dostoevsky believes there can be no order in one's life and that absence of faith hovers over both of the speakers' written testimonies.

What makes this a High Modernist text – one that anticipates later developments in modern literature such as Joyce's *Ulysses* and in modern art such as Cubism, Surrealism, and Abstraction – is that Dostoevsky undermines traditional models of resolution and wholeness and doesn't let the reader feel comfortable with one way of seeing. By having his speaker constantly shift ground in his arguments, and making him in Part I appealing at some points and disgusting at others, he doesn't allow the reader to find one perspective for seeing this maladjusted figure.

Because the Underground Man speaks in many voices and admits to contradicting himself, we as readers can't find a foothold. In a sense, by listening to him we become complicit and become underground readers. Put another way, we are being called to judgment for our inability to create a society and culture where the speaker can function, where distinctions between free will and determinism, between progress and loss of personal freedom, between romance and realism are clear.

The speaker's very telling is an indictment of the world in which Dostoevsky lived and by implication, we feel as we read, our own confused world. He raises doubts in us about ourselves and this is very much part of Dostoevsky's intention. What reader doesn't recognize some aspect of the Underground Man in himself or herself? When I teach *Notes from Underground*, every student in the class finds resonances of his or her own behavior.

As readers, we want to reconcile contradictions, but Dostoevsky won't let us. Reading Dostoevsky today, we realize that we ourselves cope with reality every day without reconciling contradictions. For example, we have the same conversations with the same people – often people very close to us – and the same unsatisfactory results. We compulsively repeat past mistakes. We make long-range plans that rarely take account of illness or accident, to say nothing of the possibility that our hopes and dreams will be trumped by actual events or frustrated by the aspirations and perhaps machinations of others.

The Opening

With few exceptions, most notably Alyosha in *The Brothers Karamazov*, Dostoevsky's characters lack modesty, balance, and gradualism. Before he begins his philosophical rant, the narrator reveals some salient facts about himself. He is a forty-year-old former civil servant who has been estranged, angry, bitter, and self-loathing for twenty years. The Underground Man is not speaking orally but rather using his pen to define his thoughts and himself. On occasion, it is almost as if he wants readers to think he is presenting an unedited written stream of consciousness, but we can't be sure that this is true. He is writing in the present tense or says he is; thus, writing for the moment or in real time, he is more a diarist than a memoir writer. After writing something that he realizes is in bad taste and at cross-purposes to his desire to appear intelligent, he parenthetically writes: "A bad witticism, but I won't cross it out. I wrote it thinking it would come out very witty; but now, seeing for myself that I simply had a vile wish to swagger – I purposely won't cross it out!" (I.i.4). Isn't he showing off his free will, his ability to make his own rules, even at the expense of diminishing his stature as a writer, a decent human being, an intellectual, and a wit?

Our reading begins at the end of the Underground Man's story, after his aspirations have been trumped by events. Put another way, the discourse rearranges the story to stress the effects in Part I before examining the causes in Part II in the form of events that took place sixteen years ago. What on a first reading we find frightening, too, is how the speaker accepts, indeed embraces, defeat at the age of forty when he writes. But, in fact, didn't he embrace defeat sixteen years before when the events in Part II took place? Indeed, in the opening he dates his estrangement and alienation from the age of twenty.

Texts reveal as they conceal, conceal as they reveal. As the Underground Man opens his monologue in brief, almost abbreviated sentences, we notice the gaps between sentences, the lack of entailment.

. . . .

> I am a sick man.... I am a wicked man. An unattractive man. I think my liver hurts. However, I don't know a fig about my sickness, and am not sure what it is that hurts me. I am not being treated and never have been, though I respect medicine and doctors. What's more, I am also superstitious in the extreme; well, at least enough to respect medicine. (I'm sufficiently educated not to be superstitious, but I am). No, sir, I refuse to be treated out of wickedness. Now, you will certainly not be so good as to understand this. Well, sir, but I understand it. (I.i.3)

. . . .

What could be more off-putting and distancing than the opening? We notice that he has not been a "spiteful" official – as in some translations – but a "wicked" one when he describes taking pleasure in rudeness and asking his imagined audience in his conversational tone: "But do you know, gentlemen, what was the main point about my wickedness? The whole thing precisely was, the greatest nastiness precisely lay in my being shamefully conscious every moment, even in moments of the greatest bile, that I was not only not a wicked but was not even an embittered man" (I.i.4).

The Underground Man is a divided self who is tortured by the dialogues he has with himself and with his audience. No sooner does he tell us he was a "wicked official. I was rude and took pleasure in it" than he claims that he has "lied" to us and, due to his repressed better qualities, couldn't be a "wicked official" (I.i.4). Among other genres, *Notes* is a confession; the Underground Man's conscience tormented him into self-conscious shame and guilt for his past behavior. As with many diaries – and *Notes* is a kind of diary – part of the risk and danger of writing is the possibility that the text might be read by someone in the future. As readers to whom the editor has made the diary available, we are a third audience, watching how the Underground Man is trying to convince himself even as he is trying to convince his imagined audience of "gentlemen."

Objecting to the modernist tendency to put Dostoevsky's work in a psychological context, Pevear insists on the correctness of his and Volokhonsky's translation of the second sentence, "*Ya zloy chelovek*," as "I am a wicked man." In his view, to substitute, as most translations did, "I am a spiteful man" "speaks for that habit of substituting the psychological for the moral, of interpreting a spiritual condition as a kind of behavior, which has so bedeviled our century, not in the least in its efforts to understand Dostoevsky."[6] But we can respect the authorial reading without discarding a more resistant psychological reading that takes account of what we have learned about how the human psyche works.

We should be aware of how the "sir" of the opening paragraph, implying one listener, becomes the imagined audience of "gentlemen" as well as of how the short staccato of the opening contrasts with the convoluted logic and circumlocutious prose of much of what follows in Part I.

The Underground Man lives in a world where the men of action measure their lives in terms of career trajectory rather than the quality of self-knowledge, and he does not fit into such a world: "Not just wicked no, I never even managed to become anything: neither wicked nor good, neither scoundrel nor an honest man, neither a hero nor an insect. And now I am living out my life in my corner, taunting myself with the spiteful and utterly futile consolation that it is even impossible for an intelligent man seriously to become anything, and only fools become something" (I.i.5).

The Underground Man defines himself in negatives as if he were reading himself out of the social text in which he was born. It is as if he lacks a coherent self, and this at a time in Russia – and Europe – of the nineteenth century when a man of character was expected to present to the world a consistent personality.

The Underground Man's Divided and Incoherent Self

Now in part because of Dostoevsky and, most importantly, Freud, we realize that we have myriad selves, which is why we all have something of a heteroglossic discourse, borrowing discourses from different kinds of speech and written texts – religious, sports, popular culture, family tradition, ethnicity – to which different aspects of our self have become familiar. The Underground Man borrows language and style from contemporary science, Enlightenment philosophy, the confession tradition, romance, seduction stories, and, in his dialogue between aspects of himself and his audience, Socratic dialogues.

Speaking to the "gentlemen" he imagines himself addressing – almost as if they were a jury that he is trying to convince – he continually tries to anticipate their response as if he were a defense attorney measuring the effects of his words. In some ways he is dependent upon the judgments that he fears others are making. Yet at the same time he is the defense attorney trying to convince himself that he is a privileged man of superior consciousness whose behavior is explicable, if not justified, by his wider and deeper understanding of human nature. He speaks as if he were continually thinking about possible objections; as Bakhtin puts it, "The tendency of these anticipations is toward the constant withholding of any final word."[7]

In his introduction, Pevear insists on the repetition of "consciousness" in his and Volokhonsky's translation: "The editorial precept of avoiding repetitions, of gracefully varying one's vocabulary cannot be applied to this writer."[8] Consciousness is both a condition of awareness and a curse; the speaker emphasizes the disjunction between what he, as the putative hyperconscious man with his full and more intense understanding, knows, and what others – Lilliputians, some of whom pretend to consciousness – know. Claiming to be more perspicacious and sensitive than others, he is actually the pathetic, self-deluded victim of his own self-conscious inadequacy and uncontrollable masochism and sadism. That he compulsively repeats words and constructions is itself a verbal metonymy for his obsessive personality.

The Underground Man continually looks for a position of superiority, but that quest is undermined by his own apparent self-knowledge of his limitations. For he senses that he is a bundle of inconsistencies and that his self-definition is in continual flux. We realize that he knows a good deal less about himself than he thinks.

Yet, even as he demonstrates that he is haunted by self-delusion and absurd rationalization, he also writes a searing satire of a sham meritocracy in a city with more than its share of miserably poor and unfortunate citizens that so-called progress has passed by, as the Liza episode illustrates.

Part II: The Underground Man and the Prostitute Liza

Liza, the destitute, miserable prostitute whom the Underground Man visits to have sex, is the product of a socio-economic system that has broken down. By implication, she represents the failure of reason and the Enlightenment to provide for humanity. Within the text, the metonymy for the Enlightenment is the Crystal Palace, the 1851 London structure that was built for the Great Exhibition celebrating the triumphs of the Industrial Revolution. The title of Part II, "Apropos of the Wet Snow," refers to the anonymous death and impersonal burial of the have-nots, and specifically prostitutes.

With Liza the narrator knows he is acting, but he is out of control, acting differently than he consciously wills and responding to darker impulses; even while speaking to her of an alternative life to her whoring, he thinks: "It was the game that fascinated me most of all" (I.vi.93). He is a ventriloquist, channeling other voices, but he cannot choose the voice he uses as he alternates spasmodically between "the beautiful and lofty" of romanticism and his own deep-rooted anger and cynicism (I.vi.19).

As we reread, we may think of the craziness of the self-dramatizing speaker in Edgar Allan Poe's "The Tell-Tale Heart." Writing is for the narrator a present-tense action. He uses writing as a means of thinking. Although Pevear speaks of us hearing him, he is mistaken on this point: "What we see is a man glancing at us out of the corner of his eye, very much aware of us as he speaks, very much concerned with the impression his words are making."[9] Raskolnikov often defines himself by speaking – although he relied on a published article to get conceptual control of his superman theory – but the Underground Man is writing at his desk alone, without any social contact. His isolation defines him and he is *writing* to an imagined audience as a way of bridging the huge divide between himself and others.

The Underground Man's moral chaos results in a telling marked by fragmentation, obsessive repetition, and finally, aesthetic chaos. As Pevear writes: "He is a passionate amateur, a condition that marks the style and structure as well as the content of the book. Where the master practitioner would present us with a seamless and harmonious verbal construction, the man from underground, who literally cannot contain himself, breaks decorum all the time, interrupts himself, comments on his own intentions, defies his readers, polemicizes with other writers."[10] We know that we are in the presence of an imperceptive narrator who is imprisoned by his own inability to move forward; we think of the narrator's emotional disarray in contrast to the controlled structure of *Crime and Punishment* or *The Brothers Karamazov*. We draw a moral and aesthetic circle of judgment around the speaker's testimony, even while recognizing that we all – to our embarrassment – have seen ourselves at times in his inchoate and ungenerous thoughts.

Let us examine the speaker at his best and worst. Even when he seems to be trying to talk Liza out of being a prostitute and speaking eloquently about love as an alternative to what he calls "debauchery" (II.vi.88), he thinks of his eloquence as a game and reflects: "[H]ow can I fail to get the better of such a young soul?" (II.vi.93). He is always a divided self, watching his own behavior from a distance rather than fully participating in it. He becomes an actor in his own play, one in which he is author and director. Yet the speaker, we learn, is an actor who on many occasions does not know when he is acting; when he does know, he cannot control his actions. Just as in Part I he responds to an imagined audience, here his words are shaped by his need to manipulate; he requires empowerment and control.

Yet, despite his inability to sustain the images of married love he eloquently presents to Liza – whom he seduces by his Machiavellian manipulation of language to hang on his every word – the Underground Man's words often do reflect Dostoevsky's beliefs: "Where there is no love, there is no reason," and he speaks of God's blessing upon a functional married family. Indeed, more and more he links love and God: "Love – is God's mystery, and should be hidden from all other eyes, whatever happens. It's holier that way, and better" (II.vi.95, 97). Yet he invents the narrative and uses his rhetorical power to convince Liza of his heroic nature even while knowing he cannot sustain such a self-image and doesn't want to. That his motives are malign may be why Pevear and Volokhonsky want to be sure that the retrospective speaker acknowledges that he is "wicked."

The reader soon sees that in contrast to the speaker's verbosity, even logorrhea, Liza's simple language, which first appears to be inarticulateness – recalling Cordelia in *King Lear* – reveals the purity of her soul. In a sense, her simplicity and decency, rendered in spare, sparse diction, are trumped by the complexity of the Underground Man's rhetoric. She becomes hostage to the power of his words, as if Dostoevsky is showing that faithless modernists such as the speaker have polluted, despoiled, and corrupted language by kidnapping it for their own purposes. She is caught in the thralls of the Underground Man's words, especially when she visits him. Unlike when he writes from underground in Part I, he feels with Liza empowered by his spoken language. Never in full control, he doesn't know what he is going to say and yet speaks eloquently about love. But he doesn't believe in the power of his own words. When he writes his "Notes" – the "Notes" that are the text – he erases, defaces, and deforms his own eloquence by his behavior and the discourse in which that eloquence appears.

Our sympathy for Liza makes the narrator much less sympathetic when we reread Part I because we realize that, for all his objections to a society organized to favor the men of action and his desire to differentiate himself as a man more conscious than others of the actual conditions of human life, he is a moral dwarf.

The Function of the Editor

At the outset of Part I, the editor has signed "Dostoevsky" to the note accompanying the title. Therefore we assume that the closing intervention is that of the author, or perhaps a version of the author who clearly wishes to distance himself from his character's monstrous and manipulative behavior towards Liza.

....

Both the author of the notes and the *Notes* themselves are, of course, fictional. Nevertheless, such persons as the writer of such notes not only may but even must exist in our society, taking into consideration the circumstances under which our society has generally been formed.... [The writer] is one representative of a generation that is still living out its life. In this fragment, entitled "Underground," this person introduces himself, his outlook, and seeks, as it were, to elucidate the reasons why he appeared and had to appear among us. In the subsequent fragment will come this person's actual "notes" about certain events in his life.

– *Fyodor Dostoevsky* (I.i.3)

....

One aspect of the irresolution of *Notes* is the ending, or lack of it, as the narrator returns to the retrospective present: "Even now, after so many years," and his expressed regret for writing what he calls his own "corrective punishment" (II.x.129).

At this point the editor – now in the guise of a reasonable and dispassionate surrogate for Dostoevsky who both introduces and complements the perverse autobiographical speaker – intervenes in such a way as to confirm the reality of the first speaker and to underline what Dostoevsky feels is necessary to the formal verisimilitude in which the narrator bitterly recapitulates his various rationalizations, often disguised as half-baked theories, along with his more credible protests against the Enlightenment's faith in reason: "However, the 'notes' of this paradoxicalist do not end here. He could not help himself and went on. But it also seems to us that this may be a good place to stop" (II.x.130).

We realize that the editor is a character whose role is to present the story and, by doing so, give it credibility. Perhaps inadvertently, he becomes a doubleganger, because while exposing the Underground Man, he is also giving him a forum. Because the Underground Man can't write a fully coherent text, he uses – and the editor accepts – the term "*Notes*." In doing so, does not the editor somewhat become a secret sharer to the Underground Man's analyses and purpose?

Conclusion

What Geoffrey O'Brien says of Gogol could be said of Dostoevsky's narrator in *Notes from Underground*, but also of his major characters in *Crime and Punishment* and *The Brothers Karamazov*: "Gogol builds a narrative line, crosses it out, starts again at another point. At any moment the world that he builds sentence by sentence can be taken apart and put back together in a different and not necessarily tolerable shape. Language is something that has the power to make worlds and also the capacity to warp and reverse them, thus a medium of permanent insecurity and, not the least, unlimited potential cruelty."[11]

Study Questions for *Notes from Underground*

1. With reference to specific passages, how should we define the psyche and values of the narrator?
2. Is the narrator reliable and, if so, in what sense? Is he perceptive? Is there an oscillating distance between Dostoevsky and the speaker?
3. What is the text's chronology?
4. How can we explain the title of Part II?
5. What is the relation between Part I and Part II?
6. Why is section ix of Part I pivotal to the structure and themes of *Notes from Underground*?
7. What is Liza's relationship to the speaker and what is her role in defining Dostoevsky's values?
8. What is the function of the editor?
9. What is the relationship between "romanticism" and "realism" in *Notes from Underground*?
10. How does the speaker of *Notes from Underground* anticipate Raskolnikov in *Crime and Punishment* and Ivan in *The Brothers Karamazov*?

2. *Crime and Punishment*: Raskolnikov's Descent and Rebirth

Dostoevsky's Imagined World

When one opens the pages of a Dostoevsky novel one enters into an imagined world defined by intensity, passion, idiosyncrasies, and extremes, whether they be alcoholism and its ravages, poverty to the point of starvation, or clothing reduced to rags, as well as fantastic dreams and nightmares. The reader is called upon to digest a maelstrom of action, thinking, and dialogue, usually in long paragraphs that almost overwhelm his capacity to hold everything in his mind at once. The reader is caught up in a torrential flow of words, images, and events.

It is as if the novel overflows the borders of Western expectations and Western sensibility.

Where in Western literature do we find the energy and speed that take us through days so hectic that it is hard to believe the action in *Crime and Punishment* takes place in only nine and one half days? More specifically, as the plot and often rapid-fire dialogue rush forward in one dramatic scene after another, the continuing resonances of the murders ricocheting in the reader's mind leave little room for the reader to step back and think about the pell-mell pace. Throughout, the resonances and echoes – within the structure of events, including intersecting plots and the verbal texture of the dialogues – put the reader in a whirlwind as well as in a closed world where there is no exit from poverty and where the strong prey upon the weak.

If, as we shall see in Volume 2 of this study, Thomas Mann is something of a Mannerist who creates a pure Mannerist in Aschenbach and Franz Kafka is a Surrealist, isn't Dostoevsky a Baroque writer who recalls Caravaggio? Along with Stendhal, especially in *The Charterhouse of Parma*, Dostoevsky relies on qualities of the Baroque: violent, high-pitched emotional episodes; richly detailed psychological and physical realism; and dramatic, highly theatrical visceral scenes with striking contrasts between light and dark. What could be more Baroque than the scenes in *Notes* between the speaker and Liza or in *Crime and Punishment* between Raskolnikov and Sonya, or even between him and his mother and sister, to say nothing of the scenes with Porfiry Petrovich?

Crime and Punishment – which originally appeared in 1866 in twelve monthly installments – is a great detective novel. We watch Porfiry Petrovich discover that Raskolnikov is the murderer and close in on him while Raskolnikov compulsively puts himself in the line of sight of the police. But unlike most detective fiction, we know from the outset who the perpetrator is. The novel much depends on the simple dramatic irony of our knowing what Raskolnikov has done and the characters in the novel not knowing. We wait for the detectives and others to discover what we know.

One of Dostoevsky's strengths is what Bakhtin has called Dostoevsky's dialogic imagination, meaning he can enter into the perspective of a bevy of characters, many of whom are far from admirable, most notably the speaker in *Notes from Underground* and Raskolnikov. As Bakhtin puts it, "The hero interests Dostoevsky as a *particular point of view on the world and on oneself.*"[12] I would substitute "protagonist" for "hero."

Since we know from the outset who the murderer is, our interest is in both his psychological responses and the process by which he is identified as the criminal as well as in his redemption. But we need to acknowledge that most twenty-first-century readers may be less interested than the author and his narrator in the murderer's Christian conversion. Indeed, it is a legitimate aesthetic question to ask, "Does the Christian ending work for those of us who are not Christians?" Are we, we might ask if we are not believers in Dostoevsky's mystical vision, resistant to his focus on suffering as the road to repentance and moral resurrection?

The novel is a study of social psychosis in which a destitute ex-student on the margins of society confirms his free will and sense of identity by killing and robbing an elderly lady pawnbroker. Using interior monologues – on occasion set off by parentheses – Dostoevsky shows us the distinction between what he sees and what Raskolnikov thinks. Over and over Dostoevsky reminds us of why Raskolnikov behaves as he does towards his mother, sister, friend (Razumikhin), doctor (Zossimov), and those seeking to know the truth about the crime.

Dostoevsky respects the intelligence and perspicacity of his readers, and knows that they need to be attentive to nuances. According to Joseph Frank, "A decisive moment in the creation of [*Crime and Punishment*] occurred in November 1865, when Dostoevsky decided to shift from a first-person narrator telling his own story to a carefully defined third-person narrator external to the events themselves."[13] The third person narrator allows Dostoevsky to dramatize Raskolnikov's perspective, but also to step back and watch other characters, provide commentary, and examine other points of view as well as shift time back and forth. Such time shifts as placing the tavern scene, which occurred six weeks before the murder but within the text right before the murder, create, as Frank puts it, "a profound effect of dramatic irony that works both backward and forward in the text."[14]

Georgy Chulkov argues that Dostoevsky burned the original text "because the first person narrative was insufficiently suited to give the reader an impression of all the complexity of psychology and plot."[15] In fact, in contrast to Tolstoy or even the self-dramatizing narrator in *Notes from Underground*, there is little overt narrative commentary in *Crime and Punishment*. Yet the third person narrator on whose focalization the reader depends is more of a character than many critics realize. By selecting and arranging and highlighting events, doesn't the narrator create the pace? And his quiet irony informs every scene and description, even when he simultaneously empathizes with multiple perspectives within a scene.

Who is Raskolnikov?

Raskolnikov is a twenty-three-year-old university dropout who has separated himself from the socio-economic world and is on a kind of private strike. His family is not of the peasant class but rather from the gentry, although his family has come upon hard times. Thus he is now living like a peasant or even worse. Except for Razumikhin, Raskolnikov is friendless (1.iv.51).

Raskolnikov reflects Dostoevsky's view of the nihilistic movement of the 1860s that urged casting aside traditional morality. He owes something to Bazarov, who in Turgenev's *Fathers and Sons* (1862) placed himself above traditional moral laws and social conventions and exhibited contempt for the ordinary Russian. Yet after his murders, Raskolnikov discovers within himself a more humane side, what Frank describes as "instinctive kindness, sympathy, and pity."[16] He needs to grow beyond, to cite Frank, "idealistic egoism that has become perverted into a contemptuous disdain for the submissive herd."[17] Such egoism allows him to regard the old woman pawnbroker, Alyona Ivanovna, as useless, thus justifying his murdering her; he also kills her half-sister Lizaveta, who arrives unexpectedly during the murder.

Dostoevsky oscillates between sympathy and judgment when presenting the most pathetic figures. He takes the reader into the minds of sociopaths and psychopaths. We might remember that not only are there no therapists in nineteenth-century Petersburg, but also that Dostoevsky does not have modern psychological terms to describe characters driven by obsessions, compulsions, and unacknowledged needs. By showing the misery, degradation, and self-torture of Raskolnikov, he almost makes the character of the poor, starving, unemployed former student sympathetic, even as Raskolnikov plots the murder of his hated pawnbroker. More strikingly, we are somewhat empathetic even after the murder because of Raskolnikov's physical and mental illness, his love for his mother, sister, and, later, Sonya, and his generosity with the pittance of money that he does have.

Raskolnikov is imprisoned by his actions even before he is caught. He becomes aware that he is completely separate from everyone: "[I]t suddenly became perfectly plain and clear to him that he had just uttered a terrible lie [namely, that he and his mother and sister "will have time to talk"], that not only would he never have the chance to talk all he wanted, but that it was no longer possible for him to *talk* at all, with anyone, about anything, ever" (3.iii.229). Perversely, Raskolnikov seems to masochistically enjoy the cat and mouse game he plays with the clever police detective, Porfiry Petrovich, even while knowing that he is losing, as when in 3.v he is the last of the old lady's clients – or so says Porfiry – to come forward and claim his pawned possessions. Dostoevsky strongly hints that Raskolnikov and Porfiry – who stresses that he is a bachelor – act out a latent homosexual attraction, perhaps a result of the loneliness of both. At times, it as if they were verbally – and at times physically – stalking one another, for a reason that neither fully acknowledges.

Once he has crossed the line and murdered, Raskolnikov is estranged from conventional social discourse by his secrets, his guilt, and at times his shame. The reader understands that words are essential to what differentiates humans from other creatures, namely the ability to communicate. Raskolnikov's estrangement from words is all the more underlined by our reading words – indeed, being immersed in the overwhelming rush of Dostoevsky's prose so that we can barely put down the book.

Dostoevsky's Response to Darwin: "The Living Soul"

The year 2009 was the 150th anniversary of *Origin of Species* and the 200th anniversary of Darwin's birth. Even though Darwin had many important predecessors in pointing the way for his scientific explanations of nature – including the geologist Charles Lyell (*Principles of Geology*, 1830–1833) and his contemporary Alfred Russell Wallace, who also formulated the theory of evolution by natural selection – it is fair to say Darwin did the most to show that the Bible was historically obsolete and simply wrong in terms of offering an account of Creation.

Richard Lewontin has argued that part of the appeal of Darwinism is that it could also be used to explain the survival of the human fittest during the Industrial Revolution and to align natural theory with political economy: "The theory of evolution by natural selection … is meant to explain the adaptation and biological success of an entire species as a consequence of the disappearance of the less fit."[18] But what if, as Lewontin puts it, this becomes a justification for competitive socio-economic or even racial success? "The theory of competitive socioeconomic success is a theory about the rise of individuals and individual enterprises as a consequence of their superior fitness."[19] And this view informs *Crime and Punishment* where one strand of characters consists of characters resembling at times predatory animals – Luzhin, Svidrigailov, and Raskolnikov – while others resist this survival of the fittest behavior and form a diametrically opposite strand, namely Sonya and Razumikhin.

Of the novelists I am writing about in Volume 1 of my two-volume study of major European novels, Dostoevsky has perhaps the most inclusive view of the human psyche. As much as any of the novelists I discuss in this volume, he understands that nature includes the irrational, the inexplicable human psyche, and the uncanny as well as the biological and instinctive needs of humankind.

Let us turn to the words of Razumikhin – Raskolnikov's closest friend whom he regards as a "little fool" (3.vi.274) – who is often a Dostoevsky surrogate in *Crime and Punishment*: "[T]he *living* process of life[,] … the living soul will demand life, the living soul won't listen to mechanics," and for that reason he rejects the view that logic and social formulae explain nature, including human nature: "Nature isn't taken into account, nature is driven out, nature is not supposed to be!" (3.v.256). For Dostoevsky and his character Razumikhin, Darwin represents mechanism, the idea that everything can be explained by reason and science so that eventually we will know everything about how human life works. For him nature means not only the mysteries of how humans behave, but also how the world is organized by God. Reason and logic are limited and there is much more to know, some of it intuitively and spiritually.

St. Petersburg

Crime and Punishment is a book about the horrors of urban life. St. Petersburg, referred to in nineteenth-century Russia simply as Petersburg, is itself a character in the novel, and it has strong resemblances to the city of nineteenth-century fiction that we see in Balzac, Dickens, and Flaubert, with poverty, drunks, vagrants, criminals, swindlers, whores, opportunists, social climbers, flâneurs, as well as corrupt and incompetent officials. Urban life is a moral tangle in most European fiction, although provincial life is no better in Flaubert and Stendhal.

Dostoevsky stresses misery as a function of the teeming city where the have-nots live in terrible circumstances. With its grinding poverty, abusive and abused people, rampant alcoholism, tiny and overpopulated apartments, and crowded streets swarming with people who are struggling for survival, Petersburg is dirty, nasty, ugly, and malodorous. Violence lurks in every corner, and it is not safe for women to walk the streets, according to Razumikhin. Its sounds – "[t]errible desperate screams" when drunks leave the taverns (2.i.89) – often define human degradation. In Petersburg, the radial circle of misery is Haymarket. Out of necessity, people seem to gravitate to Haymarket, "where there is filth and stench and all sorts of squalor" (1.vi.73).

Because *Crime and Punishment* focuses on urban poverty, money hovers over the text. We take for granted that in an urban world where people don't raise their own food, it is necessary to have money. Dostoevsky is conscious of the relationship between income and need in the city where many of the citizens are peasants, often serfs freed as recently as 1861. Women turn to prostitution, as Sonya does, to survive. Street performers eke out an existence as virtual beggars.

I am not a word counter, but "roubles" and "kopecks" are ubiquitous; Raskolnikov is always counting his tiny amounts of money. Luzhin and Svidrigailov are conscious of how much they have; the latter married for money as Raskolnikov's sister Dunya was about to do by marrying Luzhin.

Dostoevsky set himself against materialism, but in this novel he shows how poverty is a major enemy of the human spirit. If Milton in *Paradise Lost* is of the devil's party without knowing it, Dostoevsky in *Crime and Punishment* is of money's party without knowing it. Outside the police world where power dominates – that is, one person's power over another – money is the espoused motive of much of the action.

Dostoevsky's world is defined by a struggle for economic survival, a world where the hunted and the hunters reside. In Raskolnikov's case, economic jealousy and economic rage play a role in his hunt that results in the murder of the pawnbroker. Most characters in the novel play both roles of hunter and hunted, except Sonya and sometimes Razumikhin, and even the latter is not above manipulating Raskolnikov's landlady. That marriage is usually more an economic arrangement than a coming together of lovers who are best friends is emphasized not only in the behavior of Luzhin and Svridrigailov, but also in that of Raskolnikov's mother and sister, who belong to a family whose economic fortunes are in devolution.

When Raskolnikov implies that if his sister marries for money she is no different than other whores, she responds, "I haven't gone and put a knife into anyone yet," suggesting not only to Raskolnikov, but also to the reader, what separates him from others (3.iii.233). Virtually every character is concerned about money and beset by what we now call stress and depression, but only he has "stepped over" and taken the life of other members of the human community. His punishment consists of physical illness, guilt, depression, and "[t]otal apathy" (2.vi.170).

Raskolnikov's Theory of Exceptional Humans

In the novel's crucial chapter, 3.v, Porfiry Petrovich not only makes clear that he strongly suspects Raskolnikov, but also gets Raskolnikov to articulate his philosophy – presented in his obscure article – that some exceptional humans are beyond traditional moral and legal prescriptions. Rather brilliantly and subtly, Porfiry gets Raskolnikov to explain why he could justify such a murder. Lest we miss this, his functionary, Zamyotov, chimes in: "Might it not have been some future Napoleon who bumped off our Alyona Ivanovna with an axe last week?" (3.v.266).

Napoleon hovers over the tale Raskolnikov tells himself. Napoleon looms very large in the nineteenth-century European imagination as someone who made his destiny out of whole cloth. For many of the novels in my first volume, Napoleon represents a paradigm for gall, transgression, arrogance, social transformation, and will to power. In *The Red and the Black* and *The Charterhouse of Parma*, he becomes a reference point for self-creation and self-measurement, for transcending the limitations of everyday existence and becoming a heroic and historically important figure.

As Raskolnikov mentally reviews the conversation with Porfiry Petrovich in 3.v, he has Napoleon in mind as a shining example of the personality who transcends law and morality to shape his destiny, although he had mentioned others in discussing his obscure article that Porfiry had found (3.v.260; 3.vi.274).

Ironically, Raskolnikov thinks, relying on "will and reason," he can commit the perfect crime, but he is in fact a bumbling, self-deluding incompetent (1.vi.70). He believes criminals give themselves away, but he will be immune. He fulfills in every way the criminal pattern he despises:

. . . .

[T]he criminal himself ... experiences at the moment of the crime a sort of failure of will and reason, which ... are replaced by a phenomenal, childish thoughtlessness ... [It] turned out that this darkening of reason and failure of will take hold of a man like a disease, develop gradually, and reach their height shortly before the crime is committed; they continue unabated during the moment of the crime itself and for some time after it, depending on the individual; then they pass in the same way as any disease passes. (1.vi.70–71)

. . . .

We see the irony of Raskolnikov – the man who would be a Napoleon and *Übermensch* – being in the throes of a feverish illness that not only makes him sleep countless hours and feel cold in the summer heat, but also feeds delirious nightmares. In his dream about a peasant beating his own horse to death, Raskolnikov is both the pained young child watching the sadistic scene and the aggressive drunken peasant. The dream becomes a foreshadowing of his killing of the pawnbroker and her half-sister (1.v.57). After the repellent dream he asks, "[C]an it be that I will really take an axe and hit her on the head and smash her skull" (1.v.59). Within this dream is a division among three roles: Raskolnikov as a sympathetic observer (the young child watching the scene in disgust before running to the dead horse out of pity); as a perpetrator of violence (the aggressive drunken peasant senselessly beating his own horse); and – identifying with the horse – as a tortured object. Does not this division prevail throughout *Crime and Punishment*?

In fact, Raskolnikov hardly has the makings of a Napoleon, and the former's ineptitude is the source of noir humor. Immediately after the murders, he "loath[es]" himself; he thinks "that he had fallen into madness and was unable at that moment either to reason or to protect himself" (1.vii.80). He never asserts full control over himself and is prey to every circumstance that might reveal his guilt. Within his rather wide-ranging perspective, he finds a measure of sympathy for Marmeladov, who confesses his self-destructive, obsessive drinking that leads to their daughter Sonya's turning to prostitution, and certainly for Marmeladov's victimized, albeit abusive, second wife Katerina Ivanovna, who is dying of consumption.

Finally, Raskolnikov despises himself because he cannot be whom he wants to be, a Napoleon freed from conscience. He cannot be "the true *master*, to whom all is permitted" (3.vi.274). While Raskolnikov articulates an *Übermensch* philosophy, he lacks the ego to maintain it. He wants to confess, and some compulsion drives him to it; he can't cast off the old morality.

He realizes that he is no less a "louse" than the people he kills: "I chose the most useless louse of all and, having killed her ... [ultimately] I am a louse ... because I myself am perhaps more vile and nasty than the louse I killed and I had *anticipated* beforehand that I would tell myself so *after* I killed her. Can anything compare with such horror? Oh, triteness! Oh, meanness!" (3.vi.275). He had hoped to establish himself as a Napoleon by killing as a principle: "The old woman was merely a sickness ... I was in a hurry to step over ... it wasn't a human being I killed, it was a principle! So I killed the principle, but I didn't step over, I stayed on this side" (3.vi.274). According to his credo, the free man makes his own rules and own morality: "[L]ife is given to me only once, and never will be again – I don't want to sit waiting for universal happiness. I want to live myself; otherwise it's better not to live at all" (3.vi.274).

But what he discovers is that he is a meek and cringing nobody who cannot manage his emotions. He despises himself as a "trembling creature," even as the narrator emphasizes here and elsewhere that he trembles when he feels unsure of himself (3.vi.275). He is haunted more by shame than guilt. In a sense his punishment begins even before his crimes; he is punishing himself throughout the narrative for failing to live up to his Napoleonic ideal.

The reader understands that whatever Raskolnikov's illusions, he acts out of weakness, alienation, and, finally, social psychosis rather than strength. His justifications are no different than those of other murderers, and that is a stain he wears for the twenty-first-century reader even after his Christian conversion.

Dostoevsky understands the role of social conditions in creating humans, but he would take issue with twenty-first-century evolutionary psychology, which argues that we are born with certain traits that we seek to maximize in the struggle for survival. As David Brooks observes, such a theory "organizes all behavior into one eternal theory, impervious to the serendipity of time and place."[20] By contrast, Dostoevsky realizes that individual history, economic circumstances, where one lives, and the system of government under which one lives, shape each of us. Basically agreeing with Dostoevsky, Brooks argues:

[O]ur brains are fluid and plastic. We're learning that evolution can be a more rapid process than we thought. It doesn't take hundreds of thousands of years to produce genetic alterations.... [W]e've evolved to adapt to diverse environments. [Even within a single individual] [d]ifferent circumstances can selectively activate different genetic potentials. Individual behavior can vary wildly from one context to another.… Evolutionary psychology leaves the impression that human nature was carved a hundred thousand years ago, and then history sort of stopped. But human nature adapts to the continual flow of information – adjusting to the ancient information contained in genes and the current information contained in today's news in a continuous, idiosyncratic blend. (ibid.)

While reading *Crime and Punishment* and adapting to the flow of information, we may temporarily walk on the wild side with sociopaths and psychopaths. Thus at least we partially participate in Raskolnikov's and others' – Marmeladov's, Luzhin's, Svidrigailov's – weird perspectives, until suddenly (and sometimes without warning) the narrator steps in and makes a definitive judgment on his characters. In this way, the narrator in *Crime and Punishment* – as well as in both *Notes from Underground* and *The Brothers Karamazov* – implicates us readers who have sympathized with explanations and motives that our rational daytime selves know are unacceptable.

But this phenomenon of taking a temporary vacation from our moral selves exists in other texts, too. Within this study, Stendhal's Julien Sorel is a prime example, but we could also cite his Count Mosca and Gina. Closer to our world we see this with such gangster chic works as the Damon Runyon Broadway stories as well as their offspring, the TV series *The Sopranos* and the Godfather films.

After Raskolnikov commits his second murder in the apartment – that of Lizaveta, half-sister of Alyona Ivanovna, the pawnbroker – the narrator observes: "And if [Raskolnikov] had been able at that moment to see and reason more properly, if he had only been able to realize all the difficulties of his situation, all the despair, all the hideousness, all the absurdity of it, and to understand, besides, how many more difficulties and perhaps evildoings he still had to overcome or commit in order to get out of there and reach home, he might very well have dropped everything and gone out at once to denounce himself, and not even out of fear for himself, but solely out of horror and loathing for what he had done" (1.vii.79–80). The narrator's words mirror the complexity of Raskolnikov's thoughts but are his own, for he is rendering what Raskolnikov, caught in the heat and terror of the moment – including his fear of being caught on the spot – is too confused to understand.

The Opening Chapters

When we begin reading a novel, we enter into an imagined world with its own geography, time scheme, historical cause and effect, and grammar of how people behave. The opening of *Crime and Punishment* is one of the great openings in world fiction. At the very outset the narrator introduces us to Raskolnikov, who is a very troubled, neurotic, angry, desperate, destitute to the point of nearly starving – albeit handsome – young man who has retreated into himself: "He was so immersed in himself and had isolated himself so much from everyone.... He had entirely given up attending to his daily affairs and did not want to attend to them" (1.i.3).

Unable to distinguish dream from reality, Raskolnikov is on the borderline of madness. He trembles and talks to himself, not only in whispers but out loud (1.iii.40). Like the Underground Man, he has retreated to a corner and harbors secret plans of vengeance, even as he doubts that he will carry them out. What he is contemplating is stepping outside the boundaries of morality and killing Aly-ona Ivanovna, the woman pawnbroker whom he regards as a predatory excres-cence who does not deserve to live. What he hates more than the pawnbroker is his own muddled situation. He despises himself for hesitating. Thinking about his plan after pawning his watch and leaving her apartment, he exclaims out loud: "Could such horror really come into my head? But then, what filth my heart is capable of! ... Above all, filthy, nasty, vile, vile" (1.i.9).

What he lacks, we understand as we reread, is faith. Unlike Sonya, he is a hopelessly divided self without moral compass. "The feeling of boundless loathing" is for himself and his situation but also for his inability to act and thus to follow through on his plans to murder (1.i.9). Defined and "crushed" by poverty, and pawning whatever he possesses for a pittance, he thinks of his room as a closet and, later, a kennel, but this is hardly surprising since on the first page, after calling the room a closet, the narrator observes that it "was more like a cupboard than a room" (1.i.3); later he describes it as "more resembl[ing] a cupboard or a trunk" (1.iii.40).

For two days he has eaten "almost nothing," and his clothing is in tatters (1.i.4). Yet, because "so much spiteful contempt was already stored up," he seems to take a masochistic pleasure in wearing "rags in the street" (1.i.5). Later, he understands that "he had regarded himself as a man to whom more was per-mitted than to others" (Epilogue.ii.544).

The introduction of the alcoholic, dissolute, and self-loathing former offi-cial Marmeladov – the first of Raskolnikov's many doublegangers – in 1.ii sus-tains not only the presentation of grinding poverty in Petersburg, but also that of the outsider who has lost his bearings and is estranged from the social and economic axis of the city. Unable to hold a job – only five days ago he turned towards drink and away from his last chance – or provide for his family's basic needs, Marmeladov lives in a tiny, shabby apartment.

His compulsive drinking has once again cost him his job, and his daughter Sonya is prostituting herself to support his abusive, unstable, and consumptive second wife, Katerina Ivanovna, and her three children. Were it not for Sonya, they would have nothing to eat. He has been sleeping among drunks and derelicts for five days. Mirroring Raskolnikov, he is badly dressed and ill kempt: "He was dressed in an old, completely ragged black frock coat, which had shed all its buttons.... It was quite possible that he had not undressed and washed for five days" (1.ii.12–13). Indeed, he is described as a "ragamuffin" (1.iv.47). Dostoevsky mocks Marmeladov's reductive faith by which he rationalizes that Christ will forgive him.

As he walks with Raskolnikov, Marmeladov confesses that he feels better when his wife beats him, another instance of violent abuse in the novel. While he says it "ease[s] her soul," in truth it eases his (1.ii.24). No sooner do we think we have seen the worst of human degradation than we are introduced to Marmeladov's disordered one-room apartment presided over by the severely disturbed Katerina Ivanovna. Other tenants have to walk through the Marmeladovs' apartment to get to their own (1.ii.25).

Without realizing it, Marmeladov speaks to Raskolnikov's plight before and after the murder: "It is necessary that every man have at least somewhere to go.... Do you understand, do you understand, my dear sir, what it means when there is no longer anywhere to go" (1.ii.14, 17). Raskolnikov thinks of the very same words when he reacts with anger to his mother's letter about his sister's forthcoming marriage to Luzhin and then leaves his tiny cupboard of a room. Raskolnikov, of course, has nowhere to go, as Porfiry Petrovich knows. More than his own room, his "closet" and "kennel" are his own thoughts.

We recall these words, too, when Raskolnikov comes across a drunken female teenager whom he takes for sixteen; she seems to have been manhandled and will probably soon become a prey to the well-dressed man who is following her. After Marmeladov is run down by a horse-drawn carriage and Raskolnikov makes sure that he is taken home, we recall these words about needing a place to go, just as we recall, too, Raskolnikov's dream of the abused horse that is beaten to death. The more we reread, the more we see that the novel's efficacy depends on echoes and resonances.

Sonya

It is important that Sonya makes her entrance into the novel after she is fetched to visit her father Marmeladov: "Timidly and inaudibly, a girl came in, squeezing through the crowd, and her sudden appearance was strange in that room, in the midst of poverty, rags, death, and despair. She, too, was in rags, a two-penny costume, but adorned in street fashion, to suit the taste and rules established in that special world, with a clearly and shamefully explicit purpose" (2.vii.183). The stakes for the novel's themes are high here. On one hand, Dostoevsky wants to put Sonya in the context of the predatory world where men prey on helplessly poor women. But on the other, he wants to place her among the meek who will inherit the earth and to stress her timidity and inaudibility, as opposed to the commotion in which her mother plays such a major role. Although dressed in cheap, gaudy clothes, we know Sonya is different, in part because she is silent. Her outfit is out of place but her presence is not. To emphasize that she is incorruptible, Dostoevsky gives her "remarkable blue eyes"; he knew that his nineteenth-century Russian reader would remember that blue is the color of the Virgin Mary (2.vii.183).

When Raskolnikov kills the women, he kills himself. Yet rebirth is possible in Dostoevsky's cosmology. Because of his religious transformation – which is in part a function of Sonya's unconditional love – and his suffering, he can be reborn. Although an unbeliever, Raskolnikov had called on "God" to protect him in the hours after the crime (2.i.93). In a sense his problem is estrangement from God. When he is contemplating the crime, he "pleaded": "Lord … show me my way; I renounce this cursed … dream of mine!" Raskolnikov disbelieves like only a former believer can and that disbelief is vulnerable to Sonya's influence (1.ii.60).

In a memorable scene, when Sonya reads the Lazarus passage of the Bible to Raskolnikov, Dostoevsky foreshadows Raskolnikov's spiritual rebirth. By offering him an alternative vision in words and deeds, she becomes his spiritual bridge and counselor. Raskolnikov intuitively understands that he is dependent on Sonya – "I understand. I need you, and so I've come to you" (4.iv.329). He thinks they have both "stepped over" accepted moral lines but he doesn't realize the irony of his use of that term: "You, too, have stepped over … were able to step over. You laid hands on yourself, you destroyed a life … *your own* (it's all the same!)" (4.iv.329). In fact, after entering Sonya's room and at first sounding like the Underground Man with Liza – in dialogues which Dostoevsky is deliberately echoing – Raskolnikov is awakening in his soul, "stepping over" to Christianity. Sonya doesn't fully understand what is going on – how she is spiritually building a bridge to another world – but Dostoevsky expects the reader to be more perceptive than she is.

When Raskolnikov kisses Sonya's feet, we think of the Lazarus passage in which Mary of Bethany falls at Jesus's feet after her brother has died (4.iv.321). But we also recall that, according to legend, Mary Magdalene, knowing Jesus will die, washes his feet. (In *Luke* the woman is identified only as a "sinner.") In this scene, Raskolnikov also learns that Lizaveta was a treasured friend of Sonya's. Only at the end of the episode do we learn that Svidrigailov has rented the adjoining room and has been listening; he has heard Raskolnikov say that "[I]f I come tomorrow, I'll tell you who killed Lizaveta" and strongly hint that it was himself: "I've chosen you. I won't come asking for forgiveness, I'll simply tell you" (4.iv.330).

Punishment

Doesn't Raskolnikov's self-punishment begin even before he commits the crime, in part because he despises himself knowing that he has the capacity to commit the murders? Later, unable to escape echoes of his crime, Raskolnikov is the agent of much of his punishment, including Porfiry's pursuit. What George Eliot says of Bulstrode is appropriate to Raskolnikov, whose every minute is defined by his consciousness of his past crimes as well as his awareness that others suspect him: "A man's past is not simply a dead history, an outworn preparation of the present; it is not a repented error shaken loose from the life: It is a still quivering part of himself."[21]

Resonances of his crime in dreams and conversations weave an ineluctable net around Raskolnikov. His dreams are saturated with the crucial murderous event. It seems as if everywhere he goes and every conversation he hears has echoes of it. He becomes increasingly paranoid and is often sure discovery is a moment away.

To show how Raskolnikov is caught in the net of his own crime and that his punishment is within his head, Dostoevsky has him repeat his thoughts and his physical responses. It is as if he were revisiting the same dreams in his small apartment, or, put another way, as if he were regularly visited by the same uninvited and unexpected callers. Having similar interviews and conversations, it is as if Raskolnikov were in the throes of an obsessive repetition compulsion. Do we not see a strong similarity among his encounters with Porfiry Petrovich and even Ilya Petrovich (nicknamed "Gunpowder") on the one hand, and with Luzhin and Svidrigailov on the other?

The man who would commit the perfect crime is out of control as soon as he commits his crime. On his very first visit to the police station, where he has been summoned to deal with a promissory note he had signed for his landlady, he is worried that he will confess: "I'll walk in, fall on my knees, and tell them everything" (2.i.94). The non-believer is calling on God for help. The person of superior intelligence is cowed by every minor functionary within the police establishment. The man who prided himself on being a community of one, who had left behind traditional values when he had "stepped over" the needs of others so as take care of his every psychic need, is crippled by his isolation.

On first seeing the place where Raskolnikov lives, his mother remarks that his "awful apartment" resembles "a coffin" (3.iii.231), suggesting to us that murders have separated him from the rest of humanity, no matter what their shortcomings and faults. In Dostoevsky's cosmos, only suffering and repentance can bring Raskolnikov back from the morally dead.

On Raskolnikov's first visit to the police station, the narrator focuses on Raskolnikov's sense of isolation: "A dark sensation of tormenting, infinite solitude and estrangement suddenly rose to consciousness in his soul.… What was taking place in him was totally unfamiliar, new, sudden, never before experienced" (2.i.103). His every thought is fixed on the murder; instead of "stepping over" he has fallen into an abyss populated by nightmares, anxieties that he will be discovered, the need to confess, and the weight of his guilt.

Dostoevsky dramatizes a man driven by compulsions and doing exactly what his reason tells him not to do. Without any provocation, he actually says playfully to Zamyotov, the police clerk, in a tavern, "I confess," in part because the crime has become a "fixed, heavy" weight (2.v.153; 2.vi.161); he needs to lift the weight by confessing. He quickly modifies "I confess" to "I give testimony and you take it" to "I was looking – and that is the reason I came here – for news about the murder of the official's old widow" (2.vi.161). While telling Zamyotov how he, unlike some arrested counterfeiters, would be wily enough to get away with criminality, he continues to reveal himself in foolish ways that he cannot control. But he soon goes further: "And what if it was I who killed the old woman and Lizaveta?" (2.vi.165).

Raskolnikov's relation to language has changed and that is part of his punishment. He continually hears echoes of his crime. When Nastasya proposes that blood clotting is responsible for his dreaming of Ilya Petrovich beating his landlady – another resonant iteration of his guilt – and utters the word "blood," Raskolnikov thinks of the bloodstains on his clothing: "Blood! … What blood?" (2.ii.116).

In *Crime and Punishment*, punishment does not always fit the crime and is not always meted out to those deserving it, as in Sonya's suffering for the crimes of others, or as in Marmeladov's inadvertent accident created by the victim's weaknesses and setting off a concatenation of punishments, not just for him but for his family.

As we read, the text itself asks the reader to continually judge and condemn Raskolnikov as if it were trying him for the murders. It is almost as if he is captured in the reader's mind – and surely in the rereader's – before he is captured, because the reader sees how much evidence has been left behind. Specifically, once the painters and the two other visitors to the pawnbroker's apartment are discarded as perpetrators, there are no other possible murder suspects. Clearly, the obvious suspect is none other than Raskolnikov, the misanthropic former student who has been a customer of the deceased and who has written that some superior beings have the privilege of killing the less worthy. That the student is penniless, derelict, and physically and emotionally ill – if not deranged – further casts suspicion on him.

The oft-mentioned "axe" is the murder weapon that Raskolnikov takes, hides under his coat, and returns to the caretaker of his residence. Invoked by Dostoevsky as a metonymy for Raskolnikov's brutal murders, the axe hovers over our reading of the text. Raskolnikov uses the butt of the axe handle to kill the pawn-broker; she is called "the old woman" in the murder scene as if to emphasize that to Raskolnikov she is not a living person. (If he thought of her as Alyona Ivanovna, she would have a claim on her own human identity.) He uses the cutting end of the axe to split Lizaveta's head as if she were a piece of wood; she is more a stock character than a living person to Raskolnikov.

Rereading the murder scene, we see that Dostoevsky repeats and repeats the word "axe" to emphasize the horror, violence, and brutality of the crime and plant in the reader's mind the vicious premeditation of the murder. The very recurrence of the word "axe" within the text reminds us how Raskolnikov is imprisoned by his actions and awaits the axe of retribution to fall and cut through his lies and evasions. It awakens the reader's judgment and keeps the reader from being overly forgiving of Raskolnikov's plight or sympathetic to his perspective. It is not too much to say that it is Porfiry Petrovich who, although also hiding his metaphorical axe – the weapon of legality and justice – wields it against Raskolnikov.

The crime of the novel's title is not limited to Raskolnikov. Many other criminal acts take place, including those of Luzhin, Svidrigailov, and, of course, Marmeladov, whose alcoholism has destroyed his family and driven his daughter into prostitution. Luzhin's planting of a one hundred-rouble note on Sonya and then accusing her of stealing it parody the way that Raskolnikov self-justifyingly and narcissistically makes his own rules, including killing the pawn-broker and her sister.

Nor should we forget Mikolka, who suffers for a crime he thinks he has committed, or the young student who advocates killing the woman pawnbroker, or Katerina Ivanovna's abuse of Sonya and neglect of her children. Svidrigailov's wife, Marfa Petrovna, died after he hit her twice with a riding crop, recalling Raskolnikov's dream of the horse being whipped to death. We might say that the horse beating, Marmeladov's accident, and Marfa Petrovna's death constitute a metonymic series in which one violent act begets another, echoing Raskolnikov's murders on almost very page.

Doublegangers

What is powerful and frightening in *Crime and Punishment* is how characters seem to get inside one another and know their secrets even before they are told. Porfiry reads the text of Raskolnikov's life as if it were a literary text, and so, in a very different way, does Sonya. Of course, ironically Raskolnikov is a strong misreader of himself, and despises himself for not being the *Übermensch* who can step over the barriers of morality. And this failure to be the person he wishes to be makes him vulnerable to those who would claim significant parallels to his life, empathy, and/or intuitive knowledge of his thoughts.

We realize that for Raskolnikov, often delirious, the line between dreams and actuality is a dotted one. He is not always sure if he sees real people or physical apparitions. Dostoevsky dramatizes that what we see and what we dream depend on who we are. In a sense, we encounter some aspect of our past in many, if not most, present moments and even more so in our dreams. For Raskolnikov, these characters mysteriously entering his fraught, harrowing, guilt-ridden world are a source of intense psychological anxiety. R. P. Blackmur has remarked that coincidental and fatal encounters are "the artist's way of expressing those forces in us not ourselves." Such encounters "create our sense of that other self within us that we can neither quite escape not quite meet up with."[22] But that other self is really another version of ourselves brought out by a confluence of personality and character with particular circumstances.

Marmeladov, Svidrigailov, Porfiry Petrovich, Ilya Petrovich, Luzhin, Razumikhin, even Mikolka, who confesses and suffers guilt for a crime he didn't commit, and, yes, Sonya, are versions of Raskolnikov. Thus, much of the tension of the novel depends on our understanding that Raskolnikov is, at the same time as he is having a dialogue with other characters, also having a colloquy between self and soul, between who he is and who he might be. By having such figures as Svidrigailov, Porfiry Petrovich, and Razumikhin mysteriously appear in Raskolnikov's room when he awakes, Dostoevsky emphasizes how these characters are not only Other, but intimately connected to Raskolnikov's very self.

Dostoevsky uses the doubleganger as a means of probing Raskolnikov's consciousness. The word comes from the German *Doppelgänger*, literally meaning "double-goer." At various times, these doubles of Raskolnikov include Luzhin, Svidrigailov, Marmeladov, Razumikhin, and Porfiry Petrovich. Doubles also include Raskolnikov's mother, who has a propensity for madness, and his sister Dunya, whose displaced idealism resembles his own in her willingness to marry Luzhin in what Raskolnikov insists is a crude financial transaction that will make her the "benefactress" of the family (3.iii.232). Because Raskolnikov has not been able to provide for her destitute and economically declining family, Dunya is willing to marry as a kind of self-punishment, a socially accepted kind of prostitution that recalls Sonya's plight. There is a hint that she may have compromised herself with Svidrigailov.

Even minor characters are Raskolnikov's doubles, like the student in the tavern who speaks of his desire to kill Alyona Ivanovna and his claim that such a murder would be a just homicide: "I could kill and rob that cursed old woman, and that, I assure you, without any remorse.... [O]n the one hand you have a stupid, meaningless, worthless, wicked, sick old crone, no good to anyone, and, on the contrary, harmful to everyone" (1.vi.64–65). Raskolnikov's doubles include both Mikolkas. Isn't the Mikolka who confesses to Raskolnikov's crime a poignant counterpart to the man with the same name who in Raskolnikov's dreams beats his horse to death with whips and a crowbar and who – reflecting what is in the sleeping Raskolnikov's consciousness – is urged by observers to use an axe (1.v.58)?

Razumikhin as Counterpart and Double

In Dostoevsky's imagined world, most characters are in some sense counterparts to Raskolnikov. With his innocence, generosity, and straightforward, open manner, at first Razumikhin seems Raskolnikov's opposite and a kind of idealized Russian. One might say he is the man Raskolnikov would have been had he followed his better impulses. His "simplicity concealed both depth and dignity" (1.iv.51). Although poor, he does not give in to despair and, unlike Raskolnikov who has given up on work now that he is no longer a student, "supported himself decidedly on his own, alone, getting money by work of one sort or another" (1.iv.51). Razumikhin "had the property of speaking the whole of himself out at once, whatever mood he was in, so that everyone soon knew with whom they were dealing" (3.i.200). Yet, when the drunken Razumikhin calls Luzhin "a Jew and a mountebank," we would be remiss not to notice Dostoevsky's anti-Semitism (3.i.204).

To understand how Razumikhin becomes a doubleganger, we need to examine the pivotal scene at the inn (5.ii) where in Raskolnikov and Razumikhin's presence, Raskolnikov's sister Dunya dismisses Luzhin. Announcing his mysterious withdrawal from the company of sister, mother, and closest friend, Raskolnikov had said, "Leave me ... but *don't leave them*," meaning his sister and mother. In this intense scene, in which Raskolnikov assigns his own family to his better self and double – emphasized by the shared initial "R" with four syllables following – there is a strong hint that Razumikhin understands why: "Razumikhin remembered that minute all his life. Raskolnikov's burning and fixed look seemed to grow more intense every moment, penetrating his soul, his consciousness. All at once Razumikhin gave a start. Something strange seemed to pass between them.... Razumikhin turned pale as a corpse" (4.iii.314). Knowing that Raskolnikov is the murderer, Razumikhin, Raskolnikov's secret sharer, obeys: "Razumikhin became their son and brother" (4.iii.314).

Razumikhin is the polar opposite of the Machiavellian and stingy Luzhin, who creates a philosophy to justify selfishness and gets his intended and her mother – Raskolnikov's sister and mother – a place in a nasty rooming house. But he reveals himself as a scoundrel. He plants a one hundred-rouble note on Sonya and then accuses her of stealing it as a way of getting revenge on

Raskolnikov. Luzhin recalls the Underground Man in arguing that what makes man human is his free will to be an individual: "Lying is man's only privilege over all other organisms.... Lying is what makes me a man.... Lying in one's own way is almost better than telling the truth in someone else's way" (3.i.202). What he objects to is a theory of "total impersonality" – which puts him in some agreement with Raskolnikov's idea of "stepping over" limitations and constraints – as if man were caught up in an historical process that he could not control. On the face of it, he is more Raskolnikov's double than Razumikhin, but he, unlike Raskolnikov, lacks the potential for transfiguration.

Svidrigailov: Raskolnikov's Baser Self

Svidrigailov is presented as a revolting fungus who insinuates himself into Raskolnikov's tiny quarters at the end of Part Three. Later, after he overhears Raskolnikov confessing the murders to Sonya, Raskolnikov meets him – seemingly accidentally – at a tavern and thinks: "[T]he man has some hidden power over him.... [H]e had really seemed to need the man for something" (5.v.436; 6.iii.462–463).

Arriving in the very middle of the novel at the end of Part Three and dominating the first chapter of Part Four, Svidrigailov is both a doubleganger and parody of Raskolnikov. He notes a "common point" between himself and Raskolnikov (4.i.287) and speaks of their being "apples from the same tree" (4.i.290). He lives by his own code – flouting social convention – and is perhaps responsible for the death of his wife. His offer of 10,000 roubles to Dunya, Raskolnikov's sister, ironically mirrors Raskolnikov's generosity to Sonya. Svidrigailov writes to Dunya that he knows Raskolnikov is the murderer. She meets him and he threatens "force" as if he might rape her.

If Razumikhin represents Raskolnikov's better self, Svidrigailov represents his baser self. Like Raskolnikov, he makes his own rules. It is Svidrigailov who argues that "reason is the slave of passion" (4.i.282). Like Raskolnikov and Luzhin, he acts according to his own morality. He is an example of a man who uses freedom from conventional morality to make his own rules, whether in whipping women with whom he is involved or disdaining the opinions of others: "I'm not particularly interested in anyone's opinions" (4.i.284). He is a narcissistic sex addict whose depravity ironically disgusts Raskolnikov, although we know that the latter's depravity includes murder. Svidrigailov does commit suicide, while a combination of fear, love for Sonya, and some unacknowledged desire to live constrains Raskolnikov.

In dialogues with Svidrigailov, Raskolnikov plays the interrogator's role of Porfiry and Svidrigailov plays Raskolnikov's role. Dostoevsky deftly renders the psychological interplay between the two, an interplay that becomes even more intense after Svidrigailov has overheard Raskolnikov's confession to Sonya that he is the murderer.

In a sense Svidrigailov defines himself by the bitterly cynical view of eternity that he proposes during the dialogue in Raskolnikov's room with which Part Four opens: "[I]magine that there will be one little room there, something like a village bathhouse, covered with soot, with spiders in all the corners, and that's the whole of eternity" (4.i.289). Doesn't this image hover over our reading of *Crime and Punishment* and become associated not only with Svidrigailov, but also with Luzhin and even the socialist ideologue Lebezyatnikov, and of course Raskolnikov, until, with Sonya's help, he transforms himself into a Christian?

Crime and Punishment as a Detective Novel: Porfiry Petrovich Burrowing into Raskolnikov's Psyche

Crime and Punishment is a great detective novel and 4.v is as great a scene between investigator and perpetrator as I have ever read. Alternatively obsequious and condescending, solicitous and imperious, seemingly empathetic and ostentatiously manipulative, Porfiry Petrovich not only disarms Raskolnikov and cracks his defenses but also brings him within a hair's breadth of a complete confession.

Dostoevsky dramatizes how Raskolnikov is caught in a net and can't escape, no matter which way he tries to move. Dostoevsky's genius is in making us feel the pain of someone we ought to despise by focusing on the murderer's dilemma rather than on those individuals, including the lead detective Porfiry Petrovich, who are involved in unraveling the puzzle of two mysterious deaths.

In the mental chess game he plays with Raskolnikov in his office, Porfiry Petrovich makes one triumphant move after another. Raskolnikov, the self-described superior man, is no match for the police functionary. For example, Porfiry Petrovich mockingly describes how the legal investigator will "lull [the suspect's] prudence, and then suddenly, in the most unexpected way, … stun him right on the head with the most fatal and dangerous question" (4.v.334). That is in fact what Porfiry Petrovich, always two steps ahead, does, along with putting words in Raskolnikov's mouth, showing exaggerated and patronizing concern for his mental and physical health, using terms of endearment that imply not only intimacy but also personal concern for Raskolnikov's welfare (calling him "my dear"), and surprising Raskolnikov with how much he knows about him:

. . . .

[A]nd you know, really, my dear ... these interrogations frequently throw off the interrogator himself more than the one who is being interrogated ... As you, my dear, so justly and wittily remarked a moment ago.... Tell me, really, who among all the accused ... doesn't know, for instance, that they will first lull him with unrelated questions (to use your happy expression) and then suddenly stun him right on the head, with an axe, sir – heh, heh, heh! – right on the head, to use your happy comparison, heh, heh! (4.v.337)

. . . .

But Raskolnikov didn't invoke the axe. The reader thinks that Raskolnikov is caught, especially when Porfiry Petrovich mentions to Raskolnikov a second time how, in conducting his interrogation, he would have "lulled *your* suspicions ... and then suddenly to have stunned *you* on the head as with an axe (to use your own expression)" (4.v.347; italics mine). In the last quotation, we should note Porfiry Petrovich's use of the second person pronoun to burrow into Raskolnikov's psyche.

Although self-conscious about his obesity and nervous, Porfiry Petrovich is always in control; Raskolnikov – the man who wanted to be "free" – is, ironically, hopeless putty in his hands. While being interrogated, he obeys Porfiry Petrovich's every order; thus he realizes "with pain and hatred that he was unable to disobey the order ... to speak more softly" (4.v.349).

At this very moment, as Porfiry Petrovich is about to reveal the presence of an important accuser who has been behind the partition throughout the interview, Mikolka (sometimes called Nikolai) confesses. That accuser is the man who had stalked Raskolnikov the previous day and called him a murderer. But even at that moment, although taken aback and losing full control for the first time in the dialogue, Porfiry Petrovich says with some certainty of Mikolka's confession: "He's not using his own words!" (4.vi.352).

As if to emphasize the common humanity and frailty of both men, Dostoevsky's narrator stresses how, in this moment of high tension, both Porfiry and Raskolnikov are shaking in the face of challenges to their expectations. Yet what Porfiry Petrovich remarks to Raskolnikov is far truer of himself: "You notice everything!" (4.vi.354).

Porfiry has been insinuating his familiarity as a friend and asserting his difference as a police official. Assuming the guise of humility, he assures Raskolnikov of his own faults and vulnerabilities – he ingratiatingly defines himself as old (although only thirty-five), a "buffoon" who laughs uncontrollably, as well as being ill ("Hemorrhoids") and fumblingly inept: "I am, you know, a bachelor, an unworldly and unknowing man, and, moreover, a finished man, a frozen man, sir, gone to seed" (4.v.336). Yet we gradually become fully aware that Porfiry is a man of superior intellect, a man who seizes opportunities, a master psychologist, a magician with language who attributes remarks to Raskolnikov that he has never made, and a clever person in control. Ironically, he, too, is a double-ganger in the sense that he has qualities that Raskolnikov would have needed – and wanted to believe he possessed – to be a superior man committing the perfect crime.

At the beginning of 4.v, the focalization seems to be on Raskolnikov's interior monologues to reveal his complex responses. At times, the narrator describes what Porfiry is doing in a way that simultaneously renders Raskolnikov's puzzled perspective and Porfiry's artistry: "The talk was simply pouring out of [Porfiry Petrovich], now in senselessly empty phrases, then suddenly letting in some enigmatic little words, and immediately going off into senselessness again. He was almost running back and forth now, moving his fat little legs quicker and quicker, looking down all the time, with his right hand behind his back and his left hand constantly waving and performing various gestures, each time remarkably unsuited to his words" (4.v.337).

More and more Raskolnikov's responses become subsidiary to his physical responses and verbal outbursts. We see less of his reasoning as he loses control. He becomes less like the rationalizing intellect that informs Part One of *Notes from Underground*, and more like the figure who loses control when trying to assume the stance of sincerity in the face of Liza's earnestness and trust in Part Two. In 4.v, Dostoevsky deliberately evokes his earlier novella through Porfiry's words: "I would like to get hold of a piece of evidence that's something like two plus two is four! Something like direct and indisputable proof! … [S]omething with a mathematical look to it" (4.v.338–339). Are these not terms that the Underground Man – in rebellion against logic – would find repulsive?

Porfiry embraces the laws of nature against which the Underground Man and Raskolnikov, as "free" men, rebel. He speaks of a hypothetical "criminal" who "*psychologically* … won't run away on me by a law of nature…. [He] himself will prepare some sort of mathematical trick for me, something like two times two…. And he'll keep on, he'll keep on making circles around me, narrowing the radius more and more – and whop! He'll fly straight into my mouth, and I'll swallow him, sir, and that will be most agreeable" (4.v.340).

As Porfiry Petrovich is showing Raskolnikov out, Porfiry uses the term "confess" as if to plant the suggestion of confession in Raskolnikov and to warn Raskolnikov that he will not let him off no matter who else confesses: "I have a venomous character, I confess, I confess!" (4.vi.353). In a wonderful moment they repeat the same phrase but with completely different meanings:

··

"And finally get to know each other?" Raskolnikov picked up. "And finally get to
know each other," Porfiry Petrovich agreed. (4.vi.353)

··

But we know that they do know each other in the ways that matter and that
what will happen has essentially happened. At some level Raskolnikov is aware
that having gotten to know the relentless, clever Porfiry Petrovich means that he
will be completely exposed without defenses. Indeed, Raskolnikov knows him
well enough already. And Porfiry Petrovich is aware that he will prove what he
knows, namely that Raskolnikov is the murderer.

The foregoing scene has resonances the next time Porfiry Petrovich and
Raskolnikov meet, specifically when Porfiry enters his room without announce-
ment, something he has done before, we learn, in Raskolnikov's absence. In
terms of the verbal texture, we might note how, after Mikolka had temporarily disrupted his closing in on Raskolnikov, Porfiry Petrovich drops by Raskolnikov's "kennel"-like apartment to "confess" his error in presuming Raskolnikov
is the killer when what he is really doing is putting pressure on Raskolnikov
to confess (6.ii.451). For a few minutes it looks as if they had reversed roles
and Porfiry is asking for forgiveness, but it soon becomes clear that he knows
Mikolka is not the murderer. It is not long before Porfiry tells Raskolnikov that
"You killed them" (6.ii.456) and makes clear, in this second great interview
scene, that he is awaiting Raskolnikov's confession, which he mentions three
times, and *knows* he will get it.

Dostoevsky's Other Reality: God and Spiritual Rebirth

The day-to-day business of living – and having the necessary money to do so –
is inflected by Raskolnikov's coming and going to and from his closet-size
room, people entering his rooms, and, indeed, the entire packed, rushed action
of the novel prior to the epilogue. For most of the novel, we are in the world of
chronological, linear time, where we hear the clock ticking and ask what will
happen next.

However, within the novel, there is another reality, the timeless reality of God
and salvation, a principle of inner order, patience, and tranquility represented
by Sonya; this is the world of faith and the Bible, specifically the passage about
the resurrection of Lazarus. What is proposed is an alternative to Svidrigailov's
dark vision of eternity as a village bathhouse filled with soot and spiders. This
is vertical time, what the Greeks called *kairos*, when the tick-tock of passing

time doesn't matter. Even for Dostoevsky, it is difficult to enact the kind of transformation from immersion in the chronological world to awareness of this alternative, richer reality, in which love between humans is linked to God. When Raskolnikov throws himself down at Sonya's feet in an act of humility, we are to understand that he rises up: "Infinite happiness lit up in her eyes; she understood ... that he loved her, loved her infinitely, and that at last the moment had come.... [I]n those pale, sick faces there already shone the dawn of a renewed future, of a complete resurrection into a new life. They were resurrected by love; the heart of each held infinite sources of life for the heart of the other" (Epilogue.ii.549).

A resistant reader asks what happens to the day-to-day business of life. Yes, a moment is described when, as Yeats might put it, "the soul clap[s] its hands and sings," but is such a moment realized if we are non-believers? Where is the sensory, sexual part of intimacy that is part of the human world? Is there something in Dostoevsky's final vision – with its serene immobility – that makes it difficult for him to describe any aspect of the life Sonya and Raskolnikov will be leading? Does Dostoevsky end the novel because time has been suspended and Raskolnikov and Sonya are stepping into eternal time? Despite the aforementioned ending, is there finally something inarticulate about Dostoevsky's description of the transformed state? We might ask whether any writer – albeit Dante, Milton, and Yeats have been partially successful – can dramatize the eternal worlds and whether perhaps music and visuals are better suited for access to a timeless world beyond words and time?

Study Questions for *Crime and Punishment*

1. What is Raskolnikov's motivation for killing? What does he mean by "stepping over?"
2. How is *Crime and Punishment* a novel about St. Petersburg?
3. How is *Crime and Punishment* a detective novel and Porfiry Petrovich a prototype of such later fictional detectives as Sherlock Holmes and Raymond Chandler's Philip Marlowe?
4. How and why are various characters such as Luzhin, Razumikhin, and Svidrigailov doublegangers of Raskolnikov?
5. What are some of the similarities and differences between Raskolnikov and the Underground Man?
6. How do the opening chapters establish the degradation of the poor?
7. Is Raskolnikov a sociopath? Does physical illness bring on his bizarre behavior? Is he bipolar?
8. How does the narrator function?
9. What is Sonya's role? How is she a Magdalene figure?
10. Does the Christian ending work?

Notes

1. Richard Pevear, "Introduction," in Fyodor Dostoevsky, *Notes from Underground*, trans. Richard Pevear and Larissa Volokhonsky (New York: Vintage, 1994), xii–xiii. Quotations from the text are taken from this edition.
2. Fyodor Dostoevsky, *Notes from Underground*, ed. with an introduction by Robert G. Durgy, trans. Serge Shiskoff (New York: Thomas Y. Crowell, 1969), xi–xii.
3. Joseph Frank, *Dostoevsky: The Stir of Liberation, 1860–1865* (Princeton, NJ: Princeton University Press, 1986), 333.
4. *Notes from Underground*, ed. Durgy, 205.
5. *Notes from Underground*, ed. Durgy, 153–154.
6. Pevear, "Introduction," xxii.
7. *Notes from Underground*, ed. Durgy, 206.
8. Pevear, "Introduction," xxii.
9. Pevear, "Introduction," vii.
10. Pevear, "Introduction," viii.
11. Geoffrey O'Brien, "Giving Gogol His Head," *NYR* 57:7 (April 29, 2010), 20–23; see p. 22.
12. M. M. Bakhtin, *Problems of Dostoevsky's Poetics*, ed. and trans. Caryl Emerson, intro. Wayne Booth (Minneapolis: University of Minnesota Press, 1984), 47.
13. Joseph Frank, *Dostoevsky: The Miraculous Years, 1865–1871* (Princeton, NJ: Princeton University Press, 1995), 80.
14. Frank, *Dostoevsky: The Miraculous Years*, 112.
15. Georgy Chulkov, "Dostoevsky's Technique of Writing," in Fyodor Dostoevsky, *Crime and Punishment*, ed. George Gibian (New York: Norton, 1964), 548. Hereafter references to this edition are cited as *Crime and Punishment*, Norton. All quotations from the text are from this edition.
16. Frank, *Dostoevsky: The Miraculous Years*, 101.
17. Frank, *Dostoevsky: The Miraculous Years*, 101.
18. Richard Lewontin, "Why Darwin?" *NYR* 56:9 (May 29, 2009), 19–22; see p. 20.
19. Lewontin, "Why Darwin?" 20.
20. David Brooks, "Human Nature Today," *New York Times*, June 25, 2009.
21. George Eliot, *Middlemarch* (New York: Collier Books, 1962), 369.
22. R. P. Blackmur, *Eleven Essays in the European Novel* (New York: Harcourt, Brace and World, 1964), p. 126.

Chapter 7

Hyperbole and Incongruity in Dostoevsky's *The Brothers Karamazov* (1880)

Excess and Turmoil as Modes of Being

Introduction

The Brothers Karamazov is Dostoevsky's last novel. Written over almost two years, it was serialized in *The Russian Messenger*; he thought it would be part of an epic entitled *The Life of a Great Sinner*, but he died four months after its completion.

The novel has a biographical dimension. Within it, we discover echoes of Dostoevsky's life. While Dostoevsky was working on the novel, his three-year-old son Alyosha died of epilepsy, a condition he inherited from his father. Smerdyakov, the murderer of his father, Fyodor Karamazov, has epilepsy and knows how to fake symptoms. The poignant death of Ilyusha is a function of Dostoevsky's own grief. Dmitri owes a good deal to a man named Ilyinsky who was convicted for killing his father but who was later exonerated. Dostoevsky met him while doing forced labor in Siberia for distributing political pamphlets.

As we have seen in our discussion of *Notes from Underground* and *Crime and Punishment*, Dostoevsky doubted that the clarifying light of reason could effectively organize human behavior. He was skeptical of political ideologies such as utilitarianism and even democracy that made such claims. Indeed, Dostoevsky was skeptical about the place of reason and logic – which he believed had mistakenly dominated the thought of Western Europe since the Enlightenment – in

Reading the European Novel to 1900: A Critical Study of Major Fiction from Cervantes' Don Quixote *to Zola's* Germinal, First Edition. Daniel R. Schwarz.
© 2014 John Wiley & Sons, Ltd. Published 2014 by John Wiley & Sons, Ltd.

explaining individual actions and historical patterns. With few exceptions, most notably Alyosha in *The Brothers Karamazov*, Dostoevsky's characters not only lack modesty, balance, and gradualism but also quite often behave irrationally, without regard to their own self-interest. Dostoevsky believed that the only way to contain darker human instincts, including self-love, passions, desires, and impulses to narcissistic and destructive behavior, was to believe in God.

While reading *The Brothers Karamazov*, one lives in the imagined world of the novel as intensely as in any novel I have read. Each time through, I find myself wanting to reread chapters before continuing on to new ones. My last reading of *The Brothers Karamazov* followed a rereading of *Don Quixote*, which has a relaxed pace, often playful voices, and interpolated tales that have an oblique relationship to one another. Coming to *The Brothers Karamazov* after *Don Quixote* is to enter into a far more intense world where the stakes seem higher. In *The Brothers Karamazov*, emotional life is at a fever pitch. Yet *The Brothers Karamazov* is also a paradigm of significant form because every scene resonates with every other scene as well as having a place within the whole. It as if every sentence is a hall of mirrors, each mirror reflecting every other one.

The imagined world of *The Brothers Karamazov* teems with intensity, passion, unpredictability, sensuality, spirituality, unbelief, selfishness (narcissism), generosity, and naïveté. Dostoevsky does not like to be pinned down to one point of view. Each episode represents self-dramatizing characters speaking from a particular perspective and giving the reader a reason to see their points of view and understand – albeit incompletely – how their psyches work. Dostoevsky's characters have idiosyncratic ways of seeing the world and of thinking. Each has his or her own special way of voicing emotions. With obsessions and fixations that seem exaggerated – almost epic in scope – the characters appear larger than the space they occupy.

One needs to imagine Dostoevsky's characters sitting around a large circular table, each articulating his or her own unique point of view, often in the form of self-justification. Perhaps some characters like Alyosha will earn a special place at the head of the table, but only after we have heard each of them.

Cognitive psychologists have speculated that the mind is particularly drawn to triangulation for evolutionary reasons. That is, a person needs to try on various possibilities to see if he or she is attracted to prospect A or B or C. And it may be that our interest in complex narrative derives from the fun of simultaneously exploring different ways of seeing. What makes Dostoevsky exciting and challenging is that he, like Virginia Woolf, asks us to keep in mind several different mental states at once; good examples are the chapter entitled "Over the Cognac," where Alyosha, Dmitri, Ivan, and their father are present along with the narrator (I.iii.8.132ff.), and the chapter entitled "The Sensualists," with Katerina Ivanovna and Grushenka along with Alyosha and the narrator (I.iii.10.143ff.).

We live in the minds of these extraordinary characters. We feel excitement about what they will say and do next. They walk on an emotional tightrope. Take the novel's denouement. Katerina hysterically reverses her testimony in such a way as to ensure that Dmitri receives a guilty verdict; reading Dmitri's letter to Katerina becomes strong evidence for his guilt since it was written two days before his father's death (see IV.xii.5.688).

Conversations and Dialogue

In *The Brothers Karamazov* the characteristic scene is a conversation, sometimes between two people and sometimes more, as in the extended opening scenes at the monastery. While each character has his or her own distinct vocalization, the conversations are mostly among men. Such conversations take place within the frame of an often judgmental narrative presence who has his own distinct voice and point of view. An example is when the narrator underlines his antipathy to Fyodor Pavlovich, even while acknowledging the complexity of the human psyche: "Old Liars who have been play-acting all their lives have moments when they get so carried away by their posing that they indeed tremble and weep from excitement, even though at the same time (or just a second later) they might whisper to themselves: 'You're lying, you shameless old man, you are acting even now'" (I.ii.6.73).[1]

What is compelling is the unexpectedness of the characters' behavior, including the self-dramatizing narrator who is himself a character. We live in their worlds and in the dizzying hyperbolic passions that motivate them. While not withholding judgment, we experience their often atavistic and primordial passions, their emotional complexity, their inability to understand themselves, and their dependence on obsessions and fixations.

Each character is engaged in a continuing process of defining himself or herself. But complex characters have what Bakhtin thought of as "unfinalizability" because they cannot be clearly defined and labeled as if they were inanimate objects. Characters are always evolving, changing how they act and speak, according to circumstances and with whom they are interacting. The sheer energy of what characters say and think, along with their unpredictability and the hyperbole of their conversation and internal thoughts, overwhelms the reader.

A surprising example of how characters improvise speech in unexpected and even incongruous ways is when Alyosha modifies his speech in his discourse with Nikolai Snegiryov, the captain whom Dmitri has insulted (II.iv.7.203ff.). Alyosha, in his desire to set things right, can be just as excessive in his vocalization as his father and brothers, as when he urges Snegiryov to accept Katerina

Ivanovna's two hundred roubles as a kind of compensation for Dmitri's dragging him by the beard: "She entreats you to accept her help … you have both been offended by one and the same man.… She thought of you only when she suffered the same offense from him (the same in intensity) as you! It means that a sister is coming to the aid of a brother" (II.iv.7.208). Note how he improvises and embellishes and becomes loquacious in the face of a need to do so.

Just as Dmitri uses language as a weapon and talks to offend, Alyosha often talks to ease pain. But at times he has the Karamazov proclivity to overstate, exaggerate, delude himself, convince himself by iteration, continue the redefinition of the truth of what he is saying, and use language to define a position before it is formulated in his head. Because he so often is silent, his overspeaking is all the more dramatic. Such an occasion is when he accuses Katerina Ivanovna of feigning her emotion by pretending to love Grushenka whom she is trying to manipulate.

Bakhtin uses the term "carnival" to describe a social context for times when the interaction between diverse voices breaks through ordinary conventions of discourse and the voices begin to shape one another. For Dostoevsky, speaking is a crucial action. The reader hears not one voice but a polyphony of diverse voices and this complexity is itself one of the pleasures of reading. Often these multiple voices derive from different aspects of the same character. Another pleasure is to see characters willing to wrestle continually with who they are, even when who they are contains dark impulses.

Richard Pevear emphasizes the comic aspect of *The Brothers Karamazov*, but I would underline that the comic element is noir at its most noir, as when Fyodor performs his buffoonery in front of the dying father Zosima in I.ii.6 ("Why is Such a Man Alive?"), and Dmitri, although only twenty-eight, self-dramatizes himself as hardly less tortured and lustful than the father he despises. I would stress that while *The Brothers Karamazov* contains noir scenes, to laugh at such scenes is to collaborate with insensitive and sometimes brutish behavior, including that of Fyodor and Dmitri, who regard women as sexual toys.

Alyosha as Hero

The passion felt by characters is not merely between humans but between humans and God. A secular reader must do his best to enter into a world view that depends on the vertical link between heaven and hell. Sexual rivalry, desire, broken promises, debts, and family discord are of our world. Thus within a secular epistemology we may find understandable psychological reasons for Alyosha's choosing Zosima not only as his surrogate father, but also as his spiritual mentor and paradigm. But Alyosha also lives in an epistemology that allows for heaven and miracles and teaches – indeed, requires – obedience to God's will and his representatives as well as unconditional love for fellow humans, no matter what their failings. If one cannot imagine what it is to live in eternal time rather than the tick-tock of passing time, the following sentence is difficult to grasp: "[T]he promise of hearing [Zosima's] last word on earth, and above all that it would be a bequest, as it were, to him, Alyosha, shook his soul with rapture" (II.iv.1.170).

For Alyosha, human behavior is measured on a vertical standard in which God is the ultimate authority. To fully understand the concept of rapture as Alyosha experiences it – a state later evoked by Dmitri and Grushenka – secular readers must put aside their ironic perspectives on Dostoevsky's world view and accept his profound fear of not believing. The same temporary suspension of secular irony is necessary for understanding how Dostoevsky regards Ivan's spiritual crisis, a crisis caused by his estrangement from God and the experiences of living with the pain and terror of unbelief.

Dostoevsky creates for his secular reader what is at stake for the soul and that depends not only on whether the character believes or disbelieves, but also on the quality of lived life. The novel depends on the ironic distance between the apostasy of the unbelievers and the Christian belief of the narrator and Alyosha. For Dostoevsky, the renunciation of apostasy on the part of Dmitri and Grushenka is an important part of the plot. The stakes for unbelievers are high, as we see in Ivan's breakdown when he imagines he is being visited by devils – and for Dostoevsky he in fact is experiencing devils, even if they are in psychological terms of Ivan's own creation.

The spirituality of Father Zosima, the elder, shapes Alyosha, but Alyosha lives among "tormenting contradictions" that he as a sensitive soul encounters every day (I.iii.10.143). Notable among these contradictions is the tension between his brother, Dmitri, and his father, Fyodor, over Grushenka; that tension is a main cause of Dmitri's beating his father. Grushenka is a flirtatious and exploitive woman as well as an emotional sadist who has deflected Fyodor's sexual advances even while taking satisfaction in them.

In his admiration for Alyosha and his investment in Alyosha as hero, the narrator is a surrogate for Dostoevsky. Alyosha has a vast capacity for sympathy and compassion and a reluctance to judge: "[H]e did love people; he lived all his life, it seemed, with complete faith in people.… [H]e did not want to be a judge of men and would not condemn anyone for anything" (I.i.4.19). By contrast, Dostoevsky has created a narrator who judges not only Dmitri and Ivan, but also most of the other characters.

Unlike Zosima, Alyosha does not retreat from the day-to-day emotions and passions that confront him in the world outside the monastery, and this engagement shows why he is more than Zosima's disciple; as Joseph Frank writes, in

The Brothers Karamazov Dostoevsky portrays "the power of the human personality to break free from the bonds of egoism and to transform itself, if not the world, into a personal realization of Christ's law of love."[2]

For Alyosha faith is a compass and he lives in a universe imbued with God's love. But he also recognizes his common humanity with Dmitri: "I'm the same as you" (I.iii.4.109). He says this less because he is a Karamazov than because he is of this world rather than the protective world of the monastery. Dmitri, we recall, had just confessed that "I loved depravity; I also loved the shame of depravity. I loved cruelty: am I not a bedbug, an evil insect? In short – a Karamazov!" (I.iii.4.109).

Interestingly, in my most recent rereading of *The Brothers Karamazov* I began – perhaps in part because of the Pevear and Volokhonsky translation – to know a different Alyosha, a more humane, evolving character with an important teacherly role to play for his brothers, the women they love, and boys who are a half-generation younger.

Alyosha's blessing and burden are that he feels more intensely than others. He acutely feels the pain and humiliation of others. He is especially drawn to children. He cares deeply about the pathetically ill and destitute Snegiryov family, including the handicapped mother, Arina Petrovna, and daughter, Nina; the socially marginalized son, Ilyusha; and the older, angry, cynical daughter, Varya.

Almost as silent as Christ in Ivan's Grand Inquisitor parable, Alyosha, in one of the novel's crystallizing moments, kisses Ivan, who regards him as Christ-like. When Alyosha kisses Ivan on the lips, after listening to Ivan's parable in which Christ without speaking kisses the Grand Inquisitor, Alyosha is demonstrating to Ivan his unique understanding as well as his capacity for forgiveness and humility. We may recall Zosima's bowing before Dmitri at the monastery (I.ii.6.74). As a spiritual source and figure who has a special intuitive understanding, Alyosha plays the role for other characters and the reader that Zosima plays for him, and it is for this reason that he is the novel's hero. When present, Alyosha plays that mystical role for the rest of the family and most of the other principals, but when he is absent, neither family members nor the other characters can sustain faith in him or in God.

Let us turn to III.vii, the book entitled "Alyosha." The first chapter of III.vii.1 foregrounds the corrupting body of the deceased Father Zosima as well as Father Ferapont's denunciation and Father Paissy's and Alyosha's response. Zosima not only represents the quintessence of Alyosha's faith but is also his father figure; Zosima is "the person he loved more than anything in the world" (III.vii.2.340). To see that person – his surrogate father in contrast to his drunken, materialistic, lustful, mean-spirited real father – demeaned and removed from a pedestal is difficult.

Temporarily confused, Alyosha lets the corrupt monk Rakitin take him to the home of Grushenka, unaware that she has paid Rakitin twenty-five roubles to bring him to her house where she will, out of malice, humiliate and "eat him up" in order to "ruin [him]" (III.vii.3.353–354). Letting her sit on his lap, Alyosha is tempted in this scene by lust and worldliness, but overcomes that. He and Rakitin leave the monastery together and he returns alone (III.vii.3).

At the end of Book Seven's final chapter, entitled "Cana of Galilee," Alyosha has a crucial epiphany. After returning to the monastery and to the room where Zosima lies in his coffin, he goes outside and embraces the earth, and his faith is fully restored. Alyosha experiences rapture: "He fell to the earth a weak youth and rose up a fighter, steadfast for the rest of his life, and he knew it and felt it suddenly, in that very moment of his ecstasy. Never, never in all his life would Alyosha forget that moment," and he departs, as the elder instructed, to "'sojourn in the world'" (III.vii.4.363). Even if hyperbole is the rhetorical mode for how Dostoevsky depicts larger-than-life emotions, the reader cannot be ironical about Alyosha's simple, inclusive faith.

Later, after Dmitri's arrest, Alyosha believes in Dmitri's innocence, in part because he disbelieves in evil and refuses to believe that his family is beyond redemption. He believes in human brotherhood and community under God. Alyosha's enthusiasm for doing the right thing sometimes leads him to hyperbole and exaggeration and to promise more than he can personally deliver. When he tells Captain Snegiryov, whom Dmitri has insulted and humiliated, that Dmitri will repent "in the most sincere, the fullest manner, even if it means going down on his knees in that very square," and says, "I will make him [repent], or he is no brother of mine," we know that Snegiryov is exactly right to observe that Alyosha's sentiment "proceeds not directly from him, but only from the nobility of your fervent heart" (II.iv.7.204). And we know that this "nobility of heart" frequently directs Alyosha's behavior, whether he is listening to Ivan or believing in Dmitri's innocence or fulfilling the demands of those who insist upon his running errands for them.

Alyosha, like Christ, seeks the company of those in need. Alyosha is not interested in worldly gratifications but rather in being present for those in search of solace. An empathetic and sympathetic listener, he is drawn to those in any kind of trouble, especially to the economically disadvantaged, the handicapped, and the meek. For him, the needy include those in his family who have emotional, moral, and spiritual needs as well as the morally and spiritually confused women who are involved with his father or brothers, namely Katerina and Grushenka. He takes upon himself his brothers' and father's pain and forgives them for their smallness. To his father's provocative renunciation of God he says: "You're not an evil man, you're just twisted" (II.iv.2.174).

At first we think he goes along with the fantasy of Liza (Lise) Khokhlakov – who is consigned to a wheelchair and has an unstable mother – that he will marry her (II.iv.4). But we realize that Alyosha and Lise have considerable understanding of each other and that Alyosha shares his thoughts and feelings more with her than with anyone else. In part because of his consciousness of his kinship to his father and brother as "a Karamazov" and thus, because of this heritage, "earthy and violent, raw," he expresses doubts to her about his faith. In the mock betrothal scene, he says to Lise: "[Maybe] I don't even believe in God" (II.v.1.220). He feels the conflict between his doubts about his spirituality and his participation in a world so different from the monastery and his identity with his role as a monk. But we later learn from Zosima's story that to know God, one has to know the world, and that, we realize, is what Alyosha is doing.

Finally, Dostoevsky believed in what Pevear calls "the purifying effect of suffering,"[3] although in *The Brothers Karamazov* there is somewhat less stress on the necessity of redemptive suffering than in *Crime and Punishment* and more of an appreciation of nature and human life. While *Crime and Punishment* seems to value suffering as purifying, this theme is far less clear in *The Brothers Karamazov*, where suffering is, well, suffering. What makes Alyosha heroic is how he both embraces God and recognizes the value of life.

Pevear remarks, "The coexistence of faith and unbelief indeed remained with Dostoevsky all his life; its final artistic expression appears in *The Brothers Karamazov*, in the opposed figures of the elder Zosima and the Grand Inquisitor."[4] But within Dostoevsky's value system, there is no viable alternative to belief in God. As Zosima teaches, "all things are good and splendid," in part because Providence works through every aspect of life, even when humans cannot understand the purpose of events (II.vi.2.295). Dostoevsky knew that humans are drawn to pleasure and self-satisfaction, and are often motivated by impulses they can neither control nor understand.

Dostoevsky is a Slavophil. He thinks Russia must not follow the Enlightenment or pursue socialism. As Aileen Kelly puts it, Dostoevsky, taking issue with Alexander Herzen's belief that life within this world was what mattered, "expressed in ever more extravagant terms from the mid-1850s, that the Russian people had a historical mission to bring about a reconciliation of all European nations in a new Christian world order.... Dostoevsky's reading of Herzen is said to have influenced his assault on historical determinism in *Notes from Underground*: but by then the other Dostoevsky had already begun preaching the predestined mission of the Orthodox Russian people to bring about Europe's rebirth."[5]

Notwithstanding his Christian perspective, Dostoevsky shows us what Stephen Greenblatt, speaking of John Milton and Richard Wagner, calls "the stained, muddled, and sinful world that humans have created for themselves."[6]

Dostoevsky's focus is the mortal world of passions, obsessions, and unacknowledged needs and the behavior that results.

Thus Dostoevsky lets Fyodor, Ivan, Smerdyakov, and Miusov give voice to other perspectives. As if he were Hugh Hefner or Silvio Berlusconi, Fyodor speaks for hedonism as a mode of living but he does so in terms that embrace evil intentionally and obsessively; thus he says to Alyosha: "I want to live in my wickedness to the very end. Wickedness is sweet; everyone denounces it, but everyone lives in it, only they all do it on the sly and I do it openly.… I don't want your paradise" (II.iv.2.173).

Characters are continually enclosed in their solipsistic and narcissistic world. Anticipating Beckett, where characters talk past one another, Dostoevsky in *The Brothers Karamazov* dramatizes dialogues of the deaf; an extreme example is when the Poles speak Polish and the Russians speak Russian in the chapter entitled "The Former and Indisputable One." While he is far from perfect, Alyosha listens better than other characters. Even Zosima is at times in his own universe and reminds us – like Forster's Godbole in *A Passage to India* – of his remoteness from ordinary daily life.

The characters' limited understanding of their own secrets is often at odds with the narrator's – and, even more so, the reader's – larger perspective. Their self-dramatizing behavior and words reveal to us readers what is concealed from characters within the fictive world of Dostoevsky's creation. Even Alyosha suffers at times from this myopic inability to understand his own behavior, as when, disappointed in the stink of Zosima's dead body, he allows Rakitin to direct him to Grushenka's house. Retrospectively, such very occasional and incongruous lapses teach Alyosha what Zosima understood, namely that perfection is the enemy of the very good on this earth. Furthermore, clarity about how God works eludes humans. Thus humans may be puzzled by why, in contrast to Zosima's corpse, the body of Ilyusha, the young boy who dies and who has not lived a saintly life, does not stink. But Zosima's smell reminds us, as Zosima himself preached, that monks are human.

Ivan's Turmoil and His Parable of the Grand Inquisitor

Ivan is ultra-sensitive not only to the world's failings but also to his own; he cannot accept a supreme being who allows suffering, especially to children. Ivan's cynicism is presented in the parable – he calls it a "prose poem" – of the Grand Inquisitor. According to the parable, the Grand Inquisitor acts in the best interests of humans by shepherding them with all their pathetic inadequacy, even while feeling the pain of apostasy by foreclosing the very freedom Christ gave them. By providing a kind of spiritual security policy, the Church replaces the terrible burden of freedom to consciously choose – that is, by individual free will – whether or not to follow Christ. Showing forgiveness, Christ kisses the Grand Inquisitor and the Grand Inquisitor lets him go.

Following Christ means imitating Christ by saying "No" to the three major temptations: bread to solve hunger; a miracle to show that he was the son of God; and power in the form of control over the kingdoms of the world. Ivan implies that the Church rightfully recognizes that humankind is not capable of handling the burden of free will and of making the right choices. According to Ivan's parable, by substituting its rites and institutions for free will and thus appeasing man's conscience, the Church is recognizing human limitation and thus doing Satan's work.

But where does this leave Ivan, a doubter who can in his parable evoke a yearning for mystery and faith? Does he himself not suffer and bear the pain of the Grand Inquisitor's knowledge of humanity's limitations, even as his brother Alyosha sees humanity's potential?

The Grand Inquisitor is probably modeled on Tomás de Torquemada (1420–1498), who was a fifteenth-century Spanish Dominican friar, first Inquisitor General of Spain, and confessor to Isabella I of Castile. He was described by the Spanish chronicler Sebastián de Olmedo as "The hammer of heretics."

Dostoevsky has a grimly cynical view of the human condition. Because humans cannot handle the awful freedom of choosing Christ, the world is perpetually beset by human misery and exploitation. If Christ returned in the Second Coming, he implies in the Grand Inquisitor episode, we not only wouldn't welcome him, but we would take him out of circulation in order to preserve what little happiness we "pitiful, blind" humans have when we succeed in our pursuit of "earthly bread" (II.iv.5.254, 261). After threatening to burn Christ at the stake, the Grand Inquisitor lets him go with the instruction, "Go and do not come again … never, never!" (II.iv.5.262).

What has happened, according to Ivan's cynical view – a view that reflects at least one aspect of Dostoevsky's thinking – is that the Church has organized itself as a replacement for each person's choosing Christ's way of life and saying "No" to temptation: "Oh, we will allow [humankind] to sin, too; they are weak and powerless, and they will love us like children for allowing them to sin. We will tell them that every sin will be redeemed if it is committed with our permission; and that we allow them to sin because we love them, and as for punishment for these sins, very well, we take it upon ourselves…. And they will adore us as benefactors, who have borne their sins before God…. [T]hey will have no secrets from us" (II.iv.5.259).

Stressing the need for a sense of belonging to the universe that is created by God and is infinitely more important than one person, Dostoevsky sees isolatoes such as Ivan as dangerous. Ivan, "gloomy and withdrawn" since childhood, seems "so learned, so proud, and seemingly so prudent" (I.i.3.15, 17). But we learn Ivan is not prudent at all; as a rational skeptic, Ivan is in Dostoevsky's cosmology a self-hating, tortured soul. Like his half-brother Dmitri, Ivan believes in the essential corruption of the Karamazovs (what Ivan calls "the force of the Karamazov baseness") and that, in a godless world, "everything is permitted" (II.iv.5.263).

Parables play a role in the narration, and they are lessons in the need to believe in God and follow Christ's lessons. As a parabolist, Ivan plays the role of Christ, even while Dostoevsky sees his cynicism as the path to suffering. We need to remember that in *Notes* and *Crime and Punishment*, Dostoevsky had critiqued the very ideas Ivan expresses. Dostoevsky plumbs the darkest impulses of human behavior. But he believes only faith in God can be a compass and that each of us can make the most difficult choice of following Christ's example. Ivan, like the Grand Inquisitor and the devil who visits him – both versions of himself – disbelieves in man's capacity to love. But the novel presents Alyosha to refute Ivan's skepticism and cynicism.

The devil in Ivan's tale is an intellectual juggling actor who mesmerizes Alyosha and the reader. We hear the tale and are most conscious of Ivan the man telling or performing it. Juxtaposed to his tale is Zosima's testament of faith, which is interpolated a few pages earlier and is assembled and written by Alyosha (II.vi.1). This interpolation slows down the pace of the novel.

Ivan believes in evil but not in God. In the Grand Inquisitor he imagines a man-god and his version of Satan is in terms of dark human motives. In Ivan's case evil is emptiness, the inability to believe even though part of him desperately wants to. While Rakitin and Smerdyakov are cynical versions of Ivan, both the prosecutor and especially the defense attorney Fetyukovich weave stories about Dmitri that resonate in Ivan's narratives. In the chapter entitled "Disputation" (I.iii.7), Smerdyakov's sophistry as well as his intellectual arrogance and cynicism anticipate Ivan's Grand Inquisitor parable. But Ivan has a moral identity and humane feelings that make it difficult for him to sustain positions that isolate him from his fellow man; indeed, his morality leads him to dream of Satan's visiting him.

Let us examine Alyosha's behavior in light of Ivan's Grand Inquisitor parable. Alyosha's gentleness does deflect the sensual, materialistic, and conniving Grushenka from seducing him. By sitting on his lap, she throws the inexperienced Alyosha into confusion when he is fighting to understand God after smelling Zosima's decomposing body almost as soon as he dies. Yet even with Ivan's words from the Grand Inquisitor on his mind, he, following Christ, practices the universal love that he has been taught. Or does he? Isn't he taking Grushenka's pain on himself because she by her own free will cannot choose God? In other words, which path is he following? Doesn't Alyosha take on the burden of free will for others? Are the two paths so different? Isn't he, like the Grand Inquisitor in Ivan's parable, suffering the pains of others and in doing so falsely assuming that others will follow him into holiness by example? And didn't Alyosha see Zosima do something similar when he bows to Dmitri?

Grushenka is prepared to abase herself when the man she loves will take her back after his wife dies; yet she is so roiled that she thinks of herself crawling back like a dog as well as of killing herself and stabbing him. When she speaks bathetically of choices – "If I choose, I won't go anywhere or to anyone" (III.iii.3.356) – we think not only of Ivan's parable, in which the Grand Inquisitor contends that humankind is not worthy of free will, but also of Dostoevsky's belief that much of humankind has befouled the concept of choice by focusing on this world rather than God.

Ivan and Smerdyakov

Motivated by self-interest, Fyodor's illegitimate son Smerdyakov, Ivan's double-ganger, is a self-hating sociopath who is the murderer; he has no moral center and slyly imposes himself upon others. As the novel progresses, the reader cannot quite forget Grigory's dismissive if pained view of Smerdyakov and his origins, including his mother: "You are not a human being, you were begotten of bathhouse slime" (I.iii.6.124).

The physical location of their first dialogue – Ivan meets Smerdyakov when the latter is sitting by the gate to the entrance to Fyodor's house – is a crucial clue for the reader to the identity of Fyodor's murderer. With revulsion and disgust, Ivan feels that Smerdyakov is part of him, that "this worthless scoundrel ... [sits] in his soul" (II.v.6.266). In their three encounters, Smerdyakov obsequiously calls Ivan "Sir" far more than necessary, as if to call attention to their social difference. But Smerdyakov is also expressing his not so latent hatred of Ivan, who by his legitimacy is recognized by society as Smerdyakov's better.

Ivan's three meetings with Smerdyakov, suggesting Peter's denial of Christ three times, anticipate the appearance of the devil in "The Devil: Ivan Fyodorovich's Nightmare." Ivan says to Smerdyakov in the third meeting: "You know what: I am afraid you're a dream, a ghost sitting there in front of me" (IV.xi.8.623). Smerdyakov, the objectification of everything Ivan hates in himself, says to Ivan: "You're like Fyodor Pavlovich most of all, it's you of all his children who came out resembling him most, having the same soul as him, sir" (IV.xi.8.632).

Smerdyakov is as much a double at this point as he is an independent self, when he says to Ivan: "There's no ghost, sir, besides the two of us, sir, and some third one.... That third one is God, sir, Providence itself, sir, it's right here with us now, sir; only don't look for it, you won't find it" (IV.xi.8.623). Ivan is evil as emptiness, the absence of good, and Smerdyakov knows it. He claims that Ivan is complicit in their father's murder because Ivan put him, Smerdyakov, up to killing their father, in part by preaching "[E]verything is permitted" (IV.xi.8.632).

Culturally produced by a faithless contemporary world, Ivan is the arrogant rational skeptic who believes we make our own rules. For Dostoevsky it is the Ivan mind – judgmental and analytic – that produces human solutions like socialism and utilitarianism, solutions he associates with the overly rational and secular West and with the Enlightenment. The defense attorney's closing speech is another version of intellect and reason operating on their own terms. So, too, is the behavior of the worldly and corrupt monk Rakitin. By contrast to these characters, Alyosha, the man of faith and intuition, judges no one and can respond compassionately to almost anyone.

Ivan's brain fever is a moral breakdown. His punishment is to be visited by the devil, who is a double not only of Smerdyakov, but also of himself. The devil proclaims to Ivan, even as the latter covers his ears, a philosophy that has echoes of Herzen's belief that improving life in this world is what matters:

. . . .

> Once mankind has renounced God, one and all … then the entire old worldview will fall of itself, without anthropophagy, and, above all, the entire former morality, and everything will be new. People will come together in order to take from life all that it can give, but, of course, for happiness and joy in this world only. Man will be exalted with the spirit of divine, titanic pride, and the man-god will appear. Man, his will and his science no longer limited, conquering nature every hour, will thereby every hour experience such lofty delight as will replace for him all his former hopes of heavenly delight…. [A]nyone who already knows the truth is permitted to settle things for himself, absolutely, as he wishes, on the new principles. In this sense, "everything is permitted" to him. Moreover, since God and immortality do not exist in any case, even if this period should never come, the new man is allowed to become a man-god, though it be he alone in the whole world, and of course, in this new rank, to jump lightheartedly over any former moral obstacle of the former slave-man…. (IV.xi.9.648–649)

. . . .

The devil's argument reminds the reader of Ivan's cynical parable focusing on the Grand Inquisitor's rationale for creating a Church to intervene between pathetic humankind and God. According to Ivan's parable, the Grand Inquisitor claims that the Church assuages the conscience of humans by taking on itself the burden of human guilt. According to Frank, "Ivan's dialogue with the devil plays on the continual fluctuation between the stirrings of his conscience and the amorally nihilistic conclusions that he has drawn from his refusal to accept God and immortality."[7]

The Narrator as Character and His Role in the Novel

What Geoffrey O'Brien writes of Gogol's *The Nose* is applicable not only to Ivan's tale of the Grand Inquisitor, but also to the intense dialogues in the novel and to the narrator's voice:

> But the mind that tells the story exists only as a bit of free-floating intellectual energy, scarcely embodied, sustaining itself in an invulnerable force field consisting of language alone. We are always made to feel that for Gogol, words are all he has. Outside of that bubble there is only the terror and bewilderment and self-contempt (sometimes masked as self-adulation) that are the common traits of his characters.[8]

In *The Brothers Karamazov*, the narrator, like the other characters, uses words to define himself in a dynamic never-ending process of proposing a position, undermining it – sometimes by poignant efforts at erasure – and then reconfiguring it in new terms.

We feel Dostoevsky himself self-consciously takes risks by calling attention to the fictionality and necessary artistry of novels. An example is when he has both the prosecution and defense attorney invoke the world of novels, as if asking us to believe in his novel even while making fun of the genre: "[T]he triumphant novelist can be brought up short and demolished by details, those very details in which reality is so rich, and which are always neglected by such unfortunate and unwilling authors, as if they were utterly insignificant and unnecessary trifles" (IV.xii.9.721). And at times this description defines the persona of an inexperienced author that Dostoevsky has created; at the trial, when Ivan is taken away for losing his composure and throwing the marshal to the floor, the narrator recalls: "I do not remember everything in order, I was excited myself and could not follow" (IV.xii.5.687).

We are conscious of the narrator's psyche and values. But it is important that we differentiate the narrator from Dostoevsky. The chatty narrator is very much a self-dramatizing character and not the traditional authoritative omniscient voice. Pevear writes, "The first voice to be heard ... is the narrator's. Needless to say, he is not Dostoevsky.... [W]ithin his scope, which is that of an amateur writer, and more of a talker than a writer, he has his own artistry.... There are stretches when the person of the 'author' seems to recede and be replaced by a more conventional omniscient narrator, but his voice will suddenly re-emerge in a phrase or half-phrase, giving an unexpected double tone or double point of view to the passage." [9]

The narrator makes no claim to omniscience. Selecting and arranging what he sees and hears, he becomes a character living in the district where the events take place. When speaking about a suicide attempt by Fyodor Pavlovich's second wife when she was a young girl, he observes, "I do not know the details but have only heard" (I.i.3.13).

The novel's setting is Skotoprigonyevsk and the narrator is a citizen of that area. Skotoprigonyevsk is based on a Russian town called Staraya Russa in Novgorod Oblast, located on the Polist River. The town, where Dostoevsky lived when he wrote the novel, originated in the tenth century.

The narrator is part of the community he describes; he knows its culture, its eccentricities, and its gossip. Speaking of the rumors and gossip about the case in Moscow and St. Petersburg newspapers, he reveals the name of the town in which he and the Karamazovs live as if he were speaking inadvertently and couldn't erase what he wrote: "Today's item in the newspaper *Rumors* was entitled 'From Skotoprigonyevsk': (alas, that is the name of our town; I have been concealing it all this time) 'Concerning the Trial of Karamazov'" (IV.xi.2.573). Is he being ingenuous or disingenuous? That the name translates as "cattle-roundupville" or "stockyardville" underlines the provinciality of the town and the narrator. For them Moscow and especially St. Petersburg are part of another, more cosmopolitan world; for the more prosperous denizens of the little town, those cities are places of glamour, excitement, elegance, and mystery. Indeed, speaking of the jurors, the narrator notes: "Our Skotoprigonyevsk tradesmen are almost peasants themselves, they even handle the plow" (IV.xii.1.660).

As a self-described "superfluous" introduction, "From the Author" should be regarded as a fictional border crossing with one foot in the real world and one foot in the fictional (4). With his apparent supercilious attitude to "Russian critics," whom he ironically regards as overly conscientious, the "author" recalls the narrator of *Notes from Underground*: "I have been wasting fruitless words and precious time, first, out of politeness, and second, out of cunning" (4). Anticipating questions about why he has chosen Alyosha as a hero, the narrator begins with a discussion of how we should regard "my hero" Alyosha. Soon within the novel he identifies himself as a writer presenting "my first introductory novel" (I.i.2.12) and Alyosha as "my future hero to the reader" (I.i.4.18).

In "From the Author," the narrator is already a character, telling us he already has in mind the sequel to the events in *The Brothers Karamazov*, events that took place thirteen years ago. In his putative first introductory novel, he will tell us about Mitya's brothers, Alyosha and Ivan (I.i.2.12). Of course this novel was never written. The second will address Alyosha's life in the present. Since the events of *The Brothers Karamazov* took place years ago, the second novel is also unwritten.

In terms of the novel's structure, the digressive nature of the narrator's short monologue entitled "From the Author" prepares us for his sustained digressions such as Zosima's biography, which is the main focus of Book Six.

While the first person narrator does not identify himself by name, he is a more important presence than is usually realized, a choral voice of the community but also an idiosyncratic figure with spiritual and moral values and intense curiosity about the vagaries of life. Using the first person pronoun "I" to give us a sense of his presence, the self-dramatizing narrator introduces himself as someone familiar with the characters and the culture and history of the provincial area in which they live. The narrator identifies himself as a contemporary who knows the area. In the first chapters, he speaks of "our little town," "our district," and "our famous neighboring monastery" (I.i.1.7; I.i.2.10).

The narrator presents himself as something of a small town, provincial figure. Speaking of Dmitri, he mentions the opinion of him he had heard expressed "at one of our gatherings" (I.ii.6.68). By showing the narrator to not always have encyclopedic knowledge, Dostoevsky paradoxically establishes the narrator's efforts at reliability when he is recalling an event: "I do not know how it is now, but in my childhood I often used to see and hear these 'shriekers' in villages and monasteries" (I.ii.3.47). As to the narrator's judgments, the reader feels that while the narrator has his values and biases, he is doing his best to be fair.

At times he implies that he is personally acquainted with the characters of whom he speaks, especially Alyosha, whom he introduces as if he knew him quite well: "[H]e rarely cared to confide this memory [of his mother's face] to anyone" (I.i.4.19). As if he has interviewed Alyosha, the narrator even knows that Alyosha does not remember every word of Zosima's speech the day he died (II.iv.1.163). Yet the narrator does not have all the basic facts; in Chapter 4 of Book One, Alyosha is twenty years old and in the very next chapter he is nineteen (I.i.4.18; I.i.5.25).

As we learn in the very first sentence of the novel, Fyodor's murder took place thirteen years ago and the narrator's telling is a retrospective narration. He does have full knowledge of the basic plot that took place years ago, but there are limits to his knowledge. For example, it is curious that the narrator does not reveal what happened subsequently – that is, since the events of thirteen years ago – to any of the characters.

While the narrator can be annoyingly quirky, he leaves no doubt that we are dependent upon him and that he will tell his story in whatever order he wishes and reveal what he wishes in good time. For example, he withholds information about the actual murderer Smerdyakov after telling us he is Fyodor Pavlovich's son. Of Smerdyakov, the narrator disingenuously says: "I ought to say a little more about him in particular, but I am ashamed to distract my reader's attention for such a long time to such ordinary lackeys" (I.iii.2.100). Isn't the narrator's patronizing term "lackey" applied to a lower social class figure not only facetious but also atypical, and therefore something of a clue to his villainy? After all, he has not been distinguishing the virtuous and the evil characters by class. He has exposed the excessive and dissolute behavior of Fyodor Pavlovich and Dmitri, who are among the gentry, while presenting the generally honorable Grigory and his wife Marfa without disdain for those who serve the Karamazovs.

The narrator is opinionated, judgmental, loquacious, and fascinated by the diversity of human behavior but also sentimental and compassionate. Disgusted with excessive and abusive behavior, his disapproving presence introduces normalcy and control and counterbalances the novel's incongruity and hyperbole.

That the narrator places himself in the courtroom as an observer of Dmitri's trial gives authenticity to his report, including the presentation of the prosecutor's and defense attorney's speeches. Yet he warns us that his reporting may not be fully accurate: "I will say beforehand, and say emphatically, that I am far from considering myself capable of recounting all that took place in court, not only with the proper fullness, but even in the proper order.... Therefore let no one grumble if I tell only that which struck me personally and which I have especially remembered. I may have taken secondary things for the most important, and even overlooked the most prominent and necessary features" (IV.xii.1.656). And, following the rule that the maximum revelation of a speaker's shortcomings and interests affects our entire response, we realize that the narrator's reliability and perspicacity need to be questioned throughout.

That he is a self-dramatizing part of the social community – and at times talkative to the point of garrulousness – gives him the credentials to speculate on behavior such as Ivan's arrival: "Why Ivan Fyodorovich came to us then is a question I even recall asking myself at the time" (I.i.3.16–17). Speaking of how Ivan and Fyodor live together and get along, he remarks knowingly as if he were speaking as a member of the larger social community: "This last fact especially astonished not only me but many others as well" (I.i.3.17).

The narrator is defensive about Alyosha's temporary loss of faith: "This new *something* that appeared and flashed consisted of a certain tormenting impression from his conversation with his brother Ivan the day before.... [It demanded] more and more to come to the surface" (III.vii.2.340). Yet he approves of Alyosha's anger at God's hiding his finger: "I am glad that at such a moment my young man turned out to be not so reasonable" (III.vii.2.340); the "my" is indicative of the narrator's stake in defining a Christianity which balances the spirituality of Zosima with engagement in this world. On occasion, the narrator is more sympathetic to Ivan than he – and perhaps Dostoevsky – realizes.

Alyosha is often our eyes and ears and seems as much as the narrator to be in the position of receiving information. In some sense the novel is a *Bildungsroman* about the education of Alyosha, and we take part in his growth, as we watch Dostoevsky's narrator weighing and sifting different positions and ways of being.

As a self-dramatizing narrator, describing Alyosha's and, later, Dmitri's response to the erratic and quixotic Grushenka, he presents himself as someone who is particularly familiar with intimacy, sexual feelings, emotional manipulation, and jealousy; an example is when he invokes Pushkin's reading of *Othello* in III.viii.3.380–381 and discusses jealousy: "It is impossible to imagine all the shame and moral degradation a jealous man can tolerate without the least remorse" (III.viii.3.380).

We need to ask important questions about the narrator. Can the reader construct a coherent human mind from the teller? As we read, do we need to construct the narrator into a coherent presence? Do we need to reconcile contradictions within the narrator, or should we consider him another complex character who resists simple explanations? If characters don't behave logically, why should we require it of narrators? Specifically, if Dostoevsky's characters indulge in special pleading, are inconsistent, and have obsessions and fixations – and quirks and idiosyncrasies – why should we be surprised that his narrators behave in similar ways?

In keeping with Dostoevsky's desire to find typifying qualities within individuals, the narrator has a categorizing sensibility that sees the representative quality of individual behavior. In the very first paragraph he makes clear what he thinks of Fyodor Pavlovich: "[H]e was a strange type, yet one rather frequently met with, precisely the type of man who is not only worthless and depraved but muddleheaded as well" (I.i.1.7). When Fyodor's first wife, Adelaida, dies some time after abandoning Fyodor, the narrator observes that the reported versions that Fyodor rejoiced and wept could be true: "In most cases, people, even wicked people, are far more naïve and simple hearted than one generally assumes. And so are we" (I.i.1.9). But this categorizing sensibility can have an off-putting side. For the narrator is an anti-Semite, at times using the term "Jew" pejoratively (III.vii.3.344; III.viii.3.386).

When characters speak they are expressing inward conflicts and improvising feelings they often don't understand. Yet the paradox for the reader is that Dostoevsky creates characters so unique and idiosyncratic that they often cannot typify anything. Not surprisingly, echoing themes that are part of both *Notes from Underground* and *Crime and Punishment*, the narrator stresses that we humans are inconsistent, have diverse and contradictory selves, and often act contrary to our own rational interest. Isn't the narrator reminding us not to patronize his characters because, with all their obsessions and fixations as well as foibles and idiosyncrasies, they are who we are? Indeed, with his various voices (chronicler, archivist, moralist), doesn't the narrator indulge in role-playing?

The reaching out and inclusion of us readers as sharing the same human nature as his often bizarre and always idiosyncratic characters implies that we need to understand not only that we have much in common with these strange characters, but also that we fail to recognize that kinship at our peril. In these early chapters the narrator insists on these links: "[A]ll his life ... Fyodor Pavlovich was fond of play-acting, of suddenly taking up some unexpected role right in front of you, often when there was no need for it, and even to his own real disadvantage.... This trait, however, is characteristic of a great many people, even rather intelligent ones, and not only of Fyodor Pavlovich" (I.i.2.11). Fyodor Pavlovich obsessively acts the buffoon – without any self-control, self-respect, or judgment – and humiliates himself in the monastery in front of Zosima and Alyosha (I.ii.2). Do Dmitri and Ivan, who become actors in their own monodramas, follow their father's example? Dmitri certainly does, but Ivan also takes a turn at buffoonery when he has his breakdown.

In *The Brothers Karamazov* as in *Notes from Underground* and *Crime and Punishment*, each character's psyche and values are revealed by his or her idiosyncratic speech, including that of the narrator. Pevear emphasizes how Dostoevsky differentiates each character's distinctive way of speaking: "The style of *The Brothers Karamazov* is based on the spoken, not the written word.... Dostoevsky was not interested in typical, regional, or class differences of expression, as many writers of his time were; what he sought in the voicing of his characters was the singular expression of the person."[10] That is why I stressed that it is Ivan who tells the Grand Inquisitor story.

Thus we can agree with Pevear when he observes: "There is indeed no absolute authorial voice in *The Brothers Karamazov*. Every scene is narrated from at least some personal angle, and where the narrator seems effaced, we find that his voice has shaded into the equally distinct verbal element of the character he is describing."[11] Pevear wisely cites the description of Dmitri's response to his father just before the murder: "Mitya watched from the side, and did not move. The whole of the old man's profile, which he found so loathsome, the whole of his drooping Adam's apple, his hooked nose, smiling in sweet expectation, his lips – all was brightly lit from the left by the slanting light of the lamp shining from the room."[12]

Pevear could have cited the amazing dialogue between Dmitri and Alyosha in Chapters I.iii.3–5. In that dialogue, Dmitri's tortured garrulousness reflects his emotional self-flagellation as he discusses his obsessive love for Grushenka, whom his father also loves. Dmitri's "insect sensuality" (I.iii.4.109) and his betrayal of Katerina Ivanovna contrast with the simplicity of Alyosha's response when he stumbles into a meeting with Dmitri in his father's neighbor's garden

(I.iii.3.103). As with the speaker in *Notes*, Dmitri is a bundle of contradictory emotions and doesn't know what he will say next. He is about to insult Katerina, who has come to have sex with him as a way of saving her father from the embarrassment of being short on the funds he needs to turn over to the government. But to his own surprise, Dmitri gives her the money she needs: "I silently showed it to her, folded it, handed it to her, opened the door to the hallway for her, and, stepping back, bowed deeply to her, with a most respectful and heartfelt bow, believe me! She was startled, she looked intently at me for a second, turned terribly pale – white as a sheet – suddenly, also without saying a word, not impulsively but very gently, deeply, quietly, bent way down and fell right at my feet – with her forehead to the ground, not like an institute girl but like a Russian woman!" (I.iii.4.114). Alyosha opens the next paragraph with a characteristically straightforward response: "Now … I understand the first half of this business" (I.iii.5.115).

Manipulating his readers, the narrator often doesn't tell us what he knows, with the result that *The Brothers Karamazov* is a detective story. We see Dmitri rushing from his father's house but we do not see what happened in the house. This crucial fissure leaves the reader puzzled, particularly when the narrator tells us that we will learn more about how Dmitri deals with the shame that results from his stealing Katerina Ivanovna's money: "What this beating on the chest, *on that spot*, meant, and what he intended to signify by it – so far was a secret that no one else in the world knew, which he had not revealed then even to Alyosha, but for him that secret concealed more than shame, it concealed ruin and suicide…. All this will be perfectly well explained to the reader later on" ("Gold Mines," III.viii.3.388). We are teased into thinking Dmitri will kill his father but in fact he does not commit patricide.

The Structure of *The Brothers Karamazov* as a Detective Story of Patricide

Structurally, *The Brothers Karamazov* consists of four parts, twelve books, and an epilogue. Dostoevsky's book and chapter titles – informative and provocative – help direct the reader. Thus the title of Book Twelve, "A Judicial Error," makes us aware that Dmitri will be wrongly convicted. Chapter titles, too, are rich with meaning: "The Old Buffoon" (I.ii.2) to describe Fyodor or "A Seminarist-Careerist" (I.ii.7) to describe Rakitin offer memorable descriptions.

Beginning with the ironic title of Part I, Book One, "A Nice Little Family," *The Brothers Karamazov* is beautifully structured and exemplifies the concept of significant form. Introducing Fyodor Pavlovich, the children he neglected, and the elder Zosima, who has a crucial effect on Alyosha, Book One is a foundation comprised of essential building blocks.

Fyodor, fifty-five years old, has been pursuing sensual pleasures and advancing his material interests; by the time of his death – only days off – he had accumulated 100,000 roubles. He is the father of three legitimate sons – Dmitri, Ivan, and Alyosha – and one bastard, Smerdyakov. Fyodor is described as a "muddle-headed madcap"; he is a prodigious drinker and womanizer and has amassed considerable means (I.i).

From the outset, the Karamazovs are larger than life and dominate the pages. Except for Alyosha, they live lives of excess and their passions and vices are gigantic. Dmitri ("Mitya") is the son of Fyodor's first marriage to a wealthy woman who ran away with a seminarian when Dmitri was three. Fyodor took no interest in Dmitri, who was moved several times, ended up a military school, and has since lived a dissolute life worthy of his father.

The other two sons are children of Fyodor's second wife. The younger son, twenty-year-old Alyosha, is a believer. Ivan, the middle son, is twenty-four and an atheist who tells Alyosha that he "cannot bear … messengers from god," yet imagines himself being visited by the devil (IV.xi.v.602). Smerdyakov, whose mother Lizaveta was a mute street woman and whose name means son of the reeking one, is correctly rumored to be Fyodor's illegitimate son.

In fact the actual plot is brilliantly simple. It is the dialogue that is special and why so many of the novel's episodes are like scenes in a play. In every conversation the stakes are so high that the characters are struggling for their very existence as human beings, fighting for air to survive as the people they are or want to be. Scene after scene is dramatized at a feverish pitch to the point where one feels impelled to take a break. Of course, the book's length and the need to savor every word and look back to recall past scenes also slow down the pace.

Hyperbolic speech, marked by emotional or sensual excess and incongruous emotional and sensual behavior that is out of bounds or inconsistent with expectations, defines the world of Dostoevsky. From the outset, this is particularly true of *The Brothers Karamazov*. The tense dramatic scenes in the monastery in Book Two – aptly titled "An Inappropriate Gathering" because they take place in Father Zosima's presence – show us the Karamazov family's usually hyperbolic cacophony of voices. Such scenes also introduce the behavioral incongruities that are, in terms of driving the novel's structure, the counterparts to the digressions in *Don Quixote*. Take Fyodor Pavlovich's buffoonery in the monastery or his drunken dialogue about God's existence with Ivan and Alyosha (I.iii.8). Or, in terms of outrageous behavior, his fathering a child with Lizaveta (I.iii.2). Isn't Ivan's parable about the Grand Inquisitor an instance of intellectual hyperbole, while the arrest of Christ is an instance of deliberate moral incongruity and spiritual disruption?

Like their father, Ivan and Dmitri live in a world of exaggerated feeling and emotion. Describing Ivan's last night in his father's house, when he watched his obsessed father prowling about in expectation of a visit from Grushenka, the narrator tells us: "All [Ivan's] life afterward he referred to this 'action' as 'loathsome' and all his life, deep in himself, in the inmost part of his soul, he considered it the basest action of his whole life" (II.v.7.276).

We are prepared from the outset for Dmitri's exaggerated speech and incongruous behavior. When introducing Dmitri, the narrator alerts us readers: "something sickly, as it were, showed in his face" (I.ii.6.67). Dmitri doesn't know himself; his eyes have a "vague" look: "Even when he was excited and talking irritably, his look, as it were, did not obey his inner mood but expressed something else, sometimes not all corresponding to the present moment" (I.ii.6.67).

Dostoevsky dislikes the wealthy, slick, urbane, self-regarding, Western-orientated Pyotr Alexandrovich Miusov, who is very much present in I.ii in a chapter entitled "An Inappropriate Gathering" and whose bad manners and pettiness are as much on display as the buffoonery of Fyodor Pavlovich. That he patronizes Zosima underlines his superficiality: "To all appearances [Miusov is] a malicious and pettily arrogant little soul" (I.ii.2.40). Miusov is a cynical figure, motivated by self-interest, who rationally measures which way the wind is blowing and finds no place for passion or faith. Miusov's ideal city is Paris, hardly surprising since Dostoevsky uses him to express his disdain for the Enlightenment and its negative effect on Russia.

Dostoevsky postpones introducing Katerina Ivanovna, Dmitri's fiancée, and Grushenka to the second to last chapter of Part I (I.iii.10), even though we increasingly hear about them before we meet them. When we do meet Katerina and Grushenka, they are together, and Katerina is trying to convince Grushenka – age twenty-two and sexually appealing to Fyodor and Dmitri, both of whom are obsessed with her – to give up Dmitri for Ivan, her former lover. Katerina is focused, even fixated, on Dmitri, although Ivan is also in (unconsummated) love with her. But Grushenka proves unreliable and flighty; she enjoys the supplications of Katerina, a person of superior social position, as much as she enjoys flouting Katerina's wishes.

Grushenka's play-acting for an audience, her erratic and weird emotional behavior, and her continually changing attitudes recall the buffoonery and incongruous, exaggerated, and excessive behavior as well as hyperbolic speech of both Dmitri and Fyodor Pavlovich. Yet isn't Katerina, who really loves Ivan, also play-acting? Isn't she competing for Dmitri in part for competition's sake, that is, not only to placate her ego but also to assuage her shame for going to him for money to save her father's reputation? Alyosha realizes that Katerina loves Ivan – or thinks she does – and is "tormenting herself with her affected love for Dmitri, out of some kind of supposed gratitude" (II.iv.5.186).

Dostoevsky is much aware of – and revels in – how the novel's seemingly discrete parts fit together. For example, the chapter entitled "An Onion" (III.vii.3) describes a fable that Grushenka heard as a child in which a selfish woman whom the devils have placed in the lake of fire will not share an onion held out to her by her guardian angel for the purpose of pulling her out; she falls back into the lake. The onion was God's choice to test the woman because her one good deed was to give a beggar the onion; but because the woman kicked others who were trying to grab on, the onion broke (III.vii.3.352–353). What Dostoevsky is implying is that we all have an onion – a gift from God, in his cosmology – and we need to make the choice to take advantage of it. It is another version of free will to choose God. In a sense, Grushenka's later love and loyalty to Dmitri after she sees the folly of running off with her former lover combine to be her onion.

Let us turn to Book Four, which is subtitled "Strains." Without a Freudian vocabulary, Dostoevsky uses the term "strain" as an elastic umbrella concept to explain inconsistent, often bizarre, behavior. By contrast, in the first part of the twenty-first century we might use the concept of extreme emotional pressure to explain neurosis, if not psychosis, or we might rely on cognitive psychology or even genetics.

By means of his characters' hyperbolic speech and incongruous behavior, Dostoevsky demonstrates what he calls "strain" and we might define as being "out of control." Thus "Strains" covers erratic behavior on the part of Ivan, Katerina, and mother and daughter Khokhlakov in Katerina's drawing room. Take, for example, Ivan's mockery of Katerina because he doesn't know how to love or to express his feelings directly. For all his intelligence, Ivan lacks self-knowledge. Dostoevsky wants the reader to understand that Ivan's moral confusion is both the result of and the punishment for his professed atheism: "He spoke decidedly with a sort of malice, evidently deliberate, and even, perhaps, not wishing to conceal his intentions – that is, that he was speaking deliberately and in mockery" (II.iv.5.190). Or take the Snegiryov cottage. With a disturbed mother, erratic father, crippled daughter, and dying young son Ilyusha, isn't the pathetic and destitute Snegiryov family a structural echo of the dysfunctional Karamazov family, if not a reverse mirror image? For the Karamazov family has two morally disabled children, Dmitri and Ivan, and the decadent drunk and lecher Fyodor, who is economically competent but does not fulfill the father role. Snegiryov, former staff captain, is a kind of ironic double of Dmitri, who is not only a superior officer to Snegiryov but also someone who physically abuses him.

Let us look more closely at the subplot involving Ilyusha and his family, the Snegiryovs, as well as the precocious Kolya. Ilyusha asks his father, Snegiryov, an ingenuous question – but one based on his own experience and observation – that resonates through all Dostoevsky's work and almost all the nineteenth-century novels I am discussing: "[P]apa, is it true that the rich are stronger than anybody in the world?" Snegiryov responds: "Yes, Ilyusha … no one in the world is stronger than the rich" (II.iv.7.207). Economic determinism, while secondary to the presence of an immanent God, is an important aspect of Dostoevsky's world.

Desperately needy Snegiryov renounces the two hundred roubles that Katerina has sent. Had he accepted, he would have had the means to become a more capable father and husband, for that money would have enabled him to make his crippled if eccentric and disturbed wife and daughter more comfortable and send his hardened older daughter, Varvara, back to school in St. Petersburg (II.iv.7). Yet, whether from pride or eccentricity, he refuses to accept the money.

Kolya is almost fourteen, extremely bright and clever, but somewhat bored with life and without direction. He seeks thrills through mischief, opposes sentimentality, tries to be an independent thinker, but spouts hackneyed post-Enlightenment Western ideas. Even before Alyosha calls Kolya "perverted" because he is a disbeliever (we suspect that Alyosha has his brother Ivan in mind), the reader understands that Kolya is a kind of junior Ivan with a touch of the undisciplined wildness of Dmitri (IV.x.6.556). Notwithstanding Kolya's tough, prickly veneer, he has, like Alyosha, an ability to feel the pain of others. But, until he becomes Alyosha's pupil, he lacks moral bearings and direction.

Although still in the process of developing, Kolya represents the potential of Russia. To date, his potential is not yet fulfilled and could go for naught. Alyosha speaks to him the way that Zosima had spoken to Alyosha. Alyosha predicts: "Listen, Kolya, by the way, you are going to be a very unhappy man in your life" (IV.x.6.558). Although Alyosha may be issuing an oblique warning about nonbelief, it seems at first an uncharacteristic harshness on Alyosha's part, for there is no reason to say this to Kolya, unless – as we come to realize – he believes in Kolya's uniqueness to make a difference. As if Alyosha knows he has erred in the way he spoke to Kolya, he continues: "But on the whole you will bless life all the same" (IV.x.6.558).

Playing an important structural role with its suggestions of violence and redemption, the Zosima interpolation – Part II.vi is entitled "The Russian Monk" – underlines Dostoevsky's spiritual values. Zosima's story about his transformation is a tale of spiritual and moral redemption through the realization of the unity of the world. Zosima had abusively hit his military servant before refusing to duel after being shot by his rival.

Zosima's brother, who died at seventeen, lived Christ-like in infinite love for God's creation and anticipates Alyosha, who reminds Zosima of his brother. Zosima's story about the man who killed his wife and confessed – II.vi.2.d ("The Mysterious Visitor") – is a story of redemption through suffering that recalls Raskolnikov in *Crime and Punishment*. The man had almost murdered Zosima because he had previously told Zosima the secret that might have been his undoing had he not confessed.

With his dialogic method in which he questions the very answers he tentatively provides, even when those answers seem to be rooted in his Christian belief, Dostoevsky eschews dogmatism. In terms of the reader's process of sorting out Dostoevsky's values – or, more importantly, the more complex nuances of the novel's presentation, whatever Dostoevsky's personal values – Zosima raises as many problems as he presents solutions.

Dostoevsky introduces skepticism about the concept of the elder as a kind of hierarchical spiritual figure. Does not the resistant Father Ferapont, who in fact claims to be much more spiritually gifted than Zosima and the skeptical Obordorsk monk, ask the reader to pause before accepting anyone as a spiritual paradigm? Yet Dostoevsky wants us to see, too, that Father Ferapont's pride raises questions about his zealous holiness.

Is Zosima a paradigm of spiritual faith or are his words of comfort simple bromides from someone who has withdrawn from the world and is playing a role? Is there arrogance in the elder's assumption of holiness? Is the corruption of his body a reminder that no one can aspire to sainthood? Why does he bow down to Dmitri and bless Ivan, while insisting that Alyosha go out into the world? Is Zosima's simplistic view of forgiveness and possible redemption and his stress on spirituality and the importance of the next world – what Ivan regards as a falsehood – something Ivan is critiquing as a reductive solution to the human predicament in his Grand Inquisitor parable? Dostoevsky believes that Christianity needs to account for human impulses towards reason and sensuality, community and selfishness, as well as nobility and baseness.

Dmitri Accused: Dostoevsky as a Detective Story Writer

As we know from *Crime and Punishment*, Dostoevsky writes compelling detective stories. Hovering over the novel is Dmitri's threat of patricide. Responding to his father's buffoonery in the monastery, Dmitri proleptically and ominously asks out loud, "Why is such a man alive!" (I.ii.6.74). During Dmitri's intense dialogue with Alyosha – while he is keeping watch over his father's house – he tells Alyosha that if Grushenka visits his father, he, Dmitri, will kill him, although as soon as Alyosha says, "[W]hat are you saying?" Dmitri responds, "Maybe I won't kill him, and maybe I will.... I feel a personal loathing" (I.iii.5.122).

When, while speaking to Ivan and Alyosha in his house, a drunken Fyodor Pavlovich sees and hears Dmitri arrive amidst a commotion and break through the guard of both Grigory and Smerdyakov, his first response is hysterically fearful: "He'll kill me, he'll kill me! Don't let him get me!" (I.iii.8.138). Dmitri beats and kicks him until Ivan and Alyosha intervene. After Ivan shouts, "Madman, you've killed him!" Dmitri cries, "Serves him right! ... And if I haven't killed him this time, I'll come back and kill him. You can't save him" (I.iii.9.139).

Lest the reader suspect only Dmitri, we hear Ivan asking Alyosha: "[D]o you consider me capable, like Dmitri, of shedding Aesop's [Ivan's facetious nickname for his father] blood, well, of killing him?" (I.iii.9.143). And he adds ambiguously and cynically, "But as for my wishes in the matter, there I reserve complete freedom for myself" (I.iii.9.143). Ivan the non-believer – for whom immortality is a "complete zero" and who rejects the devil at this point with certainty – has no more moral and spiritual compass than Raskolnikov in *Crime and Punishment*. He is simply less violent and less economically desperate.

Beginning with Alyosha's conversation with Rakitin in I.ii.7 and Rakitin's insinuations about a forthcoming "crime," the novel gradually shapes the reader to anticipate that Dmitri is the "murderer" who will "even put a knife in his own papa" (I.ii.7.78–79). Rakitin gives us many hints that it will be Dmitri who murders his father (I.ii.7.78–79), but he also casts some suspicion on Ivan: "The three of them are at loggerheads." With insinuating suggestiveness that recalls Svidrigailov in *Crime and Punishment*, Rakitin adds, "and maybe you're the fourth" (I.ii.7.79). According to Rakitin, whose words resonate with Alyosha's darker thoughts, "[T]hese three sensualists are now eying each other with knives in their boots" (I.ii.7.79). That Rakitin at this point observes that Alyosha is "shaking all over" and that he doesn't deny the substance of Rakitin's analyses encourages the reader to believe that violence among Dmitri, Ivan, and Fyodor might happen (I.ii.7.79).

Dostoevsky seeds Book Eight with many strong hints that Dmitri has murdered his father. We might cite Fenya's crying, "he'll kill somebody" (III.viii.3.390) and Grigory's shouting "Parricide!" (III.viii.4.394) as well as someone in the tavern that the police official Pyotr Ilyich Perkhotin visits immediately after leaving Dmitri remembering that Dmitri had boasted that "he'd kill his father" (III.viii.5.408).

Yet Dostoevsky the detective novelist ensures that we suspect Ivan as well as Dmitri as characters with homicidal intentions. Fyodor is also afraid of Ivan; he is not entirely facetious when he asks Alyosha when Ivan has been visiting him for three weeks, "It can't be that he's come to put a knife in me, too" (II.iv.2.173). It is quite some time before we realize with Dmitri that it most likely is Smerdyakov who is the murderer because he knew where the money was and knew the code for Fyodor's opening the door.

In Part III.viii.5, at the very center of the book entitled "Mitya," a manic, disoriented, and obsessive Dmitri – also called Mitya – who is stained with blood, visits Pyotr Ilyich to get back the pistols he has pawned. We don't know at this point that the blood came from his collision with the old servant, Grigory; nor do we know where the wad of money – identified as 3,000 roubles by Mitya – has come from (III.viii.5.401). With loaded pistols and with champagne and party supplies purchased on a spending spree, Dmitri irrationally follows Grushenka to Mokroye where she is rendezvousing with her recently returned lover.

In order to emphasize the moral difference that divides Dmitri from Alyosha and cast suspicion on the former, Dostoevsky reminds us that Dmitri makes this journey on "the same night, perhaps the same hour, when Alyosha threw himself to the earth 'vowing ecstatically to love it unto ages of ages'" (III.viii.6.409). In his oeuvre, Dostoevsky brilliantly dramatizes manic and obsessive behavior, and nowhere better than in the scene where Dmitri unfolds a piece of paper in front of Pyotr Ilyich that reads, "For my whole life I punish myself, I punish my whole life!" (III.viii.5.403). This written riddle – a chiasmus which strongly hints at suicide and perhaps murder of his rival – frightens Pyotr Ilyich as well as the reader. The riddle strikingly illustrates Dmitri's inability to move forward and becomes an emblem of his obsessive behavior revolving around his father – his rival for Grushenka – Grushenka herself, and Katerina Ivanovna, whose 3,000 roubles he has misappropriated. At this point, the narrator inflects Dmitri's erratic if not sociopathic behavior: "Though Mitya began bustling about, making arrangements, he spoke and gave commands somewhat strangely, at random and out of order. He began one thing and forgot to finish it" (III.viii.5.404).

Dostoevsky wants us to see that there is something sad about Dmitri's sexually obsessive desire for Grushenka. The ironic title of Chapter III.viii.7 when Dmitri meets Grushenka's lover is "The Former and Indisputable One," and we realize that as Grushenka observes the two of them together, the "Indisputable One" is Dmitri with all his faults and excesses. The sardonic chapter title describes Dmitri's place in Grushenka's fickle and unstable heart as if the title were describing a king who returned to power.

The Brothers Karamazov gives a sense of a Russia filled with mean-spirited scoundrels, including some of the judicial and legal officials such as the young district attorney Nikolai Parfenovich Nelyudov; the Poles – the two card sharks, one of whom is Grushenka's lover – are even worse. When Dmitri arrives at the inn, despite his manic behavior, he is a more attractive and sympathetic figure than Grushenka's Polish lover who – in another scene marked by incongruity, extravagance, excess, and hyperbolic speech – is not only a dishonest gambler seeking Grushenka for her supposed wealth, but a pathetic man in physical stature with a huge Polish bodyguard.

Book Eight concludes with "Delirium," a chapter presenting a wild party at which Mitya experiences great joy as Grushenka affirms her love. But the party is brought to a close when he is arrested for murdering his father. In the first chapter of Book Nine, a book entitled "The Preliminary Investigation," the reader is taken back a few hours in time to the young Pyotr Ilyich's role and his perspective in determining what happened. After the various police and legal officials arrive at Mokroye and arrest Dmitri, he acknowledges smashing Grigory's skull but denies killing his father.

The narrator casts Dmitri in a sympathetic light because Dmitri naïvely believes that if he tells the truth he will be believed. He takes the high ground in refusing to say how he came upon the funds for his spree and acknowledges that he is a thief, the worst kind of scoundrel, but not a murderer. He ingenuously thinks that if he opens up to those local officials he considers his peers, he will get a sympathetic hearing: "It is a noble man you are speaking with, a most noble person; above all – do not lose sight of this – a man who has done a world of mean things, but who always was and remained a most noble person, as a person, inside, in his depths" (III.ix.3.462).

The chapter titles at the center of Book Nine – "The Soul's Journey through Torments. The First Torment," "The Second Torment," "The Third Torment" – emphasize Dmitri as a guilty and tormented victim of his own disreputable and disgraceful behavior, but not as a man who committed patricide. We think of Christ's crown of thorns and other physical abuse such as flogging and pulling his beard at the hands of Roman officials prior to his actual crucifixion. Book Nine's climax is Dmitri's moving dream of exploited, impoverished peasants with whom he feels a kinship and whom he cares for and wants to help: "[H]e also feels a tenderness such as he has never known before surging up in his heart" (III.ix.8.508). Dostoevsky's use of the present tense emphasizes Dmitri's epiphanic moment. Such awareness and transformation – the result in part of Grushenka's declaration of love ("I will go with you for the rest of my life") – align Dmitri with Alyosha, Zosima, and, of course, Dostoevsky himself, who felt deeply for the downtrodden and victimized Russian peasant (III.ix.8.508).

The Ending of *The Brothers Karamazov* and its Implications

Book Twelve is entitled "A Judicial Error." The chapter in which the verdict is given – the last chapter before the epilogue – is entitled "Our Peasants Stood Up for Themselves," as if the peasants rejected the elaborate arguments of Fetyukovich, the defense attorney from Moscow. The latter is a secular version of the Grand Inquisitor, using sophistry and twisting Christ's words to suit his purposes. Fetyukovich often takes logic and reason to reductive absurdity to try to exculpate Dmitri, for whom he shows little human concern. The prosecutor's use of logic and reason to argue for Dmitri's conviction as well as the specious erudition of the law courts contrast with Zosima's faith as well as with Alyosha's simple humanistic love. His love is based in large part on faith and intuition but also on human decency and caring for people. Testimony from

Dmitri that is both humanistic and Christian aligns Dmitri with Alyosha. We learn that Dmitri remembers all his life the act of kindness on the part of Dr. Herzenstube, who gives him a pound of nuts and teaches him to say in German, God the Father, God the Son, and God the Holy Ghost ("Gott der Vater, Gott der Sohn und Gott der heilige Geist!" [IV.xii.3.675]).

With long paragraphs of judicial argument in the form of monologues, the pace slows down with the trial. The narrator is a presence, revealing the verdict – also disclosing the name of the town, something he had withheld – and telling the reader he is editing the trial up until the prosecutor and defense attorney's statements. Because we already know the identity of the murderer, the recapitulation of what we know, even if inflected by eloquence, sarcasm, and wit, gets a little tiresome for some readers.

Ivan the skeptic has brain fever but he is in the care of Katerina Ivanovna. Like Ivan and Dmitri, she is a tempestuous soul who lacks coherence, consistency, and self-regard. Her testimony against Dmitri is an act of vengeance from a rejected lover. After testifying in a way that supports Dmitri's story, and after Ivan's breakdown, Katerina becomes hysterical and produces a crucial letter – the smoking gun – that sways the jury. She reveals the letter from a complex mixture of motives, including wanting to undermine Ivan's self-sacrifice. She betrays Dmitri, the lover who rejected her, and Ivan, her current lover. As readers, we both sympathize with her suffering even as we realize how much misery her pride causes herself and others. She betrays Dmitri and Ivan because she fears if she shows joy at Dmitri's being saved, Ivan would be jealous.

Dostoevsky gives us a thematic epilogue but not a fully satisfactory ending. As we have been seeing, this is a novel that leaves the reader with more questions than it answers. Dmitri is convicted but plans for escape have been arranged. Alyosha seems sure Dmitri is going into exile, but does he mean escape or prison? To be sure, redemption is an important part of the finale. After Dmitri's arrest, Grushenka becomes more spiritual under Alyosha's tutelage. At the trial Katerina abandons Dmitri, but she, too, eventually undergoes some spiritual redemption.

Since the events took place thirteen years ago, we want to know what happened in the interim to the central characters – what the effects of their experience are on their psyches – and we don't know. That, except for Alyosha, they are all tortured souls, ever-changing and unable to live up to their resolutions and ideals, may in some way be the point of Dostoevsky's omitting a traditional ending. Ivan has brain fever; Dmitri is poised between hard labor and exile with Grushenka; and both are without the full emotional tools to cope with day-to-day life. Unreliable in her behavior, Katerina is still brooding about Dmitri.

The three chapters of the epilogue of *The Brothers Karamazov* are humanistic as much as Christian. Dostoevsky's lessons are (1) Humans must draw on their good memories – and their best impulses – even when tempted by wickedness and (2) humans must love one another. Unlike Zosima, Alyosha's influence is as a practical mentor to the young adolescents he has brought together; after Ilyusha's funeral, he affirms: "You must know that there is nothing higher, or stronger, or sounder, or more useful afterwards in life, than some good memory, especially a memory from childhood, from the parental home" (Epilogue.iii.774). When Kolya asks if we will arise after death, Alyosha, "half laughing, half in ecstasy," affirms that too: "Certainly we shall rise, certainly we shall see and gladly, joyfully tell one another all that has been," and Kolya, his jejune pupil, cries ecstatically, "And eternally so, all our lives hand in hand!" (Epilogue.iii.776). Aileen Kelly remarks that "in his more self-questioning moods, … Dostoevsky express[es] the fear that his vision of the transformation of the terrestrial world is incompatible with the Christian doctrine of the heavenly Kingdom of God."[13] In other words, Dostoevky's real interest is often in the here and now and undercuts his simple theological propositions. Isn't this part of his dialogic method, where no sooner does he present an apparent truth than he calls it into some question?

Study Questions for *The Brothers Karamazov*

1. In his parable of the Grand Inquisitor, what are Ivan's points about the human condition, faith, and free will?
2. What are Zosima's values and how are they a response to Ivan's parable about the Grand Inquisitor?
3. Why does Zosima's corpse smell and how does it affect Alyosha? How does the smell affect our response to Alyosha?
4. What is the role of Christianity in the novel? How does Dostoevsky convey to his secular reader what is at stake for each soul, whether a character is a believer or a skeptic?
5. Why does the narrator designate Alyosha as the novel's hero?
6. How is the narrator a self-dramatizing character and how reliable and perceptive is he?
7. How is *The Brothers Karamazov* a detective story? When do you as a first-time reader begin to suspect Smerdyakov? When are you certain he is the murderer?
8. What is Dostoevsky implying about the effects of parenting and early childhood?
9. Why is Dostoevsky's technique of presenting character called "dialogic" by the Russian critic Bakhtin?

10. What is the function of the three chapter epilogue?
11. Is the ending satisfactory or do we expect the narrator, who is describing events that took place thirteen years ago, to tell us more?
12. Why does Dostoevsky postpone introducing Katerina Ivanovna and Grushenka to the second to last chapter of Part I (I.iii.10)?

Notes

1. Fyodor Dostoevsky, *The Brothers Karamazov*, trans. Richard Pevear and Larissa Volokhonsky (New York: Farrar, Straus and Giroux, 1990; New York: Vintage, 1993). Quotations from the text are taken from this translation.
2. Joseph Frank, *Dostoevsky: The Miraculous Years, 1865–1871* (Princeton, NJ: Princeton University Press, 1995), 300.
3. Richard Pevear, "Introduction," *Brothers Karamazov*, xiii.
4. Pevear, "Introduction," *Brothers Karamazov*, xiii.
5. Joseph Frank, "The Millennium & Dostoevsky: An Exchange," reply by Aileen Kelly, *NYR* 50:15 (Oct. 9, 2003); http://www.nybooks.com/articles/archives/2003/oct/09/the-millennium-dostoevsky-an-exchange (accessed February 14, 2014).
6. Stephen Greenblatt, "The Lonely Gods," *NYR* 57:11 (June 23, 2011), 6–10; see p. 10.
7. Frank, *Dostoevsky: The Miraculous Years*, 678.
8. Geoffrey O'Brien, "Giving Gogol His Head," *NYR* 57:7 (April 29, 2010), 20–23; see p. 22.
9. Pevear, "Introduction," *Brothers Karamazov*, xv–xvi.
10. Pevear, "Introduction," *Brothers Karamazov*, xv–xvi.
11. Pevear, "Introduction," *Brothers Karamazov*, xvi.
12. Pevear, "Introduction," *Brothers Karamazov*, xvi.
13. "The Millennium & Dostoevsky: An Exchange."

Chapter 8

Tolstoy's *War and Peace* (1869)

The Novel as Historical Epic

On (Re)Reading Tolstoy's *War and Peace*

I
Living with the Rostovs and Bolkonskys
for several months as I wend my
way through early nineteenth
century Tsarist Russia;
over twelve hundred pages
opens the door to genius.

II
My mind lives in another time,
takes part in the loves, disappointments,
losses and grieving of an immense cast.

III
War's terrible cycle:
its human cost, exhilaration
horrors, triumphs,
pain, pleasures.
Victory for one side is
defeat for another.
Is peacetime, with its winners,
its losers, any different?

Reading the European Novel to 1900: A Critical Study of Major Fiction from Cervantes' Don Quixote *to Zola's* Germinal, First Edition. Daniel R. Schwarz.
© 2014 John Wiley & Sons, Ltd. Published 2014 by John Wiley & Sons, Ltd.

IV
History as accident:
A compilation of a grammar
of motives and chance
coalescing retrospectively
into perceived patterns.

V
Tolstoy reads character in every
physical gesture, facial feature;
understands serendipity
of military history, even as generals
think they tightly control
crisscrossing European armies.
In his vast sweep, doings of
seemingly minor characters matter.

VI
War defines males;
women stay behind, often
wrenching meaning from
lives of male relations.

VII
Peace: inheritance and position
provide context for idle social prattle –
lonely, vapid "little princess" Lise,
for example, all but discarded
by bored husband Andrei Bolkonsky,
who touchingly loves
his cranky, eccentric father;
bacchanalias of Anatole
Kuragin's circle;
Nikolai Rostov's
naïve integrity.

VIII
Obese, cuckolded, bumbling, gauche,
puzzled, questing Pierre overcomes his faults,
winning our sympathy with his
simplicity, decency, and lack of guile.
loving Natasha,
heartfully.

(Daniel R. Schwarz, "On (Re)Reading Tolstoy's *War and Peace*")

Introduction

Reading – indeed rereading – *War and Peace* has been one of the great experiences of my reading life. *War and Peace* challenges the reader's memory and, indeed, reading skills. Multiple narratives and large swathes of social and military history need to be kept in mind. The sheer length and number of characters mean the reader lives within the imagined world a long time and watches history unroll. In a sense, like most of the truly great novels, *War and Peace* not only is a novel that keeps speaking to its readers, but it is a novel about how and why we read.

Writing about Richard Pevear and Larissa Volokhonsky's authoritative translation of *War and Peace*, James Wood observes:

. . . .

Literary translators tend to divide into what one could call originalists and activists. The former honor the original text's quiddities, and strive to reproduce them as accurately as possible in the translated language; the latter are less concerned with literal accuracy than with the transposed musical appeal of the new work ... Pevear and Volokhonsky ... are closer to the originalist camp than to the activist.... [T]hey want the English to sound as close to the Russian as possible, and they are fervent about the importance of "roughening up" their versions when the Russian demands it.[1]

. . . .

Tolstoy wants us to rethink the meaning of the terms "War" and "Peace" not as simple polar opposites but as profound concepts informing the entire novel and, indeed, the broad sweep of history. When we open *War and Peace*, we are in a world where political and personal intrigues percolate beneath social rituals, where wealth and family heritage shape personal history, and where international events and public discourse matter. In the opening chapter, many if not most of the guests attending Anna Pavlovna's vapid salon have their eyes on improving their social and economic statures.

From the outset, Tolstoy demonstrates that the interval between wars that we call "peace" is frequently insidious and invidious and takes the form of often sordid warfare without weapons. An early example is the scrambling for the wealthy courtier Count Bezukhov's fortune, which goes to his illegitimate son Pierre. We soon realize that stratagems for making economically and socially desirable marriages and manipulating the social system to get the best possible positions for adult children are both kinds of aggressive warfare. Both the aforementioned stratagems often yield, like wartime stratagems, unintended consequences. Tolstoy also makes clear that the sudden deaths of the young and the consequent disruptions to families are not restricted to war. For example, Lise, Andrei's wife, dies in childbirth.

Tolstoy understands that a dotted line sometimes separates peacetime from war; if peace has its social conquests and duels, military life has its idleness: "In this obligatory and irreproachable idleness consists and will consist the chief attraction of military service" (2.IV.i.488).[2] Yet, finally, the horrors of war are quite different from the rivalries of peace.

Peace, including diplomatic maneuvers and bivouac respites, can take place within the context of war. War, either in aggressive self-seeking behavior or in the form of a duel, can take place within the domestic world where one might expect peace. An example of the former is the comfort of home Nikolai Rostov feels when he rejoins his regiment after losing money gambling and presuming on his father to pay the 43,000 roubles debt to Dolokhov: "Rostov experienced the same feeling as when his mother, father, and sisters had embraced him" (2.II.xv.395). Ironically, despite the mortality rate in battle, he finds respite from the confusion and ambiguities of civilian life in the "distinctly defined and ordered" world of the military with its "definite conditions of regimental life" (2.II.xv.395).

The Rostov family has been betrayed by one of the novel's most predatory scoundrels, Dolokhov, who was the Rostov houseguest after Nikolai befriended him. Dolokhov uses a card game to put the naïve Nikolai in enormous debt to him as a way of getting even with the Rostov family after he realizes that he cannot win Sonya's hand; he won the 43,000 roubles from Nikolai Rostov as revenge for Sonya's refusal.

Dolokhov is always at war, a restive soul with malicious intent. He has an affair with Pierre's wife followed by a duel with Pierre. Later, in battle, he is indifferent to the death of sixteen-year-old Petya Rostov as if he still hated the Rostovs; "with a cold smirk," Dolokhov speaks disparagingly of "the little sixteen year old count" and seems to gloat when Petya is killed (4.III.viii.1049). Dolokhov, we realize, is a moral idiot, if not a psychopath, driven by inner demons that would be at home in a Dostoevsky novel. Yet often Tolstoy eschews the absolute and surprises us. For Dolokhov becomes slightly sympathetic when we learn that he lives with a hunch-backed sister and an elderly mother to whom he is quite solicitous.

The Napoleonic Period

In the combination of the characters' empty social prattle, family ambitions, and manipulative and self-serving discourse, we readers see startling similarities with contemporary cocktail parties of influential people and wannabes.

With powerful politically connected families and titled princes, this is a very different salon from Austen's provincial English drawing room, but not without similar caste distinctions. Even as the upper classes speak French, the gathering storm is Napoleon's expanding empire. Quite ironically, the first words we hear are Anna Pavlovna's French. As Count Rastopchin sarcastically remarks in 1811 when the restive Napoleon is proving an unreliable and patronizing ally: "[F]ar be it from us to fight the French.... The French are our gods, and our kingdom of heaven is Paris" (2.V.iii.545).

Tolstoy wanted to render the truth about the Napoleonic period as he understood it and to show the folly in seeing it in reductively romantic terms as good versus evil or the fulfillment of God's ordained teleology. He detests Napoleon's megalomania, ambition, solipsism, and self-immersion. Tolstoy's narrative voice is that of a Russian patriot speaking of "our army." But the narrator is also a human being who pities those killed and wounded on all sides and understands the terrible costs of war and how individuals are pawns of political and historical forces. While Tolstoy dramatizes battles, he refuses to give credit for military strategies because he believes that so much depends on accident.

Tolstoy presents Napoleon as a vain, foolish man who is in over his head. He is derisive of Napoleon's actions in Moscow; he sarcastically calls Napoleon "that genius of geniuses" (4.II.viii.1001) and thinks every decision Napoleon made was wrong-headed. But Tolstoy is also doubtful that any course of action Napoleon could have taken would have saved the French from humiliating defeat. For Tolstoy is skeptical about the Great Man theory and is something of a New Historian in his stressing the importance of understanding how history percolates upward from the soldier in service and the peasant working the land. Thus Napoleon's "personal activity, having no more power than the personal activity of each soldier, merely coincided with the laws according to which the phenomenon was accomplished" (4.II.viii.1002).

Tolstoy's Philosophy and Historical Perspective

To understand *War and Peace*, we need to realize that the novel contains strong assertions of Tolstoy's bedrock philosophy as well as hints of his later philosophy. Thus we need to read with awareness of three perspectives: Tolstoy's understanding of the period about which he is writing, his retrospective view of that period, and his philosophy of history and of life which he is in the process of defining but which is often not yet fully realized.

Even before the epilogue, Tolstoy proposes his philosophy of history and of life in metafictional essays, such as the opening reflections in 3.II.i about history as a result of myriad causes – including chance – that interact in a specific way at a particular spatial-temporal locus: "Providence made all these people, while striving to achieve their personal aims, contribute to the fulfillment of one enormous result, of which not one man (neither Napoleon, not Alexander, still less any of the participants in the war) had the least expectation" (3.II.i.682).

As the novel evolves, Pierre and Andrei grow morally and come to embrace Tolstoy's values, values that balance a sense of community with private happiness. Well before he marries Natasha, Pierre believes that "[T]he pleasure of doing good is the only certain happiness in life" (2.II.xi.384). He is committed to bettering the circumstances of the serfs who live on his land.

By contrast, at this point, Andrei wants to live for "myself alone" (2.II.xi.384). Andrei had returned from war to see his son born and his wife die. The combination of these events led him to refocus on himself and his immediate family. He is suffering from what we now would call depression. But he awakens "in his inner world" to "a new life," after Pierre – under the influence of the Freemasons, but speaking from his heart – points to the sky and tells Andrei, "We must live, we must love, we must believe … that we do not live only today on this scrap of earth, but have lived and will live eternally there, in the all" (2.II.xii.389). When he falls in love with the much younger Natasha in 1809, Andrei feels "an unexpected tangle of youthful thoughts and hopes, contradictory to his whole life" (2.III.ii.422). His loving Natasha becomes the catalyst to his wanting to participate in public life.

Tolstoy had a profound sense of history. He understood what has become known as F. W. Maitland's rule for understanding history: "[A]lways remember that events far in the past were once in the future."[3] In other words, we can look back and see what a general might have done, but he was facing events that hadn't yet taken place and had to guess what would happen. Yet Tolstoy also understood that, as Geoffrey Wheatcroft puts it, "Because something happens does not mean it had to happen."[4]

Tolstoy's narrator is a character and is often a surrogate pressing the author's views: major events do not depend upon a hero's will but upon a confluence of causes; humans seek simple explanations and need to isolate a comprehensible concatenation of events from the historical mess; history is an accident informed by God's will, which humans cannot understand; military action is more farcical than planned. What makes life meaningful is human love, but finally we return to God's more majestic world. We think we control far more in our personal life than we do. Selfishness is bad and self-immersed narcissism is worse, but some self-love is necessary to act effectively. Tolstoy's conservative view of Russia's social structure regards the great families as necessary guardians of serfs and peasants.

Great events, Tolstoy knew, may have insignificant causes, or may depend on individual misjudgments. For Tolstoy, much of history is accident or, to put it better, history is a compilation of infinite grammars of motives – often leading to misjudgments and misunderstandings – and chance (including weather, landscape) coalescing into what, from the vantage point of retrospectively looking backwards, is a pattern.

Tolstoy takes for himself the liberty of reflection on actual events that took place as well as those events he imagined and dramatized. Tolstoy moves between history and fiction, sometimes introducing himself into the text and displacing the omniscient narrator's rendering of individual characters' points of view. While fictional characters can be part of historical events and often are, the degree to which in *War and Peace* they are either entwined in historical events – most notably Napoleon's attack on Moscow – or are illustrating behavioral patterns that reflect Tolstoy's current and emerging philosophy is unusual.

Some of our reading pleasure may even be in watching Tolstoy chafe against the conventions of the novel, even the subgenre of the historical novel.[5] We are aware that the author's stakes are higher in the essayistic comments than in many novels. There is something going on in these self-conscious metafictional intrusions of Tolstoy's thoughts and feelings that we wouldn't see in, say, Dostoevsky or Joyce or Conrad. Do not these essayistic intrusions – this presence of the author that eludes our usual sense of what fiction is – represent a difference not merely in degree but in kind? Rather than dramatization, plot, and attempts at verisimilitude, we have reflections on events that put aside novelistic conventions.

The structure of *War and Peace* oscillates between a narrow focus on paradigmatic families that typify historical patterns and a hawk's eye view of military and social history. The novel proceeds by expansion – widening the lens on major historic events – and contraction to individual lives. Tolstoy alternates between the grim details of war and the triviality of social life as well as the excitement of love during peacetime; peacetime even at times includes the domestic front during wartime.

Tolstoy focuses on Pierre Bezukhov, Andrei Bolkonsky, and Nikolai and Natasha Rostov as well as their parents and families. John Bayley succinctly observes: "Pierre is the representative of the future, so old Bolkonsky [Andrei's father] is of the past."[6] Ironically, to a resistant reader, the long view can also become nominalistic – rather than, as Tolstoy urges, typifying – when focusing on the details of the lives of his central figures. Moreover, the narrow view can become representative when dealing with how war ensnares everyone in its grasp. But this is another way that *War and Peace* overflows the borders of its teleology, even as it challenges the expectations of the novel form.

Despite its historical sweep, plot takes a back seat to character in *War and Peace*. At times, without worrying about what we now call organic development, Tolstoy manipulates characters so that they reappear or disappear. When he loses interest, he simply – as he does with Hélène – kills them off; or he forgets them, as he virtually does with the detestable Berg.

It is almost as if the forward motion of the novel is arrested when Moscow is emptied and burns. It burns, according to Tolstoy, less because of French and Russian arsonists than because it is made of wood. We readers are suspended in stasis while the narrator presents the chaotic remnants of Moscow life in the form of almost anonymous figures and anecdotes: the tall Russian left behind who is both perpetrator and victim of violence, French and Russian looters, those few Russians defending the Kremlin, and the "murder" of the Russian factory worker and four others by the "criminals" of the French conquering army (4.I.xi.967). The French army – a third of which is left – dissolves into looting once it enters Moscow, although the Russians who are left behind are not immune from looting.

Tolstoy's focus is on the dissolution of civility and social behavior in Moscow after the city is abandoned by both the army and almost all people of rank. According to Tolstoy's conservative views, the social structure depends on the leadership of responsible great families; he implies that in their absence the poor become rabble, especially if led by demagogues like Count Rastopchin, whom Tolstoy despises. The Machiavellian Count Rastopchin remains behind for a time, presiding over chaos, but even he leaves after instigating mob violence upon the supposed traitor Vereshchagin.

Tolstoy regarded *War and Peace* more as an historical epic than a realistic novel, although we surely put it in the latter category. In a fine essay in the *New Yorker*, James Wood observes:

> Whatever Tolstoy's precise intentions, in 1865 he began to shape the quiet "English" novel – at this point still called "All's Well That Ends Well" – into a Russian epic about Alexander and Napoleon; by 1867–68, he was writing about the savage national trauma of 1812, and beginning to add long essays on warfare, freedom and determinism, and the philosophy of history. Here was the most flagrant strike against the "pure" European form of the novel.[7]

According to Pevear, Tolstoy "was acutely aware of the inadequacy of all human means of speaking the truth, but his artistic intuition told him that those means might be composed in such a way as to allow the truth to appear."[8] Tolstoy's concept of an artist was that of someone who understands more than the historian and relies on imagination to see deeply into the gap between human motives and human behavior. Tolstoy stresses the complexities of human psyches and how individuals can shape – and be shaped by – historic events. As Pevear puts it, "[T]he artist sees not heroes but people, not results but facts, and considers a person not in terms of a goal."[9]

Character development is Tolstoy's strength. He deftly presents a complex grammar of motives for his characters, especially such major characters as Natasha, Andrei, and Pierre. He shows us choices they make and why, the stories and rationalizations they tell themselves but that they don't recognize. For example, his narrator explains why the Rostov family doesn't feel joy at Berg's proposal to the twenty-four-year-old Vera: "In the feelings of the family regarding this marriage confusion and abashedness could be noticed. It was if they were ashamed that they loved Vera so little and were now so eager to get her off their hands" (2.III.xi.446–447). The translation captures the full force of the Rostovs' wanting to marry her off, in spite of her father's embarrassment about his financial affairs. The narrator stresses that Berg's interest is in promoting his own well-being since he comes from a relatively obscure family, even though he knows the Rostovs' affairs are "in great disorder" (2.III.xi.446). Thus Berg extracts – perhaps we could say extorts – a larger dowry from the Count than the latter can afford when he agrees to marry Vera.

Micro-history and Macro-history

Anticipating New Historicism, Tolstoy thinks it folly to focus only on the Great Men. Not only do accident and chance play an important role in historical patterns controlled by God, but so, too, do the anonymous soldiers and serfs take part in these patterns. Humans – their leaders and followers – think they have more control than they do. For Tolstoy, as Wood notes, God is a mystery, but finally – even if it means some obfuscation – a presence and even a value: "[Tolstoy] emits that characteristically vague growl of nineteenth-century doubt in which God is no longer describable but impossible to abandon. War, rendered so painstakingly in all its senselessness and evil, finally serves only to confirm God's benevolent presence, however spectral."[10]

Tolstoy's focus is not on the anonymous soldiers and serfs who comprise the ninety-nine percent, but on the one percent and perhaps even on the wealthiest one-tenth of a percent. He also enjoys dramatizing and satirizing those striving to join the ethereal social worlds of princes and counts, such as Boris, Berg, and Dolokhov, either by marriage, adultery, and/or by toadying to those in that elite class. In Tolstoy's Russia, a few flourish at the expense of the many; as a realist he is committed to showing us how things are. We notice, too, that this is a society without a middle class, and the best way to win position is through marriage or by forming relationships with powerful people in peace or wartime. Indeed, "campaigns" to move up the social ladder in peacetime can be as ugly as those in wartime.

It is difficult to categorize Tolstoy's views, although he usually seems to speak to what he believes are the interests of the Russian nation. Tolstoy understands the role of self-interest in motivating much of the aristocracy – and often their self-delusion – even while believing that the titled class has an important social and political role to play. Prince Vassily is a schemer without being conscious of who he really is. But the narrator bitterly forewarns us of how Vassily will prey upon Pierre: "If Prince Vassily had thought out his plans beforehand, he would not have had such naturalness in his dealings and such simplicity and familiarity in his relations with all people, whether of higher or lower station than himself. Something constantly drew him to people more powerful or richer than he, and he was endowed with the rare art of seizing the precise moment when he should and could make use of people" (1.III.i.201). Here, in these balanced sentences, Tolstoy gets to the essence of the titled aristocrats who have become dedicated to their own self-interest.

Tolstoy believes parents and their milieu have a strong influence on shaping children. Vassily's offspring are the worst sort of parasites: Hélène, who trades her sexuality for wealth and influence; Anatole, a complete scoundrel who seduces Natasha for his own amusement; and the negligible and physically unpleasant-looking Hippolyte (sometimes called Ippolit) Kuragin, who takes after his father.

In some cases, such as belief in God and the place of the tsar or emperor, Tolstoy is quite conservative. Tolstoy's conservatism includes his deep religious faith. While he is impatient with what he regards as Princess Marya's fanaticism, he shows that those among the privileged class who lack faith in God are often without direction and moral principles. In other matters, such as the freeing of the serfs, he is, by contemporary Russian standards in the first years of the nineteenth century, quite liberal. Andrei is much praised for taking steps to turn peasants into landowners.

Tolstoy does not have much interest in the psyche and thought processes of serfs who live in social and economic bondage, even though he founded schools for the serfs in the period when he was writing the novel. In fact more than twenty-three million serfs were freed in 1861, eight years before the book's publication. Serfs now had full rights of free citizens, gaining the rights to marry without having to get the consent of their landlords, to own property, and to own a business. (Peasants living on state land were not serfs.) At times what is lacking within the novel is feeling for the servants and have-nots such as the "wanderers" whom Princess Marya welcomes.

Understanding the role of memory and how past encounters between people feed into the next ones, Tolstoy sees private relationships as a concatenation of small events. Tolstoy emphasizes the place of private and personal human events within the larger historical scheme – that is, how macro-history comments on micro-history and reduces it to blips on a cosmic screen – even while acknowledging that it is individuals' micro-histories that matter. Thus Andrei and Anatole are fatally wounded in the same battle and are in the same hospital, although Andrei lives with his wounds for some time. Pierre thinks Andrei is dead, but the latter is with the Rostovs and is, before his death, poignantly reunited for a brief time with Natasha, who later becomes Pierre's wife.

Much of the novel is rendered through the eyes of the male characters, who are relatively close in age. Tolstoy likes two of them – Pierre and Andrei – because they both have what Andrei describes in Pierre and Marya describes in her brother Andrei as "heart[s] of gold" (2.III.xxiv.481; 2.III.xxv.484). On the other hand, Tolstoy does not hold Nikolai in high regard: "He had that common sense of mediocrity" (2.IV.i.489).

We think of Tolstoy as the ultimate realist, but there is a strong aspect of romanticism in his awareness within his characters of the inner child who relies on fantasy and imagination to make sense of the world. Andrei discovers in himself a romantic side in his attraction to the much younger but ebullient Natasha: "[W]hile I'm alive, I must live and be happy" (2.III.xix.467). To be happy one has to, like Natasha, discover the original child within oneself, including the capacity for wonder and pleasure in being. Tolstoy's major characters, Andrei and Pierre, do best when they respond to their intuitions, their inner voices; in the case of Andrei, within that intuitive self can be found "a sudden, vivid awareness ... of something infinitely great and indefinable that was in him" as opposed to "something [that was] narrow and fleshly" (2.III.xix.467).

For males, happiness in personal relations at times needs to be balanced by some sense of doing good. Yet the promise of love within a stable nuclear and extended family matters far more than political committees where "everything to do with the essence of the matter was carefully and briefly dispensed with" (2.III.xviii.466). Finally, Andrei turns his back on politics, commissions, and the machinations of Speransky and turns towards love: "[H]e felt astonished that he could have been occupied with such idle work for so long" (2.III.xviii.466).

Tolstoy also understands how immaturity and childishness can lead to the kind of narcissism and flightiness that lead Natasha astray with the predatory solipsist Anatole Kuragin. During the three weeks Natasha doesn't hear from Andrei after they declare their love for each other, the narrator speaks of her returning "again to her favorite state of love and admiration for herself" (2.III.xxiii.477).

How *War and Peace* Begins

Each novel has its own genesis. Every time I begin reading *War and Peace* or *Anna Karenina*, I marvel at how Tolstoy takes us into his imagined world and gradually introduces his readers to the major characters.

While war is on the horizon, the book opens in peacetime. With young men about to go off to war, it is a time for flirtations and regrets. Tolstoy's narrator, a surrogate for Tolstoy, oscillates between being a worldly and distanced observer and being an innocent and naïve onlooker experiencing with his characters their wonder at events he cannot understand. The narrator can be either an empathetic or cynical participant, as well as a rhetorical bully of both the reader and his characters when they deviate from his sense of what is right. At times, too, he is a self-dramatizing presence trying to define his values as the circumstances of reality change and evolve through time within the fictive world he describes. Always, whether describing humans or nature, he has a wonderful eye for detail. Without using psychological language, Tolstoy is a great observer of human behavior and, while interested in types, never loses sight of individuality in all its tics and quirks.

Tolstoy's Russia is a social space based on vertical hierarchies and extreme inequalities, often made visible by the characters' gestures and nuanced ways of addressing one another in salutations and in ensuing conversations. The opening of *War and Peace* stresses the resistance of the narrator to the prevailing social snobbery. Prior to his inheriting a large fortune, the soon-to-be Count Pierre Bezukhov, who is now regarded simply as the present Count's illegitimate son, receives a perfunctory nod from Anna Pavlovna. But the narrator observes that Pierre has an "intelligent and at the same time shy, observant, and natural gaze which distinguished him from everyone else in that drawing room" (1.I.ii.9).

At times for Tolstoy, physiognomy is psychology. He often uses physical descriptions to reveal not only his opinion of characters but also their essential psychology. Their facial expressions, even posture, tell us a good deal about their inner selves. A good example is the way Prince Andrei Bolkonsky's unhappiness is rendered when he is married to the "little princess," Liza, whom he is "sick of": "Everything in his figure, from his weary, bored gaze to his quiet measured gait, presented the sharpest contrast with his small lively wife" (1.I.iii.14). When Andrei, who has "a consciousness of his own superiority," confesses to Pierre what a mistake it was to marry, "His dry face was all aquiver with the nervous animation of every muscle; his eyes, in which the fire of life had seemed extinguished, now shone with a bright, radiant brilliance" (1.I.vi.28–30). When Liza complains of being left alone while Andrei goes off to war, the narrator describes a self-indulgent, whiny woman: "Her tone was querulous now, her little lip rose, giving her face not a joyful but an animalish, squirrel-like expression" (1.I.vi.26). Tolstoy has little patience with unattractive women. With her face showing "sagging and deadened contours" (1.III.iii.219), the pregnant "little princess" becomes ugly.

Tolstoy does not use the terminology of modern psychology but he has a wonderful insight into human nature. He shows us complex social situations – and often the manipulativeness and cynicism underlying them – but also the puzzlement of those, like Pierre and Andrei, who are less cynical and who try to make sense of what they see. Even after Pierre becomes the heir to his father's immense wealth and everyone's demeanor to him changes, he is still confused. When he arrives at his father's deathbed, he sees that "He was being shown a respect no one had ever shown him before" (1.I.xix.78). Pierre is oblivious to the machinations of Prince Vassily Kuragin and Catiche, the niece of Pierre's father, to destroy the will, and of Anna Mikhailovna's intervention.

A keen observer of human behavior, Tolstoy is a master of the revealing detail that defines a character; it may be a gesture, a phrase in dialogue, or a crucial, often seemingly insignificant nuance, within an interior monologue. Thus he captures the self-satisfied narcissism of Hélène, who enjoys staring at her own body parts (1.I.iii.12), and the face of her brother Ippolit, "clouded by idiocy and invariably express[ing] a self-assured peevishness.... His eyes, nose, and mouth all seemed to shrink into an indefinite and dull grimace" (1.I.iii.13). Berg explains to his wife Vera, a Rostov, that his success derives "Mainly by knowing how to choose my acquaintances" (2.III.xx.468), and we realize that the Rostovs maintain their position in a similar way. Or, observing the rapprochement between the Russians and the French, Nikolai Rostov "remembered Denisov with his changed expression, his submission, and the whole hospital with those torn-off arms and legs, that filth and disease. He imagined so vividly now that hospital stench of dead flesh that he looked around to see where the stench could be coming from. Then he remembered that self-satisfied Bonaparte with his little white hand" (2.II.xxi.416). It is also through Nikolai Rostov's eyes, when he visits Denisov, that we see first see the horror of the military hospital; in the midst of a typhoid epidemic, Rostov is "enveloped by the stench of rotting flesh" (2.II.xvii.402).

Beneath the slow, stately pace of early chapters revealing the hierarchical society that is in place is the beginning of a tumultuous social transition in which power and authority begin to move to the next generation. In the opening scene Tolstoy shows us Prince Vassily, an ineffectual father but one concerned with marrying off his wastrel son, Anatole, in part because the latter costs him 40,000 roubles a year. We meet the impoverished widow Anna Mikhailovna, who is obsessed with the welfare of her son Boris; she has no shame in begging for Vassily's intervention to get her son a good military assignment or asking anyone for help: "Let them think whatever they like of me, it really makes no difference to me, when my son's destiny depends on it"(1.I.xi.48). (Proving Tolstoy's view that the acorn often does not fall far from the tree, Boris becomes even more of an opportunist than his mother.)

Tolstoy's narrator deftly satirizes the pretensions and superficiality of Prince Vassily and his wayward children, Anatole and Hélène. Vassily is a manipulative time-server and his children – perhaps consequently – lack values. Vassily's pose is indifference but he is looking out for his own economic advantage and hopes someone else will take responsibility for his son, Anatole. By contrast, Count Rostov presides over his family drawing room "with the look of a man who loves life and knows how to live it, spreading his legs dashingly and putting his hands on his knees" (1.I.vii.36). Yet his beautiful narcissistic elder daughter Vera "had such an irritating, unpleasant effect on everyone" (1.I.xi.46).

The narrator despises the dashing Anatole, whose handsome appearance is in contrast to one of the most self-denying characters in the novel, Marya Bolkonsky. Even while pretending to woo Marya, he is arranging an affair – his own cynical "peace" campaign – with her paid companion Mlle. Bourienne. Anatole loses the marriage to Marya's fortune that his father sought because he and Bourienne are caught embracing the very hour in which Marya would have said "yes." Not wanting to lose his daughter, whom he depends upon even as he abuses her, Prince Bolkonsky had deliberately turned his eye from what was going on between Anatole and Bourienne. Poignantly and pathetically, the naïve Marya devotes herself to trying to arrange a marriage between Anatole and Bourienne: "She loves him so passionately. She repents so passionately.... She is so unhappy, a stranger, lonely, helpless!" (1.III.v.232).

Pierre

Pierre is the novel's most important character and often a focal point. As witness and surrogate, Pierre becomes Tolstoy's eyes and ears at Borodino and even more so when the French invasion results in the fall of Moscow.

Obese, alcoholic, cuckolded, bumbling, gauche, Pierre overcomes his faults, winning our sympathy with his simple decency, lack of guile, and heartfulness. Like Andrei, Pierre tests and discards many ways of being. Pierre wants to do the right things for the peasants, but he has little business sense and is blocked by the desires of his stewards; the latter disguise what is happening from him and make him believe that the serfs' lot has been improved when that is not the case. In a bitingly ironic passage in which he repeats the phrase "He did not know," the narrator ironically stresses the difference between what Pierre sees on his tour of his estates and what the reality is (2.II.x.380).

Pierre is not very good at getting his life in order. Although he continually makes mistakes in judgment and is often rather pathetic, Tolstoy is forgiving and sympathetic. Pierre, the narrator remarks, "experienced the unfortunate ability of many people, especially Russians – the ability to see and believe in the possibility of goodness and truth, and to see the evil and falsehood of life too clearly to be able to participate in it seriously" (2.V.i.537–538). For Tolstoy, who is attracted to absolutes even while knowing the difficulty of defining them and even more of living them, it is important that one believes in such abstractions as goodness and truth and understands their opposites, namely falsehood and evil.

Even when the often ironic narrator is hard on Pierre's failures, he is empathetic with Pierre's quest to discover himself and the values by which he needs to live. Until Pierre inherits his wealth and title, he is a bastard in a socially ambiguous position. Awkward but not manipulative, his virtues are stressed by the narrator: "But all his absentmindedness and inability to enter a salon and speak in it were redeemed by his expression of good nature, simplicity, and modesty" (1.I.v.22). Yet no sooner do we think favorably of Pierre than we learn he is profligate and is part of Anatole's circle.

Nevertheless, notwithstanding his faults, the bumbling, gauche, obese, and binge-drinking Pierre gradually wins the narrator's and the reader's heartfelt sympathy. Naïve to the point of resembling Don Quixote and well-meaning, Pierre doesn't know himself, and because of this he is a ready victim to Vassily Kuragin's machinations to get him married to his daughter Hélène. Pierre is easily gulled. Once Pierre inherits great wealth, everyone makes him feel loved and important; according to the ironic narrator, "[H]e was sincerely beginning to believe in his extraordinary kindness and his extraordinary intelligence, the more so because, deep in his heart, it had always seemed to him that he really was very kind and very intelligent" (1.III.i.202). Pierre is drawn to Hélène as much by the seeming inevitability of social expectations – created by Vassily and his wife – as by her beauty. Yet Pierre knows Hélène is "stupid" and worthless: "And again he said to himself that it was impossible, that there would be something vile, unnatural, as it seemed to him, and dishonest in this marriage" (1.III.i.207). Realizing that she is "depraved," Pierre characteristically blames himself for marrying her (2.I.vi.318).

Although he doesn't fully believe in God, Pierre always has a generous soul and wants to do what is right. Pierre flails about, intermittently immersing himself in Freemasonry. After he breaks with Hélène he is drawn to the Freemasons, but Tolstoy has an ironic view of the Masonic rites and despite some sympathy for their idea of the brotherhood of man – which he realizes in Russia is mostly the brotherhood of the elite – he finds much of their doctrine to be gibberish. After Pierre has with regret taken Hélène back but no longer is sleeping with her, he represses as much as possible thinking of her taking Boris as a lover and later a Prince. As a way of avoiding the pain brought on by his wife's behavior, he strives to reignite his Masonic zeal. Tolstoy does not use the Freudian vocabulary of repression and denial but he understands what is going on in Pierre's psyche (2.III.x.440).

Pierre's quest is an important part of *War and Peace*. As soon as Andrei is engaged to Natasha, Pierre begins to fall apart and his inner life revolving around the Masons collapses. Pierre does not realize that he himself is in love with Natasha. Note the opening sentence of 2.V: "After the engagement of Prince Andrei and Natasha, Pierre, without any obvious reason, suddenly felt the impossibility of going on with his former life" (2.V.i.535). Pierre seeks refuge in drink because it enables him to escape what Tolstoy's narrator calls "the tangled, terrible knot of life": "Drinking wine became more and more of a physical and at the same time moral need for him" (2.V.ii.538). Finally, he finds fulfillment in his marriage to Natasha, whom he has loved silently even while married to the self-indulgent and promiscuous Hélène.

An instance of the epic influence on *War and Peace* is the way that Tolstoy's narrator stresses the response of the cosmos to turns in Pierre's life. When the appearance of the "huge bright comet of the year 1812" signifies to Pierre the possibility of a new life, we think of the cosmos responding to or anticipating heroic events in an epic: "It seemed to Pierre that this star answered fully to what was in his softened and encouraged soul, now blossoming into new life" (2.V.xxii.600).

Seeking refuge in the house of his Freemason mentor when the French take Moscow, the now zealously patriotic Pierre gives his life definition in the form of his insane fixation on a bizarre plan to assassinate Napoleon (3.III.xxvii). The narrator renders Pierre's realization of the moral cost of the French invasion of Russia to both the conquered and the conqueror: "On all the Russian faces, on the faces of the French soldiers and officers, on all without exception, he read the same fear, horror, and struggle that were in his heart" (4.I.xi.966).

A patriot with a deep love for Russia and pain for its dead and wounded and its military and political humiliations, Tolstoy believes the Russian soul saved Russia. The Russian soul is a somewhat mystical collective entity represented in part by Platon Karataev, the peasant soldier whose presence deeply affects Pierre when he is imprisoned with him by the French. Pierre's transformation into a peasant during his imprisonment is really the discovery that he is part of the Russian soul. He discovers "peace and contentment" and "that feeling of … moral fitness" in the simplicity of life (4.II.xii.1012, 1014).

Platon Karataev remained "forever in Pierre's soul as the strongest and dearest memory and the embodiment of everything Russian, kindly and round…. [Karataev's] life, as he looked at it, had no meaning as a separate life. It had meaning only as a part of the whole, which he constantly sensed" (4.I.xiii.972, 974). In a sense he discovers freedom in captivity: "And yet afterwards and for the whole of his life Pierre thought and spoke with rapture of that month of captivity, of those irrevocable, strong, and joyful sensations, and above all of that full peace of mind, that perfect inner freedom, which he experienced only in that time" (4.II.xii.1013).

Yet Tolstoy's ideal Russian soul is composed of many parts, including qualities that are represented by Prince Andrei, Natasha, and Sonya, an orphaned Rostov cousin. Although hopelessly in love with Nikolai, Sonya is a paradigm of steadiness, stability, and loyalty. As the conscience and moral compass that saves Natasha from Anatole and is on to Hélène from the outset, the aristocratic matron Marya Dmitrievna is something of a choral figure standing in for the narrator and Tolstoy.

War

For most readers, the novel's military history can at times become tedious, particularly in the latter pages, although the depiction of the human cost of war and the transformation of humans into impersonal killing machines is compelling and haunting and a lesson that is still relevant. As John Bayley observes, "Tolstoy's military narrative is remarkably flexible and capable of unexpected variations."[11] He is referring to how Tolstoy can invent incidents out of whole cloth or follow an extended historical account in great detail.

Tolstoy never lets the reader forget the horrors of war, epitomized by Emperor Alexander's ingenuous yet heartfelt reaction to seeing a dying soldier: "What a terrible thing war is, what a terrible thing!" (1.III.x.255). A vital element of Tolstoy's strategy for rendering war is to focus on the perspective of the young men of four major families, Count Nikolai Rostov – and later his brother, Petya – Prince Andrei Bolkonsky, and, to a much lesser extent, Prince Anatole Kuragin, as well as on Pierre's.

If at first Tolstoy seems to extol the excitement of war – the thrill and exaltation, even bluster – felt by male troops, especially younger ones, he soon (and at times almost simultaneously) exposes its pain and folly. His versions of the scars of battle are as graphic as Goya's. It is almost as if he bathetically reduces war to the incoherent, often animalistic struggle it is. We learn that seventeen of the forty men in Captain Tushin's gun crew "had been eliminated" (1.II.xx.192). The wounded are often abandoned without receiving medical attention, and what medical attention others receive is minimal. After an intense battle, the "groans [of the wounded] and the gloom of that night were one" (1.II.xxi.196). We learn how in battle men lose all sense of proportion, as when the brave and daring Tushin disappears into "a fantastic world of his own…. He pictured himself as of enormous size, a mighty man, flinging cannonballs at the French with both hands" (1.II.xx.193).

Tolstoy understood that war was an elaborate game with fatal consequences. Thus he juxtaposes Andrei's youthful excitement, exhilaration, and his "feeling of animation" as the major battle begins with a Cossack's death a few paragraphs later (1.II.xvii.179–180). The rereader knows Andrei is going to be fatally wounded. Nor does Tolstoy's narrator omit reminding the reader of the "certain alarm and fear of something" that Andrei notices a little further from the front lines (1.II.xv.174).

The Russian defeat at Austerlitz in 1805 at the hands of Napoleon reveals the cost of war. The narrator describes "crowded men disfigured by the fear of death, crushing each other, dying, stepping over the dying, and killing each other, only to go a few steps and be killed themselves just the same" (1.III.xviii.289). Or, using one of Tolstoy's epic similes: "Over the field, like sheaves on good wheatland, lay dead or wounded men, ten to fifteen to an acre. The wounded crept together by twos and threes, and one could hear their unpleasant cries and moans" (1.III.xviii.286). Tolstoy saw the ravages of combat during his own military service during the Crimean War, an experience that formed the underpinning of *Sevastopol Sketches* (1855), comprised of three historical short stories that show the futility of war.

Tolstoy understands how hero worship underlies the enthusiasm for war. In terms that suggest homosocial if not homosexual attraction ("He was as happy as a lover who has obtained a hoped-for rendezvous" [1.III.x.254]), the narrator describes how Nikolai Rostov is awe-struck by the "beautiful" young Emperor Alexander, whose face to Nikolai suggests "a boyish fourteen-year-old friskiness" (1.III.x.254–255). Later, the narrator compares Nikolai Rostov's being captivated by Emperor Alexander's presence to "a young man in love [who] trembles and thrills, not daring to utter what he dreams of by night" (1.III.xviii.287). By comparing a response to a male public figure with the response of a young man in love, isn't Tolstoy also hinting at the erotic – and in this case the homoerotic – aspect of hero worship? The reader realizes that such magnetism also energizes the French, who have their own emperor.

By focusing on the first military action by Nikolai Rostov, a character whom we knew as a playful youth in his home environment, Tolstoy brings war home to the reader. Rostov is wounded moments after feeling "merrier and merrier" and rushing into battle (1.II.xix.188). He soon gives flight "with the feeling of a hare escaping from hounds" and a "feeling of fear for his young, happy life" (1.II.xix.189). Fortunate to have Tushin on the battlefield, the wounded Rostov is not left to die. While awaiting medical aid, Rostov "dragged himself to the fire. A feverish trembling from pain, cold, and dampness shook his whole body" (1.II.xxi.196). In great pain and neglected, Rostov thinks: "There's nobody to help me or pity me. And once I was home, strong, cheerful, loved" (1.II.xxi.200). Note that in these war scenes he is not "Nikolai" to the narrator but the impersonal "Rostov," who is even further depersonalized after being wounded as "a pale hussar junker" or "this junker" as if he had no name that mattered (1.II.xxi.195). It is as if Tolstoy is implying that war reduces its participants to interchangeable bodies.

Although Nikolai will survive and ultimately marry Princess Marya Bolkonsky, the narrator stresses the ironic juxtaposition of the ending of 1.II with Nikolai's own memories of peace in the world of his family home: "He looked at the snowflakes dancing above the fire and remembered the Russian winter with a warm, bright house, a fluffy fur coat, swift sleighs, a healthy body, and all the love and care of a family. 'And why did I come here?' he wondered" (1.II.xxi.200).

Tolstoy's second focal point in wartime is Prince Andrei Bolkonsky, intelligent, mature, but arrogant. Prince Andrei was excited going into battle, but, in the close to 1.II, after it is over he is disillusioned; he "felt sad and downhearted. All this was so strange, so unlike what he had hoped for" (1.II.xxi.199). Certain that he will make a difference, Andrei is wounded and captured at Austerlitz while serving as an adjutant for General Kutuzov. With the expectation of imminent death, Prince Andrei faces the self-satisfied Napoleon, who once was his hero; at this point, Prince Andrei moves towards a larger view of the world: "Nothing, nothing is certain, except the insignificance of everything I can comprehend and the grandeur of something incomprehensible but most important" (1.III.xix.293).

While Tolstoy does praise the behavior of Russian troops in contrast to that of the French, he is aware that war brings out the worst in humans. Tolstoy shows the horror of war on those who actually do the fighting – Andrei's death is a long goodbye; Petya, the younger brother of Natasha and Nikolai, is killed; and countless others are maimed and die. In the terrible military hospital to which Denisov is sent and even in the lack of care Nikolai Rostov receives when he is wounded, we see war before such modern medicines as antibiotics and effective anesthetics. Tolstoy never forgets the effects of war – the agony and painful loss – endured by surviving members of the families of those killed.

Even in relatively minor matters, or at least in less serious matters than life and death, the worlds of war and peace bleed into one another. Within the army, Boris discovers that social rank takes precedence over military rank: "[B]esides the subordination and discipline that were written in the regulations and known to the regiment, and which he knew, there was another more essential subordination" which made a general deferential to Prince Andrei, an adjutant (1.III.ix.249).

War exposes not only a man's mettle but also his capacity for self-delusion. War creates illusions and lies. After one of the regimental commanders reports to General Bagration on his, the regimental commander's, wise and successful decisions, the narrator remarks: "The regimental commander had so wanted to do that, he had been so sorry that he had had no time to do it, that it seemed to him that all this was exactly so. And perhaps it really was so? As if one could make out in that confusion what was and was not so?" (1.II.xxi.198). Many know Zherkov's report is a "lie" about seeing an attack by the Pavlogradsky hussars – Rostov's troop – but no one contradicts him; the narrator reminds us "[Zherkov] had not seen any hussars that day" (1.II.xxi.198).

War also illustrates, for Tolstoy, the Law of Actions Having Unforeseen Consequences. After the confusion of battle, Tushin's bravery and important role in holding off the French are almost lost; unpretentious, socially awkward in the face of superiors, he would have been chastised for losing two guns – and indeed feels "guilt and disgrace" despite acting heroically – were it not for Prince Andrei's intervention, and even that intervention is not fully believed by Prince Bagration (1.II.xxi.199). In another instance of unforeseen consequences, Zherkov, the jokester, disguises his failure to deliver Bagration's crucial message to the general of left flank that they must "retreat immediately"; that failure has a role in Nikolai Rostov's injury: "An insurmountable fear came over [Zherkov], and he was unable to go where there was danger" (1.II.xix.186). A second cause of Rostov's injury is a conflict between two officers, a Russian general and a German colonel, about the positioning of troops.

Tolstoy knows that leadership includes not only courage and self-confidence, but also the appearance of controlling events: "Prince Andrei noticed that, in spite of the chance character of events and their independence of the commander's [Bagration's] will, [Bagration's] presence accomplished a very great deal" (1.II.xvii.182). Tolstoy's narrator commends the elderly Field Marshal Kutuzov as a leader for keeping Russian interests paramount and foregoing egotistical confrontations with the enemy. The narrator ironically contrasts Kutuzov's behavior with the "greatness" of the egocentric Napoleon, who is oblivious to the terrible losses of human life in battle. Moreover, at Borodino Napoleon's confidence wavers; he imagines "a countless number of unlucky chances, and he expected them all. Yes, it was as in a dream, when a man sees a villain coming at him, and in his dream, the man swings and hits the villain with terrible force, which he knows should destroy him, and he feels his arm fall strengthless and limp as a rag, and the terror of irresistible destruction takes hold of the helpless man" (3.II.xxxiv.804).

This may be a good place to interject a comment about Tolstoy's use of similes. They are crucial to the verbal texture of *War and Peace* and help give the novel its epic stature. Tolstoy uses the kind of similes we expect to find in epics, but often in strikingly original ways. Often similes can play an evaluative role, as in the above comparison in which Napoleon's failure of nerve is compared to a dream of ineffectiveness.

It as if human drama inflected by war – and invasion of the homeland and its rebuff – cannot be described in realistic terms, and the realistic novel needs to be supplemented by the rhetorical tools of epic. Thus Tolstoy uses a proliferation of epic similes when describing the Moscow retreat. Similes are used to stress Tolstoy's basic ideas, such as the notion that historical forces are components of a machine whose workings humans cannot understand; nor can humans even determine what their own individual function is within the mechanism. After Pierre is arrested by the French, he, experiencing Kafkaesque irrelevance and confusion, "felt like an insignificant chip of wood fallen into the wheels of a machine unknown to him but functioning well" (4.I.x.963). Thus capable but not flamboyant generals like Konovnitsyn and Dokhturov are "inconspicuous gears which, without clatter or noise, constitute the most essential part of the machine" (4.II.xvi.1024).

Tolstoy views with irony Kutuzov's epithet "his serenity." Yet he stresses that, no matter how ridiculous his appearance or temporary miscalculations, he is always focused on the main task of saving Russia. Indeed, Kutuzov is depicted comically as a fat lecher who at times is barely aware of the chaos surrounding him. After Austerlitz, Kutuzov is not spared from criticism as "a court weathercock and an old satyr" (2.I.ii.307). By 1812, he is "decrepit old" Kutuzov (4.II.v.995), a farcical figure whose strategy is contradicted by events and who often has to put up with disrespectful officers.

We need to remember one of Tolstoy's goals is to rewrite military history – *Russian military history* – by simultaneously defending Kutuzov, who supposedly "deprived the Russian army of the glory of a complete victory over the French" even as he removed Napoleon from the pedestal of Great Man (4.IV.v.1084). Kutuzov is one of those "rare, always solitary men who, discerning the will of Providence, submit their personal will to it" (4.IV.v.1084–1085). By contrast, according to Tolstoy, Napoleon is "that most insignificant instrument of history, who never and nowhere, even in exile, displayed any human dignity" (4.IV.v.1085). Kutuzov is a "simple-hearted" and "good-natured" "old man" who crystallizes what is best in the Russian soul (4.IV.vi.1089): "The source of this extraordinary power of penetration into the meaning of events taking place lay in that national feeling, which he bore within himself in all its purity and force" (4.IV.v.1086–1087).

If we think of Vietnam and General Giap's assertion that the Vietnamese would fight to defend their homeland for hundreds of years against the US – as they had defended Vietnam against the Chinese for centuries – and that it could withstand great human loss, and if we think of the underground Cu Chi tunnels close to Saigon and men living there in tiny man-made cells, we get an idea of the fervor of the Russians defending their homeland against Napoleon and the French invasion of Russia that climaxed in the Battle of Borodino. According to Tolstoy, what determines victory is "the spirit of the army," that is, "the greater or lesser desire to fight and subject oneself to danger" (4.III.ii.1034–1035). In 1812, the Russians, motivated by "the feeling of outrage and revenge," ferociously defended their homeland: "The French were the fencer who demanded a fight by the rules of the art; the Russians were the adversary who dropped his sword and picked up a club" (4.III.i.1031–1032).

Peace

Tolstoy is a great novelist of manners and understands – not so unlike Jane Austen – that marriage and preservation of family fortune are often intertwined, and that social arrangements are often disguised economic arrangements.

As we have been stressing, *War and Peace* is, among other things, a family chronicle of three families – the Bolkonskys, the Rostovs, and the Kuragins – and a fourth if we include Pierre's, the Bezukhovs. Others lurk close to the foreground, notably Princess Anna Mikhailovna, who will do almost anything to forward her interests and those of her son, Prince Boris.

Tolstoy hates predators, those who take without giving: the careerist Berg; the self-seeking Boris who, following his mother's example of using people to best advantage, marries Vera, the elder Rostov daughter; Dolokhov, a scoundrel and parasite who thrives on destruction; the cynical solipsist Anatole; and Marya's French companion, Mlle. Bourienne, who depends on sexual wiles to seduce Marya's father, the old Prince. Hélène is consistently a slut and is about to slip out of her marriage via conversion to Catholicism until Tolstoy tires of a lewd character who violates his paradigm for women and marriage and conveniently has her take ill and die.

The novel opens in July 1805 and focuses on life during peacetime. But the storms of war are in the background, and war takes up the entirety of 1.II. Tolstoy returns to the domestic world in 1.III for the first seven chapters. Then he takes us back to events leading to the Battle of Austerlitz, concluding with Prince Andrei's capture after he is wounded. The next volume (2.I) begins with Nikolai's return home and a lighter atmosphere of family reunion, although that atmosphere is disrupted by Sonya and Nikolai's breaking off of their adolescent commitment. Thus peacetime is not immune to heartache, strife, and even violence. Andrei returns to see his wife die in childbirth. When the often obsequious Prince Vassily visits Pierre and tries to speak on behalf of his daughter Hélène, whom Pierre has thrown out after her affair with Dolokhov, Pierre refuses to listen to his entreaty.

Tolstoy admires those with noble souls even when they go astray: Marya, Andrei, Nikolai, Pierre, and most of all Natasha, who would elope with the despicable Anatole. Forgiving Natasha's narcissism, Tolstoy makes her a heroine when, as the family abandons their home in the face of the French invasion, she creates space for the wounded by discarding possessions. In the sense of letting his characters evolve and voicing contradictory emotions, Tolstoy is dialogic. What makes Natasha somewhat consistent is her impulsiveness, her need to be loved, her romantic gloss on life's circumstances, and her desire to be of decent character, qualities her brother shares.

Tolstoy is even forgiving of their parents, Count and Countess Rostov; the former is generous – even if an occasional sycophant – and the latter's entire world revolves around herself and her children. Eventually, Countess Rostov borders on senescence and Count Rostov irresponsibly dissipates his family estate and spends his money foolishly. For example, he wastes thousands of roubles on a dinner in honor of General Bagration after Austerlitz when the Russians attempt to rationalize their defeat as the fault of anyone but themselves. Yet Rostov's decency and patriotism come through when the wounded need to be transported out of the Moscow area.

Within the framework of peace, threatening physical confrontations, especially duels such as the one between Pierre and Dolokhov, his wife's lover, may occur. Dolokhov is a warrior in war and peace – a cruel man, a "notorious duellist and scapegrace" as well as an adulterer who brags in front of Pierre that he is his wife's lover (2.I.iv.312–313).

For some of the novel's social climbers and self-seeking opportunists as well as its adulterers and those who are cuckolded, peace is another form of war, conducted insidiously and invidiously. Indeed, Tolstoy understands that in social transactions, there are often winners and losers. Sometimes, as when Pierre marries Hélène, those whom society sees as winners are really losers. In their own way the aforementioned Anna Mikhailovna, Boris's mother, and Prince Vassily are winners according to society, albeit Tolsoy exposes them as reprehensible human beings. During peacetime, virtually every social event is an aggressive campaign with a purpose.

Thus, at the beginning of 1.III Prince Vassily Kuragin, whom Tolstoy despises, carries out a campaign when he manipulates Pierre into marrying his daughter. For to the reader's astonishment Pierre never proposed to Hélène, but is entrapped by Vassily. Before Vassily rushes into the drawing room to congratulate Pierre on asking his daughter Hélène for her hand in marriage – which Pierre has not done – Vassily's "cheeks twitched with an unpleasant, coarse expression peculiar to him" (1.III.ii.213). Not knowing how to love, the narcissistic Vassily is not even tender to his own children, and "only approximated [affection] by means of imitating other parents" (1.III.ii.213).

Vassily's next campaign is to marry his son Anatole to Marya Bolkonsky. For Anatole, who has learned his father's cynicism, life is an amusement: "He looked upon his whole life as a ceaseless entertainment, which somebody for some reason had taken it upon himself to arrange for him" (1.III.iii.218). In 1.III the narrator almost nastily stresses Princess Marya's plainness; her face is described as "pitiful and unattractive" (1.III.iii.219). Her own campaign for fulfillment is conflicted. Her desire for earthly passion ("her forbidden earthly dream") seems to conflict with her self-abnegation espoused in her devotion to God (1.III.iii.221).

Tolstoy's Artistry in *War and Peace*

The greatness of *War and Peace* lies not only in its vast historical sweep, but also in the accretion of great little moments that endure in our memory, including the dramatization of Andrei's dying and its effects on both Marya and Natasha. Tolstoy understands death as subtraction; Andrei, like Mrs. Moore in *A Passage to India*, loses interest in life but paradoxically moves (or, to a resistant reader, thinks he does) to a more spiritual realm; he concludes, "[A]ll these thoughts of ours, which seem so important to us – … they're *unnecessary*. We cannot understand each other" (4.I.xv.981). Tolstoy imposes his somewhat reductive Christian ideology on Andrei; "He experienced an awareness of estrangement from everything earthly and a joyful and strange lightness of being" (4.I.xvi.982). Here Tolstoy uses what Bakhtin would call a monologic perspective in contrast to the polyphony he found in Dostoevsky and a polyphony that I believe is present in much of *War and Peace* until Volume 4 and the epilogue.

Whatever his epic pretensions, Tolstoy is fundamentally writing in the realist tradition. He is a master of characterization based on observation of crucial physical and psychological traits, including idiosyncrasies, hypocrisies, and unacknowledged motives and desires. Tolstoy's wisdom and understanding of human nature are impressive. Without using the Freudian vocabulary that we know, Tolstoy understands the role of obsessions, fixations, repression, emotional compensation, and subconscious needs. While later in life he himself was perhaps dominated by rigorous religious and moral theory, at this time Tolstoy could write: "Pfuel was one of those theorists who so love theory that they forget the purpose of the theory – its application in practice; in his love for theory, he hated everything practical and did not want to know about it" (3.I.x.640). Tolstoy realized that we each are individuals with our own unique grammar of motives.

Like other great realists from Dickens and Dostoevsky to Flaubert and Thackeray, Tolstoy shines his light on virtually every conceivable way of being, including religious zealotry in the person of Princess Marya and her faithful "wanderers." Tolstoy's ironic, satiric, critical, and empathetic evolving narrative voice sifts through alternatives in his search for values. He tests – often through Pierre and sometimes through Andrei – and discards positions from Freemasonry to Russian Orthodoxy as well as from political engagement to standing aside.

The narrator is often sympathetic towards Pierre's and at times Andrei's quests for values in much the same way, as we shall see, that the narrator in *Anna Karenina* is empathetic to Levin's quest. Pierre's engagement with Freemasonry is taken seriously, while Andrei, one of the first landowners in Russia to free serfs by recognizing peasants as free plowmen, has "that practical tenacity, lacking in Pierre, which kept things in motion" (2.III.i.418).

Recalling not only the great evocation of the old oak (2.III.i.418–420) and its transformation (2.III.i.423), but also the nightscape when Andrei falls in love with Natasha, we realize that Tolstoy is not only an historian of politics, culture, and the military, but also a great nature writer.

The Problematic Ending of *War and Peace*

As Bakhtin concludes, Tolstoy can be monologic, and this is true particularly in the later pages when Pierre and Nikolai Rostov discover their inner peasant and inner husbands, even as Natasha and Marya discover their inner wives and Pierre and Andrei discover God. As Wood observes:

> [T]he epilogue concludes not with the fictional narrative but with a final, dragonish blast from the flaming, irritable, essay-writing Tolstoy, eager to put us right about freedom and predestination. "War and Peace" is "not a novel" but a frequently essayistic national epic, and this side of the story also involves two families and an outrider – the two "families" of the French and Russian nations, and Napoleon, who forced them together when he invaded Russia and took Moscow, in 1812. "War and Peace" vibrates with anti-Napoleonic anger; the irony is that this novel about great egotists and solipsists (Pierre and Andrei are just the chief representatives), written by perhaps the greatest egotist ever to put pen to paper, is a cannon aimed directly at the egotism of Napoleon.[12]

Nikolai marries Marya and Pierre marries Natasha, with both males feeling a kind of transformation from unlikely women. Pierre feeds off Natasha's joy, Nikolai off his belief in Marya's higher moral character and mature stability as well as knowledge that her wealth will save his family from economic disaster. Natasha has an intuitive capacity for joy, but she is a flighty, often selfish, self-immersed girl who disregards others until she undergoes a moral transformation to a mature woman.

The epilogue oscillates between the macro view of Tolstoy's historical reflections and the micro view of the two main families, Pierre and Natasha and Nikolai and Marya, and their households, with some glance at Pierre's politics. In many ways, Tolstoy is quite conservative. To a resistant reader, Natasha and Marya are confined by male expectations, if not presumptive male privilege that expects married women to have babies and create circumstances for their husbands' comfort and leisure.

Tolstoy dramatizes family happiness, as he understood it, in the form of a supportive wife whose place is in the home presiding over children and house serfs, and while seeming to defer to the husband, managing the household. Marriage is a source of joy when organized this way by couples who want to please each other. Tolstoy also accepts the master–subject relationship between, on the one hand, household serfs and muzhiks and, on the other, landowners, and he sees this as part of the Russian way of being. When the master–subject relation defines a marriage, the modern reader becomes uncomfortable.

For Tolstoy everything human – war, love, and politics – takes place under God's auspices: "Man is the creation of an almighty, all-good, and all-knowing God" (Epilogue.II.viii.1202). He believes that the Russian soul is unique and not only gives Russian nationhood a special unity but is blessed by God and responsible for saving the Russian nation. Yet Tolstoy is also humble in terms of claiming to have human understanding of the complex causes of human events. He is as skeptical of the Great Man theory of history, with its implications of genius, as he is of attributing the outcome of major events to chance.

Once Tolstoy has shown us the happy families (Pierre and Natasha, Nikolai and Marya) – and even the presentation of the families at home is more tableau and set piece than complex narrative – he would have been better off exiting his novel rather than insisting over and over again on a few points, namely the historian's overemphasis on heroes and the impossibility for humans to understand all the causes of an action as well as their tendency to overestimate freedom of will as opposed to historical necessity.

Thus the epilogue also oscillates between anti-climatic plot to tedious polemic, with the latter dominating the epilogue's Part Two. As Wood puts it, "Tolstoy barges into his own work, and unloads his years of reading and thinking about history on the reader, with an autodidact's sleepless certitude."[13] To say that Part Two of the epilogue – pages 1179–1215 – is tiresome and repetitious is an understatement. A mostly abstract rant, it is a disappointing ending to a fabulous reading experience. Yet we need remember that in *War and Peace*

Tolstoy at times strays far from the traditional forms of the novel and that part of the experience of reading him includes essayistic intrusions, which transgress those forms.

Study Questions for *War and Peace*

1. What are Tolstoy's values? How does he use his narrator to present them?
2. What is the function of the epilogue? In what ways is the ending satisfactory and in what ways unsatisfactory?
3. Why do we forgive Pierre his failures and misjudgments? What are Natasha's failures and misjudgments?
4. What is Tolstoy's view of military strategy?
5. How is Tolstoy a social satirist?
6. What techniques does Tolstoy use to help the reader understand what it is like to have one's country's entire culture and history hang in the balance?
7. How does Tolstoy differentiate between the Russians and the French?
8. How does Tolstoy depict Napoleon and his counterpart Kutuzov?
9. What is Tolstoy's attitude to the Kuragin family? The various Rostovs? The various Bolkonskys?
10. How would you define Tolstoy's religious views? What troubles him about Marya?
11. Do characters evolve and change in *War and Peace*? If so, in response to what personal and historic causes?
12. How is the paradoxical relation between the concepts of War and Peace a crucial component of the novel's theme and form?
13. Is Tolstoy sufficiently critical of class structure?
14. What is your favorite chapter and why?
15. Why is the book divided into four volumes and an epilogue?

Notes

1. James Wood, "Movable Types: How 'War and Peace' Works," *New Yorker*, Nov. 27, 2007; http://www.newyorker.com/arts/critics/atlarge/2007/11/26/071126crat_atlarge_wood#ixzz1er49SpJH (accessed February 14, 2014).
2. All quotations from the text are from Leo Tolstoy, *War and Peace*, trans. Richard Pevear and Larissa Volokhonsky (New York: Alfred A. Knopf, 2007).
3. Quoted in Geoffrey Wheatcroft, "Hello to All That!" *NYR* 58:11 (June 23, 2011), 30–32; see p. 31.
4. Wheatcroft, "Hello to All That!" 32.
5. See James Wood, "Reality Effects," *New Yorker* (Dec. 19 & 26, 2011), 134–138.
6. John Bayley, *Tolstoy and the Novel* (London: Chatto and Windus, 1966), 171.

7. Wood, "Movable Types."
8. Richard Pevear, "Introduction," *War and Peace*, xii.
9. Pevear, "Introduction," *War and Peace*, xiii.
10. Wood, "Movable Types."
11. Bayley, *Tolstoy and the Novel*, 165.
12. Wood, "Movable Types."
13. Wood, "Movable Types."

Chapter 9

Tolstoy's *Anna Karenina* (1877)

Exploring Passions and Values in Nineteenth-Century Russia

Introduction: History

If possible, I recommend reading *Anna Karenina* immediately after *War and Peace*. This will enable readers to better understand Tolstoy's evolving values and changing approach to fiction. Tolstoy is writing about a far different Russia. The threat of the country being invaded and dominated by a foreign power is no longer foregrounded. Nor do major male characters face imminent death in war.

Tolstoy's protagonist – or at least one of the major ones – is Russia in the late nineteenth century after the freeing of the serfs but still in the time of the tsars. Konstantin Levin is a typifying character with historical resonance, struggling with moral and economic issues facing large landowners once the serfs are freed. In 1861 Alexander II had issued his Emancipation Manifesto freeing the serfs and allowing peasants to buy land from their landlords. The payments would be advanced to the landlords by the state, and the money would be repaid to the state in forty-nine installments.

Among the historical themes in nineteenth-century novels that recur in *Anna Karenina* are the transformation of agrarian life due to machinery and the concomitant effect on traditional rural communities; the rise of capitalism; the evolution of the modern city; and the attraction and disappointment of urban life, with a focus on, as in the case of Tolstoy, its utter frivolity. Equally important are deepening class divisions, including the creation of a class of underemployed and marginally employed workers whose safety is not taken seriously, as in the

Reading the European Novel to 1900: A Critical Study of Major Fiction from Cervantes' Don Quixote to Zola's Germinal, First Edition. Daniel R. Schwarz.
© 2014 John Wiley & Sons, Ltd. Published 2014 by John Wiley & Sons, Ltd.

case of the railroad watchman accidentally killed when Anna meets Vronsky for the first time.

Absent, of course, in *War and Peace*, trains play an important role in *Anna Karenina*. The Moscow–St. Petersburg line began in 1851. Writing of the role of railroads, Tony Judt observes: "[After 1830] trains – or, rather, the tracks on which they ran – represented the conquest of space."[1] Trains transformed the landscape. They made possible movement from place to place that was once unthinkable. In a matter of hours, Vronsky and Anna quickly transport themselves back to their St. Petersburg homes after they first meet at the Moscow station. Coming to *Anna Karenina* after reading *War and Peace*, we realize that the pace of life has changed.

Invented in the 1760s, the steam engine was the quintessence of the Industrial Revolution, but the steam engine didn't drive trains until 1825. The steam engine depended on coal, the subject of Zola's *Germinal*, to make it run. We see trains in *Anna Karenina* and in *Sentimental Education*. As Judt puts it, "[M]ost of the technical challenges of industrial modernity – long distance telegraphic communication, the harnessing of water, gas, and electricity for domestic and industrial use, urban and rural drainage, the construction of very large buildings, the gathering and moving of human beings in large numbers – were first met and overcome by railway companies."[2] The railroads were a bridge to urbanization and the modern city. What the railroads did was move people pursuing jobs into urban centers; as cities spread out and suburbs developed, more people returned to their homes after work. Draining the rural areas of workers and communities, the railroads added to the urban underemployed and unemployed.[3]

Tolstoy's Themes and Values

Why is Tolstoy's novel entitled *Anna Karenina*? Why not *Anna Karenina and Konstantin Levin*? Within the satire and polemic that hover over Anna's demise, Levin is as much a major character as is Anna. It is Levin's values that resonate with those of the other Tolstoy surrogate, the narrator. To an extent, Levin is the cultural answer to the triviality of the world of Oblonsky, Vronsky, Anna, and her husband, Alexei Karenin. But the novel is entitled *Anna Karenina* because this is a novel of manners in which sexual ethics are a crucial subtext. For Tolstoy sexual ethics are a metaphor for all ethics, and the stakes are much higher than who is sleeping with whom, for Tolstoy's concern is how Russia is to organize itself morally and spiritually.

Certainly from the marvelous opening paragraph (one of the great openings in all fiction), the early chapters – focusing on Oblonsky's adultery and its consequences as well as Vronsky's seduction mentality that he disguises as courting – serve as overtures to the theme of sexual ethics: "All happy families are alike; each unhappy family is unhappy in its own way" (I.i.1).[4] Whether Tolstoy, given his polemical impulse, would agree or not, we learn from what Tolstoy shows us that such reductive oversimplifications do not speak to the gray areas most people inhabit; happiness has many forms and even happy families have troubled times, as Kitty's parents do and as do the Rostovs in *War and Peace*. Yet Tolstoy's narrator reverts to the opening sentence when, at the oncoming of Anna's breakdown and demise, he reductively observes: "In order to undertake anything in family life, it is necessary that there be either complete discord between the spouses or loving harmony" (VII.xxiii.739).

For Tolstoy, technique is inextricably linked to values. Tolstoy condemns those like Anna and Vronsky, and the philanderer Stiva Oblonsky, who put family at risk. By introducing Oblonsky at the outset, the reader is placed in, as John Bayley notes, "the situation of an adulterer."[5] Anticipating our entering into Anna's perspective and consciousness, we see adultery from his point of view. Indeed, the name Oblonsky is a homophonic foreshadowing of Vronsky. As Bayley rightly observes, "With Stiva, Tolstoy raises to its highest art his practice of letting the individual appear in the light of his own point of view."[6] Oblonsky gets away with being like Vronsky much of the time, but his good nature and dissembling leave him within the social ken. He controls his flirtations so they don't become passions that jeopardize who he is.

Tolstoy understands sexual attraction; even Dolly is taken by Vronsky's passion and animation and understands how her sister-in-law Anna could be captivated by him. But Tolstoy realizes the need to keep sexual attraction at bay unless it is confined – as is Levin's attraction to Kitty – within the rules and conventions of courtship and marriage.

As we shall see, Tolstoy admires and respects Levin – like Pierre, something of a surrogate – just as much as he hates Vronsky and Alexei, Anna's husband, both of whom suffer from the results of too much self-love. While seeming opposites – one a passionate dandy, the other a self-important functionary who thinks he is more of a factor in governance than he is – Vronsky and Alexei are both narcissists. Vronsky actually does more good than Alexei by building hospitals and attending to his land. Tolstoy strongly disapproves of Anna's flirtation, selfishness, and lack of self-discipline and often regards her behavior with ironic disdain. But he is not completely unsympathetic to her in the face of Alexei and Vronsky's behavior. He never lets us forget that Vronsky, whether it be in his relations to Kitty or Anna or the horse Frou-Frou that he rides to its death by a shift in his saddle – a metaphor for his protean, inconsistent, and inconstant nature – is a destructive and parasitic presence.

We might recall Bayley's observation: "Tolstoy's worldliness is absolutely comprehensive, with the confidence that suggests an understanding all the more complete for being tacit."[7] Thus Bayley is correct that Anna and Vronsky "were unaware of the extent to which they were created by the society they lived in, and of how much they needed it."[8]

Tolstoy believes in family and the inculcation of values within family. For him, the acorn does not fall far from the tree. Kitty is caught between a superficial mother and a strongly grounded father, but Vronsky "had never known family life" (I.xvi.56). Like Pierre's wife Hélène, Vronsky's mother had public affairs – if there is one thing Tolstoy has even less tolerance of than adultery, it is public sluttishness – and Vronsky didn't know his father.

From the outset Tolstoy detests Vronsky as a self-indulgent solipsist unaware of the consequences of his behavior, an irresponsible flirt and adventurer, a person without class or character, and a moral idiot concerned with his own pleasure. Of his behavior to the eighteen-year-old Kitty, the narrator tells us with scathing satirical irony: "He did not know that his behavior towards Kitty had a specific name, that it was the luring of a young lady without the intention of marriage, and that this luring was one of the bad actions common among brilliant young men such as himself" (I.xvi.57). Notice that Tolstoy, employing his characteristic repetition, uses not "courting" or even "flirting" but the more damning "luring," as if Vronsky were leading her into a moral transgression, which in fact he is since he is interested in seducing her but not in marrying her and finds family life "alien, hostile, and, above all, ridiculous" (I.xvi.57). To Tolstoy, Vronsky's dismissive use of the word "boring" to categorize winter in the country – where Levin lives – says much about the speaker's patronizing and superficial attitudes. And Oblonsky, cynically cheating on his wife with a former governess, at first seems no better. Both remind us of Anatole Kuragin, his sister Hélène, and their father, Prince Vassily Kuragin.

Levin

Oblonsky and Vronsky are contrasted to Levin, who loves deeply and loyally. But the real contrast is between frivolous Anna, who lives by her senses without regard to responsibility, and conscientious Levin, who lives by values and feels a strong sense of responsibility to others. For Tolstoy, Levin is the epitome of the Russian soul and the figure in the novel on whom Russia depends.

The distance between Tolstoy and Levin is never great and narrows as the novel progresses. Despite Levin's pomposity and self-righteousness, he espouses Tolstoy's values in that he is committed to work, uses his time well, and has an active mind. Levin can be aggravatingly self-righteous, pedantic, and judgmental, but he has a good heart and a strong sense of responsibility to family, as when he is dealing with his decadent and ill brother, Nikolai. Love, parenthood, and finally his acceptance that he lives in a vertical universe informed by God's presence transform Levin into a fully functional person. Tolstoy believes in God, and, by the close, so does his surrogate Levin. Tolstoy and Levin also believe that the Russian (Slavic) temperament and soul are different from those of Europeans.

Tolstoy can be a snob and elitist, but he also believes that the nobility have special responsibilities towards the less fortunate, although he sometimes seems to consider them different in kind, not in degree. He is scathingly critical of the wasteful and dissolute ways of living of people of privilege who, like Oblonsky, are living beyond their means. (Even Levin has some money concerns.) At other times Tolstoy eulogizes simple rural life, as when Levin visits a wealthy muzhik whose "farm was flourishing" and who gives Levin an "impression of well-being" (III.xxv.324–325). Levin's visit takes place on the way to see his friend Sviyazhsky, "the marshal of nobility," with whom he has an agricultural debate. Tolstoy contrasts the aforementioned instinctive and intuitive muzhik with Sviyazhsky, whose "reasoning" about life was inconsistent with how he lived his own life and whose inconsistency troubles Levin (III.xxvi.326).

In the Introduction to his and Larissa Volokhonsky's translation, Richard Pevear writes:

. . . .

Levin is [Tolstoy's] most complete self-portrait. He has the same social position as his creator, the same "wild" nature, the same ideas and opinions, the same passion for hunting, the same almost physical love of the Russian peasant.... Levin's estate reproduces Tolstoy's ... and his marriage to Kitty duplicates Tolstoy's marriage to Sophia Andreevna in the minutest details....

Levin also goes through the same religious crisis that Tolstoy went through while he was writing the novel, and reaches the same precarious conversion at the end.[9]

. . . .

When we join Levin in the country in Part Two, Chapters xii–xvii (151–173), it is as if Tolstoy takes us into a different, cleaner, and clearer world than the urban world of Part One. Tolstoy's lyrical description of the beginning of spring on Levin's property – rebirth and new life that is an ironic comment on Anna's "new life" – is almost a suspension of time within the tick-tock of passing time as well as great nature writing (152–153).

Tolstoy is extremely impatient with political dialogue and polemics other than his own, and makes fun of what passes for electoral politics among the landowning class. Indeed, Tolstoy has a wonderful comic imagination, although the comedy can be poignant, as when he describes the reception, or lack of it, of the book by Sergei Ivanovich, Levin's half-brother, entitled *An Essay in Survey of the Principles and Forms of Statehood in Europe and Russia*, on which he had worked six years. The response is "complete indifference" (VIII.i.769).

Tolstoy's view of urban life, contemporary fashions, and political machinations is very much that of Levin. We need to stress that Tolstoy can be as much a comic social satirist in the Thackeray mode as a realist; often he combines both: "[Princess] Betsy, dressed after the very latest fashion, in a hat that hovered somewhere over her head like a lampshade over a lamp, and in a dove-gray dress with sharp diagonal stripes going one way on the bodice and the other way on the skirt …" (IV.xix.422).

Indeed, perhaps because of Tolstoy's compulsion to teach and perhaps because he doesn't quite trust his readers to understand the implications of what he is showing, the Levin sections have a great deal of telling and far less dramatic action; the result is that these sections become polemical and repetitious. For example, we can see that Levin enjoys working with the peasants or muzhiks on agrarian tasks. But because Tolstoy wants to be sure that the reader is aware of Levin's naïveté and good will in considering "himself part of the peasantry," he describes Levin's feelings in detail: "In his methodical mind certain forms of peasant life acquired a clear shape, deduced in part from peasant life itself, but mainly from contrast [to the life he did not love]" (III.i.238).

At times, to a resistant reader Levin is perhaps more comical than Tolstoy realizes, although his narrative voice does show with gentle irony that Levin, like Pierre in *War and Peace*, is socially awkward and disdainful of many urban social customs. At first when rejected by Kitty in favor of Vronsky, he withdraws and becomes something of an isolato. Feeling sorry for himself at this point, Levin goes into a tailspin. Intuitive more than he realizes since he thinks of himself as a rationalist, he undergoes on occasion rapid transformation. Later the narrator tells us: "[T]he thought came clearly to Levin that it was up to him to change that so burdensome, idle, artificial and individual life he lived into this laborious, pure and common, lovely life" (III.xii.275). Spending a night sleeping on a haystack helps change Levin's mind about farming; he realizes that his modern ideas are at odds with the peasants' desire "to work as pleasantly as possible, with rests, and above all – carelessly, obliviously, thoughtlessly" (III.xxiv.321). As is often the case, the resistant reader feels a tad bludgeoned by the polemical, if not viral, impulse in Tolstoy's intended irony.

Tolstoy draws a strong contrast between what he sees as the superficiality of urban life and the substantive family-oriented life of those who live on the land. It is almost as if the Russian soil is a mystical presence shaping character. Of course Tolstoy's focus is on the privileged class, but the quality of agricultural life for the peasants is nonetheless better than that of those born to comfortable circumstances. Urban officials are self-important time servers even when, like Alexei Karenin, they have prominent positions.

Reflecting his creator's beliefs, Levin's view of hunting is positive. In a way, hunting is part of Tolstoy's paean to human interaction with nature, although many contemporary readers may be disgusted by the killing. Even though hunting demands and requires the cooperation of highly trained dogs, sometimes it seems a weird form of man's demonstrating superiority and control over the animal kingdom. Like English foxhunting, it is an aristocratic diversion with its own customs. The thrill of the chase is important and competitive – one wants to outshoot one's cohorts – and the quarry matters. Rituals seem less important than killing the animal or bird, but the killing is less for food than for triumphing over the bird or animal and being more proficient than fellow hunters.

Genre: What Kind of Novel is *Anna Karenina*? What Kind of Fiction is Tolstoy Writing?

If *Anna Karenina* were a British novel, it would be in the subgenre of novels of manners called country house novels. As R. P. Blackmur puts it in his essay on *Anna Karenina*, "[M]anners are the medium in which the struggle between the institutions of society and the needs of individuals is conducted…. [In *Anna Karenina* it] is through manners that the needs and possibilities of each person are seen in shifting conflict with the available or relevant institutions."[10] But Tolstoy's and his surrogate Levin's raising of intellectually profound versions of the question, "For what purpose do we live?" is something quite different than a country house novel or a novel of manners. Indeed, Tolstoy satirizes both the very nature of the country house tradition and its inhabitants. For Tolstoy Anna's deviation from the ideals he holds to be central to civilized social life is more serious than it might be in a novel of manners.

Put a different way, the moral and political stakes are higher in Tolstoy than is often the case in the novel of manners. Because Tolstoy is defining the essential values that humans live for, Levin plays a different role in the imagined world of Tolstoy than Knightley plays in the sequestered world of Austen's *Emma* where manners are values. Anna's and Vronsky's behavior – and the frivolous behavior of their circle – is far more a challenge to the heart of a nation's social, economic, and political structure than anything that happens in an Austen novel.

Anna Karenina, like *War and Peace*, mixes several genres: realistic novel, novel of manners, social satire, psychological study, political novel, scathing satire, polemic, and, in the close association of Tolstoy with Levin, autobiographical inquiry. As a political novel, like Dostoevsky's *Crime and Punishment* and even more so *Notes from Underground*, it asks, "Whither Russia?" – that is, how in the mid-nineteenth century should Russia evolve from its agrarian, religious, cultural, and class-stratified past? Sometimes this mixture of genres relieves the tension that we find in, say, *Madame Bovary*, where another woman rushes downhill to her demise. But in *Anna Karenina*, the organic plot is relieved by digressions, not only in the form of polemics on Levin's quest for values amidst his self-imposed rustification, but also in scathing commentary on the idleness, self-indulgence, and hypocrisy of the upper classes.

That *Anna Karenina* contains much more about agricultural economy, hunting, and horse racing than would interest many readers is an example of the kind of over-determinism we saw in the protracted and intricate discussions of military operations and iterative philosophizing in *War and Peace*. These subjects become tedious reading for many contemporary readers, especially the discussions of farming along with those on how the nobility is dealing with the muzhiks now that the serfs have been freed. One might say with a smile that these aforementioned subjects are to *Anna Karenina* what cetology is to *Moby Dick*. And, of course, a minority of readers like both Tolstoy's and Melville's digressions and find them essential.

In Tolstoy's view, one must have more than a good heart; one must do something substantive for the betterment of Russia, and one must have within oneself a capacious Russian soul. Not only are Anna and Stiva's adulteries violations of sacred responsibility, but so also is the immoral and amoral quality of life pursued by Stiva, Anna, and Vronsky. Inability to feel purely, foppery in dress or behavior, insincerity, lack of ideals, social guile, performance of emotions that are expected – whether done so disingenuously or from an inherent dearth of feelings or the corruption of impulses caused by a faulty upbringing – are causes for Tolstoy's disdain. Even the naïve Dolly knows that "there was something false in the whole shape of [the Karenins'] family life" (I.xix.66).

As John Bayley observes, Tolstoy asks, "What happens when you cut yourself off from society, or are cut off by it? … [Anna and Vronsky] were unaware of the extent to which they were created by the society they lived in, and of how much they needed it. Once they have gone against it they can never be in the same easy and unconscious relation to it again. Lacking society, lacking the family, they are destroyed by a conflict of wills that arises with appalling inevitability. Without the freedom of society, their passion becomes a prison."[11]

What Vronsky and Anna have is a sense that their pleasures matter more than their commitments to family and society; this narcissism is shared by most of the characters inhabiting their social sphere. Vronsky's mother, who had many affairs, is the paradigm for being absorbed in her own constricted world, most notably after Anna's suicide. She praises the Serbian war as "God's help to us … [I]t's been sent him by God," because Vronsky will be distracted from his depression over Anna (VIII.iv.779). According to Vronsky's mother, Vronsky had tried to shoot himself, although we have learned that we can't quite trust her. She has no thought of those who will be killed and maimed in war, and her thinking the world revolves around herself and her son is comic and pathetic. She is a reductive example of how we see the world through tinted glasses: "But my poor son gave her all of himself. He abandoned everything – career, me – and even so she took no pity on him but deliberately destroyed him completely" (VIII.iv.778).

Tolstoy emphasizes that if we challenge social strictures and set out on our path, "We live, as we dream – alone," as Conrad puts it in *Heart of Darkness*. Vronsky and Anna become socially isolated; yet they cannot live with one another as a self-contained unit of two. As Bayley notes, "Not only is nothing permanent in the world of *Anna Karenina* – nothing is seen in the same way by any two people."[12]

It is rare to read a novel in which satiric vitriol plays such a large role. But this is another area where Tolstoy's techniques are inexorably tied to his values. To be sure, a novel of manners often depends on the ironic distance between narrator and characters, but in *Anna Karenina* Tolstoy scathingly dissects upper-class frivolity and its waste of human and economic resources. In a way, his subject is waste, the detritus of a social class that dissipates its energy in immoral behavior.

Tolstoy asks what will happen to Russia if the highest social classes are immoral, narcissistic, and decadent. His narrator tells us, as Vronsky becomes infatuated with Anna, that Vronsky "knew very well that for [his wealthy cousin Princess Betsy, who is having an adulterous affair, and all the other society people] the role of the unhappy lover of a young girl, or a free woman generally, might be ridiculous; but the role of a man who attached himself to a married woman and devoted his life to involving her in adultery at all costs, had something beautiful and grand about it and could never be ridiculous" (II.iv.128–129). It is as if sexual fealty were an obsolete convention. Mentioning the word "adultery" for the first time as a possibility for Anna, the aforementioned sentence is an ironic inversion of Tolstoy's bedrock beliefs about family, marriage, and moral behavior. Moreover, the sentence defines Vronsky and Anna's behavior as acceptable within an important strand of the "highest circle in Petersburg" (II.iv.126), one with ties to the court.

That pleasure is Anna's and Vronsky's one motivation and that they are indifferent to whom they hurt is underlined by the preceding scene in which we see the twin misery of the eighteen-year-old Kitty, who has been misused by Vronsky, and her sister Dolly, misused by Oblonsky, who subscribes to the same selfish and hedonistic standards as Vronsky. The following scene in which a young wife and her husband are harassed shows Vronsky and the fellow members of his regiment as disrespectful drunken skirt chasers. In this world passions are for affairs; as Princess Betsy says during a soiree attended by Anna and Vronsky: "I think that in order to know love one must make a mistake and then correct it" (II.vii.138). For Princess Betsy affairs are essential to corrections.

Princess Betsy's circle specializes in "malicious gossip." In a great but simple metaphor, Tolstoy catches the circle's essence: "Each had something demeaning and derisive to say about the unfortunate Mme Maltishchev, and the conversation began to crackle merrily, like a blazing bonfire" (II.vi.134). The image of a bonfire suggests a large family in a rural community, the antithesis of what is going on in this society without any decorum or moral standards, a community where each person has her own illicit shadow.

Tolstoy juxtaposes agrarian life with urban life, to the detriment of the latter. In I.xxvi and I.xxvii, we first see Levin at his rural estate home, and see him revitalized and stabilized after Kitty's refusal: "He felt that something in the depths of his soul was being established, adjusted and settled" (I.xxvii.95). We quickly see him lose his sense of "shame" and plan for "a new, better life," even while deceiving himself that he can be happy without a wife (I.xxvi.92–93).

For Tolstoy, home – and home means wife and children, just as in *War and Peace* – is an oasis of peace, a refuge from the world beyond home that we cannot control. Tolstoy places a heavy stress on commitment to marriage, children, and maintaining a stable social structure because for him they are the underpinnings of a stable political structure.

Tolstoy's Artistry

Tolstoy sometimes deviates from what we expect of an organic plot and on occasion the plot can seem like a shaggy dog story, as when Anna almost dies and then we see her happy with Vronsky in Italy. The more we reread, the more we see how tightly structured and organic a novel Tolstoy has written, but the structure revolves around central themes – and, to an extent, major characters – more than the development of plot. Yet the underlying unity – yes, organic unity but not in the traditional plot-centered way – is often in the thematic interplay rather than the linear story.

To Henry James the paradigmatic "loose baggy monster" was *War and Peace*. But within *Anna Karenina* – and indeed, to an extent, in *War and Peace* – the unifying glue holding the novel together is Tolstoy's dramatization of the to-and-fro struggles that underlie marriages and relationships as well as his belief that children are important in holding marriages together. As Pevear writes in his Introduction, for Tolstoy, "marriage and childrearing were a woman's essential tasks, and family happiness was the highest human ideal."[13]

Anna Karenina is capacious enough for digressions about agrarian life, the joys of hunting, the qualities of the Russian muzhiks or peasants, the wonders of nature, and the necessity for Christian belief to give life shape and meaning. Henry James's "loose baggy monsters" include moments that fray at the edges of connectivity and concatenation and puzzle our need for entailment; this fraying occurs in part because of such novels' sheer amplitude, in part because even rereaders and re-rereaders cannot hold the whole of the novels in memory.

When rereading, we see how our early view of Anna and Vronsky captivated by each other at the train station anticipates Anna's throwing herself under the train at the end. We recall that they were both present when a train watchman is killed by an oncoming train. It is as if the confused and illicit journey towards disaster began then and as if the words elicited by this accident apply to their entire story as well as – except for the male pronoun "himself" – to Anna's end: "What? … What? … Where? … Threw himself! … run over!" (I.xviii.64).

The seven major characters form three intersecting units, namely: (1) Stiva and Dolly; (2) Anna (Dolly's sister-in-law), Vronsky, and Karenin; and (3) Kitty and Levin. Each takes his or her meaning from his or her place in the constellation of major characters and we are always measuring one character by the others and understanding character in terms of the other six major ones.

Unlike English novels – those of Dickens, Thackeray, Woolf, Conrad, or Lawrence – or even Tolstoy's Russian counterpart Dostoevsky, Tolstoy in *Anna Karenina* gives the reader little sense of characters' pasts. We need to look carefully for hints as to how they have been produced in terms of family and culture. Tolstoy's characters don't arrive with biographies. Yet the reader has a sense that while his third person narrator may not be omniscient, he knows more than he tells. Put another way, the narrator doesn't look backwards or forward, but rather puts his characters in the immediate present in each scene and lets us see their values and idiosyncrasies as they respond to circumstances and other characters.

The reader knows and doesn't know at the same time, and needs to be attentive to new and often surprising information. We know something about characters from prior scenes, but little about their past. Because Tolstoy's characters evolve and change, we can't always guess how a character should behave based on deductive and inductive evidence from prior scenes.

Yes, Tolstoy can be a polemicist – he hates triviality, licentiousness, and sloth – but he understands intuitively that human behavior cannot always be controlled by reason and that characters break out of the molds in which he puts them. Notwithstanding Tolstoy's rigid moral scruples, he asks, "What is Anna to do, given who she is as a distinct individual human being, once she is married to an Alexei Karenin?"

Tolstoy has a deft understanding of psychology – of the grammar of motives – and of social situations to which characters respond. Lacking Freudian terminology but a keen student of human behavior, Tolstoy writes brilliantly about anxiety, depression, drug abuse (Anna's morphine use), and physical ailments (Levin's brother, Nikolai).

While Bayley is not incorrect that Tolstoy "does not forget that most human beings are incapable of feeling one thing for long,"[14] we need to be aware that Bayley has a tendency to attribute his own view of human nature to Tolstoy. For example, Bayley argues, "For the men in *Anna* it is the body that leads and the feelings that follow…. Tolstoy was well aware of the destructive potential of this joyful solipsism."[15] While this may be true of Stiva and Vronsky, perhaps it is best to exclude Levin and to observe that Karenin lives in a self-deluding bubble that is not joyful solipsism but rather pleasureless masochism. Or as R. P. Blackmur puts it, drawing an insightful parallel between Dolly and Karenin, both "are never equal to their situation and still struggle with it, however pitifully or pretentiously, and lose power over others as over themselves with each successive act."[16]

One of the most compelling incidents and an example of Tolstoy's deft understanding of human psychology occurs when Levin meets Anna. When we might expect Levin to be judgmental, he is captivated by her:

....

[He] felt a tenderness and pity for her that surprised him…. Levin admired her all the while – her beauty, her intelligence, her education, and with that her simplicity and deep feeling. He listened, talked, and all the while thought about her, about her inner life, trying to guess her feelings. And he who had formerly judged her so severely, now, by some strange train of thought, justified her and at the same time pitied her, and feared that Vronsky did not fully understand her. (VII.x.700–701)

....

Tolstoy enjoys deconstructing reductive oppositions like that between Anna and Levin. We might say Levin's sympathy reveals something about Tolstoy, who may be more of Anna's party than he knows. Not only do we see that Levin, too, is not immune to her flirtation and sexuality, but also that he is growing less wooden in his arch responses and more human in his empathy and sympathy.

Levin's response to Anna is also an example of Levin himself creating what he sees, but it might be also a kind of shadow plot – a hint of what might have been – if Anna had met a man like Levin before she married Alexei Karenin. The might-have-been or story manqué – a term I use for a direction that the plot suggests but doesn't take – is when Levin is so overcome by his Everlasting

No, that is, his inability to define what he should live for, that he contemplates suicide: "And, happy in his family life, a healthy man, Levin was several times so close to suicide that he hid a rope lest he hang himself with it, and was afraid to go about with a rifle lest he shoot himself" (VIII.ix.789). But the narrator's next sentence reveals a great deal about the difference between Levin's temporary despondence and Anna's despair: "But Levin did not shoot himself or hang himself and went on living" (VIII.ix.789).

Tolstoy often uses a double optics alternating the microcosmic perspective of characters, often driven by self-interest and psychic needs, and the macrocosmic perspective of a mature narrator aware of the larger moral and social contexts. For the most part we are aware of the omniscient narrator's mature and insightful perspective. Yet, because we often view characters through the limited perspective of the narrator's focalization on a particular character – say, Anna or Vronsky or even Levin – at times we may feel that the narrator is somewhat limited in his perspicacity. Certainly, his presentation urges us to trust some characters far more than others. As the novel progresses, the reader has more and more confidence in Levin – although he puzzles us with his sympathy for Anna and his thoughts and fears of suicide – and less and less in Anna as she becomes unhinged in the later chapters.

Tolstoy is not only a great observer of human behavior but also a master of complex and deft characterization, and this awareness of complexity can even extend to his sometime surrogate, Levin, particularly early in the novel. Thus he understands that Levin found it "pleasing, because [Kitty], who had made him suffer so much, was suffering herself" (II.xvi.166). He shows us that Levin can be something of a bully to his employees, and that he has a pedantic and polemical side, as when he chides Oblonsky for selling his words cheap. He understands that Kitty has to be ultra critical of her husband, "holding him guilty for everything bad she could find in him and forgiving him nothing, on account of the terrible fault for which she stood guilty before him" (II.xxiii.189).

If ever a novel depended on a combination on the part of the narrator of bitter, judgmental irony and at other (less frequent) times nuanced irony, it is this one. The narrator begins by showing us the false notes of the social world he despises. From the opening scenes of Oblonsky's adultery and the gruesome accidental death at the railroad station, Tolstoy's plotting of his basic theme and story is near perfect. When Vronsky gives 200 roubles to the family of the deceased, he may or may not know Anna will learn of it, but he is presented as someone who buys self-satisfaction and for whom everything is for sale.

Tolstoy creates one of his characteristically great moments of narrative focalization when we see at the ball through Kitty's eighteen-year-old eyes what is going on between Anna and Vronsky: "Kitty was overcome by a moment of despair and horror ... [A] terrible despair pained her heart.... No one except herself understood her situation, no one knew that a few days before that she had refused a man whom she perhaps loved, and had refused him because she trusted another" (I.xxiii.82). The narrator is showing us Kitty's response as she awaits Vronsky's proposal after she has refused Levin and in her mind chosen Vronsky. Paralleling how Levin felt in the company of Vronsky and Anna, Kitty now becomes the outsider. The reader sees through her eyes that Vronsky and Anna are completely captivated by one another as if no one else exists: "She saw that they felt themselves alone in this crowded ballroom. And on Vronsky's face, always so firm and independent, she saw that expression of lostness and obedience that had so struck her, like the expression of an intelligent dog when it feels guilty" (I.xxiii.82–83). Of course, due to the narrator's greater awareness of what is going on – what we might call his cosmopolitan focalization as opposed to Kitty's local and ingenuous focalization – we realize it is Anna who saw Vronsky as "firm and independent" because, as a self-serving solipsist enjoying his bachelorhood with no model of family life, he does not commit to Kitty.

Tolstoy renders Kitty's deflation and does so through her eyes and mind. Her triumphant, self-satisfied presence at the ball turns into an awareness that she has nothing, and that her hopes have been betrayed by her putative husband and a woman she had "loved" in an adolescent way, but of whom, in her disgust, resentment, and jealousy she thinks, "Yes, there's something alien, demonic, and enchanting in her" (I.xxiii.83). Paradoxically, even while recognizing that "there was something terrible and cruel in [Anna's] enchantment," "Kitty admired her even more than before" (I.xxiii.83).

Tolstoy is both a master storyteller and an innovative artist. He not only brilliantly renders interior monologue but also presents stream of consciousness, as when he dramatizes Levin's thoughts, upon returning home, in a series of associations: "Well, all right, electricity and heat are the same.... It'll be especially nice when Pava's daughter is already a spotted red cow.... Splendid! To go out with my wife and guests to meet the herd ... My wife will say: 'Kostya and I attended this calf like a child'" (I.xxvii.96). These excerpts from a longer passage capture the essence of Levin's intellectual curiosity, desire for family, practicality (cows need to reproduce), and rhapsodic view of agrarian life.

For Tolstoy, style is value and Pevear and Volokhonsky's translation is alert to this. Their wonderful translation enables us to appreciate the richness and succinctness of his prose, including Tolstoy's tendency to repeat crucial words, but in ways that develop nuanced and inflected meanings.

Tolstoy stresses how guilt and shame play a major role in Anna's demise. The word "shame" is crucial in *Anna Karenina*. "Shame," the self-conscious awareness that one has transgressed personal and societal moral boundaries, is a major concept in Tolstoy's moral universe. Tolstoy tells us so much about human character in one sentence: "Kitty looked into [Vronsky's] face, which was such a short distance from hers, and long afterwards, for several years, that look, so full of love, which she gave him then, and to which he did not respond, cut her heart with tormenting shame" (I.xxii.80). Intuitively hurt, she isn't ready then to acknowledge what the narrator has made us aware of, namely that in her rejection of Levin, she has made a terrible choice.

Levin, to whom Tolstoy has his narrator turn so we can see his response, feels "shame and dissatisfaction with himself" after being rejected. But when Levin returns to his country life, these feelings drop away, and he begins to recreate his dream of a family and regain his own sense of worth (I.xxvi.92).

By contrast, Tolstoy's striking focalization presents Anna's subtle and evasive thoughts with which we are not unsympathetic as she takes the train journey back from Moscow to St. Petersburg. Anna rejects shame, even though she has been flirting with Vronsky to the point of captivating him and turning his attention away from her sister-in-law, Kitty. "There was nothing shameful," she repeats as if to assure herself (I.xxix.100). But the reader judges Anna severely, in part because her behavior suffers by comparison with Kitty's straightforward if not ingenuous response and along with Kitty's pained awareness of how she has been marginalized by Anna and Vronsky. Tolstoy shows us what a complete narcissist Anna is – how she can rationalize any behavior that feeds her own pleasure – and how Vronsky is her secret sharer in his devotion to self-gratification. When Vronsky meets her at a train stop – having taken the train only to be near her – and declares, "I am going in order to be where you are," she "sensed that this momentary conversation had brought them terribly close, and this made her both frightened and happy" (I.xxx.103).

Our first view of Anna and her husband reveals that theirs is a strained if not failed marriage. Her first perception is to see his weariness and mockery, but she is attributing to him what she feels herself; seeing "his habitual mocking smile" as he meets her at the station, "Some unpleasant feeling gnawed at her heart as she met his unwavering and weary gaze" (I.xxx.104). Is this a version of what Austen calls "Myself creating what I saw" (*Emma* III.v)? Clearly, her dissatisfaction with his disengaged ennui has fed her wandering eye and need for adventure. But are we sure that any marriage would have satisfied her?

Anna's erratic changes of mood speak to her emotional instability and her boredom with her husband: "[T]he feeling of dissatisfaction with herself that she experienced on meeting him. This was an old, familiar feeling, similar to that state of pretence she experienced in her relations with her husband; but previously she had not noticed it, while now she was clearly and painfully aware of it" (I.xxx.104). We had hints before that something was radically wrong; when Anna reads, she wants to be the characters: "She wanted too much to live herself" (I.xxix.100). (We might note Tolstoy's ironic textuality in the form of his narrator warning readers of the difference between literary characters and life and of the need for us readers to retain our judgment when reading.)

Remarkably unperceptive, Alexei Karenin lacks imagination and passion. He is a careerist who has organized every moment to maximize his potential within his work. He is a parody of the Enlightenment man who has organized his life around reason and rules. He has no way of understanding what is "illogical" and "senseless" to him such as his wife "loving someone else besides him" (II.viii.142). Within his mind is a debate between his desire to believe "nothing" – a word he keeps repeating – had happened and feelings of confusion and jealousy (II.viii.143). He despises his own jealousy because in his logic it is humiliating to his wife, even while he cannot help dancing around it. His life is measured by "proper" and "improper": "improper" is his word for what others see in Anna's behavior before he realizes that they might be right. As Tolstoy's narrator puts it, "All his life Alexei Alexandrovich had lived and worked in spheres of service that dealt with reflections of life. And each time he had encountered life itself, he had drawn back from it" (II.viii.142).

With one of Tolstoy's spare, straightforward, and amazingly effective metaphors, the narrator continues: "Now he experienced a feeling similar to what a man would feel who was calmly walking across a bridge over an abyss and suddenly saw that the bridge had been taken down and below him was the bottomless deep. This bottomless deep was life itself, the bridge the artificial life that Alexei Alexandrovich had lived" (II.viii.142–143). With characteristic play on crucial and repeated terms, Tolstoy shows us how Alexei, self-absorbed narcissist that he is, explores the bottomless deep – that is, life; the term is not his but Tolstoy's narrator: "For the first time [Alexei] vividly pictured to himself her personal life, her thoughts, her wishes, and the thought that she could and should have her own particular life seemed so frightening to him that he hastened to drive it away. It was that bottomless deep into which it was frightening to look" (II.viii.143–144).

Alexei depicts himself as one who doesn't struggle with emotions or look into the life of feelings: "I'm not one of those people who suffer troubles and anxieties and have no strength to look them in the face" (II.viii.144). Alexei is emotionally challenged in much the same way as Tolstoy's Ivan Ilych is in *The Death of Ivan Ilych*. His preoccupation with the vertical pronoun "I" when he takes stock of his marriage is another telling way that Tolstoy's focalization exposes him. The irony is that he is an emotional child without self-knowledge or the capacity for sympathy or empathy. In fact he is like Dr. Seuss's Grinch with a heart that is too small. The reader wonders how Anna could be attracted to this man so opposite to herself other than by his potential for providing a safe haven. But within Tolstoy's world, the safe haven offered by marriage is a necessary and sufficient condition for the best women, namely, Kitty, Natasha, and Marya.

Tolstoy is fascinated with the parallels between Vronsky and Anna's husband and how their solipsism and self-indulgence, despite seeming differences, echo one another. Anna's lover and her husband have the same name Alexei, and indeed they are each other's doubleganger: "One dream visited her almost every night. She dreamed that they were both her husbands, that they both lavished their caresses on her.... [S]he would wake up in horror" (II.xi.150). Tolstoy uses the term "new life" to describe her transformation, and for Anna it is ironic, because she has lost her moral moorings and knows it, even while the term "new life" anticipates her pregnancy with Vronsky's child: "[S]he could not put into words her feeling of shame, joy, and horror before this entry into a new life" (II.xi.150). Unlike Betsy and others in that circle, Anna is tortured by guilt and – a feeling embodied in a word that almost becomes a metonymy for her – "shame."

While Tolstoy understands the nuanced complexity of motives that drives human behavior in a way that resembles the subtleties of Henry James's late fiction, he can at the same time be judgmentally direct. No sooner does Alexei forgive Anna and Vronsky after learning of Vronsky's abortive suicide attempt than his forgiveness competes with darker impulses which he does not understand and derive from his anger and hurt: "[Alexei] felt that, besides the good spiritual force that guided his soul, there was another force, crude and equally powerful, if not more so, that guided his life, and that this force would not give him the humble peace he desired" (IV.xix.419). Tolstoy is not as sympathetic as we might expect with the cuckolded Alexei, who, as we have seen, he regards as a self-important functionary without much capacity for feeling.

Tolstoy's presentation of Anna's collapse contains some of the great passages in world literature. Tolstoy's dramatization of Anna's breakdown – her paranoia, her fixations, and her compulsive and destructive behavior – is the work of genius. Rendering Anna, he dramatizes a mind unable to concentrate and to focus on one thing at a time. We see Anna losing touch with herself and her surroundings and feeling increasingly isolated. She forgets where she is going and loses the strands of her thoughts. As she gets on the train with hopes of finding Vronsky, we recall how earlier he had boarded the train in Moscow hoping to encounter her; because he was oblivious to anyone else, everyone seemed repulsive and ugly. (It could hardly be an accident that both incidents take place in the thirty-first chapter of the Part – to use Tolstoy's term for dividing *Anna Karenina* – in which they appear: VII.xxxi; I.xxxi.)

Yet she also has moments of perfect clarity. As Anna falls apart, one of the crystallizing moments is when she, riding back from visiting Dolly and inadvertently discovering there her former rival and Dolly's sister, Kitty, sees a group going out of town and thinks, "You won't get away from yourselves"

(VII.xxx.762). She knows that she is imprisoned by her past actions from which she can't flee and knows that she is separated from the self she wished to become. Anna invested everything in Vronsky, but she is sure he hasn't reciprocated: "Our lives are parting ways, and I have become his unhappiness and he mine, and it's impossible to remake either him or me. All efforts have been made; the screw is stripped" (VII.xxx.764). She realizes that she has driven him away. Vronsky seems to realize, too, how morphine is contributing to skewing her perceptions. Because she has abandoned family values, she has nothing to prop her up morally. She rushes relentlessly towards suicide like the very train that kills her. Isn't her dream of "[a] little old muzhik" doing something "dreadful" over her with "iron" both a foreshadowing of the train and a more mystical, uncanny image – and in her mind! – of Russia's retribution for her neglecting its moral center (VII.xxvi.752)?

Tolstoy often presents his characters' psychological effects as resulting in part from sociological and cultural causes, and those causes include the Russian Orthodox Church. Crossing herself before jumping and calling on the Lord as the train rolls over her, Anna returns to religion as if Tolstoy wanted to punctuate his point that, finally, belief in God is a necessity for moral stability.

The Ending of *Anna Karenina*: Enter Tolstoy, Stage Right

With Anna on the verge of a headlong leap into madness, the relaxed pace of Chapters xx–xxii (728–738) of Part Seven may surprise us. Stiva visits decadent St. Petersburg and falls asleep watching Anna's husband, Alexei Alexandrovich, as part of a coterie led by Countess Lydia Ivanovna. The latter follows a French quack named Landau practicing a weird combination of spiritualism and Christianity that does not require good works. If these chapters have any relationship to the main plot it is to show that, despite his pretensions, Alexei Karenin is shallow, foolish, and dependent on Anna for his social identity, and thus to make Anna marginally somewhat more sympathetic. Hasn't he always been oblivious to what Blackmur calls "the nature and the springs of human action"?[17] Like Mme. Stahl and Varenka, whom Kitty meets when she goes abroad to restore her health, he suffers from a diminished soul, in Blackmur's words, "the negation of vitality."[18] A second purpose of these chapters, central to Tolstoy's polemical answer to "Whither Russia?" is to show that Christianity is more than superficially professing belief.

Why does the novel conclude anti-climatically with Levin's discovery that the meaning of life resides in the soul and that science, reason, and the material world is a dead end? In some ways, Levin and his creator Tolstoy are re-enacting the mechanism–vitalism debate that was foregrounded in Western

Europe. Levin thinks his overly intellectual brother, who is always talking about "the common good" and believes in the materiality of words as efficacious substance that can do something like rally people to fight on the side of the Serbs against the Turks, has "a lack of life force" (III.i.239). A despairing unbeliever, Levin finally undergoes an epiphanic conversion experience. Before this he had been haunted by the purposelessness of his life: "So he lived, not knowing and not seeing any possibility of knowing what he was and why he was living in the world, tormented by this ignorance to such a degree that he feared suicide, and at the same time, firmly laying down his own particular, definite path in life" (VIII.x.791). He overcomes his Everlasting No and, by abandoning reasoning, feels and affirms his Everlasting Yea by discovering in his soul "the one obvious, unquestionable manifestation of the Deity … disclosed to the world by revelation" (VIII.xix.815).

Formally, what is happening is that Tolstoy is re-establishing equilibrium and showing an alternative to Anna and Vronsky's quality of life. But the resistant reader may feel that these are preacherly pages that distract from the power of Anna's suicide, and that the quality of Levin's agrarian life, in contrast to Anna's and Vronsky's life, has already been established in the early chapters of Book III (237–256). It is true that until the end Levin seems to not be in a direct relationship with God, but his religious awakening could have been managed earlier and more efficiently. Yet, Tolstoy needed to stress that the answer to the question "Whither Russia?" is in the enrichment of Levin's capacious and growing soul, enlarged by marriage and the birth of a son, and, finally, a vibrant sense of God. Levin becomes more in tune in Tolstoy's odd combination of agrarian, community, and elitist *noblesse oblige*. His growth and rebirth, we realize, are juxtaposed to the shrinking of Anna's world when she intuitively and gradually understands that she cannot always be a young girl in love and has been ostracized by society and dies.

As resistant readers, whether we are coming to *Anna Karenina* for the first time or the fourth time, but knowing something about subsequent Russian history, we understand the reasons for the February and October Revolutions of 1917. For we see why Tolstoy's acceptance of flagrant class divisions – especially of the privileges and elitism of the nobility – and his stress in his conclusion on spiritual awakening were for most people a dead end to the question "Whither Russia?"

Study Questions for *Anna Karenina*

1. What genres do we find in *Anna Karenina* and how does that mix of genres shape the novel's structure?
2. What are Tolstoy's values? His sexual ethics?

3. What is Levin's role in the novel and how is he a surrogate for Tolstoy? How does Tolstoy humanize him?
4. Why does the novel open with Oblonsky and Dolly? How does Tolstoy use the novel's beginning to define his ethics of love and marriage?
5. What is the function of Varenka?
6. What are the major and distinguishing features of Tolstoy's artistry? How does he use the narrative voice to point up his themes and values? How does the narrator's focalization work? How do themes and characters become central structural principles rather than plot?
7. Why do Karenin and Vronsky have the same name, Alexei? Can you define their failures and shortcomings, including what they have in common?
8. How does Anna seduce the reader in the early pages and seduce Levin later?
9. How do *Anna Karenina*'s major characters change and why?
10. In what way is Tolstoy a social satirist? Is he also an iconoclast and an elitist?
11. What is Tolstoy's solution for the future of Russia? Why does the twenty-first-century reader resist some of his views as naïve? Do we see Tolstoy differently in light of subsequent Russian history?
12. How does Tolstoy view the muzhiks or peasants now that the serfs have officially been freed?
13. What is Tolstoy's view of the military and political leadership in this period?

Notes

1. Tony Judt, "The Glory of the Rails," *NYR* 57:20 (Dec. 23, 2010), 60–61; see p. 60.
2. Judt, "The Glory of the Rails," 60.
3. See Tony Judt, "Bring Back the Rails!" *NYR* 58:1 (Jan. 13, 2011), 34–35.
4. All quotations from the text are from Leo Tolstoy, *Anna Karenina*, trans. Richard Pevear and Larissa Volokhonsky (New York and London: Penguin, 2000–2001).
5. John Bayley, *Tolstoy and the Novel* (London: Chatto and Windus, 1966), 206.
6. Bayley, *Tolstoy and the Novel*, 207.
7. Bayley, *Tolstoy and the Novel*, 209.
8. Bayley, *Tolstoy and the Novel*, 201.
9. Richard Pevear, "Introduction," *Anna Karenina*, xiii–xiv.
10. R. P. Blackmur, *Eleven Essays in the European Novel* (New York: Harcourt, Brace and World, 1964), 8.
11. Bayley, *Tolstoy and the Novel*, 201.
12. Bayley, *Tolstoy and the Novel*, 206–207.

13. Pevear, "Introduction," *Anna Karenina*, ix.
14. Bayley, *Tolstoy and the Novel*, 227.
15. Bayley, *Tolstoy and the Novel*, 222.
16. Blackmur, *Eleven Essays in the European Novel*, 14.
17. Blackmur, *Eleven Essays in the European Novel*, 13.
18. Blackmur, *Eleven Essays in the European Novel*, 13.

Chapter 10

Emile Zola's *Germinal* (1885)

The Aesthetics, Thematics, and Ideology of the Novel of Purpose

Introduction

Writing about the later nineteenth century with a specific focus on France, Anka Muhlstein observes, "The modern artist resolutely turns his back on the past (and therefore on traditional subjects, either religious or historical), choosing instead to paint his contemporaries. [As Baudelaire puts it, he] 'has a spirit of a mixed nature, that is to say, a strong literary element enters into it.... Observer, flaneur, philosopher ... he is most like a novelist or a moralist. He is the painter of both the passing moment and everything in that moment that smacks of eternity.'"[1]

To understand the French novel in the nineteenth century, we need to read four authors: Balzac, Stendhal, Flaubert, and Zola (1840–1902). While human passions are the main focus of the first three, Zola focuses on social and economic conditions that he believes are the main determinants of character and personality. Unlike Balzac, who does have a strong interest in class movement and capital formation – both economic and social – Zola's interest is in the lower classes and the permanent have-nots, the people on the margins of society who have not benefited from urbanization, industrialism, and capitalism.

As a novel of purpose, *Germinal* aimed to expose the abuses – indeed, the human exploitation – perpetuated by the mining industry and, by extension, capitalism. *Germinal* foregrounds aesthetic and ideological issues to a lesser degree than Tolstoy who, as we have seen, intrudes with his polemics in *Anna*

Reading the European Novel to 1900: A Critical Study of Major Fiction from Cervantes' Don Quixote *to Zola's* Germinal, First Edition. Daniel R. Schwarz.
© 2014 John Wiley & Sons, Ltd. Published 2014 by John Wiley & Sons, Ltd.

Karenina and, even more so, in *War and Peace*. But in *Germinal*, how we respond to both Zola's polemics and the underlying, somewhat doctrinaire, dramatization of his purpose is more central to how we respond to the novel than is the case with Tolstoy.

I consider Zola important enough to include in my first volume on the European novel, and I consider *Germinal* a suitable work to represent his achievement. But as will be clear in what follows, I do not consider *Germinal* quite on a par with the other works discussed in this volume, except *Sentimental Education*, and I have some reservations about the heavy-handedness of Zola's artistry.

Given specified conditions, including heredity and the external social, economic, and physical environment, Zola believed one could scientifically predict the specific kind of human nature that will emerge. In his essay "The Experimental Novel," he wrote:

. . . .

The novelist is equally an observer and an experimentalist. The observer in him gives the facts as he has observed them.... Then the experimentalist appears and introduces an experiment, that is to say, sets his characters going in a certain story so as to show that the succession of facts will be such as the requirements of the determinism of the phenomena under examination call for.... In fact, the whole operation consists in taking facts in nature, then in studying the mechanism of these facts, acting upon them, by the modification of the circumstances and surroundings, without deviating from the laws of nature. Finally, you possess knowledge of the man, scientific knowledge of him, in his individual and social relations.[2]

. . . .

Given Zola's commitment to this positivistic philosophy, it is not surprising that his novels, including *Germinal*, become doctrinaire. For the most part, he is repelled by the haves, notably the mine owners and managers as well as the religious and political establishment.

Revolving around political themes and fueled by Zola's anger – even rage – at social and economic injustice and not without a strong polemic, *Germinal* may be the least subtle novel in my book. Zola rarely creates great complex characters, even though in individual episodes they can be wonderful, as when Maheu speaks eloquently, yet simply, on behalf of the miners in a meeting with management. At this moment, Zola captures the wonderful stillness in Maheu's quiet dignity. What Zola does do is create memorable and sustained larger-than-life figures that take their place in our visual imagination (almost like Diego Rivera's murals) and stay with us as if they were figures in a graphic novel or a film.

254

Zola's Scathing Critique of the Mining Industry

Zola did considerable research into the conditions of the mines in northern France and visited the mining area in 1884. He knew that in 1869 the French army had fired into a crowd of strikers and that all strikes were treated as illegal. But labor laws were making slight inroads on behalf of the rights of laborers. By 1874 women could not be employed underground and children couldn't work in the mines.[3] Thus Zola, who set his novel in the 1860s, was describing some conditions that no longer were present.

Yet today we periodically read about world mining disasters – on occasion in recent years in the United States – and we realize that the safety of miners still takes a back seat to human greed. In 1907 more than 3,200 miners were killed worldwide, 358 in one explosion in West Virginia. In 2009 there was a record low of thirty-four deaths in the US, but in recent years there have still been mine collapses and methane explosions. In May 2014, there was a major mining disaster in Turkey, killing more than 300 miners. About a century later in November 2009 in Hegang in Heilongjiang province, China, over a hundred miners were killed. These mining death figures do not include those dying from chronic respiratory disease, which plagues miners everywhere and is another focal point in *Germinal*.

Contemporary events may shape our responses to imaginative literature and surely the events in West Virginia in April 2010 brought Zola's *Germinal* into our conscience. I was in the midst of one of my rereadings of *Germinal* when that event took place. Could the explosion of methane gas killing twenty-five people have been avoided? Massey Energy Company – one of the larger mining companies in the nation – had a significant history of safety violations, including not properly ventilating the highly combustible methane. They had paid a fine for a 2006 fire that trapped twelve miners, two of whom suffocated; on that occasion, they admitted that two permanent ventilation controls had been removed and not replaced. They also paid a $20 million fine for polluting waterways.

Zola's Dramatization of the Mining World

Grinding poverty reduces humans to an animalistic survival of the fittest. Conflicts – and often confrontations (including those among family members and friends) – brought on by human needs and human deprivation are at the heart of *Germinal*. Zola stresses not only the struggles to obtain adequate food and shelter and to keep healthy, but also the concomitant struggles between those who have and those who do not and between those who control the mines and those who eke out an existence to survive. He also dramatizes the conflicting approaches among those who want to raise the consciousness of the miners, a conflict represented by ideas expressed by the anarchist Souvarine, the more moderate Rasseneur, and the increasingly radicalized Etienne, who tries on a number of positions.

At times in *Germinal* Zola is a muckraking journalist, at other times a political polemicist, at still others a prophet. In *Germinal*, we can say that Zola's main focus is on class struggle between the bourgeois and the working class. Zola exposes capitalism as predatory. Poor people, Zola emphasizes, have little chance to live comfortable lives. *Germinal* is a pervasively violent novel where labor struggles to survive in the most egregious conditions; family life is punctuated by hunger, illness, injury, and death in the mines; sex is often submission to the male will or to animal desire; nature is indifferent, if not hostile, and life expectancy is shortened by the conditions in the mines. Zola knew that helplessness could be the catalyst for violence.

Zola demonstrates repeatedly that bad working conditions accompanied by lack of food and warmth can deprive people of their humanity. We see this when the strikers, stimulated by Etienne's rhetoric, become a "mob": "And in this growing ferocity, in this old need of revenge which was turning every head with madness, the choked cries went on, death to traitors, hatred against ill-paid work, the roaring of bellies after bread" (5.IV.305).

Zola and Darwin

As William Pfaff observed, "When, as a result of the Enlightenment, religion ceased to play its former central part in society, at least among the intellectual and political classes of Europe, one or another version of belief in scientific progress usually took religion's place, plausibly supported by the evidence of technological and material accomplishment."[4]

Writing in the wake of the Darwinian revolution, Zola, along with other naturalists like Theodore Dreiser, Stephen Crane, and Thomas Hardy, and, later, modernists like Conrad and Joyce, stressed that we should think of humans not as linked to God in a great chain of being that rose upward from plants to animals to humans to angels to God Himself, but rather as part of the natural world.

For Zola, the dichotomy between humans and animals breaks down. Zola understood that humankind was very much part of nature along with animals and plants. Humans may be the most sophisticated creatures in the natural world with larger, more effective brains and the ability to talk, but, nonetheless, they are more different in degree than kind from other animals. Poverty can create conditions that further blur the difference in degree.

He also knew that nature in a post-Darwinian universe can no longer be regarded as in tune with human fulfillment and optimism but is instead inherently an indifferent if not hostile presence. Thus Zola understands human behavior – human desires, anxieties, and unacknowledged needs – as responses to the world in which we find ourselves.

But Zola, along with many of his contemporaries, misunderstood Darwin. The contemporary impact of Darwin's two major ideas – evolution and natural selection – was mixed. As David Quammen reminds us, "[T]he idea of natural selection seemed profoundly materialistic and gloomy – that is, it was both literally and figuratively dispiriting," while evolution itself could be – mistakenly – reconfigured as an upward teleology and "could be reconciled with belief that a divine Creator had established laws governing the universe, had set life in motion, had allowed species to change over time, and then – at some magical moment – had injected a unique spiritual dimension into the primate species that was later to be known (by its own self-naming) as *Homo Sapiens*."[5] But this, as we now understand, is a misreading of Darwinism.

Zola's error was to focus on a gloomy reading that stresses that under certain conditions humans devolve backwards. What Zola didn't quite grasp is, as Quammen puts it, "Insofar as mutation and recombination [of existing genes] – which are the main sources of variation – are accidental processes, variation is undirected by need or purpose." In addition, Mendel's theory of inheritance "prevents the results from being blended away."[6] Natural selection, then, is a mindless editing process, and heredity in humans does not necessarily create either downward spirals of devolution – as Zola sometimes seems to imply – or an upward teleology. Perhaps influenced by Lamarck's theory that acquired characteristics shaped by environment are inherited, Zola misunderstood Darwin and that misunderstanding informs *Germinal*. For example, Etienne may have inherited, we now know, a tendency to alcoholism, but it is not inevitably determined that violence deriving from alcoholism will be passed from generation to generation. Nor is it inevitable that Bonnemort's degeneration and Jeanlin's physical repulsiveness and moral idiocy are genetically determined since environmental conditions – including hunger, bad diet, and breathing bad air in the mines – play such an important role.

Even though Zola fancied himself something of a Darwinian and even though Etienne invokes (and simplifies) Darwin in arguing that the world was a "battlefield, where the strong ate the weak" (7.VI.481), we should note the presence of Lamarckian evolutionary theory where environment shapes heredity. Etienne's murder of his rival Chaval is almost as shocking as Bonnemort's senseless murder of Cécile: "The need to kill seized him irresistibly, a physical need, the bloody stimulus of mucus which causes a violent spasm of coughing. It rose and broke out beyond his will, beneath the pressure of the hereditary disease…. All his struggles came back to his memory confusedly, that useless fight against the poison which slept in his muscles, the slowly accumulated alcohol of his race" (7.V.463–464).

Etienne had begun his wanderings after hitting a foreman at a railway workshop, and Etienne himself attributes this outburst of violence to alcohol. In other words, Etienne's family of middle-class degenerates – including his alcoholic mother and ne'er-do-well father – speaks through the genes to cause the murder. This is deterministic claptrap under the guise of naturalism. To be sure, earlier when he had attacked Chaval with a knife, alcohol was a factor: "This stirred in him the whole of that unknown terror, the hereditary ill, the long ancestry of drunkenness, no longer tolerating a drop of alcohol without falling into homicidal mania" (6.I.346).

Yes, we now know, a propensity to alcoholism is inherited. But alcohol surely has nothing to do with his desire to kill Chaval, his sexual rival as well as an abusive bully, when they are both trapped deep beneath the earth. What we do see throughout is that poverty and desperate conditions – Etienne, Chaval, and Catherine are trapped below the earth and almost certain to die – cause humans to revert to bestial behavior.

Is anything more disturbing in the novel than the senseless murder of a soldier committed by the predatory, sociopathic, and physically repulsive child Jeanlin whose only response when Etienne asks him, "[W]hy have you done this?" is "I don't know; I wanted to" (6.IV.380)? The narrator concludes: "[N]o one had pushed him on, it had come to him by himself, just as the desire to steal onions from a field came to him" (6.IV.381). The implication here, too, is that environment – generations living in poverty and breathing bad air in the mines – played a role in shaping heredity in Bonnemort's grandson.

The Mine as Beast Devouring Men

In terms of form and rhetoric, *Germinal* depends on a strong visual synecdoche – writ large by Zola's apparent repetition compulsion – in which the mine is imaged as a gigantic living beast feasting on the blood of the miners. It is a kind of land version of the biblical Leviathan. At various times, the mine is described as having intestines, bowels, lungs, and mouths; it "swallowed men by mouthfuls of twenty or thirty" (1.III.25): "For half an hour the shaft went on devouring … with more or less greedy gulps … but without stopping, always hungry, with its giant intestines capable of digesting a nation" (1.III.26). In a sense, the mine becomes a metonymy for predatory capitalism that is devouring all the poor in France.

Zola, who wrote art criticism, was influenced by the painters of his time, especially Manet and the Impressionists who observed the contemporary world in all its detail and wanted to capture the ephemeral moment in a scene rather than, as say Ingres would, a polished and finished tableau. Like them, he was, as Anka Muhlstein puts it, interested "in capturing the fleeting moment in which an artist depicts on canvas his contemporaries exactly as they are, with their clothing, their gestures, their way of life."[7] Like many of the painters, he noticed the effects of the Industrial Revolution and how it undermines community and creates loneliness and isolation. Not only in *Germinal* but also in other novels such as *L'Assommoir* (1877) and *Nana* (1880), he especially focused on those left behind by so-called progress. Manet's *Nana* (1877) derives from the young Nana who first appeared in *L'Assommoir*.

No sooner do we enter into the imagined world of *Germinal* than Etienne sees the Voreux mine – playing on the French *vorace* (in English voracious) – as a living creature: "This pit, piled up in the bottom of a hollow, with its squat brick buildings, raising its chimney like a threatening horn, seemed to him to have the evil air of a gluttonous beast crouching there to devour the earth.... He could explain even the escapement of the pump, that thick, long breathing that went on without ceasing, and which seemed to be the monster's congested respiration" (1.I.7). As Zola closes Chapter I, the narrator underlines Etienne's impression: "And the Voreux, at the bottom of its hole, with its posture as of an evil beast, continued to crunch, breathing with a heavier and slower respiration, troubled by its painful digestion of human flesh" (1.I.14). The mine is an anthropomorphized monster, ingesting and digesting its contents; as the equipment lowers the men down through the monster's alimentary canal, "The cages rose and sank with the gliding movement of a nocturnal beast, always engulfing men, whom the throat of the whole seemed to drink" (1.III.30).

With its resonances and echoes of the beginning, Part Seven takes us back to Part One. As if to recall the Voreux as an untamed monster devouring all who enter and to anticipate the terrible deaths to come as a result of Souvarine's murderous re-rigging of the mine's safety controls, the narrator speaks of "the blood the Voreux mud had yet scarcely drunk up" (7.I.413). With references to mud, Zola emphasizes the Darwinian context – recall that Etienne has an interest in Darwin – suggesting that like prehistoric creatures, the miners are towards the bottom end of the evolutionary cycle.

When the Voreux collapses, due to the sabotage of Souvarine, its demise is described in terms of a monster dying – "the pit bleeding at the neck" (7.III.434) – even as it continues to wreak destruction on its victims, namely the men who cannot escape: "It was done for; the evil beast crouching in this hole, gorged with human flesh, was no longer breathing with its thick, long respiration. The Voreux had been swallowed whole by the abyss" (7.III.438). As the men "spread over the neighboring ground, ... the weather cock on the steeple creaked in the wind with a short, shrill cry, the only melancholy voice of these vast buildings which were about to die" (7.III.436).

The Voreux even devours the mine's horses, notably Bataille, who drowns in the catastrophe deliberately created by Souvarine: "[T]his pit was murdering him after having blinded him. The water which had pursued him was lashing him on the flanks and biting him on the crupper" (7.V.456).

Once the Voreux is dead, it is replaced by another monster ready "to swallow down men[,] ... rows of men trotting with faces bent towards the earth, like cattle led to the slaughterhouse" (7.VI.475, 478). Etienne "found the monster again swallowing his daily ration of human flesh, the cages rising and plunging, engulfing their burden of men, without ceasing, with the facile gulp of a voracious giant" (7.VI.475).

Germinal as Family Drama

The narrator describes the residents of the Company's houses in the Settlement as "inmates." Often living in houses filled with children, no one has any privacy. No detail of family life – sex or bathroom or intimate conversation – remains hidden, even from the youngsters.

Zola is much better in the architectonics of *Germinal* than in either stylistic nuances or editing iterative and overly detailed passages, especially on the intricacies of mining. He wisely chooses one family as his focal point. When the novel begins, ten people live in Maheu's and Maheude's tiny house. In addition to Maheu and Maheude are Maheu's father and seven children. All but the four youngest (one of whom is a "humpback") go down into the mines. The children range from the twenty-one-year-old Zacharie – who has two children of his own with a girl-friend – to the baby Estelle and include the fifteen-year-old Catherine, who is reaching sexual maturity, and Jeanlin, who is physically repulsive and morally deficient.

The Maheu family has worked in the mines for 106 years. Bonnemort – whose nickname derives from his having been three times pulled out of near-death situations in the mine – speaks of the mine, in the opening chapter when Etienne first meets him, as if it were a punishing God whose ways are unknown to humans: "His voice assumed a tone of religious awe; it was as if he were speaking of an inaccessible tabernacle containing a sated and crouching god to whom they had given all their flesh and whom they had never seen" (1.I.13). The miners live in an insular world barely touched by traditional Christianity, notwithstanding the presence of the Catholic Church. Superstition, ritualized customs, animal desires and needs – all exacerbated by poverty – form the basis of the mine's Settlement culture.

When we look back on our reading, we see that Chapter II.i introducing the family is important. The novel grew on me as I reread it and I began to root for Catherine – the barely pubescent fifteen-year-old who is pushed into sex by Chaval before she is ready, even while a more traditional kind of human intimacy would be possible with Etienne – and Maheu, who, despite drinking too much on occasion, works with dignity, and his wife Maheude.

Although bullied and abused by Chaval, Catherine defends him from Etienne's drunken attack on the day of the rampage when Etienne has become a kind of lord of misrule: "And she planted herself before her man to defend him, forgetting the blows, forgetting the life of misery, lifted up by the idea that she belonged to him since he had taken her, and that it was a shame for her when they so crushed him" (5.IV.311). Zola is aware how the miners are reduced to bestial behavior and that Catherine's defense of Chaval is not motivated by love but by the most primitive kind of loyalty.

Gradually we learn how the family lives and survives. Zola's narrator strongly underlines the juxtaposition between the dignity – and monogamist intimacy – of Maheu and his wife Maheude, and the sexual casualness and promiscuity of many of the Settlement women. He also highlights and contrasts two opposing responses to the mining and Settlement world: the indifference of the family's eldest son, Zacharie, and the criminal sociopathology of the next son, Jeanlin.

With one pampered daughter, the Grégoire family is the Maheu family counterpart. For the senior Grégoire, the mine is not a monster but a god to be worshipped for providing comfort to his family: "God himself was not so solid. Then with this religious faith was mixed profound gratitude towards an investment, which for a century had supported the family in doing nothing. It was like a divinity of their own, whom their egotism surrounded with a kind of worship, the benefactor of the hearth" (2.I.73).

Zola's narrator stresses the grotesque distinction between, on the one hand, the comfort, frivolity, and superficiality of the Grégoires and their bourgeois counterparts, the Hennebeau family, and, on the other hand, the misery of the Maheu–Maheude family. The Hennebeaus wish to marry their nephew Paul Negrel to the Grégoire daughter, Cécile.

The haves seem to be oblivious to the disparity between their lives and those of the miners and to be narcissistically immersed in their own pleasures and comforts. For example, Madame Hennebeau, the quintessence of self-gratification, "was indignant at the ingratitude of the people … [who] were lodged and warmed and cared for at the expense of the Company!" (4.I.193).

As the miners develop a collective consciousness and go on strike, the transformation of Maheu into a voice of protest is a major focus of the novel. The idea that the poor will come together has a mythic dimension derived in part from Marxism but dating back to the French Revolution. As Irving Howe puts it, "It is the myth of the people and, more particularly, of the proletariat. They who had merely suffered and at times erupted in blind rebellion; they who had been prey to but not part of society; they who had found no voice in the cultures of the past – they now emerge from the sleep of history and begin the task of collective self-formation."[8] But what begins as brave and noble action in defiance of the mine owners and the support of the state degenerates into a mob action accompanied by senseless loss of life.

In the last section, Maheude returns to the mine and concedes to Etienne, in one of Zola's most effectively poignant passages, that there is nothing but the mine for her young children, Lénore and Henri: "What would you have? They after the others. They have all been done for there; now it's their turn" (7.VI.478).

Sexuality in *Germinal*

Not only sexuality but also reproduction is rampant in the Settlement environment where humans are reduced to work animals and there is barely enough food to survive. Without sensible contraception, family size exceeds economic means, and women and children need to work in the mines to help families survive. The Maheu family needs the income of their children before Etienne becomes a lodger. Yet, paradoxically, in deterministic concatenation where early death is quite likely, the population of the poor is controlled by the living conditions, hunger, disease, and inadequate safety provisions at the mine.

The miners' lives revolve around sex – and sex without any more thought of contraception than animals would have – and alcohol and an occasional feast day when they have rabbit. We might note that by the 1870s when the book was published, pharmacies were selling chemical suppositories, vaginal sponges, and medicated tampons, but this is the 1860s when some women used the less than fully effective rubber "womb veil." But of course even if the the miners, their wives, and lovers were aware of these products, they didn't have discretionary funds to buy them. We see how food is traded for sex by the grocer Maigrat and how begging is necessary to survive, as when Maheude visits the wealthy Grégoires, owners of the mine.

Criticizing humans for pretending they are less animalistic than they think they are, Zola urges us to see sex as part of nature's rhythms. His characters flout the sexual conventions inculcated by Catholicism. Since poverty has reduced humans to their lowest common denominator of almost animal existence, why, he asks, shouldn't they have sexual pleasure?

But Zola has a leering side and enjoys describing the frequent coupling that takes place in the fields or in the depths of the mines as if it was the only antidote other than alcohol for the misery of the miners' lives. Indeed, Zola seems to enjoy describing adultery and promiscuity. Pierron's wife sleeps with a captain named Dansaert, and Levaque's wife sleeps with Bouteloup and the manager Hennebeau. Meanwhile, Hennebeau's wife looks down on him and has sex with others but not him, including her nephew, Paul Negrel. At times Zola's narrator – a surrogate for Zola – links sexual frustration and jealousy with small-minded behavior, both in Hennebeau's case and in Etienne's.

Zola's narrator captures the pathos as well as lewdness of the very active Mouquette, who makes a strong play for Etienne, for whom she does have feelings. He is accepting of – if not voyeuristically enjoying – Mouquette's enjoyment of sex: "[S]he was quite capable of being with both the trammers [coal workers] at once" (1.IV.41).

He also seems to be rather tolerant of male desires intruding upon women's space, for the women often have little to say in choosing sexual partners. Isn't Zola's narrator describing what we now would call rape? "It was the element of bestiality which breathed in the pit, the sudden desire of the male, when a miner met one of these girls on all fours, with her flanks in the air and her hips bursting through her boy's breeches" (1.IV.41).

Just as Etienne would be one of the bourgoisie at times, M. Hennebeau thinks – comically to Zola's narrator and his readers – how pleasant it would be to live as simply and promiscuously as a miner: "He would willingly have made [the miners] a present of his large salary to possess their hard skin and their facility of coupling without regret. Why could he not seat them at his table and stuff them with his pheasant, while he went to fornicate behind the hedges, to tumble over the girls, making fun of those who had tumbled them over before him!" (5.V.324).

Zola's Artistry and the Kind of Fiction He Writes; Strengths and Weaknesses

According to Georg Lukács, Zola depicts the "*outer* trappings" of life, such as the mines. These trappings "form a gigantic backdrop in front of which tiny, haphazard people move to and fro and live their haphazard lives. Zola could never achieve what the truly great realists Balzac, Tolstoy, or Dickens accomplished: to present social institutions as human relationships and social objects as the vehicles of such relationships. Man and his surroundings are always sharply divided in all Zola's works."[9] As Irving Howe notes, Zola finally doesn't fulfill Lukács's Marxist paradigms because Zola is "mechanistic and passive, lacking in revolutionary dynamism."[10] But Howe does not regard this necessarily as a shortcoming: "We have here a confrontation between a writer's honesty and an ideologue's tendentiousness, between Zola's myth of a collective entry into consciousness and Lukács's pseudomyth of 'socialist realism.'"[11]

What I want to stress is, as Howe implies, that Zola's vision is more complex than his ideology, and that he cannot simplify human behavior into dogma, whether it be determinism, Marxism, or Darwinism. In his graphic depiction of sexuality, violence, and human exploitation, we find that reductive versions of all the foregoing dogmas coexist, along with echoes of Charles Baudelaire's dark vision in *Les Fleurs du Mal* and anticipation of the Decadent movement that is epitomized by Joris-Karl Huysmans.

Henry James combines grudging admiration and disdain for Zola, whose novels have little if any of the subtlety and delicacy for which James strove: "Grant – and the generalization may be emphatic – that the shallow and the simple are *all* the population of [Zola's] richest and most crowded pictures, and that his 'psychology' in a psychological age, remains thereby comparatively coarse.... [Nevertheless] we derive from Zola at his best, the concomitant impression of the solid.... [He is] never faithless for a moment to his own stiff standard.... It is in the great lusty game he plays with the shallow and the simple that Zola's mastery resides."[12]

At times, *Germinal* cries out for greater selectivity, understatement, irony, and subtler focalization. The reader experiences a kind of over-determinism in the form of mind-numbing descriptions of the coal mining, often with technical terms. Yet we need to acknowledge that the sufferings of the Settlement people are effectively foregrounded. As we read we do feel for the individual lives. Often, the reader's mind glazes over the technical terms and detailed descriptions and moves onto the characters, perhaps the most interesting of whom is the barely pubescent Catherine, fifteen years old when the novel opens, whose strong but slight body "contrasted with the sallow tint of her face, already spoilt by constant washing with black soap" (1.II.15) and whose gums already have a "chlorotic pallor" (1.II.16). She is responsible for organizing the household at 4 a.m. and she herself goes into the mines, where she is also extraordinarily competent. Yet she awakens "with a look of painful distress and weariness which seemed to spread over the whole of her" (1.II.16).

It may be that we need to read *Germinal* at a few sittings in a relatively short time frame – rather than over quite a few sittings – to maintain our sympathy with Zola's characters. If we do so, several central characters – Etienne, Souvarine, Maheu–Maheude, two of their children, namely, Catherine and Jeanlin – are truly memorable.

As Dominique Jullien writes: "Naturalism involved the application to literature of two scientific principles: determinism, or the belief that character, temperament, and ultimately behavior are determined by the forces of heredity, environment and the historical moment; and the experimental method, which entailed the objective recording of precise data in controlled conditions."[13] In other words, given A, B, and C, Etienne, Maheu, and Maheude will behave in such and such a way. Among the problems with Zola's hyperbolic, yet reductive, naturalism are its iteration and lack of complex character psychology. Thus despite Zola's narrator's occasionally ironic take on Etienne, the contemporary reader – conditioned perhaps by James, Proust, and Joyce – on occasion seeks more complexity, more awareness, more playfulness, and more variety from the narrator. Yet the characters of *Germinal* at times do overflow the canals of A, B, and C and surprise the reader, and possibly the author.

Unlike when rereading the Balzac, Stendhal, and Flaubert texts that we have been discussing, we do not discover upon rereading *Germinal* a new underlying subtlety that is the stuff of great fiction. What Bakhtin calls the dialogic imagination – diverse voices representing ways of seeing and imagining – is missing. Too much of a dogmatic tract informs the pages. What Zola lacks is a sense of humor; even the irony towards Etienne is heavy-handed. Yet, as Irving Howe notes: "What remains vital in the naturalistic novel as Zola wrote it in France and Dreiser in America is not the theoretical gropings toward an assured causality; what remains vital is the massed detail of the fictional worlds they establish, the patience – itself a form of artistic scruple – with which they record the suffering of their time."[14] In other words, as with all significant novels, we need to allow *Germinal* to teach us how to read it.

What Zola is interested in is how excruciatingly deleterious social and economic conditions undermine the quality of human life, and in *Germinal* his focus is on the coal-mining industry, both its victims and perpetrators. *Germinal* is polemical and never playful. His narrator is rather self-righteous, angry, and sure of himself. When we think of Zola, we do not think of the stylistic elegance of a nuanced narrator hovering over the story. We think instead of characters within the story who are hampered or damaged by economic conditions.

Thinking of how Barthes and Nabokov in their own ways have liberated texts from the need for a reader responding to a structure of effects – that is, from the need for responding to thematic strategies and character portraits shaped by an author to elicit from readers particular effects – Michael Wood writes, "Barthes's view of writing liberates the reader; Nabokov's view of reading celebrates the writer."[15] But, even assuming what Wood describes happens to some degree – and I am doubtful that it ever happens more than partially – Zola is a far different kind of writer and he writes for a different kind of reader.

Germinal is an expose in the tradition of investigatory journalism that shines a light on terrible conditions. We might think of Upton Sinclair's muckraking *The Jungle*. Zola's narrator is enraged by what he knows. To an extent, the narrator lacks balance and at times gentleness. Rather than a room with a view, we have a fortress without another perspective. Describing a world where nature is as violent and unforgiving as man-made turbulence, the narrative voice is harsh and abrasive and revels in describing sex without love and work in inhuman conditions.

What works best in *Germinal* are the often eloquent descriptions of human misery in the Maheu household where people's lives – as is the case elsewhere in this novel – are reduced to the lowest common denominator. According to Jullien, "Insufficient hygiene and sanitation, combined with malnutrition, respiratory diseases, unsafe working conditions, and alcoholism, accounted for the low life expectancy (twenty-four years) and the high infant mortality rate (40 per cent of children died before their fifth birthday) in the mining regions of France."[16]

The Structure of *Germinal*

Germinal is a fast read, but it makes its points in relentless detail. Zola focuses on one place and a limited cast of characters. Zola is a master of tempo and pacing. His unit is not the sentence, like Flaubert or Proust, but, like Stendhal and Hardy, the paragraph and even the chapter. His strength is the overall, almost stately, control of the architectonics of *Germinal*'s form. He is excellent at imagining vast, complex spatial arrangements of the mine and the Settlement, but also the small spatial arrangements of a house or bar or part of the mine.

Taking place in the late 1860s, Zola's seven-part novel is made of building blocks that constitute an indictment of the mining industry and of the way capitalism exploits its workers. His structure oscillates between the macrocosmic and microcosmic. In Part One, the naïve Etienne arrives at the mine and learns about conditions there as well as in the Settlement provided by the mine for its workers. Etienne decides to stay, in part because of his interest in Catherine, the daughter of the novel's central family headed by the father Maheu and the mother Maheude.

Part Two introduces the comfortable bourgeois world of the mine owners, the Grégoires, and presents a history of their ownership. It also focuses on Etienne's discovery of the sexual hothouse that is part of the Settlement; Mouquette has been active since the age of ten. Etienne sees Chaval and Catherine copulate for the first time in a scene showing what we now would call rape.

In Part Three, Etienne moves in with the Maheu–Maheude family and becomes increasingly radicalized by what he observes in the mine and the Settlement. Zola dramatizes his debates with the more moderate Rasseneur and the anarchist Souvarine about what can be done; they all agreed that "[O]ne way or another it would have to come to an end, either quietly by laws, by an understanding in good fellowship, or like savages by burning everything and devouring one another" (3.I.133).

We might recall the two-edged meaning of the title *Germinal*. During the month of Germinal in "*an* (year) III (1795), there were bread riots in Paris, and popular protests brought down the government of the National Convention."[17] But Germinal also suggests the rebirth of plants in the spring, as well as revolution; as Jullien reminds us, "Germinal was the name of the 'seedtime' month of the Revolutionary calendar (March 21–April 19)."[18]

The rereader understands that Etienne has vague utopian impulses without a full understanding of the means or difficulties of realizing his hopes: "But now the miner was waking up down there, germinating in the earth just as a grain germinates; and some fine day he would spring up in the midst of the fields: yes, men would spring up, an army of men who would reestablish justice" (3.III.154). The image builds on Etienne's awareness of late spring: "Grass was invading the pit-bank, flowers were covering the meadows, a whole life was germinating and pushing up from this earth beneath which he was groaning in misery and fatigue" (3.I.128). Whatever the intended thrust of this metaphor, the novel offers a more skeptical perspective on the inevitability of apocalyptic splendor, or even glorious victory, for the suffering, downtrodden miners.

In political novels, characters are defined by social and economic issues. Etienne's political awakening is in response to conditions he sees and experiences. At this point in *Germinal*, Etienne's view is midway between the moderate Rasseneur, who owns a pub, and the anarchist Souvarine, whose credo is: "Set fire to the four corners of the towns, mow down the people, level everything, and when there is nothing more of this rotten world left standing, perhaps a better one will grow up in its place" (3.I.132). Follower of the anarchist Bakunin, Souvarine is – Zola knew and wanted the reader to know – a political psychotic who is misusing the growth metaphor that recalls the title.

Etienne is becoming a leader, something the narrator regards with some irony as Etienne becomes pleased with himself and enjoys his own voice. Even as the narrator tells us briefly in the second paragraph of 4.I that the strike has begun, Part Four opens, like Part Two, with a look at the comfortable bourgeois life, this time at the manager Hennebeau and his adulterous wife. Even as Maheu emerges as an articulate leader of the suppressed miners, Etienne is still the dominant figure presiding at an open-air meeting.

Zola's narrator shows us the terrible costs of the strike in terms of hunger and misery. The miners sell treasured objects for a pittance in order to have money for food. In Part Five the strikers embark on destructive behavior, smashing the mines and degenerating into a savage mob. At this point, the narrator distances himself from the political uprising. His irony gives way to disgust when, in the last chapter of Part Five, he describes the "frightful mutilation" – the castration after death – of the predatory food shop owner Maigrat, who traded food for sex, and the women marching behind Mother Brulé who is holding Maigrat's genitals, a "lump[,] … that pitiful flesh [on a stick] … like a waste piece of meat on a butcher's stall" (5.VI.338). Violence begets violence. Axe in hand, Etienne had begun the process that ended in Maigrat falling to his death.

Part Six includes Zola's dramatization of the Law of Unintended Consequences in the form of the strike's effect. The narrator presents a scene of Maheude's young children begging – something she said would never happen (6.II.364) – and ends with troops firing on the strikers and Maheu being killed.

Part Seven focuses on the effects of Souvarine's sabotaging the Voreux mine, including Catherine's death because of the mine's collapse. With Gothic sections recalling the world of *Wuthering Heights*, Part Seven dramatizes the collapse of the mine brought on by Souvarine's treachery and his sitting on a knoll cynically watching the catastrophe he has caused. The subsequent rescue is a compelling read, with its inclusion of the deaths of Catherine as well as Zacharie, Maheude's eldest son, and the death of Cécile Grégoire.

In one of the most striking passages of the novel, one which casts class struggle as a primordial and inevitable conflict, Zola describes the moment before Cécile is killed in rage by Maheu's father Bonnemort, who has metamorphosed into a coal-infested psychotic after his stroke: "Fascinated, they remained opposite each other – she flourishing, plump and fresh from the long idleness and sated comfort of her race; he swollen with water, with the pitiful ugliness of a foundered beast, destroyed from father to son by a century of work and hunger" (7.IV.452). If one recalls the sentence during the mob's riot when Bonnemort, in a moment of depravity when he is fascinated by her "white neck," grabs hold of Cécile, his murderous behavior is less a surprise: "He seemed drunk from hunger, stupefied by his long misery, suddenly arousing himself from the resignation of half-a-century, under the influence of no one knew what malicious impulse" (5.VI.332).

Zola proposes a reductive version of the future as it might be imagined by the anarchist Souvarine, even while realizing that what is imagined is destructive folly that would leave nothing to build on: "It was the red vision of the revolution, which would one day inevitably carry them all away, on some bloody evening at the end of the century…. Fires would flame; they would not leave standing one stone of the towns; they would return to the savage life of the woods, after the great rut, the great feast-day, when the poor in one night would reduce women to leanness, and rich men's cellars to emptiness. There would be nothing left" (5.V.321). Because Zola has dramatized for us the grim reality when collective action degenerates into a homicidal mob or when someone like Souvarine takes it upon himself to maniacally destroy, we understand that such simplistic ideology is a false path that Zola intended to be ironic. To a contemporary reader drenched in twentieth-century history, the ending is grimly prophetic.

Zola's (Sometimes) Ironic Narrator

What sometimes alleviates the pontifical tone and the stiff political speeches – notably Etienne's dialogues with Souvarine and Rasseneur (and the latter's more radical wife) – and the equally wooden interior monologues of Etienne is the narrator's irony towards reductive solutions and self-inflating behavior. When Etienne begins to become pleased with himself in response to his growing influence, the narrator, undoubtedly expecting the reader to recall Etienne's desperation at the novel's outset when he is starving and without work after hitting his boss, remarks with something of a smirk: "The whole settlement grouped around him. The satisfaction of his self-love was delicious; he became intoxicated with this first enjoyment of popularity…. His face changed; he became serious and took on airs, while his growing ambition inflamed his theories and pushed him to ideas of violence" (3.III.159).

While the narrator admires Etienne's idealism and his feeling for the plight of his fellow miners – Etienne "had a sudden vision of disaster; of dying children and sobbing mothers" (4.III.214) – the narrator can be ironic about Etienne's naïveté and narcissism. Thus the narrator facetiously notes: "[T]he joy of [Etienne's] being leader, of seeing himself obeyed, even to sacrifice, the enlarged dream of his power, the evening of triumph" (4.III.215) as well as the way that Etienne as "the unquestioned leader … gave forth oracles" (4.III.208). He also mocks how Etienne "was climbing a ladder … entering this execrated middle class" (4.III.208). The narrator's irony carries over into the naïveté of the workers who for a time respond to Etienne's every word, an irony that compares their faith with that of "blind" religious believers who are hypnotized by fantasies of heaven: "There was an absolute confidence in spite of everything, a religious faith, the blind gift of a population of believers…. They saw again over there, when their eyes were dimmed by weakness, the ideal city of their dream, but now growing near and seeming to be real, with its population of brothers, its golden age of labour and meals in common" (4.III.207).

The novel is more complex in those passages where the narrator's distance from Etienne oscillates because he regards Etienne's politics and rabble rousing as naïve and reductive. Zola does depict Etienne as a fallible human being, often lacking in self-knowledge, prone to the family weakness for alcohol, and feeling depressed that the strike might fail. Etienne recalls his "savage drunkenness" on the day of the strikers' destructive rampage, including his abortive effort to kill Chaval (6.I.346).

In part because of Etienne's feelings for Catherine and his disgust with his drunkenly attacking Chaval, he assumes "a feeling of superiority" towards the miners and desires to live like "one of those bourgeois whom he execrated" (6.I.346), even as he lives in Jeanlin's underground burrow – "his cavern of villainy" – and avoids starvation by eating the fruits of Jeanlin's thievery. In a sense Etienne has become a secret sharer with Jeanlin, the prepubescent and grotesque psychotic who is described as "a savage" (6.I.345) and who bullies his friends and thinks of destructive and anti-social behavior as "jokes" (5.IV.307; 5.IV.309).

Conclusion

If one understands what kind of novel *Germinal* is – namely a naturalistic novel of purpose – it will be more satisfying. But this is not to deny that the novel contains a great deal of repetition of the physical setting and working conditions. Reading Etienne's muddled interior monologues about politics – many of which cry out for clarity and tightening – as well as reading about his intermittent self-doubt punctuated by snobbery and his infatuation with Catherine can become laborious. Before the denouement, when several important characters are killed by the soldiers, Zola drags the strike out longer than aesthetically necessary until the presentation of the strike seems iterative and prolix.

Zola's characterization could be far more efficient; we know Catherine is abused by Chaval without being told countless times, just as we know without countless examples that Jeanlin is a borderline psychotic. Characters are not only underdeveloped, they are also generally one-dimensional and predictable. We also tire of the Grégoire family's complacency. To be sure, there are occasional surprises when characters change, as when Maheude becomes a zealot after her husband has been killed, before lapsing back into resignation, if not depression.

The last chapter's alleged optimism – claimed by Jullien and other critics – and the germination imagery (which may be the source of Lawrence's similar image at the close of *The Rainbow*) are called into question by the horrors that preceded it. Formally, the horrors of the mine and reduction of life to a struggle for survival undermine the last optative paragraphs, especially the concluding sentences, with their focus on growth and vegetation: "On every side seeds were swelling, stretching out, cracking the plain filled by the need of heat and light. An overflow of sap was mixed with whispering voices.... Men were springing forth, a black avenging army, germinating slowly in the furrows, growing towards the harvests of the next century, and this germination would soon overturn the earth" (7.VI.484). The closing rhetoric has not been supported by the plot.

Yet generations of readers remember the pages of human exploitation, disregard for safety, hunger, violence, death, and loveless sex. What makes *Germinal* not only worth reading, but also a minor masterpiece in spite of its faults, is the unforgettable, compelling, and graphic dark vision of poverty and misery defined by life in the mines.

Study Questions for *Germinal*

1. Does the novel fulfill Zola's goals as defined in the quoted passage from "The Experimental Novel"?
2. How is *Germinal* both a polemical and documentary novel? Do these genres work in tandem for the reader or are they sometimes at cross-purposes?
3. Is Zola ambivalent and ironic about revolutionary behavior? Why (and when) does collective action degenerate into a brute mob?
4. Are the major characters fully realized? Which of the characters are most compelling and most complex?
5. Acknowledging that this is a translation, how would you describe the stylistic features of Zola's prose in *Germinal*?
6. Why does one read this novel at a faster pace than most other novels in this study?
7. How does the seven-part structure function to shape your reading experience?
8. As we read *Germinal*, do we reference contemporary events more than we do for our other novels in this study and, if so, why?
9. What is the narrator's attitude to Etienne?
10. What are the implications of the title? Do you leave the novel with a sense of possible rebirth?

Notes

1. Anka Muhlstein, "Paris: The Thrill of the Modern," trans. Anthony Shugaar, *NYR* 60:8 (May 9, 2013), 14–15.
2. Emile Zola, "The Experimental Novel," in *The Experimental Novel and Other Essays*," trans. Belle M. Sherman (New York: Haskell House, 1964), 8–9.
3. Dominique Jullien, "Introduction," in Emile Zola, *Germinal*, trans. Havelock Ellis, intro. and notes by Dominique Jullien (New York: Barnes and Noble, 2005), xxii. All quotations from the text are taken from this edition.
4. William Pfaff, "Pure, Purifying, and Evil," *NYR* 60:11 (June 20, 2013), 58–59; see p. 58.
5. David Quammen, *The Reluctant Mr. Darwin* (New York: Norton, 2006), 206–207.
6. Quammen, *The Reluctant Mr. Darwin*, 228–229.

7. Muhlstein, "Paris: The Thrill of the Modern," 15.
8. Irving Howe, "Afterword," in Emile Zola, *Germinal*, trans. Stanley and Eleanor Hochman (New York: New American Library, 1970), 434.
9. Georg Lukács, *Studies in European Realism* (London: Hillway, 1950), 92–93.
10. Howe, "Afterword," 435.
11. Howe, "Afterword," 435.
12. Quoted in *Germinal*, 503–504.
13. Jullien, "Introduction," *Germinal*, xviii.
14. Howe, "Afterword," 430.
15. Michael Wood, "A Passage to England," *NYR* 57:4 (March 11, 2010), 8–10; see p. 8.
16. *Germinal*, 485.
17. *Germinal*, 485.
18. *Germinal*, 485.

Selected Bibliography
(Including Works Cited)

Primary Works

Balzac, Honoré de. *Père Goriot*. Trans. Burton Raffel. Ed. Peter Brooks (Norton Critical Edition). New York: Norton, 1980.

Balzac, Honoré de. *Père Goriot*. Trans. Henry Reed. New York: New American Library (Signet edition), 1962.

Cervantes, Miguel de. *Don Quixote*. Trans. Edith Grossman. New York: HarperCollins, 2003.

Cervantes, Miguel de. *Don Quijote*. Trans. Burton Raffel. Ed. Diana de Armas Wilson (Norton Critical Edition). New York: Norton, 1999.

Dostoevsky, Fyodor. *Notes from Underground*. Ed. with an introduction by Robert G. Durgy. Trans. Serge Shiskoff. New York: Thomas Y. Crowell, 1969.

Dostoevsky, Fyodor. *Notes from Underground*. Trans. Richard Pevear and Larissa Volokhonsky. New York: Vintage, 1994.

Dostoevsky, Fyodor. *Crime and Punishment*. Trans. Richard Pevear and Larissa Volokhonsky. New York: Vintage, 1993.

Dostoevsky, Fyodor. *Crime and Punishment*. Ed. George Gibian (Norton Critical Edition). New York: Norton, 1964.

Dostoevsky, Fyodor. *The Brothers Karamazov*. Trans. Richard Pevear and Larissa Volokhonsky. New York: Farrar, Straus and Giroux, 1990; New York: Vintage, 1993.

Flaubert, Gustave. *Madame Bovary*. Trans. Paul de Man (Norton Critical Edition). New York: Norton, 1965.

Flaubert, Gustave. *Sentimental Education*. Intro. and trans. Robert Baldick. New York and London: Penguin, 1964.

Reading the European Novel to 1900: A Critical Study of Major Fiction from Cervantes' Don Quixote *to Zola's* Germinal, First Edition. Daniel R. Schwarz.
© 2014 John Wiley & Sons, Ltd. Published 2014 by John Wiley & Sons, Ltd.

Stendhal. *The Charterhouse of Parma*. Trans. Richard Howard. New York: Modern Library, 2000.

Stendhal. *Courrier Anglais*, II. Paris: Le Divan, 1935.

Stendhal. *Red and Black*. Trans. and ed. Robert Adams (Norton Critical Edition). New York: W. W. Norton, 1969 (first edition).

Tolstoy, Leo. *Anna Karenina*. Trans. Richard Pevear and Larissa Volokhonsky. New York and London: Penguin, 2000–2001.

Tolstoy, Leo. *War and Peace*. Trans. Richard Pevear and Larissa Volokhonsky. New York: Alfred A. Knopf, 2007.

Zola, Emile. *The Experimental Novel and Other Essays*. Trans. Belle M. Sherman. New York: Haskell House, 1964.

Zola, Emile. *Germinal*. Trans. Havelock Ellis. Intro. and notes by Dominique Jullien. New York: Barnes and Noble, 2005.

Selective Biographical and Critical Works

Achebe, Chinua. "An Image of Africa: Racism in Conrad's 'Heart of Darkness,'" *Massachusetts Review* 18 (1977). Rpt. in *Heart of Darkness, An Authoritative Text, Background and Sources Criticism*. 1961. 3rd ed. Ed. Robert Kimbrough. London: W. W. Norton, 1988, pp. 251–261.

Bakhtin, M. M. *The Dialogic Imagination: Four Essays*. Trans. Caryl Emerson and Michael Holquist. Ed. Michael Holquist. Austin: University of Texas Press, 1981.

Bakhtin, M. M. *Problems of Dostoevsky's Poetics*. Ed. and trans. Caryl Emerson. Intro. Wayne Booth. Minneapolis: University of Minnesota Press, 1984.

Banville, John. "The Prime of James Wood," *NYR* 55:18 (Nov. 20, 2008), 85–88.

Bayley, John. *Tolstoy and the Novel*. London: Chatto and Windus, 1966.

Begley, Adam. "Stendhal in Parma, Italy," *New York Times*, Dec. 23, 2009.

Bell, Julian. "Manet: 'Sudden Sensuous Dazzle,'" *NYR* 58:12 (July 14, 2011), 16–19.

Bell, Julian. "The Angel of the Bizarre," *NYR* 60:10 (June 6, 2013), 24–26.

Benfey, Christopher. "Bend Sinister in Wales," *NYR* 60:13 (Aug. 15, 2013), 40–41.

Bermann, Sandra. "Introduction." In *Nation, Language, and the Ethics of Translation*. Ed. Sandra Bermann and Michael Wood. Princeton, NJ: Princeton University Press, 2005.

Bermann, Sandra. "Teaching in – and about – Translation," *Profession 2010*, 82–90.

Blackmur, R. P. *Eleven Essays in the European Novel*. New York: Harcourt, Brace and World, 1964.

Brooks, David. "Human Nature Today," *New York Times*, June 25, 2009.

Butterfield, Andrew. "Titian and the Rebirth of Tragedy," *NYR* 57:20 (Dec. 23, 2010), 16–21.

Campbell, James. "Creative Misreading," *New York Times Book Review*, June 12, 2011, 35.

Chabon, Michael. "What to Make of *Finnegans Wake*?" *NYR* 59:12 (July 12, 2012), 45–48.

Coetzee, J. M. "Storm Over Young Goethe," *NYR* 59:7 (April 26, 2012), 17–22.

Cohen, Patricia. "Next Big Thing in English: Knowing They Know That You Know," *New York Times*, March 31, 2010; http://www.nytimes.com/2010/04/01/books/01lit.html?src=me&ref=arts (accessed February 14, 2014).

Conley, Verena. "Living in Translation," *Profession 2010*, 18–24.

Culler, Jonathan. *Flaubert: The Uses of Uncertainty*. Ithaca, NY: Cornell University Press, 1974.

Derrida, Jacques. "Plato's Pharmacy." In *Dissemination*. Trans. Barbara Johnson. Chicago: University of Chicago Press, 1981.

Echevarría, Roberto González (ed.). *Cervantes' Don Quixote: A Casebook*. Oxford: Oxford University Press, 2005.

Ferguson, Frances. "Ralph Rader on the Literary History of the Novel," *Narrative* 18:1 (Jan. 2010), 91–103.

Frank, Joseph. *Dostoevsky: The Stir of Liberation, 1860–1865*. Princeton, NJ: Princeton University Press, 1986.

Frank, Joseph. *Dostoevsky: The Miraculous Years, 1865–1871*. Princeton, NJ: Princeton University Press, 1995.

Frank, Joseph. "The Millennium & Dostoevsky: An Exchange," reply by Aileen Kelly, *NYR* 50:15 (Oct. 9, 2003); http://www.nybooks.com/articles/archives/2003/oct/09/the-millennium-dostoevsky-an-exchange (accessed February 14, 2014).

Greenblatt, Stephen. "The Lonely Gods," *NYR* 57:11 (June 23, 2011), 6–10.

Grossman, Edith. *Why Translation Matters*. New Haven, CT: Yale University Press, 2010.

Heath, Stephen. *Flaubert: Madame Bovary*. New York: Cambridge University Press, 1992.

Howard, Richard. "Duet for Two Pens," *New York Times*, April 8, 2010; http://www.nytimes.com/2010/04/11/books/review/Howard-t.html (accessed February 14, 2014).

Howe, Irving. "Afterword." In Emile Zola, *Germinal*. Trans. Stanley and Eleanor Hochman. New York: New American Library, 1970.

James, Henry. *The Future of the Novel: Essays on The Art of Fiction*. New York: Vintage, 1956.

Johnson, Ken. "Mockery, Alive and Well Through the Ages," *New York Times*, Sept. 16, 2011.

Johnson, Ken. "Unfiltered Images, Turning Perceptions Upside Down," *New York Times*, Aug. 26, 2011.

Judt, Tony. "The Glory of the Rails," *NYR* 57:20 (Dec. 23, 2010), 60–61.

Klinkenborg, Verlyn. "Some Thoughts on the Pleasures of Being a Re-Reader," *New York Times*, May 29, 2009.

Lewontin, Richard. "Why Darwin?" *NYR* 56:9 (May 29, 2009), 19–22.

Lodge, David. "The Pre-Postmodernist," *New York Times*, Jan. 29, 2010; http://www.nytimes.com/2010/01/30/opinion/30lodge.html (accessed February 14, 2014).

Lopate, Philip. "The Best German Novelist of His Time," *NYR* 58:3 (Feb. 14, 2011), 35–38.

Lukács, Georg. *Studies in European Realism*. London: Hillway, 1950.

Lyall, Sarah. "Booker Prize Winner's Jewish Question," *New York Times*, Oct. 18, 2010.

Manet 1832–1883. New York: Metropolitan Museum of Art, 1983.

Mason, Wyatt. "David Mitchell, the Experimentalist," *New York Times Magazine*, June 27, 2010; http://www.nytimes.com/2010/06/27/magazine/27mitchell-t.html? pagewanted=1&8dpc (accessed February 14, 2014).

Mason, Wyatt. "Smarter than You Think," *NYR* 57:12 (July 15, 2010), 12.

Menand, Louis. "Regrets Only," *New Yorker*, Sept. 29, 2008, 80–90.

Mendelsohn, Daniel. "After Waterloo." Review of *The Charterhouse of Parma*, trans. Richard Howard (New York: Modern Library, 2000), *New York Times Book Review*, Aug. 29, 1999, 15–17; http://www.nytimes.com/1999/08/29/books/after-waterloo.html (accessed February 14, 2014).

Morris, Roderick Conway. "Weaving a More Modern Narrative," *IHT*, June 14, 2011.

Muhlstein, Anka. "Paris: The Thrill of the Modern." Trans. Anthony Shugaar. *NYR* 60:8 (May 9, 2013), 14–15.

Mumford, Lewis. *The Culture of Cities*. New York: Harcourt Brace and Company, 1938.

O'Brien, Geoffrey. "Giving Gogol His Head," *NYR* 57:7 (April 29, 2010), 20–23.

Pareles, John. "The Queen Pop Needs Her to Be," *New York Times*, May 22, 2011.

Parks, Tim. "Life at the Core," *NYR* 58:6 (April 7, 2011), 58–59.

Paz, Octavio. "Translation: Literature and Letters." In *Theories of Translation: An Anthology of Essays from Dryden to Derrida*. Ed. Rainer Schulte and John Biguenet. Chicago: University of Chicago Press, 1992, pp. 152–162.

Pfaff, William. "Pure, Purifying, and Evil," *NYR* 60:11 (June 20, 2013), 58–59.

Phelan, James and Richter, David. "The Literary Theoretical Contribution of Ralph Rader," *Narrative* 18:1 (Jan. 2010), 73–90.

Rader, Ralph. "Exodus and Return: Joyce's *Ulysses* and the Fiction of the Actual," *UTQ* 48 (Winter 1978/9), 149–171.

Roiphe, Katie. "The Naked and the Conflicted," *New York Times Book Review*, Jan. 3, 2010, 8.

Rowland, Ingrid D. "Having a Good Time with Ariosto," *NYR* 57:20 (Dec. 23, 2010), 86–91.

Sante, Luc. "In Search of Lost Paris," *NYR* 57:20 (Dec. 23, 2010), 54–57.

Sauerlander, Willibald. "The Genius of the Other Daumier." Trans. David Dollenmayer. *NYR* 60:3 (Feb. 21, 2013), 17–18.

Schwartz, Sanford. "Looking into the Beyond," *NYR* 58:10 (June 9, 2011), 26–27.

Simic, Charles. "Grass: The Gold and the Garbage," *NYR* 57:5 (March 24, 2011), 23–24.

Simic, Charles. "The Weird Beauty of the Well-Told Tale," *NYR* 58:9 (May 26, 2011), 18–19.

Smith, Roberta. "Sculpture in High Relief," *New York Times*, May 20, 2011.

Smith, Zadie. "Two Paths for the Novel," *NYR* 55:18 (Nov. 20, 2008), 89–94.

Venuti, Lawrence. "Translation, Empiricism, Ethics," *Profession 2010*, 72–81.

Vermeule, Blakey. "Room for Debate: Can 'Neuro Lit-Crit' Save the Humanities?" *New York Times*, April 5, 2010.

Wadler, Joyce. "Though Memory May Fail Us, What I Recall Was Truly Love," *New York Times*, Sept. 15, 2013.

Wheatcroft, Geoffrey. "Hello to All That!" *NYR* 58:11 (June 23, 2011), 30–32.

Winterson, Jeanette. "A Classic Passes 50," *New York Times*, Jan. 29, 2012.

Wood, James. *The Broken Estate: Essays on Literature and Belief.* New York: Random House, 1999.

Wood, James. *How Fiction Works.* New York: Farrar, Straus and Giroux, 2008.

Wood, James. "Movable Types: How 'War and Peace' Works," *New Yorker*, Nov. 27, 2007; http://www.newyorker.com/arts/critics/atlarge/2007/11/26/071126crat_atlarge_wood #ixzz1er49SpJH (accessed February 14, 2014).

Wood, James. "Reality Effects," *New Yorker* (Dec. 19 & 26, 2011), 134–138.

Wood, Michael. "A Passage to England," *NYR* 57:4 (March 11, 2010), 8–10.

Index

Reading the European Novel to 1900: A Critical Study of Major Fiction from Cervantes' Don Quixote
to Zola's Germinal, First Edition. Daniel R. Schwarz.
© 2014 John Wiley & Sons, Ltd. Published 2014 by John Wiley & Sons, Ltd.